1941

BACK TO

BACK TO PEACE

*Reconciliation and Retribution
in the Postwar Period*

edited by

ARÁNZAZU USANDIZAGA

and

ANDREW MONNICKENDAM

University of Notre Dame Press

Notre Dame, Indiana

Manufactured in the United States of America

Library of Congress Cataloging in-Publication Data

Back to peace : reconciliation and retribution in the postwar period /
edited by Aránzazu Usandizaga and Andrew Monnickendam.
    p.   cm.
Includes bibliographical references and index.
ISBN-13: 978-0-268-04452-7 (pbk. : alk. paper)
ISBN-10: 0-268-04452-X (pbk. : alk. paper)
1. Peace in literature. 2. American literature—20th century—History
and criticism. 3. English literature—20th century—History and criticism.
4. Peace—Social aspects. 5. Culture conflict in literature. 6. Social conflict
in literature. 7. Displacement (Psychology) in literature. 8. Soldiers in
literature. 9. War and literature. I. Usandizaga, Aránzazu.
II. Monnickendam, Andrew.
PS228.P43B33   2007
809'.93358—dc22   2006039824

Contents

Introduction

The Problematic Return to Peace

ARÁNZAZU USANDIZAGA &
ANDREW MONNICKENDAM

I am beginning to rub my eyes at the prospect of peace. I think it will require

more courage than anything that has gone before. It isn't until one leaves off

spinning around that one realizes how giddy one is. One will have to look at

long vistas again, instead of short ones, and one will at last fully recognize

that the dead are not only dead for the duration of the war.

Lady Cynthia Asquith, entry from *Diaries, 1915–18*

Western civilization has always shown an intense desire to understand war, as a necessary step toward understanding itself. But after a long history of reflection, we are today repeating the debates that have been among us since the Enlightenment. From Hobbes's "Homo homini lupus" to Wordsworth's "The child is father to the man," the arrival of modernity has been characterized by the dichotomy between recognition of a violence inherent in the very concept of humanity and the development of a proto-pacifist perspective that identifies violence with civilization. The opposition of the theory of the state developed in Hobbes's *Leviathan* (1651) and Rousseau's *Du contrat social* (1763) is also the opposition between two divergent anthropologies:

1

one that acknowledges a destructive drive in human nature and one that sees violence as cultural and institutional. Romanticism, which is to a certain extent the cultural inheritance of Rousseau, developed an approach to nature that was in itself a form of social criticism and marked the beginning of what we have come to know as pacifism.

It was at the end of the nineteenth century, with the arrival of radical cultural critics such as Friedrich Nietzsche and Sigmund Freud, that it was first possible to deconstruct the binary opposition between war and peace, destructive and creative impulses. For Nietzsche, in *The Genealogy of Morals* (1883), Western civilization itself was founded on an ongoing war, that waged by the bourgeois state against independent, "strong" selves: a war that had taken the form of democratic institutions and had assumed the ideology of religion. Nietzsche's vindication of tragedy and pre-Christian forms of art was an attempt to accept the existence of physical pain, conflict, and arbitrary violence as essential conditions of life. At the close of the nineteenth century, Sigmund Freud recognized in human nature the simultaneous passions of love and death, war and peace, in the instincts of Eros and Thanatos. Yet even he subscribed to a powerful utopian desire: in spite of having defined the ambivalent and coexisting impulses of life and death, he still claimed, in a letter of September 1932, that it was possible to contemplate the end of war: "Now war is in the crassest opposition to the psychical attitude imposed on us by the process of civilization. . . . [I]t may not be Utopian to hope that . . . the cultural attitude and the justified dread of the consequences of a future war, may result within a measurable time in putting an end to the waging of war" (362).

The twenty-first century is witnessing both the persistence of the old debates and the continuation of war. Against all odds, many thinkers imagine a more civilized view of human nature, although the persistence of war in the world continues to raise important doubts as to the accuracy of such hopes. In spite of intense discussion, it can escape no one's attention that the main questions concerning war remain unanswered: Is war the usual condition of life as suggested by Hobbes? Has it been essential to progress? Is it possible to imagine a world where wars have been abolished?

The moral and psychological effects of war have been and continue to be fraught with contradictions. Witness the extensive literature of war in the West, a literature that covers the theoretical, the testimonial, and the imaginative. In all its horror war has always exercised an intense power of fascination. It has been celebrated for the paradoxical nature of the wisdom it can provide. In the poem "Absolution," written in 1915 while he was serving on the Western front, the English poet Siegfried Sassoon wrote: "War is our scourge; yet war has made us wise" (63). Rooted in Christianity, the redemptive quality of suffering has been a justifying myth in many writers' and poets' approach to the description and representation of the experience of war. Platonic aesthetic echoes of the virtuous as beautiful, of the *pulchra sunt quae visa placent,* can also be heard on the World War I battlefield of the imagination. The American poet H.D., in "The Scene of War," suggests that war might reveal the strange quality of unexpected beauty:

> And perhaps some outer horror,
> some hideousness to stamp beauty
> a mark
> on our hearts.
>
> (85)

Our starting point is the belief that the understanding of war can be much improved by a systematic study of its aftereffects. In other words, we believe that knowledge of the different aspects of the return to peace is a necessary part of the comprehension and maybe even the prevention of further conflicts. Few scholarly approaches have taken the unifying perspective of *Back to Peace.* The discussion, representation, and memory of war, of all wars, based on the innumerable quantity and variety of existing war texts, have hardly focused on the huge corpus of postwar documents, whether cultural, historical, or literary. Neither has there been a theorizing of the return to peace, as such, capable of incorporating its many aspects and complexities. Yet we may accurately say that one of the foundational texts of Western culture, Homer's *Odyssey,* is a story about the cultural, political, and personal implications of returning to peace. Indeed, if the *Iliad* becomes the most emblematic war text of Western civilization, the *Odyssey* mythologizes the immensely difficult and dangerous adventure of returning to peace. Homer imagines for Ulysses, in his legitimate desire to recover his wife, his son, and his estate, a return that implies all kinds of difficulties and that will lead to further fighting, this time of a domestic kind, against the pretenders.

Scholars have rarely studied the return to peace as a cultural category, as the groundbreaking experience and condition common to so many lives at any time in history. The reading of these texts from such a perspective reveals that the reestablishment of peace is always ambivalent, sometimes even more dangerous than war, and that it raises a number of difficult issues.

As Clausewitz suggested, the potential for further wars is often a result of the cultural, moral, and political terms on which peace is negotiated and settled.

The purpose of this collection of essays is to initiate the pioneering work of searching for the common language of the return to peace: of finding the rhetoric, the figures of speech as well as the figures of the mind and of the heart, in which the return to peace is imagined and narrated. We provide a first approach to what we believe can become an important contribution to the understanding of war and peace, for we cannot culturally comprehend public conflict without understanding and theorizing the public and private processes of readjustment, of recrimination and reconciliation, that follow upon any war. How do combatants and noncombatants return to the forgotten fronts of everyday life? How does the postwar period reinvent the social and ideological framework? How does it suggest new forms of survival and adaptation in personal as well as national and international terms?

We also think the study of the return to peace must be interdisciplinary, just as the study of war has proved to be. As many philosophers, historians, and literary critics have shown and confirmed in the twentieth century, literature and history must work together, for literary documents can be a source of great documentary riches, and historical documentation helps the literary scholar to understand important aspects of the literary text. The illuminating work of scholars like Paul Fussell, Sandra Gilbert and Susan Gubar, Claire Tylee, Phyllis Lassner, and many others exemplifies the fruitfulness of this interdisciplinary collaboration. In the highly influential study *The Clash of Civilizations and the Remaking of World Order* (1996), Samuel P. Huntington argues that an understanding of culture is essential to the study of war. If that is so, it is also necessary to comprehend how the return to peace is represented in different cultures and different genres. This is what we have striven to achieve.

Our collection aims at initiating what we hope will become a long and fruitful discussion of war and peace. It tackles uncertainties that range from the immediate to the more general and theoretical. Some of our essays try to come to terms with the difficult justification of the violence of war once peace is reestablished; with issues such as mapping out unclear distinctions between victory and defeat; with the changes undergone in the definitions of such notions as heroism after war; or with how we reorganize our feelings toward our enemies once war is over. *Vincebamur a victa Graecia*, said

Cicero. "We were conquered by conquered Greece." Isn't that very often the situation in the moment of the return to peace? How is the personal self recovered after the period of war when the collective necessarily takes over the individual? How is war remembered and narrated by the different classes, political parties, and genders, and by combatants and noncombatants, immediately after the restoration of peace and later? How can war be made sense of from the perspective of peace? We hope that these initial steps into the uncertainties of understanding the return to peace will raise larger and more ambitious issues in the theoretical discussion of war and peace. We also hope that the reflection and articulation of the mistakes made so far in the return to peace from different wars may be of some use in understanding the prevention of further conflicts.

Our collection of essays is divided into three parts. We thought the first one should be devoted to the return of combatants, since combatants are those most obviously affected by the return to peace, though certainly not the only ones. It includes five essays, two of them focused on representations of return from the First World War, two dealing with World War II documentary and literary material, and one on the return from Vietnam. The literature of the First World War is rich, dominated by the sense of loss and sacrifice; we believe these two essays provide a fresh perspective on the study of this war's vast literary corpus. Brian Dillon's "Anticipating Commemoration: The Post–World War I Era as British Poets Imagined It" analyzes part of the extensive corpus of poetry written by some of the best-known World War I poets, such as Blunden, Sassoon, Gurney, Owen, Read, and Graves. Instead of concentrating on the better-known topics such as death or heroism, Dillon attends to the more unusual subject of how soldiers on the front line foresaw the return to peace. He argues that although some poets envisioned a peaceful return to peace, many were considerably bleaker: instead of invoking pastoral images of England, they imagined a wilderness, a world devoid of the purpose that war gave to combatants. Poets "depict survivors in the postwar era as lacking the mental, physical, and emotional rejuvenation that readers might expect peace would bring." Their verses show that adjustment to civilian life is well-nigh impossible: a remarkable vision for war poets. Although some poems, like Sassoon's "Reconciliation" (1918), envision a future in which the conflicts that underlay the war have been reconciled, they are undercut by expressions of revulsion and mistrust toward civilians who are and may continue to be blind to the realities of war. Sassoon's "On Passing the New Menin Gate" (1927), which deflates, in a highly polemical manner, national pride in sacrifice, exemplifies this mistrust, as does Siegfried Sassoon's "At the Cenotaph" (1933), in which the Prince of Darkness appears at this London memorial to the war dead to pray that citizens will forget what the memorial means and draw from it only the motivation to engage in more wars. War poets differed in their responses to the ways soldiers' deaths were commemorated: many could not accept anonymous burials in mass graves in France and drew no consolation from the official monuments of remembrance that they feared would be misused as rallying points for jingoistic and sentimental patriotism. Not all remembrance poetry is, thankfully, so despairing. For Dillon, commemoration poetry does not always meet Jon Silken's widely accepted criteria of anger, compassion, and intelligence leading to a desire for change. Such criteria are, for Dillon, overoptimistic, problematizing even further the nature of the return to peace.

William Blazek's "The War Veteran in *Tender Is the Night*" acts as a companion piece to Dillon's essay. His initial premise is that "reminders of the First World War saturate the novel in layered images of war and battle" and function as reminders of the violence war engendered—that is, the violence that has spilled over into peacetime. Many critical essays have focused on the central figure of Dick Diver in Fitzgerald's text, but the importance of Blazek's contribution is that by concentrating on the fate of two other characters, Abe North and Tommy Barban, he turns the novel into a broad portrayal of the complexities of the return to peace. Fitzgerald attributes to Abe a carnivalesque role, his humor being by its very nature subversive. The character's function is revealed in a remarkable incident when, in a sightseeing visit to the battlefields of the Somme, the epitome of the cruelty of war, Abe plays at being a soldier, mocking serious official discourse on war and its causes. Blazek argues that Abe is closely connected to the American past, "a violent history . . . fraught with the tensions between ideals and a divergent reality." On the other hand, Tommy's choice of a postwar career in stockbroking seems to be more conventional than Abe's, for, unlike Abe, Tommy is able to control his alcoholism and organize his life. However, this does not, Blazek argues, put him on a higher moral plane than Abe. Tommy appears to be a better survivor in times of war and peace, but like Abe he encounters great difficulties in accepting postwar life. Blazek further emphasizes that neither character ends up a nervous wreck, like Virginia Woolf's Septimus Smith, because both, as literary characters, are unusually consistent. In other words, Fitzgerald places his complex creations in a scenario that has too often provided oversimplified characters.

Part One continues with two essays on the return to peace after the Second World War. Their different locations and different subjects enlarge our understanding of the complex problem of readjustment; for no one can this be more difficult than for the defeated. In "Coming Home Defeated: Soldiers and the Transition from War to Peace in Post–World War II Japan," Beatrice Trefalt argues that although the Western world believes—erroneously—that Japan quickly forgot the Second World War, a belief strengthened by its rapid economic growth, in postwar Japan there was in fact "no amnesia on war issues." Japanese attitudes toward war veterans constitute her test case. Three areas are examined: the notion of surrender, changes in attitudes toward the armed forces during the Allied occupation, and the treatment of these two topics in various literary texts. Trefalt analyzes the stigma of capture, tantamount to treason in the Japanese military code, which partially accounted for the relatively low number of Japanese POWs. Returning soldiers, both POWs and demobilized troops, feared that the civilian population would treat them with great distrust. The doctrine of "no surrender" was tenacious, and society could be openly hostile toward returning combatants. This often caused soldiers to go into hiding instead. The last stragglers, who had actually been hiding, surfaced as late as 1974. Trefalt illustrates her analysis with texts virtually unknown outside Japan, such as Ōka Shōhei's *Furyoki* (Diary of a POW) and his novel *Nobi*, translated into English as *Fires on the Plain*. According to Trefalt's conclusion, even now the "ambiguity of soldiers' position has not been resolved, and their experiences are therefore difficult to discuss."

Mary Anne Schofield's "'Battle Dress to Sports Suit; Overalls to Frocks': American and British Veterans Confront Demobilization, 1945–51" analyzes two relatively unknown subgenres related to the return to peace: nonfiction written primarily for the returning American and British combatants, very often in the form of pamphlets, and fiction of the period 1946–51 written primarily for combatants' wives—in mythical terms, the literature of the modern Ulysses and Penelope. Although government documents and fiction might seem to have little in common, they do share a purpose: mapping the soldier's problematic return to the civilian world—a return that, despite social changes at home and changes within the soldier himself, they tend to portray as his task of "changing back to the boy he used to be" and readjusting to a life envisioned in prewar terms. Schofield analyzes a significant cross section of pamphlets that show awareness of the multiple difficulties of establishing "normalcy" even as they assert its eventual success. Home may not be the golden paradise that soldiers have imagined: one author warns that "no one can make your dreams come true but yourself," while another informs its readers that combatants are in no mood to be patronized. One publication has a title that is beguiling, self-explanatory, and deceptive: "Problems Have No Sex." Clearly, sexuality was a major problem, as was the upheaval war caused in gender roles. Schofield analyzes the representation of postwar gender role conflicts in both British and American novels of the period, arguing that the American novels have a more somber tone than their British counterparts. The essay is accompanied by an outstanding bibliography of primary and secondary materials for further research.

Jennifer Terry's "'When All the Wars Are Over': The Utopian Impulses of Toni Morrison's Postwar Fiction" takes us to a much more contemporary landscape, the United States after the Vietnam War. To the many African American combatants, a hopeful vision of peace inevitably involved their attainment of full citizenship, however problematic this turned out to be in a racially segregated United States, as illustrated in Morrison's novel *Jazz* (1992). Morrison's more recent novel *Paradise* (1998), which was originally going to be entitled *War,* continues this theme: for Terry, "Male departure to and return from war is a pattern that shapes Ruby's story" (Ruby is Morrison's fictional town). Terry concentrates on three major themes: what military service means to African Americans, their definitions/visions of "home," and how these two phenomena conflate in Ruby, particularly between 1968 and 1976, years haunted by the specter of the Vietnam War. Morrison does not tackle the politics of the Vietnam War head on, but she leaves us in no doubt as to how it affects the whole community. Terry concentrates on the central event, the assault on the neighboring community of Convent, arguing that the assault "represents the final perversion of the original dream of Haven. . . . The campaign of maligning and then obliterating the Convent women comes . . . to reveal the danger of assuming an imperialist position and the devastating effect of violence enacted along such lines." Morrison further suggests that in the same way that war propaganda demonizes the enemy, patriarchs demonize the other sex; no distinction is made between races. In line with contemporary feminist thought, Morrison's partly allegorical tale reinforces the link between imperialism and patriarchy. The return to peace brings about an outbreak of warlike violence in which issues of gender and race refuse to be parties to a peace treaty.

Part Two, "Reconciliation," offers five approaches to the dilemmas of coming to terms with the changes that take place after any war, especially the need to adapt to new, far more complex contexts, both in cultural terms and in terms of power. Whatever we consider the true nature of peacetime, any historian, philosopher, or political scientist has to tackle Hobbes's assumption that peace is abnormal. Janet Dawson's "Searching for Peace: John Dryden's *Troilus and Cressida or Truth Found Too Late*" crosses disciplines by reading John Dryden's play—an adaptation of Shakespeare's bitter tragicomedy—in the light of Hobbes's theory of the commonwealth as set out in his influential *Leviathan* (1651). Dryden's 1679 play must be contextualized within the Restoration, a term implying the interdependent restorations of monarchy, peace, and civil society. Dryden's use of both Shakespeare and mythical sources ensures that the issues debated have serious implications for any historical period. But unlike Shakespeare and his contemporaries, Dryden does not make revenge the dynamic of his play. The Greeks are in the end victorious because although they are at first weakened by acts of disrespect and insubordination within their ranks, they work toward and eventually establish "the Hobbesian ideal of submission to a single sovereign." The Trojans, on the other hand, are defeated because their political organization—from a Hobbesian viewpoint—is outdated, relying on patriarchy rather than sovereignty. Dawson concludes that "peace, as Hobbes understands it, . . . mediates conflict by law rather than acts of private violence"; thus Trojan values, such as family and nobility, necessarily cede to Greek—Hobbesian—values in Dryden's play. The return to peace does not restore anything, as the term *Restoration* would imply; rather, it imposes a more modern, harsher society. In this way, Dryden demythologizes a story of epic proportions, while at the same time drawing his audience's attention to the cost of the return to peace and the Restoration.

Problems of readjustment are especially intense after a civil war. Don Dingledine's "Romances of Reconstruction: The Postwar Marriage Plot in Rebecca Harding Davis and John William De Forest" uses as its point of departure romances that "captured the popular American imagination in the immediate post–Civil War era" by suggesting, through the metaphor of marriage, a union between North and South in which a submissive, female South would never again threaten the North. As Dingledine argues, the problem with such symbolic unions is that they bypass the crucial issues of race and rights. How, for example, would the emancipated slaves, both male and female, envisage peace? Some novels of the period actually provide alternatives to and variations on the stock North-South romance plot. One of these is Davis's *Waiting for the Verdict* (1867), which Dingledine contrasts with De Forest's *Miss Ravenel's Conversion from Secession to Loyalty*, published in the same year. Dingledine argues that Davis's romance of Reconstruction is of great interest for its reversal of popular paradigms: the male is a slaveholding aristocrat and the female a northern abolitionist. Further, the romance is accompanied by an ongoing struggle of discourse between the opposing sides that shows the southerner incapable of fully accepting and understanding the new order. While Davis's text debates and resolves conflict, the much more reactionary text by De Forest shows its "romantic triangle [to be] as much a struggle over the freed black body as it is a struggle for the hand of the white female." If the languages of slavery and gender mingle, then the whole project of Reconstruction, so vital to American consciousness, is open to question. Union and Reconstruction provide optimistic visions for a fruitful future on a personal, familial, and national level, but we are left with the doubt that perhaps "the very hierarchies and inequalities that led up to the Civil War" have been reinscribed.

Laurie Kaplan's "The Unpleasantness at the Chandrapore Club, and the Mayapore Club, and the Jummapur Club: Forster, Scott, and Stoppard and the End of Empire" explores how Forster's *Passage to India*, Scott's *Raj Quartet*, and Stoppard's *India Ink* all use the institution of the British club as a narrative space. The club, as its name implies, suggests fellowship, but the reality was one of social, racial, and gender tensions. The most dramatic case affected soldiers. In the war, British and Indian officers served alongside each other as colleagues, yet in India, Indian officers were barred from the clubs to which their colleagues belonged. For Kaplan, Forster's club is rife with suspicions and racial hatreds, but at the historical moment of his novel there is no sign of imperialism giving way, whereas in the later treatments of the subject the clubs "provide a vivid backdrop for dramatizations of social transition." Kaplan's essay is valuable because it deals with texts that are set at various key moments in Indian history; the two by Stoppard and Scott take place in post-Independence India, when a new period of peace was throwing up new problems. In *The Raj Quartet*, Scott uses the club for his fierce critique of British attitudes toward India and its inhabitants—a mixture of pride and prejudice that, Kaplan argues, has not changed all that much despite different political and economic conditions. Stoppard uses two locales and two periods (1930 and 1980) with the intention of suggesting connections between their scenes and characters. In his depiction, "the postcolonial period of reconciliation becomes even more complex and unstable." What Scott pictured as two nations acting in violent opposition to each other have become two nations "locked in an imperial embrace."

"Imperial embrace" is a remarkably suggestive phrase, evoking relations both loving and deadly, of equals or perhaps not. Again, as our essays have shown, the return to peace is by its very nature ambiguous, even when the objective, in this case decolonialization, is laudable and readily identifiable.

Claire Tylee's "Community and Harmony in Charlotte Eilenberg's Post-Holocaust Play *The Lucky Ones*" analyzes a recent play in the light of the premise that, as evident in current film and television, contemporary writers have at last broken with wartime stereotypes of Britons and Germans that have been deeply embedded within British culture. The play itself is of great interest, though if we call it daring we simply reinforce Tylee's thesis that old images refuse to die. It focuses on the lives of four *Kinder* who escaped from Berlin—they now form two couples—and their relationship with Lisa, who is also from Berlin but is non-Jewish. Although the four are lucky in the sense that they escaped certain death, they do not feel at home in Britain: Tylee insightfully observes that "they have inherited an impossible burden of need and obligation, and they transmit it to the next generation." Eilenberg intensifies the whole question of guilt in her account of the deeply charged sexual relationship between one of the refugees and Lisa; the metaphor of sleeping with the enemy becomes extremely suggestive. For Tylee, the play problematizes the question of Jewish identity, tackling difficult questions such as the nature of being originally German—or not, as the case may be—in contemporary Britain, as debated by the Jewish community itself. Tylee points out that even though the play ends with a funeral, the choice of music, which includes Jewish Klezmer music alongside the ultranationalist Wagner and the essentially English Vaughan Williams, provides some prospect for what Tylee calls "the hybrid third space of an eclectic new European culture." Tylee's essay is controversial, for the texts analyzed are highly critical of lingering ideas and attitudes from World War II that are still hampering a return to peace even sixty years later. Although some may believe that the essay opens old wounds, we would argue that it envisages a more peaceful future that can come about only after a deep and painful period of introspection and reflection.

The second part, like the first, closes with Vietnam and its consequences. Questions of identity emerge in Renny Christopher's "Vietnamese Exile Writers: Displacement, Identity, the Past, and the Future," which explores how the works of these writers "address the lingering impact of the war on the writers and on their country of origin and their adopted country." For younger writers, biculturality is a tenser struggle than it was for their elders; they feel that they have one soul but two hearts. Christopher's focus is Nguyen Qui Duc's *Where the Ashes Are: The Odyssey of a Vietnamese Family* and Ngoc Quan Huynh's *South Wind Changing*. Duc's book is a family history rather than a personal biography: a sizable section comprises his father's POW narrative and his mother's story, and the book itself is dedicated to his sister, whose ashes rest in Vietnam. Duc's life in the West is one of dislocation, yet his return to Vietnam is unsatisfactory: "his 'home' exists only in memory, and his memory is continually thwarted by current reality." Though he goes to Vietnam to bring his sister's ashes back to America with him, asserting that "[w]here the ashes are, one should make that home," his home remains elusive. Huynh's narrative is written by someone who has assimilated with much greater ease than Duc—to such a point, and this is where its interest lies, that it "lacks political and historical analysis to an extent that is very unusual among Vietnamese narratives and much more typical of American ones." Christopher detects a shift among Vietnamese American writers toward poetry; an outstanding instance is the Amerasian orphan Christian Nguyen Langworthy, who represents a transitional position, or the possibility of a bridge between cultures, since Vietnam is the war that "U.S. culture as a whole seems unable to leave behind."

The last part of our volume is devoted to "wars within peace"; its title extends the doubts expressed by Asquith. Three of the essays included in the section analyze women's perspectives of the end of the three European wars fought in the twentieth century: World War I, the Spanish Civil War, and World War II. The final essay focuses on women as war victims of World War II.

In the first essay, "Seeing the War through Cut-off Triangles: H.D. and Gertrude Stein," Kathy J. Phillips offers a stimulating reading of H.D.'s and Gertrude Stein's extremely critical presentations of post–World War I society. She argues that H.D.'s short story "Ear-Ring" and Gertrude Stein's play *An Exercise in Analysis* use the techniques of modernism to obliquely offer "a surprisingly large view of the effects of World War I." By reproducing the characters' apparently conventional conversations in the story, H.D. bitterly denounces the damaging effects of war. H.D. uses indirect suggestions and insinuations to lay bare the economic corruption underlying the tragedy of a war that killed millions of people and was to repeat itself nineteen years later. But more ambitiously, H.D.'s story is an experiment in a new form of art that Phillips defines as an art of "cut-off triangles." Using the freedom allowed by modernism to defy social and political detachment, H.D. provides a narrative space for the integration of the contextual in art, of the "time-in-time" neglected by modernist approaches of "time-out-of-time." Phillips argues that Gertrude Stein does something similar in her play *An Exercise in Analysis* and shows that again, in the apparently shallow speech of characters in a socialite setting, the author is actually evaluating "war and sexuality" as well as "war and gender." Stein's play concludes that war does not advance democracy, and though perhaps less radically pessimistic than H.D.'s, it also insinuates that the apparent improvement in women's situation after the war is very slight.

Aránzazu Usandizaga's "The Forgotten Brigade: Foreign Women Writers and the End of the Spanish Civil War" analyzes women's texts from a twentieth-century war little discussed in recent mainstream gender and war studies: the Spanish Civil War. She focuses on foreign women authors' writing of the end of the war, suggesting that some of these texts are valuable documents about both the end of the war and the fate of many Spaniards in the French concentration camps, initially set up to house fleeing refugees. She discusses the work of several writers, among them the autobiographical reports of two British social workers, Kanty Cooper and Francesca M. Wilson. Both authors had been involved in war work since the outbreak of the Spanish Civil War and had spent long periods of time in Spain during the war. They remained in Spain until its very end, narrating its conclusion at a time when most journalists and reporters had left Spain and were focusing on the events in central Europe that were soon to bring about the Second World War. Cooper provides one of the few accurate descriptions available of the fall of Barcelona to Franco's troops. Usandizaga also discusses the war writing of the English poet Nancy Cunard, who did much for Spain during the war. Among Cunard's best work are her passionately committed reports for the *Manchester Guardian* about the last stages of the war. The essay also focuses on the work of Martha Gellhorn, whose important career as one of the first war reporters started during the Spanish Civil War. Though she arrived in Spain in 1937 almost by chance, Gellhorn found in Spain a new perspective and a new language with which to narrate war. She became so involved in the events that she continued not only to report the conflict until its very end and beyond but also to incorporate her Spanish experiences into her writing long after the Civil War was over. These women's writings about the end of the Spanish Civil War reveal the international nature and the complexity of back-to-peace processes in both personal and political terms. Two essays included in this part contribute to the discussion of women's perspectives of World War II. In the first of these, "Wish Me Luck As You Wave Me Goodbye: Representations of War Brides in Canadian Fiction and Drama by Margaret Atwood, Mavis Gallant, Norah Harding, Margaret Hollingsworth, Joyce Marshall, Suzette Mayr, Aritha van Herk, and Rachel Wyatt," Donna Coates expands the category of war victims to include many British women whose lives were radically transformed by the war. Coates investigates the records of the forty-eight thousand mostly British women who moved to Canada as war brides after the Second World War and who narrated their very difficult and often unhappy lives there. Coates also analyzes several fictional representations of the lives of some of these foreign women by the best-known Canadian women authors—representations that, as she points out, have never been the subject of any major critical work. In the texts she studies, many war brides experience peace as more horrible than war, since the world they encounter in Canada has little in common with the glowing promises made to them before they left their own country. She says these women came to Canada for reasons very similar to many young Canadian men's reasons for joining up, and she argues in favor of considering their stories truly postwar texts that are as relevant in the assessment of the war as those of the combatants. Of particular interest is Coates's discussion of the effects of the Canadian landscape on these women; she also relates their surprise at discovering that the men who welcomed them were no longer the gallant soldiers they had seemed to be abroad. The hostility the women had to contend with leads Coates to conclude that "the aftermath of war was as destructive to women as the war years had been to men."

Camila Loew's "Ta(l)king War into Peace: Marguerite Duras's *La douleur,* History and Her Stories" also contributes to the understanding of the devastating effects of the Second World War and its aftermath by simultaneously reading two well-known French testimonies: *L'espèce humaine,* by Robert Antelme, a prisoner in the Nazi camps, and *La douleur,* by his wife, the writer Marguerite Duras, who remained in Paris during the war and worked in the Resistance. Loew studies Duras's interesting experiment in expanding the bounds of what was understood to be the "authentic" war narrative in order to erase the strict spatial and temporal distinctions between war and peace. She argues that Duras constructs her revisionist text by introducing a complex narrative pattern that includes different theoretical approaches capable of showing how "the patterns of war are deeply inscribed in the domain of what we usually call 'peace.'" Duras introduces a metatextual dimension to her text by incorporating her husband's memoir of war into the fabric of the narrative and establishing a dialogue with it. In so doing, she subverts the conventions of the narrative of war and builds her own war testimony, a text in which her husband is also a character. Duras's narrative suggests that the differences between witnessing the war at the front and writing from the perspective of a man or a woman from the home front make the woman's testimony not less powerful but maybe even more so. Her genre revisions are enlarged into ethical considerations about war and its aftermath and provide a broad reassessment of gender roles.

Together the essays offer our readers important suggestions on how to give coherence and structure to the questions we framed at the beginning of this introduction. The essays included in Part One, "Return of the Combatant," are original inquiries into the drama of the soldier's return and establish patterns articulating the main features of demobilized soldiers' reactions upon their return home. In the examples discussed, fighting a war seems to have equally destructive consequences for the victors and the vanquished. Though the essays provide examples and models from very different contexts, both historical and fictional, the conclusions they reach in relation to the soldiers' return are surprisingly similar. The difficulties demobilized soldiers face in readapting are huge; the world they return to has profoundly changed, and the experience of fighting has transformed their lives beyond a point of no return.

Even more difficult to accept are the scenarios depicted by the essays in Part Two, "Reconciliation." These five essays provide insights into the processes that make reconciliation well-nigh impossible after war across a broad range of times and places. For example, Janet Dawson's chapter on Dryden's *Troilus and Cressida* shows how, for Dryden, the actual restoration of prewar conditions is not possible; the play both draws on and modifies Hobbesian political philosophy to envision means of survival after war. The authors provide further examples of how the processes of reconciliation are fraught with complexities that distort them and of how survival takes time and enormous effort on both a personal and a collective level.

In Part Three, "Wars within Peace," gender issues are a key concern. The contributors outline how women's lives have responded to and been affected by the return to peace. Their essays show women obliquely denouncing not so much war as the return to peace and asserting their right to lament their personal suffering. Rather than concentrating on the consolations of a return to peace, the writers discussed in these essays discover the terrible moral failures of peace and, by voicing their own suffering, dare to join in the lamentation that seems to be the only consolation available after war. Indeed, for some of the women discussed in this collection the return to peace is not a bed of roses but a bed of thorns.

These essays initiate a fascinating approach to the understanding of the figures of the mind and of the heart articulated in response to the great suffering involved in any return to peace. They also investigate how a return to peace must reinvent first its social and ideological framework and second the private psychological patterns that can make some kind of tolerable survival possible. We see this volume as a beginning: our hope is that it will stimulate further studies of the very important subject of the return to peace as a central element in the understanding of war and peace. Only its incorporation can complete the overall estimation of conflict, and it may even make the needed work for peace more feasible.

Works Cited

Asquith, Lady Cynthia. Entry from *Diaries, 1915–18. Women's Writing of the First World War: An Anthology.* Ed. Angela K. Smith. Manchester: Manchester University Press, 2000. 234.

Freud, Sigmund. "Why War." An exchange of letters between Sigmund Freud and Albert Einstein, 1932–33. *Civilization, Society and Religion,* ed. and trans. James Strachey, Penguin Freud Library 12. Harmondsworth: Penguin Books, 1991.

Fussell, Paul. *The Great War and Modern Memory.* New York: Oxford University Press, 1975.

Gilbert, Sandra, and Susan Gubar. *No Man's Land: The Place of the Woman Writer in the Twentieth Century.* New Haven: Yale University Press, 1988.

H.D. "The Scene of War." Hibberd and Onions 85.

Hibberd, Dominic, and John Onions, eds. *Poetry of the Great War: An Anthology.* London: Macmillan, 1986.

Huntington, Samuel P. *The Clash of Civilizations and the Remaking of World Order.* New York: Simon and Schuster, 1996.

Lassner, Phyllis. *British Women Writers of World War II: Battlegrounds of Their Own.* New York: St. Martin's Press, 1998.

Sassoon, Siegfried. "Absolution." Hibberd and Onions 63.

Tylee, Claire. *The Great War and Women's Consciousness: Images of Militarism and Womanhood in Women's Writings, 1914–64.* Iowa City: University of Iowa Press, 1990.

PART ONE

RETURN OF
THE COMBATANT

CHAPTER ONE

Anticipating Commemoration

The Post–World War I Era as British Poets Imagined It

BRIAN DILLON

I

"Carpet slippers and Kettle-holders." That was the reply given to Siegfried Sassoon by his officer friend Barton to the question, "What were you thinking?" as they sat speechless and stupefied by the noise of exploding shells early on the morning of July 1, 1916, the opening day of the nearly five-month-long Battle of the Somme (*Memoirs* 73). Sassoon does not ridicule his fellow officer's thoughts on these emblems of comforting, mundane habits. "My own mind had been working in much the same style," he admits. If soldiers could be sustained emotionally by the trivial, then so be it. At other times, though, Sassoon seemed to distance himself from such habits. In his poem "Dreamers," his comrades are "mocked by hopeless longing to regain / Bank-holidays, and picture shows, and spats, / And going to the office in the train" (*Collected Poems* 72). In these brief excerpts, the postwar world is imagined as a recovery of safe prewar conventions. What may surprise us, though, is how rarely such images appear in the poetry written during the war. Poems by Herbert Read, Edmund Blunden, Ivor Gurney, Sassoon, Robert Graves, Wilfred Owen, and others that either attempt to foresee the postwar future or are set in the postwar era and deal with the problem of memory offer no emotional or spiritual consolations—not through participation in a community or the company of a lover, and seldom even through participation in the landscape. The poems of these six named authors, all of whom served in the military in World War I, cohere to a remarkable degree in their vision of a relatively bleak postwar era. All but Owen survived the war; Owen was killed a week before the Armistice

in 1918. The five surviving soldier-poets shaped their poetic careers to vary-
ing degrees in response to the issues of the "value" of the violence they witnessed and often performed in response to their memories of camaraderie
and trauma once they were situated in England during the years of temporary peace following the war.[1]

Typically, during the war when the poets place their speakers in the
postwar era, abstractions displace vivid, concrete images. The postwar landscape is emptied out. A sense of absence—of both people and purpose—
dominates the poets' rendering of the postwar exterior world. Read's speaker
in "My Company," an officer, presumes the future to be diminished. He
imagines himself situated in the future and looking back on his present
with feelings of intense loss:

> But, God! I know that I'll stand
> Someday in the loneliest wilderness
> Someday my heart will cry
> For the soul that has been, but that now
> Is scatter'd with the winds,
> Deceased and devoid.
>
> I know that I'll wander with a cry:
> "O beautiful men, O men I loved
> O whither are you gone, my company?"
>   (32)

In this time-bending poem where a memory of the present is projected
onto the future, Read's speaker voices his fear of the potential emotional
disorder that peace will bring for him personally. Peace will bring no solace,
nor is there any hint that he will return home strengthened by the knowledge that he fulfilled his leadership role. No English pastoral notions comfort him: the wilderness he is convinced he will enter is both his psychic
interior and the exterior landscape.

Apart from the obvious fact that "the loneliest wilderness" this speaker
"someday" will enter is devoid of his war comrades, this landscape is projected to be a wilderness because it lacks the sense of purpose that the war
created. In Blunden's "1916 Seen from 1921," a poem that, as the title indicates, is premised on the insights that the postwar perspective brings, the
speaker asserts that the dead landscape of the past embodies meaning while

the living landscape he currently moves within fails to satisfy: "the charred stub outspeaks the living tree" (Silken 113). Birdsong wakes him to no purpose, to a solitariness he has chosen:

> I rise up at the singing of a bird
> And scarcely knowing slink along the lane,
> I dare not give a soul a look or word
> Where all have homes and none's at home in vain
> (*Poetry and Prose* 113)

As is typical in Blunden's poems, these home-front civilians are not scorned. Blunden's speaker "only hear[s] / Long silent laughters, murmurings of dismay, / The lost intensities of hope and fear." For Blunden's speaker, hearing these voices from five years earlier ensures his continued solitude. Locked in the past with the laughters and murmurings that only he can hear, the speaker remains unwilling or unable to engage with his fellow villagers in the present: "I dare not give a soul a look or word." He barely alludes to a prewar past in this village. The reader is left wondering: If the once-reassuring landscape of the past dissolves, what will the speaker be left with? Whatever joys he derived from this setting are beyond recovery: his

> life drags
> Its wounded length from those sad streets of war
> Into green places here, that were my own;
> But now what once was mine is mine no more
> (112–13)

That final "no more," along with the dependence on monosyllabic words, provides a formal echo of Wordsworth's "Immortality Ode," in which Wordsworth expresses the distance he has crossed from the rich childish wonder he took in the natural world to the diminished glory he now sees as an adult: "The things which I have seen I now can see no more" (279). Wordsworth's speaker accepts as a necessity this diminished glory: "We will grieve not, rather find / Strength in what remains behind; / . . . In years that bring the philosophic mind" (284). Blunden's speaker resists such muted optimism and instead enters a daydream set in 1916 in which he and his "friend of friends" temporarily escaped the firing by sleeping from sunup until noon "in the tall grass." Contrary to Wordsworth, Blunden's speaker does not find strength for the present in his memories, yet he is not grieving either; he is too passive, too inert, to grieve. The present in 1921 is barely sketched, displaced as it is by the vividly rendered 1916 voices and setting.

In some of his poems, Blunden's speaker implicitly contrasts the odd comfort he took in the predictability of trench life with the disorientation associated with postwar peace and his failure to seek membership in a hometown community. The speaker of "The Watchers" describes how, during the war, strangers sharing the same purpose with him absorbed him into a community that satisfied him. The recollection of a brief, relatively generic scene allows the speaker to conjure a reassuring past: a sentry's "Who goes there?" followed by this same sentry's advice for the speaker's continued movement through the trenches, as commonplace an exchange as could occur during the war.

> When will the stern, fine "Who goes there?"
> Meet me again in midnight air?
> And the gruff sentry's kindness, when
> Will kindness have such power again?

The sentry's question is fine while stern; he is kind while gruff. For Blunden, the sense of belonging rests on such mundane features. The reference to the postwar present in this poem consists of a mere two lines that vaguely suggest emotional loss: "now I wake and brood, / And know my hour's decrepitude" (*Undertones* 234). As in "1916 Seen from 1921," a memory of wartime nearly cancels out the present. And it is not contemplation of the dead that prompts such cancellation.

Nearly twenty years after the war, Blunden's speaker answers the title question of another poem, "Can You Remember?" with a qualified yes. He admits that his memory now is insecure:

> Yes, I still remember
> The whole thing in a way;
> Edge and exactitude
> Depend on the day.

Place names lie beyond his recall: the landscape is enveloped by a mist that is "luminous-obscure," a makeshift term that expresses his arrival at a threshold that opens into the past, along with his inability to cross that threshold. This poem favors imprecise description and avoids reflection:

> commonly I fail to name
> That once obvious Hill,
> And where we went and whence we came
> To be killed, or kill.

(Indeed, it is the rare Great War poem that philosophizes upon being a killer.) No specific individual is conjured here—no "friend of friends" to join with to withdraw from the trenches for a morning nap, no sentry offering manly advice. Instead, the final stanza contrasts recollections of two types of soldiers with a parade of descriptive terms that do not individualize any of them:

> some are sparkling, laughing, singing,
> Young, heroic, mild;
> And some incurable, twisted,
> Shrieking, dumb, defiled.
>   (*Poetry and Prose* 221)

The subdued, reasonable tone of the speaker suggests he falls between these two extremes. Neither the speaker's postwar experiences nor his present setting is mentioned. To assert that the poem withholds any insights into how the war has shaped the speaker's identity over the past two decades may seem to be a criticism of Blunden's artistry. But it need not be. The speaker does remain nebulous about how he must reckon with his past, which should frustrate readers who want more than rhyming adjectives; yet, to his credit, he honestly admits that the passage of time requires that he repeatedly confront his war experiences even if he does not achieve any consolatory closure.

Fortunately, Blunden's depiction of the veteran in the postwar world is inconsistent. One of his poems defies in subtle but profound ways the shared traits of the postwar era as imagined in his other poems. In "The Veteran" a silver-haired beekeeper lives with quiet joy in a post-sin Eden: "He steeps himself in nature's opulence." For this man, "contentment only thrives" in his natural setting. He babbles "lovingly" over the bounty nature yields, and his babbling would prevent anyone overhearing him from imagining this beekeeper's war experiences, the "dragging years / Of drouthy raids." But no one overhears him because he remains absolutely solitary: Blunden does not hint at whether his apparent psychological stability has been achieved despite or because of his being cut off from a human community. Whatever postwar trauma he experiences is negligible. During the daytime he is satisfied with his outdoor chores; any nightmares that might visit him are abruptly dismissed:

> And if sleep seem unsound,
> And set old bugles pealing through the dark,
> Waked on the instant, he but wakes to hark
> His bellman cockerel crying the first round.
> (*Poetry and Prose* 45–46)

Rather than "The Veteran," should Blunden have titled this "A Successful Repression of War Experience"?

"What did they expect of our toil and extreme / Hunger—the perfect drawing of a heart's dream?" (Gurney 196). This question, which opens Ivor Gurney's "War Books" (written in the early 1920s), taunts readers who expect that the soldier-poets who have participated in carnage will be capable of elucidating emotional—and physical—realms outside our conventional experience. Gurney, like Blunden, Sassoon, Graves, and Owen, depicts survivors in the postwar era as lacking the mental, physical, and emotional rejuvenation that such readers might expect peace would bring. Each of these poets assesses the postwar era in his own way. The latter three wrote poems—and letters—that agree in principle with the opening statement of Gurney's best-known poem, "Strange Hells": "There are strange hells within the minds war made / Not so often, not so humiliatingly afraid / As one would have expected—the racket and fear guns made" (140). While Blunden might agree with this premise, his poems that suggest the postwar era avoid such straightforward pronouncements as Gurney's opening line. (Gurney's whole three-line sentence is itself not so straightforward, as the mental "strange hell" results in part from the soldiers' adjustment to the abnormal noise and terror of life in the trenches and the charge forward.) The poem's first two stanzas describe the stoic enthusiasm of a Gloucester regiment singing through their first bombardment "with diaphragms fixed beyond all dreads." The third and final stanza lifts the reader off the battlefield and into postwar England. Quietly traumatized, the veterans all put on a face to disguise the hell within:

Where are they now, on state-doles, or showing shop-patterns
Or walking town to town sore in borrowed tatterns
Or begged. Some civic routine one never learns.
The heart burns—but has to keep out of face how heart burns
(140–41)

The poem distinguishes three groups of people in marginalized circumstances: those on the dole, shopkeepers, and homeless wanderers (the latter,
apparently, an autobiographical reference; see Hynes 387). Yet these distinct
economic circumstances collapse into the crucial point: for members of all
three groups, the "heart burns." That the veterans must keep this burning
"out of face" indicates the lack of belonging with their community and even
their fellow veterans, an outsider status, also suggested by the cryptic frag-
ment "Some civic routine one never learns." No one returns to comforting
habits or to a landscape familiar, preserved; the solitude of the postwar era
is itself a "strange hell." In his 1917 "Bach and the Sentry," Gurney's speaker
focuses his attention, rather than distracts himself, by recalling a Bach prelude while staring through the starry mist of an October night while on
sentry duty: "my spirit rose in flood," he notes, as he thinks of the music.
But when he projects himself in the postwar future, he fears this same Bach
prelude will only reawaken thoughts of No Man's Land:

When I return, and to real music-making,
And play that Prelude, how will it happen then?
Shall I feel as I felt, a sentry hardly waking,
With a dull sense of No Man's Land again?
(32)

What is now the present gets projected into the future as a deforming
mechanism: not only will art fail to console, but it may also trigger grim
memories.

None of the poems considered so far deals with any physical damage to
the speaker. In "Does It Matter?" Sassoon poses this question three times
over with regard to loss of legs, eyes, and sanity. He answers these questions
with bitter assurance that people will be kind despite such losses. It is not
evident here—in fact, it is rarely evident in a Sassoon poem—just what
the appropriate civilian response to wounded soldiers should be. While

implicitly empathizing with the wounded veterans, regardless of whether injuries are observable, Sassoon projects inauthentic responses onto the civilians. Graves's "Recalling War" may be set up as a challenge to Sassoon's bitterness toward others. From a distance of two decades since the Armistice, Graves asserts that the physically handicapped adapt, and his silence regarding how civilians react to the wounded implies that what those who stayed at home think is irrelevant:

> The one-legged man forgets his leg of wood,
> The one-armed man his jointed wooden arm.
> The blinded man sees with his ears and hands
> As much or more than once with both his eyes.
> Their war was fought these twenty years ago
> And now assumes the nature-look of time,
> As when the morning traveler turns and views
> His wild night-stumbling carved into a hill.
>
> (*Collected Poems* 130)

The contrast between these two poets' postwar views emerges clearly in the closure to their respective poems. Sassoon's passive civilians will accept shell shock as simply necessary collateral damage: "And people won't say that you're mad; / For they'll know you've fought for your country / And no one will worry a bit" (*Collected Poems* 77). Rather than reflect on how the wounded veterans' own sense of identity is both destabilized and confirmed by the battles they have participated in, Sassoon chooses to maintain a contemptuous tone toward civilians. Graves implies agreement between soldiers and civilians that the war's consequence was a collapsing of "sublimities" and "faith," yet his closing lines direct his greatest scorn toward veterans—himself included—who shape a future distorted by their recollections of war. Graves concludes his poem by comparing the playful destruction of children's games with the machine-gunning of soldiers: this is "A sight to be recalled in elder days / When learnedly the future we devote / To yet more boastful visions of despair" (131). Graves ridicules the notion that experience in the war fortifies veterans with a moral wisdom; if they think they have acquired such wisdom they have deceived themselves.

Owen's "Disabled" contemplates subject matter similar to that in Sassoon's and Graves's poems, the postwar experience of the wounded veteran, though with more specificity and definitely more compassion for the wounded. Owen's speaker observes a young former footballer now wheel-chair bound, legless and missing one arm. Owen dwells upon the disabled man's past, including his physical vitality and his self-indulgent, apolitical motives for enlisting. The disabled man's future, sketched in the poem's final stanza, is stripped of any pleasures or meaning that the prewar era held: "Now, he will spend a few sick years in institutes, / And do what things the rules consider wise, / And take whatever pity they may dole." More to the point, this disabled young man who enlisted "to please his Meg, / . . . to please the giddy jilts," foresees he will never enter any bond of intimacy: "Tonight he noticed how the women's eyes / Passed from him to the strong men that were whole" (67–68). Superficial women provoked the young man's enlistment, then recoiled from him upon his return.

Owen does not indicate what response the disabled man or the poem's speaker would find acceptable. One scene in Pat Barker's novel *Regeneration* suggests the incompleteness of Owen's "Disabled" through the charac-ter of Sarah Lumb, a munitions plant worker who has lost one fiancé in combat and who maintains no illusions, religious or patriotic, about the war. Through Sarah, whose intellect and depth of emotion have been estab-lished earlier in the novel, we see that what Owen's disabled soldier (and the poem's speaker) presumes to be lack of compassion should be understood instead as a lack of any possible compassionate role for the former "giddy jilts" to fill. While visiting a London hospital for soldiers, Sarah inadver-tently enters a sun-filled conservatory in which wheelchair-bound men sit silently with vacant stares. Sarah is keenly alert to the intrusive force of her presence on these men. After taking in the row of lost-limbed men, one with neither arms nor legs, Sarah exits the conservatory:

She backed out, . . . feeling their eyes on her, thinking that perhaps if she'd been prepared, if she'd managed to smile, to look normal, it might have been better. But no, she thought, there was nothing she could have done that would have made it better. Simply by being there, by being that inconsequential, infinitely powerful creature: *a pretty girl*, she had made everything worse. Her sense of her own helplessness, her being forced to play the role of Medusa when she meant no harm, merged with the anger she was beginning to feel at their being hidden away like that. If the country demanded that price, then it should bloody well be prepared to look at the result. (160)

Sarah resists being objectified and found guilty of lacking compassion. Owen projects callous complacence onto young women; he presumes that only soldiers are capable of feeling real compassion, real pity. This scene from Barker's novel, though, emphasizes the narrowness of this perspective and highlights Owen's inability to recognize the depth of anguish experienced by those left behind in England.

To return to Read's "My Company," the officer speaking the poem briefly silences his own troubled thoughts about what the postwar era will be like, metaphorically stepping aside and allowing two men of his company to spar verbally over the future awaiting all the soldiers who survive. Ken, whose "sexual experience is wide and various," intends to "settle down and marry." That's the extent of his foresight, though we may speculate that his one-line claim encompasses an unsurprising collection of conventional habits and even material objects, such as carpet slippers and kettle holders. The stanza that follows undermines Ken's claims, as it forcefully denies that these soldiers will be able to expunge their emotional trauma. This stanza, spoken by a company member named Malyon, whose sexual experience—in fact, whose entire background—is left a blank, derides the prospect of quiet contentment suggested in Ken's harmless phrase, "settle down and marry":

> Old Ken's a wandering fool;
> If we come thro'
> Our souls will never settle in suburban hearths;
> We'll linger our remaining days
> Unsettled, haunted by the wrong that's done us;
> The best among us will ferment
> A better world;
> The rest will gradually subside,
> Unknown,
> In unknown lands.

(36)

Comparatively, Blunden's beekeeper in "The Veteran," though isolated, is thriving remarkably. The verbs convey the weight of Malyon's argument: *linger, ferment, subside.* And why *ferment* instead of *foment?* Both verbs express the sense of achieving positive societal change through agitation; but it is not too fanciful to note the innuendo that such agitation may be only the talk of drunks, traumatized, perhaps shell-shocked. These two stanzas were included in Read's 1919 *Naked Warriors,* then excised from his *Collected Poems.* Dropping them does allow the officer-speaker's thoughts to dominate each section. Furthermore, the officer refrains from asserting whether Ken's or Malyon's opinion deserves most merit. But we know from the poem's final stanza that implicitly he sides with Malyon:

> The men I've lived with
> Lurch suddenly into a far perspective;
> They distantly gather like a dark cloud of birds
> In the autumn sky.
>
> (37)

Their community in the mud of the trenches will not be reanimated around a warm hearth in any conceivable time of peace.

II

In his introduction to *The Penguin Book of First World War Poetry,* Jon Silken challenges the purpose or usefulness of emotionally charged Great War poetry: "Even compassion must now be circumspect, for if it doesn't try to do away with, or limit, the war that causes the suffering, it's indulgent. At best compassion like this walks behind the system" (15). Silken establishes the criteria that must be met by any individual poem to achieve the highest stage of consciousness possible for treating the subject of war: anger and compassion must merge "with extreme intelligence, into an active desire for change, a change that will re-align the elements of human society in such a way as to make it more creative and fruitful" (33). We might expect that poems written after the Armistice—and specifically those poems that reflect on commemoration, on what should be remembered—would have the greatest likelihood of reaching such a stage of consciousness. But even with this expectation we should be alert to the significant demands of Silken's criteria: effective poems of commemoration must instruct us on what to remember, as well as suggest the kind of peaceful future that individuals should actively desire. Impressive because of their idealism, Silken's criteria are useful for evaluating several poems of commemoration.

Blunden's poem "From Age to Age," first published in 1934, reflects on both a marble monument and farmlands crowded with graves. The monument evokes positive features of the dead soldiers that perhaps require the sensitive poet and veteran's illumination for the viewer/reader. Consider the first stanza:

> Retarded into history's marble eyes
> Is their quick challenge and ability;
> All the expression of their enterprise,
> The fierce, the rapt, the generous and the free.
> Behold their monument; no more is now to see.
> (*Poetry and Prose* 260)

That first line—"retarded into history's marble eyes"—suggests that the monument diminishes the positive features of the dead soldiers, that the gap between the marble artwork and the reality of the human loss must remain wide. The monument disappoints the viewer's effort to make meaning out of their deaths. This same accusation applies to Blunden's poem itself. But to give the poet credit, he seems aware of what his poem specifically cannot say and what commemorative activities cannot achieve. Speaking, apparently, both to himself and to his reader, he urges that we walk the onetime battleground and "Count farms and haycocks, think of dead event, / Count all these graves, count every pang and pain / Which put" the soldiers in their farmland graves. British soldiers who died away from home were not allowed to have their bodies returned to England for burial. In small towns in England, church bells might announce the deaths of soldiers, but the corpses of those soldiers would never be returned for burial in the churchyard. Blunden knows that for the postwar visitors to the French and Belgium farmlands transformed into battlefields, such counting of graves, if taken literally, quickly would turn into a hopeless task. Consider these staggering numbers: "By 1930 557,520 soldiers of the Empire (454,574 from the United Kingdom) had been buried in identified, that is, named, graves. Another 180,861 unidentified bodies were put each in a separate grave. . . . The names of these men, and of a further 336,912 whose bodies had simply disappeared, blown into the air or ground into the mud, are inscribed in stone on a monument near the place where they were thought to have died" (Laqueur 153–54). In the absence of home-front conventional forms of grieving—not following the coffin of one's neighbor or beloved into and out of the church doors for the funeral service, not interring the young soldier near his family's home—walking the last land that the soldier walked and locating his name on a uniform marker would become for many an alternative act of grieving, or, by 1934, remembrance.

"Their name liveth for evermore," the epitaph from Ecclesiasticus 44:14, was engraved on every "austerely classical Stone of Remembrance" that presided over each of the one thousand cemeteries in France and Belgium that held at least four hundred graves (Laqueur 153). This British government–decreed uniformity extended to the gravestones themselves, which lacked a cross or Star of David or any other religious designation or a notation of the age of the deceased. The terse statement from Ecclesiasticus begs the question, *How* does a name live, especially when that name is listed along with tens of thousands of other names? And *what* is to be remembered when a visitor walks through these battlefields become cemeteries? To return to Blunden's poem, "From Age to Age" quietly urges that we respect the land itself as a monument. Blunden does not direct his readers regarding how they should think of the "dead event." He implies that each reader's act of remembering must be private. Consequently, Blunden avoids both indulgent compassion and reflections on how his society might change to prevent further eruptions of war. And he concludes with this couplet: "Over the skeleton the grass comes creeping, / And life's too short for wondering, too aflame for weeping." Blunden denies that these two contrary responses to the "monument" of the former battlefield—wondering or weeping—are appropriate. But he does not affirm what the appropriate response might be.

Sassoon's "Reconciliation," written in November 1918, unambiguously tells English parents whose own sons died what they must also remember when they visit their "hero's grave": "Remember, through your heart's rekindling pride, / The German soldiers who were loyal and brave." Though Sassoon's two quatrains avoid commenting on political motives for the war, he judges the English parents harshly; the foundation for their pride is "hatred, harsh and blind." He closes his poem with the hope that such hatred will collapse when English parents confront German mothers on the now-quiet battlefield and in the European cemeteries: "But in that Golgotha perhaps you'll find / The mothers of the men who killed your son" (*Collected Poems* 99). The Golgotha reference suggests that soldiers on both sides were Christ-like and that pride must rest on this conciliatory foundation. In this immediate response to the end of the war, Sassoon points to the peaceful future that the sorrow-filled older generation should strive for.

But as a decade and more passes from the war's end, Sassoon's conciliatory tone dissolves into sarcasm and revulsion at how the slain of Golgotha are misremembered. Most notably in "On Passing the New Menin Gate" he directs his anger toward this Belgium war memorial to the missing:

> here with pride
> "Their name liveth for ever," the Gateway claims,
> Was ever an immolation so belied
> As these intolerably nameless names?
> Well might the Dead who struggled in the slime
> Rise and deride this sepulchre of crime.
>
> (*Collected Poems* 188)

As in "Reconciliation," he deflates swellings of pride in the sacrifice. He even refers to the tens of thousands of soldiers memorialized at this site as "unheroic" and "unvictorious." Also, the scorn Sassoon felt for the noncombatant population in his poems written during the war persists in this poem. Sassoon's contempt for the memorial and the cheapened emotions he presumes it will inspire is obvious. He should be credited for acknowledging that remembering does not mean pacifying memory, putting thoughts of the war to perpetual rest. Instead, remembering should be active, intrusive, disturbing, taking the viewer of the memorial—or the reader of Sassoon's poems—away from consolation. But what, for Sassoon, lies away from consolation? Frustration, despair, anger. "Who shall absolve the foulness of their fate," he asks of the roughly fifty-five thousand men whose names are written all over the memorial. While it would be impossible for this memorial to treat as individuals so many slain soldiers, naming them at least makes a gesture at individualizing them. Yet Sassoon disapproves: "Was ever an immolation so belied / As these intolerably nameless names?" Sassoon does not indicate what purpose a monument should serve, what the appropriate monument would look like, or even if any monument should have been constructed. The Menin Arch has been described as "decidedly not a triumphal arch"; it "evokes nothing so much as a ghostly army beyond" (Laqueur 163). If the monument does not champion the political will of the state and if it avoids promoting any religious sentiment, we might have expected that ten years after the war's conclusion Sassoon would have been pleased with it. Perhaps, though, Sassoon's poem about the Menin Arch anticipates this crucial point made by Jay Winter: "[W]ar memorials, with their material representation of names and losses, are there to help in the necessary art of forgetting" (115).

Indirectly Sassoon indicates the effect one memorial should have in his 1933 sonnet "At the Cenotaph," in which "the Prince of Darkness," with his staff, appears respectfully and offers a prayer that memories of the war be erased and that the motives for the war be revived. This memorial (*ceno-taph* is from the Greek, meaning "empty tomb") was placed in 1919 in the middle of a heavily trafficked London street in Whitehall, a very public site for a "memorial to someone whose corpse lies elsewhere"; it "accurately reflects British concern for inventing forms capable of memorializing the specific trauma of national bereavement: a million young men, vanished" (Booth 33). The abstract power of the Cenotaph, as Winter asserts, provokes the viewer's contemplation "without the slightest mark of Christian or contemporary patriotic or romantic symbolism" and in effect transforms "all of 'official' London into an imagined cemetery" (104).[2] The prayer of Sassoon's "Prince of Darkness" implies that present urgings can overpower even the strongest of cultural memories:

> Make them forget, O Lord, what this Memorial
> Means; . . .
> Breed new belief that War is purgatorial
> Proof of the pride and power of being alive.
> (Collected Poems 201)

The unsubtle poetic device of the Prince of Darkness as the speaker blatantly expresses the motives for war that are antagonistic to Sassoon's own feelings. Clearly, Sassoon does not satisfy Silken's criteria: these postwar poems do not imagine a peaceful future. Instead, Sassoon implicitly denies the merits of Silken's criteria; he rejects the principle that monuments should function as "official acts of closure" (Hynes 270); he issues a warning that disillusionment felt in the postwar world cannot be overcome by means of another war. Also implicit in this sonnet is Sassoon's concession that his own poetry—like the Cenotaph itself—has failed to convince his audience.

Less politically polemical, though disconcerting nonetheless, is Ursula Roberts's "The Cenotaph," which suggests the anguish of noncombatants. The controlling voice of Roberts's poem (it is awkward to label her the poem's speaker, since she serves as an auditor) details passengers on a London omnibus silently viewing the "relatives of dead heroes, / Clutching damp wreaths" that are to be placed by the Cenotaph. These relatives are "Dumb beneath the rain, / Marshalled by careful policemen"; the speaker does not refer to any speech by any of these relatives or government officials to mark the occasion. The only person who speaks is a "plump" woman departing the bus who comments to no one in particular on the actions of the relatives: "I wouldn't stand in a queue to have my feelings harrowed." This woman, whom the speaker parenthetically notes is "Plump of mind as well as of body," whose own personal loss in the war is not specified, then adjusts her response to demonstrate that her position is personal, not critical:

> Not my*self*, I wouldn't
> . . . But then, again,
> There's some, you see,
> As can.
> >   (Reilly 93)

The poem implicitly poses a number of painful, unanswerable questions. What mourning rites are appropriate when the bodies of the dead relatives are not returned home? Should mourning for those who died in war be conducted in private, or is there necessarily a political dimension to the act of mourning soldiers? Is consolation available for surviving relatives in the recognition that their family members' death was one of hundreds of thousands of British soldiers? The term *harrowed,* with its implication that even with the passage of a few years since the war's end (the poem was first published in 1922) the emotions of the survivors continue to distress them, expresses the emotional torment that the plump woman recognizes. A harrow first breaks up and then evens off plowed ground. Thus the term may suggest that when applied to emotional suffering such public displays of grief as laying a damp wreath at the Cenotaph might reinvigorate and then ease the distress the surviving relatives experience.

In the poem's final lines, the controlling voice asserts that her memory of this plump woman's statement of open-mindedness has served her well, not specifically with regard to the acquisition of new insights into how others grieve their war dead, but more generally as a reminder to adopt a more tolerant attitude toward the vices and virtues of her neighbors. Those who do not suffer the direct loss of a family member may acquire from the mourners a degree of tolerance toward others. In simple terms, the incident Roberts describes is a plea for peace in the everyday thoughts and habits of her readers. Whereas Sassoon alarms his readers with fears that the monument will be misused as a site for rallying eager participation in a new war, Roberts recognizes that it may function as the intersection of private and public grief. The experience of living in postwar England disturbs these poets in different ways. Granted, eleven years passed between the writing of their two poems. And no reader should expect that the criteria of consolation will be the same for a veteran and a civilian. Nonetheless, their implicit conflict regarding the purpose of the monument highlights the success in creating an architectural form that provokes such contrary responses.

It may seem to make perfect sense to conclude this survey of poems that imagine and confront the postwar era with Roberts's somber optimism. Roberts avoids indulgent compassion, which satisfies part of Silken's criteria. But her poem avoids the content of the acts of commemoration: What do those who carry the damp wreaths remember of the war or more specifically of their dead loved ones, and what have they already forgotten? Roberts's poem adds further evidence to the argument that Silken's criteria remain, not wrong, but idealistic.

Notes

1. Though it would be naive to read the first-person speakers of the poems discussed in this essay as autobiographically accurate voices, some background information on each poet may prove helpful. A decorated officer, Read addressed the effects of the war in short stories and autobiographical prose as well as poetry and in the half-century of his life postwar became, as Hugh Cecil has written, "the most influential English art critic of the century" (38). Blunden enjoyed a successful and lengthy teaching career (he died in 1974) in Japan and England. He continued to write poems about the war throughout his life. In "Preliminary" remarks written in 1924 for his well-received prose autobiography, *Undertones of War*, Blunden justified his detailed account of his war years by referring to the claims of an inner voice: "You will be going over the ground again, it says, until that hour when agony's clawed face softens into the smilingness of a young spring day" (xii). This proved to be true both figuratively and literally. In 1936, Blunden succeeded Rudyard Kipling as literary adviser to the Imperial War Graves Commission, overcoming his initial reluctance "'to play a Kipling part when it comes to incising three or four words of respect on the tombstones of those who, but for the Kipling mind, would be quietly increasing the fruits of the earth, material and immaterial'" (qtd. in Webb 43). From 1936 on, Blunden revisited the sites of battles he participated in—at the Somme, Ypres, and Passchendaele—as well as other battlefields and cemeteries in France and Flanders (Webb 211). Prior to the war, Gurney seemed to demonstrate significant potential as a musician and a composer. During the war, in which he served as a private and played in the military band, he was gassed at Passchendaele. Signs of mental instability, evident as early as 1912, increased postwar: he spent his final

fifteen years (1922–37) in a London mental asylum, where he continued to write poetry (see Kavanagh and Hurd). Owen experienced a transformative, profound burst of poetic creativity after his initial extended service in the trenches. Like Sassoon, Owen was treated at an Edinburgh hospital set up to address symptoms of "shell shock" afflicting British officers, and, like Sassoon, he eventually returned to the front and led troops in further conflicts. Sassoon's admission to the hospital followed his public declaration against the war, a bold action that complicates efforts to understand both the degree of his illness and the British officials' requirement that he be treated. Some medical professionals, such as Sassoon's doctor who treated him during the war, W. H. R. Rivers, deserve to be acknowledged for their progressive, humane response to the essentially invisible wounds of shell shock. Though the origins of this form of psychological trauma continue to be debated, as Margaret Higonnet states in her recent essay on the testimony of nurses and orderlies who worked with the wounded and dying soldiers of World War I, certain features seem consistent: "The conditions to which many doctors in 1914–1918 as well as modern psychiatrists have pointed are extreme fatigue, the continuous confrontation with death and mutilated bodies, the shock of surprise (a sudden horrifying sight), and an irresolvable conflict between fear and duty or between two equally compelling responsibilities" (95). *Good-bye to All That* remains, arguably, Graves's best known of his lengthy list of books. This prose autobiography covers his prewar schooling, his experiences as an officer during the war, and his postwar adjustment up through 1929, when he said good-bye to England and moved to Majorca, where he stayed until his death in 1985. Wounded in the lungs by shrapnel at the Somme, Graves also lived with severe psychological scars: "Shells used to come bursting on my bed at midnight, even though [his wife] Nancy shared it with me; strangers in daytime would assume the faces of friends who had been killed" (287).

    2. The cited works by Laqueur, Winter, and Booth all reflect on forms of commemoration. Laqueur defines Britain's unprecedented task of uncovering and identifying corpses and constructing gravestones of uniform design in cemeteries located where the soldiers died; his essay highlights the British government's rejection of religious and patriotic language and images on the headstones and other memorial structures, an unwillingness to direct how the living should think of the war dead. Winter and Booth both examine the implications of the war within a cultural context and illustrate their discussion with analyses of architectural and literary creations. Winter's 1995 book is one of a number of his well-informed volumes on the war. Though Booth's primary focus is on prose literature, many of her insights may apply to the poetry under discussion in my essay, including this introductory comment on her chapter treating glass objects in buildings and literary works: "I trace the tendency in both modernist literature and expressionist architecture to portray interior and exterior reality with equal vividness, arguing that the modernist attention to interior experience springs at least in part from an awareness that only when the lessons of war are rendered in imaginative terms can modernism teach the lessons of war without participating in it" (13).

Works Cited

Barker, Pat. *Regeneration.* New York: Plume, 1991.

Blunden, Edmund. *Poetry and Prose.* New York: Horizon, 1961.

———. *Undertones of War.* 1928. London: Penguin, 2000.

Booth, Allyson. *Postcards from the Trenches: Negotiating the Space between Modernism and the First World War.* New York: Oxford University Press, 1996.

Cecil, Hugh. "Herbert Read and the Great War." *Herbert Read Reassessed.* Ed. David Goodway. Liverpool: Liverpool University Press, 1998.

Graves, Robert. *Collected Poems.* Garden City, NY: Doubleday, 1961.

———. *Good-bye to All That.* New York: Doubleday, 1988.

Gurney, Ivor. *Collected Poems of Ivor Gurney.* Ed. P. J. Kavanagh. New York: Oxford University Press, 1982.

Higonnet, Margaret. "Authenticity and Art in Trauma Narratives of World War I." *Modernism/Modernity* 9.1 (2002): 91–107.

Hurd, Michael. *The Ordeal of Ivor Gurney.* Oxford: Oxford University Press, 1978.

Hynes, Samuel. *A War Imagined: The First World War and English Culture.* New York: Collier, 1990.

Kavanagh, P. J. Introduction. *Collected Poems of Ivor Gurney.* New York: Oxford University Press, 1982.

Laqueur, Thomas W. "Memory and Naming in the Great War." *Commemorations: The Politics of National Identity.* Ed. John Gillis. Princeton: Princeton University Press, 1994.

Owen, Wilfred. *The Collected Poems of Wilfred Owen.* Ed. C. Day Lewis. New York: New Directions, 1964.

Read, Herbert. *Naked Warriors.* London: Arts and Letters, 1919.

Reilly, Catherine, ed. *The Virago Book of Women's War Poetry and Verse.* London: Virago, 1997.

Sassoon, Siegfried. *Collected Poems.* London: Faber and Faber, 1947.

———. *Memoirs of an Infantry Officer.* London: Faber and Faber, 1930.

Silken, Jon, ed. *The Penguin Book of First World War Poetry.* 2nd ed. London: Penguin, 1996.

Webb, Barry. *Edmund Blunden: A Biography.* New Haven: Yale University Press, 1990.

Winter, Jay. *Sites of Memory, Sites of Mourning: The Great War in European Cultural History.* New York: Cambridge University Press, 1995.

Wordsworth, William. *Wordsworth's Poetical Works.* Ed. E. De Selincourt and Helen Darbishire. New York: Oxford University Press, 1958.

CHAPTER TWO

The War Veteran
in *Tender Is the Night*

WILLIAM BLAZEK

In his short history of the First World War, Michael Howard includes in an appendix statistics about the number of people killed from each of the ten major European combatant nations, including the British Empire (146). These estimated figures show a total of eight million dead. In another column, he lists another reminder of the scale of social upheaval caused by the 1914–18 war: over sixty-two million soldiers were mobilized. That leaves a difference of fifty-four million people mobilized but not killed in World War I. The veteran always presents postwar societies with an incongruous presence that lingers for many decades, the human reminder of a violent and chaotic past, a memory that civilians first celebrate and honor but then gradually erase. Yet many American writers of the immediate postwar decades had living relatives—grandfathers, even fathers and uncles—who fought in the Civil War, which ended less than fifty years before World War I began (the equivalent distance in time of the Korean War for us today). Americans in the 1920s were faced with the disconcerting situation of having an older generation reminding them of the only partially healed national tragedy of the Civil War and a younger generation coming to terms with the slaughter on the Western Front.

Fitzgerald's novel *Tender Is the Night* brings both past and present elements to bear in its depiction of the World War I veteran, particularly the veteran with direct experience of combat.[1] In general, the veteran characters serve in the novel to question the meaning of war and to provoke the reader into considering the consequences of war. The combat veteran, especially, is shown to be awkward to integrate back into peacetime society and to elicit mixed responses from civilians that reflect poorly on the latter's understanding and empathy. In an insightful study of the social and emotional effects of participation in battle, J. Glenn Gray points out some aspects of guilt that the veteran feels, including "the realization that he is a participant in a system and an enterprise whose very essence is violence and whose spirit is to win at whatever cost" (233). Having witnessed comrades horribly wounded, endured the psychological strain of trench warfare, and faced the prospect of sudden death, the combat veteran is marked out as a special case in postwar society. He presents a challenge to one's comprehension of warfare, and—as impossible expectations are placed on his adjustment to peace—he must devise his own strategies for survival after the kinds of experiences that are impossible to explain to outsiders. The nature of those ways of coping, of how the veteran repositions himself with direction or purpose after the war, is the main theme of this essay.

The novel's key figures in this regard are Abe North and his counterpart Tommy Barban. In passing, however, it is worth noting the inclusion in books 1 and 2 of *Tender Is the Night* of a few other characters at least presumed to be war veterans, who build the impression of a war-torn past and a present continually recovering from calamity: namely, both of the late husbands of the widow Mrs. Elsie Speers (the first a cavalry officer and the second Rosemary Hoyt's father, an army doctor) and also the shifty World War I veteran whom Dick Diver first encounters outside the Films Par Excellence Studio in Paris—a shadowy figure whose importance in the narrative will be discussed below. After learning of Abe's death, Dick Diver watches a procession of German World War I veterans: "The column marched slowly with a sort of swagger for a lost magnificence, a past effort, a forgotten sorrow" (208). The mood of that scene is filled with the melancholic certainty that the Great War's conclusion less than a decade before did not mark the end of all wars but rather is the latest link in a chain of historic inevitability in which the war veterans represent the courageous yet vainglorious endurance of humanity in its fated progress toward death.

Despite the somber tone of that scene, I will examine shortly how specific scenes in which Abe North is foregrounded at least partially refute the elegiac description of the German war veterans. First, though, consider how reminders of World War I saturate the novel in layered images of war and battle and reveal how a military discourse continues to dominate after the Great War. Milton R. Stern asserts that "no novel written in the so-called 'lost generation' more deeply or centrally probes the significance of the war's legacy," and he gives several examples of how references to warfare infuse the text and connect World War I to America's other wars, especially the Revolution, the Civil War, and the Indian wars (103, 106–7). His sampling might be extended further to show how peacetime adjustments are inseparable from memories of the war. In a well-known passage in book 3, Nicole and Tommy's postcoital minutes in a half-star hotel are accompanied by the noise of American sailors fighting and the guns of a battleship sounding recall. Within a few paragraphs of the novel's opening at the opulent Riviera, Rosemary Hoyt is warned about the sharks offshore that devoured two British sailors the previous day. In contrast to this maritime menace, the beach itself is characterized by its umbrellaed demarcations and the general immobility of its inhabitants—like a pantomime of trench warfare, with small maneuvers of advantage followed by a cross-season Christmas truce. Dick Diver's "work house" at the Villa Diana sits like a pillbox or redoubt, suitable as observation and communications center for the hilltop fortress. In his typically evocative and elusive prose, in this instance combining equal measures of comic hyperbole and psychological insight, Fitzgerald writes of Dick, "He sometimes looked back with awe at the carnivals of affection he had given, as a general might gaze upon a massacre he had ordered to satisfy an impersonal blood lust" (31). In Paris, Maria Wallis fires two revolver shots into an Englishman at a railway station, ironically once a staging post for war, now a battle site itself. On a smaller scale, Maria Wallis is described as "a tall girl with straw hair like a helmet" (87), a jarring combination of shape and texture that suggests fusions of time periods and of genders, of pastoral softness and metallic strength. Even more subtly, Abe North's eyes in Paris are "bloodshot from sun and wine"(65)—and these simple descriptive words evoke how stress and even death may come from sybaritic pleasures (sun and wine) as readily as from the battlefields of France.

Abe North is the potential victim of easily accessible postwar dissipations, and critics often have seen him as a tragic drunkard who foreshadows Dick Diver's fate. William E. Doherty's assessment is typical: "Abe, like Dick, has a strong desire for loss of self, and forgetfulness. Abe wants oblivion and seeks it in drink; he longs for death" (191).[2] But the war veteran Abe North is a more positive figure than such judgments imply, one with the potential for affirming the resilience of human life, or at least raging against dullness and death. He does so in an antiheroic and comic-surreal way akin to Dada, which uses absurdist theater and wordplay to expose the flaws in a dominant culture based on rigid ideals of masculinity and an overindulgence in commodity consumption. If his role is eventually destructive—"My business is to tear [things] apart," he says to Nicole (86)—for the most part his actions and especially his dialogue contain revitalizing energy and show him as a postwar trickster, willing to overturn traditional notions of masculine behavior. That effort is best made by a veteran, who has nothing left to prove in terms of male courage and has had his inhibitions scoured clean by combat experience.

Abe attempts to revitalize the world through the therapeutic value of silliness. His conversation on the beach with his wife, Mary, and Nicole Diver, for example, derives from vaudevillian incongruity and Dadaist nonsense: "[Mary says:] 'So Mr and Mrs Neverquiver have arrived.' 'They're this man's friends,' Nicole reminded her, indicating Abe. 'Why doesn't he go and speak to them? Don't you think they're attractive?' 'I think they're very attractive,' Abe agreed. 'I just don't think they're attractive, that's all'" (23). Abe is unwilling to accept that a revived career as a composer is the answer to his apparent lack of direction; instead, he has threatened to cut a waiter in half with a musical saw—an appropriate instrument for him, combining bizarre artistry, a sardonic act of scientific discovery, mock-violence, and the possibility of reconstruction from splitting apart two halves: perhaps his prewar and postwar selves. While Dick Diver, the orchestrator of the carnival, joins in the high jinks by wearing his "transparent black lace drawers" (24),[3] in book 1 he might be seen as a minor character in Abe's drama, playing Zeppo to Abe's Groucho. With Marx Brothers anarchy, Abe declares to Nicole his moral code: "'Of course I've got one,' he insisted, '—a man can't live without a moral code. Mine is that I'm against the burning of witches. Whenever they burn a witch I get all hot under the collar'" (37). It seems a perfect moral code in a chaotic world, both righteous and comic, equally revealing and protective of his inner conscience.

Modris Eksteins writes about the instigators of the Dada movement, begun in Zurich in 1916: "[T]hey denied all meaning, even their own. The only sense was nonsense, the only art anti-art." He adds the important injunction, however, that "it nonetheless looked on the war as the essence of meaning. Dada's nihilistic games were war games of the mind" (210). If such a reaction to the war and its erasure of meaning is applied to Abe North, his markedly American style of puns, wisecracks, non sequiturs, and related pantomime attitudes stands as the equivalent of the Dadaists' phonetic and onomatopoeic concoctions. Moreover, such outwardly useless employment of words and behavior has a purpose: to reinvest language and action with meaning.

While his wordplay can be seen as a means to encourage radically new ways of thinking, Abe also acts directly in three key episodes that help explain how his own efforts at postwar survival also serve others. By acting contrary to a resurgent heroic code, he sends a warning to those who would repeat the mistake of thinking that wars should be fought to solve problems.

The first episode is the duel between Tommy Barban and Albert McKisco, in which Abe serves as McKisco's second and defuses a farcical situation that might have turned tragic. He explains to Rosemary that the duel "certainly is coo-coo but it seems to be true" (47). Besides using Dada-like words here, the dialogue points to the absurdity of this masculine contest, fought with dueling pistols (that Tommy carries in his suitcase) on a golf course (ironically indicating the modern emphasis on leisure and display) at 5:00 AM (associating it with a predawn attack of troops going "over the top"). The duel becomes a parody of the origins and consequences of World War I: starting unexpectedly, pursued because of false pride, fought with no apparent victor, and ending in reparations—the money required by a French doctor for his medical expenses. In his quiet, straightforward, cynical way, Abe prevents anyone from being killed in the incident. "Well, we'll see there's as little damage done as possible" (50), he tells Rosemary. And he accomplishes this by drawing on his veteran status and a close understanding of his fellow-in-arms, Tommy Barban. Abe leads McKisco through the ordeal by deemphasizing himself and cutting through the sense of honor that seems at stake. Without undue condescension, he deals with the reality of McKisco's fear, copes with the distraction of Rosemary and Campion's prurient interest, and defuses the professional anger of Tommy:

> "The distance was ridiculous," [Tommy] said. "I'm not accustomed to such farces—your man must remember he's not now in America."
>
> "No use cracking about America," said Abe rather sharply. And then, in a more conciliatory tone, "This has gone far enough, Tommy." (54)

The link between America and pointless aggression will become clear in later scenes, but the keynote here is the agreement between the two combat veterans that allows the farce to end as a farce rather than a killing, even though their interpretations of what makes the situation farcical are quite different.

This empathy through shared military experience is reinforced by the conversation that follows between Abe and McKisco about the difference in facing gunfire drunk or sober: "If you can't see it, there's no use going into it," Abe says, thereby condemning the reaction of the pumped-up McKisco, who unwisely states: "Don't you know everybody was drunk all the time during the war." To this provocative statement from someone who most likely avoided military service, Abe responds, "Well, let's forget it" (55). These dismissive words might suggest that Abe has been irreparably damaged by the war, creatively and emotionally, and that he seeks forgetfulness. But it is more likely that the conversation highlights the gulf between the combat veteran's perspective and the position of others who cannot comprehend the war even on a physical level, much less on a psychological or epistemological one. This chasm in understanding between the sensitive war veteran and those outside his experience is the space Abe North tumbles into, as his efforts to show others the purposeless waste of war are never understood.

The futility of Abe's attempts to make others hear the message behind his comic anarchy is shown especially in the account of a sightseeing trip to the Somme trenches and cemetery two chapters after the duel (tellingly preceded by the chapter incorporating Nicole and Rosemary's shopping trip around Paris, in which the structures of global capitalism and America's leading role in commodity culture are laid out). Dick Diver wants to explain what happened at the Somme in 1916, "though actually Abe North had seen battle service and he had not" (61). In response to Dick's overwrought analysis of the cultural-historical foundations for what he calls "a love battle," his attempt to understand in metahistorical terms why the Somme happened, Abe focuses on the philosophical with an orientation toward the future: "'There are lots of people dead since and we'll all be dead soon,' said Abe consolingly" (62). The narrative voice in this chapter seems to swing back and forth in sympathy between the two male characters and their perspectives, so it is important to consider the war veteran's point of view carefully and interpret Abe's tomfoolery in the trenches as something more than childish insensitivity. I would argue that Dick's sentimentality about trench warfare, based on his study of battlefield guidebooks, is significantly qualified by Abe's seriously comic turn, which in turn is supported by his status as a combat veteran, a position that gives him the privilege to clown around—and in so doing to expose the absurdity of the war and of attempts to give it logical meaning or sentimental value. "The war spirit's getting into me again." Abe jokes. "'I have a hundred years of Ohio love behind me and I'm going to bomb out this trench.' His head popped up over the embankment. 'You're dead—don't you know the rules? That was a grenade'" (62). The game, which plays with physical reality and the random nature of death at the Somme, is not one that Dick can enter into: "'I couldn't kid here,' he said rather apologetically [to Rosemary]. 'The silver cord is cut and the golden bowl is broken and all that, but an old romantic like me can't do anything about it.'" To which Rosemary uncomprehendingly replies, "I'm romantic too" (62), thereby further undercutting Dick's strained efforts to elucidate and entertain—and increasing the gap between Abe's unsentimental, antiromantic outlook and the position of others in the party. Dick Diver asserts that the carnage of World War I changed everything, but Abe shows that Dick's sympathies for lost youth and high ideals are not enough to survive the war's repercussions and may only repeat the mistakes of the past—the errors of misplaced honor, rigid social conformity, and unquestioning loyalty. Moreover, even if Abe's frivolity may be the harbinger of a nihilistic future, his dark wit in this scene retains a vital spark of resilience in the face of moral doubt and physical oblivion.[4]

As the unwelcome prophet of a directionless future, the trickster who destroys outdated social paradigms, the Dadaist inventor of new language patterns, Abe North is a difficult character for his wife and female friends to explain. As an alcoholic, he is a threat to their own more single-minded need for happiness and social control. Seeing off their desperately hungover companion at the Gare Saint-Lazare, "They stood in an uncomfortable little group weighted down by Abe's gigantic presence: he lay athwart them like the wreck of a galleon, dominating with his presence his own weakness and self-indulgence, his narrowness and bitterness" (87). Like the archaic words used to describe him, Abe is misplaced and turned out of time. With Nicole, especially, he acts clumsily in the railway station at the start of a solo journey from which Mary North and the others can only faintly hope that he will start afresh by returning to his American sources of artistic inspiration. Yet particularly following the visit to the trenches and its reminders of past trauma and reinforcement of present futility he loses all sense of purpose. Pushed by Nicole, who says sharply, "I can't see why you've given up about everything," he replies: "I suppose I got bored; and then it was such a long way to go back in order to get anywhere" (86). He has nearly arrived at the terminus of Dadaist nihilism, the danger of exhausted creativity spent on a worthless effort to raise a New Man from the ashes of the war. However, "Tired of women's worlds," he is ultimately unable to fashion one of his own that could reconcile his past, present, and future—a prewar world in which his artistic imagination sought to redefine music, a World War I combat experience that neither Nicole nor Mary and certainly not Rosemary could possibly comprehend, and a postwar society traveling in a direction that he can neither join nor alter. In those circumstances, alcohol provides a spatial and temporal but only temporary escape: "The drink made past happy things contemporary with the present, as if they were still going on, contemporary even with the future as if they were about to happen again" (107–8).

"Where cynicism is not mere shallowness and show," J. Glenn Gray suggests, "it is the cry of men who have not been able to endure the tension between their inner ideal and outer reality. They resolve not to take the world or themselves seriously any longer and give themselves over to enjoyment. But everyone notices that there is a pathos about their gaiety, and their frivolity is hardly contagious" (249). Gray is referring especially to World War II combat veterans here, but just such a division between caring interior and careless exterior selves is recognizable in Abe's alcohol-fueled theatrics in Paris. Nicole, Mary, and Rosemary are "frightened by his survivant will, once a will to live, now a will to die" (87). In appearance he maintains a "noble dignity" (65), a "solemn dignity" (87); but the effort to stand out and apart from the ordinary in order to lead people away from shallow exhibitionism results in a self-destructive surrender of individuality, a form of self-sacrifice that finds no worthy object in the Jazz Age (cf. Doherty 191). No longer the emerging composer, the combat soldier, or the popular wit, Abe in his last days in Paris is just a drunk—although a spectacular one.

Even in this last phase of his modern jeremiad, Abe manages to make an impact on those around him: "There is something awe-inspiring in one who has lost all inhibitions, who will do anything." But "[o]f course we make him pay afterward for his moment of superiority, his moment of impressiveness" (112). I would argue, drawing upon this narrative comment and upon Gray's assertions above, that as a representative World War I veteran Abe must pay for his unsought status acquired during wartime, for the responsibility of killing other men, for being invested with a nation's fate. A large part of that penance is to discard one role in exchange for another, to shift from being a fighting soldier who drank to get through the war to being a drunken veteran who cannot stop fighting the battles within himself as he participates in the postwar struggles over America's potential future.

For the hedonistic gossips in the Rue Monsieur Abe is merely "the entirely liquid Mr North" (78), and his fluid nature, symbolized by his increasing alcohol intake in Paris, is reflected in his awkward and unsettling departure from the narrative. Like the man shot by Maria Wallis through his identification card, Abe steadily loses self-identity after the war, loses his love for music, and becomes less substantial and more like a malicious ghost. In happier times, Nicole remembers,

> Abe used to be so nice. . . . He'd come to stay with us for weeks and weeks and we scarcely knew he was in the house. Sometimes he'd play— sometimes he'd be in the library with a muted piano, making love to it by the hour—Dick, do you remember that maid? She thought he was a ghost and sometimes Abe used to meet her in the hall and moo at her, and it cost us a whole tea service once—but we didn't care. (104)

Described initially as having blond Nordic features, Abe becomes associated with blackness and, consequently, with the threat of social disintegration caused by crossing racial boundaries (Smith 208). Rosemary is "rather revolted at his dirty hands" (112). His name is remembered by a policeman as "Mr Afghan North" (101). He misidentifies a black man named Freeman as the person who took his money and thereby becomes the unintended cause of Jules Peterson's death. Previously he impersonated General John ("Black Jack") Pershing in a joke played on the concierge and waiters at the Ritz.

Abe trickles out of the plot after he refuses to play a "quiet game" of anagrams and leaves with a final, absurd remonstrance to Dick and Rosemary: "But remember what George the Third said, that if Grant was drunk he wished he would bite the other generals" (113). This farewell, despite its fragmentation of wordplay and collapsing of history, evokes the determination, understated courage, and sad fate of Abraham Lincoln and Ulysses S. Grant, but with a tragicomic bite: for all the efforts of Lincoln and Grant to win the Civil War, save the Union, and address the long-standing problem of slavery, America was left a deeply divided nation; and for all of Abe North's mordant humor and casually expressed concern for others after the war, he is left bankrupt of vitality and ideas and meets an unseemly death.

Abe's only compensation for his sufferings is that he can remain ignorant of such events as the shooting of Maria Wallis's lover at the Gare St. Lazare (which takes place just as his train departs) and Jules Peterson's murder (which is revealed just after Abe leaves the hotel). Associated with each of these acts of violence (Nicole leaves Abe's side temporarily to try to speak with Maria Wallis before the shooting), he is spared the direct consequences of them. However, because "the only person [the Peterson murder] didn't disturb was Abe North," as Dick informs Mrs. Speers (171), Abe's absence from such moments of dramatic postwar violence is designed in part to reinforce his earlier exposure in the army to wartime bloodshed and thereby to connect him more firmly to America's problematic and bloody past. That violent history is fraught with the tensions between ideals and a divergent reality, and Abe is meant to serve as an increasingly perverse exemplar of it to those around him, who are exposed to and often participate in contemporary battles between sexes and within families. Furthermore, in his own death, following an aimless return to the United States, he is, like Peterson, almost a footnote to events, at least symbolically a victim himself of "some nigger scrap" (115), a redundant player in the latest historical drama unfolding among the Americans in Europe.

The details in the chapters through which Abe makes his convoluted and variously delayed exit create a heady concoction, but to make complete sense of them is in part to defeat their purpose, for they are composed of America's complex and often contradictory history—beginning in revolutionary violence, devolving into the still unreconstructed aftermath of the Civil War, and leading to the impossibility of identifying an assured individual self amid the confusion of selves demanded by post–World War I consumption culture and social upheaval. No wonder, then, that Abe is frustrated in his attempts to generate a receptive audience for his Dadaist life-performance. We are told that he finally leaves Paris, after an aborted first attempt, via the Ritz Bar, on a second-choice route more directly westward to America, "[f]eeling lost and homeless" (113), a phrase that echoes Tommy Barban's earlier remark "I have no home" (33) and Nicole's scabrous outburst "Home! . . . That filth!" (198). Ironically, it is Abe North, of the two war veterans, who will not find a home to return to after all—although, as reported incidentally in Tommy and Dick's presence some eighteen chapters later, he seems to have found enough strength and dignity, before his sordid death as a result of being beaten up in a New York speakeasy, to expire at the Racquet Club—or (the newspaper report is argued about) perhaps the Harvard Club (208).[5]

Abe fades from the narrative, his departure from Paris melding like a cinematic dissolve into the next chapter scene featuring Dick and Rosemary's affair: book 1, chapter 25, begins, "When he had tottered out, Dick and Rosemary embraced fleetingly" (113–14). The connection between Abe's histrionic, almost stock-staged alcoholism and the chimerical appeal of movies is emphasized by Abe's companionship with Rosemary and becomes even more clear in light of the scenes involving the anonymous war veteran who first appears in chapter 21. This American veteran, "perhaps thirty, with an air of being scarred and a slight but sinister smile," is associated by Dick with "the dim borderland of crime" and places such as garages, barbershops, and theater lobbies (97)—to which might later be added the speakeasy where Abe is fatally injured. "I just wonder why you've got so much time to waste," Dick says to him (98), a question that recalls Nicole's critical remark to Abe, "I can't see why you've given up about everything" (86). The American veteran, who has been in Europe since the war ended over seven years before, is outwardly marked as an underworld figure but is actually more of an entrepreneur; he sells American newspapers to tourists for over 200 percent profit and wants to get into the movies: "[T]hey need guys can speak English. I'm waiting for a break" (98).

The disreputable but hopeful veteran clearly foreshadows the wastage of Dick's expatriation (and reappears like a seedy Tiresias during the final confrontation between Tommy and Dick [315]), but he also evokes the experience of war as a "borderland" social space where killing is rationalized and consequences are deferred, where moral boundaries are redrawn—an experience that will exert a lasting effect in the lives of Abe North and Tommy Barban. Fitzgerald may even be equating war with criminal activity. The veteran outside the film studio also illustrates the detached attitude of former combatants forced to readjust to life outside the military. Abe's joking explanation two chapters later that he missed his first boat to America because he wanted to read the next installment of a story serialized in the popular magazine *Liberty* makes more obvious the links between war, disorder, and modern America. Furthermore, the skulking veteran selling American newspapers and the reference to the magazine *Liberty* suggest how the mass media of print and film are also implicated in the general decline and increasing commodification of postwar culture—to which Abe's comic creativity and absurd logic offer an alternative vision.

Besides carrying a subtextual reminder of what might have been the publisher for the serialization of *Tender Is the Night* itself (Bruccoli and Baughman 98), the title *Liberty* conveys an ironic reference both to a foundational principle of the United States and to the reckless liberality that results from the debasement of that ideal. As soldiers struggled to retain human dignity under the barbarous conditions of the Western Front, libertine attitudes to personal behavior and social interaction opened up in the territory behind the lines. Fitzgerald's expatriate Americans in Europe after the war are even more free to follow their urges and most often (or eventually) choose pleasure and entertainment over duty and sacrifice, opportunism and self-interest over honesty and loyalty. The dissolution of the Divers' marriage is the key sign of the arrival of a fragmented and unscrupulous social order that is also suggested by Nicole's "white crook's eyes" (297), the criminal threat of the unnamed war veteran, the decline and fall of Nicole's once-fondest companion Abe North, and the dubious attractions of Tommy Barban. When Nicole and Dick's marriage finally breaks down, the chapter-ending sentence "Doctor Diver was at liberty" (307), besides dismissing him from duty and suggesting that he does not want others' compassion, carries allusions to the war veterans as Dick joins them on the liminal ground of Liberty-libertinism-liberty.

A comparison of Abe North with Tommy Barban provides further support for the view that their position as war veterans is crucial to an understanding of the dynamic historical realignments of the postwar era portrayed through the narrative about the Divers' marriage. Besides illuminating the importance of the veterans in the structure of the novel, I hope to show why Tommy's enhanced survival is possible amid the ruins and reconstructions of the 1920s and 1930s.

The similarities between Abe and Tommy are as intriguing as the differences. Both men focus on Nicole romantically: Abe "had been heavy, belly-frightened, with love for her for years" (86), and Nicole "knew, as she had always known, that Tommy loved her" (282). The two tall men sit on either side of her at the table during the party at the Villa Diana as if they were festive colossi guarding her at a ritual banquet (36). Their mutual respect is shown on two pertinent occasions: during the duel scene, as discussed above, when their sense of alliance as fellow veterans helps resolve the conflict without bloodshed; and after Abe's death is disclosed, when Tommy briefly defends the musician's reputation as an innovator and pioneer (107). Although they are both present in the opening eleven chapters of the novel, after the duel Tommy disappears for thirty chapters, resurfaces unexpectedly in a Munich café, where the two men's stories cross as Abe's fate is revealed, and then returns unannounced eleven chapters afterwards to participate in all except one of the concluding nine chapters of book 3— comparable to Abe's presence in eleven of the final fourteen chapters of book 1.

These structural parallels are further reinforced by thematic balances and counterbalances between the two veterans. Both men alternately lose and find direction for their lives in the course of the narrative, both at times resist the pursuit of commercial opportunities for their financial stability, and both are associated with theater and film. For Tommy, the life of a mercenary soldier fighting for reactionary causes is exchanged for a temporary foray into stockbroking—an occupational shift that requires him to change from an outlandish suit, designed by the Polish court tailor, "of a cut and pattern fantastic enough to have sauntered down Beale Street on a Sunday" (206), into a conventional one. His adventures fighting in Morocco or rescuing a prince from Russia and his plans to prostitute himself in the 1920s stock market boom suggest a Gatsby-like pursuit of wealth that has Nicole as the distant object. Although Tommy is too restless and intense to adapt well to the marketplace and although he soon tires of work as a stockbroker, he readjusts his talents and disposition in a way that Abe North cannot do: he channels his merciless energies into capturing Nicole from Dick, gaining both the American princess and her Riviera-based kingdom. Appropriately, the shift in his financial intentions and the beginning of his affair with Nicole take place on the *Margin*, the motor yacht of T. F. Golding.

The significant differences between Tommy and Abe explain why the former successfully negotiates a route through the aftermath of World War I. Abe loses his battle with alcohol while Tommy applies his military discipline to control his drinking and thereby reaps the advantages and disadvantages of remaining in real time. Tommy "[does] not like any man very much or feel his presence with much intensity," while Abe covers his empathy with a nonchalant demeanor and impish behavior. I have argued above for recognition of Abe's essential morality, but Tommy's moral constitution is more ambiguous—mainly because of his hybrid American-French background and his attitudes toward war and sexuality.[6] If Abe struggles with his reaction to the futility of war, Tommy accepts the persistence of human conflict and applies his calm courage and "the complexity of his training" to that fact (39). He tells Rosemary, "'I suppose there's a war—there always is.' 'Don't you care what you fight for?' 'Not at all—so long as I am well treated'" (33). Note that he does not say "well paid": profit is not his chief motivation in wearing uniforms of more than eight different countries. Tommy is a professional soldier, while Abe is presumably a product of America's emergency call to arms, either enlisted or drafted in 1917 after the U.S. entry into the war, an amateur who would expect to return to civilian life if he survived the fighting. Less well prepared for what he had to encounter, Abe went through the experiences of combat but was then left with the kinds of moral and psychological problems that Tommy's mental armor more easily deflects.

Tommy is the one male protagonist to remain employed in his profession during the majority of the narrative's chronology. "I am a soldier," he tells Rosemary. "My business is to kill people" (39).[7] He is admired and feared in equal measure for the distinguishing characteristic of his occupation: he is granted the license to kill other people in exchange for the risk of being killed or injured himself. When he turns away from soldiering, it is because that risk has become too high: "Recently an eighth of the area of his skull had been removed by a Warsaw surgeon and was knitting under his hair, and the weakest person in the café could have killed him with a flip of a knotted napkin" (205). Dick asks if he has ever been frightened; "'When I was cold,' Tommy said. 'I always get scared when I'm cold. During the war I was always frightened when I was cold'" (207). The inwardly brittle but outwardly imperturbable persona of a soldier sustains him as he turns from fighter into lover, from the café in Munich during his wintertime recuperation to the party yacht anchored offshore at Nice in the heat of a Riviera summer.

"Tommy Barban was a ruler, Tommy was a hero," the chapter set in Germany begins, and continues: "As a rule, he drank very little; courage was his game and his companions were always a little afraid of him" (205). For my argument, the most relevant words here are *ruler* and *rule,* expressing the dominance of his personality and the self-discipline that underpins it, and *game,* which connects to Abe North's Dadaist games and explains how war heroes such as Tommy must behave to survive: "he was all relaxed for combat; as a fine athlete playing secondary defense in sport is really resting much of the time, while a lesser man only pretends to rest and is at a continual and self-destroying nervous tension" (205–6). Lesser men, in this sense, such as Abe and Dick, are neither rulers nor heroes. Tommy is the better player in the postwar power games with love and money because he knows instinctively that his authority is gained partly through skill and partly through bluff, partly from action and partly from playacting. His ability to disengage his feelings in what becomes a successful performance is akin to the necessary detachment of acting that Dick explains to Rosemary: "In the theatre all the best comédiennes have built up their reputations by bur*les*quing the correct emotional responses—fear and love and sympathy.... You go all *out* of character—you understand?" (293–94). The essential detachment of the physical from the psycho-emotional comes from Tommy's military background, and only in extremis is that gap breached.

When next encountered, Tommy has resuited himself to play the role of hero. On Golding's yacht he boasts about himself, self-consciously trying out his new persona for the first time with Nicole, initially in French and then in English (although, as she explains, "in English you can't be heroic and gallant without being a little absurd"):

> "After all, I am a hero," Tommy said calmly, only half joking. "I have ferocious courage, *u*sally, something like a lion, something like a drunken man."
>
> Nicole waited until the echo of his boast had died away in his mind—she knew he had probably never made such a statement before. (276)

Fitzgerald is able to resurrect here the question about the nature of courage raised by McKisco's insinuation that soldiers were drunk all the time while fighting in the Great War (55), and with it a reminder of Abe North's drunken heroism in peacetime. Furthermore, Tommy's mispronounced "*u*sally" points to the complexity of heroic action, which flows from a jumble of human motivations, often including fear, self-preservation, and anger. "Pure" heroism can be found only in the cinema, as Tommy indirectly acknowledges. When Nicole asks, "Is it all like the movies?" he replies: "The movies aren't so bad—now this Ronald Colman—have you seen his pictures about the Légion Étrangère? They're not bad at all" (276). By contrast, Abe North shows his indifference and perhaps derision toward the illusions of movie culture at the start of the screening of *Daddy's Girl* as he "coughed convulsively and blew his nose" (74). Yet both veterans respond to the contemporary influence of cinema by seeing through the artifice because as soldiers they learned how to confront the unnatural demands of the twentieth-century battlefield. Paul Fussell points out, "Seeing warfare as theater provides a psychic escape for the participant: with a sufficient sense of theater, he can perform his duties without implicating his 'real' self and without impairing his innermost conviction that the world is still a rational place" (192). Abe and Tommy have been shaped by such combat experience to remain both actors and spectators in the lives they create following the war.[8]

Tommy's willingness to accept the artificiality of the cinema as the modern representation of heroic action illustrates both the atrophy of the meaning of heroism and a shift in Tommy's own perceptions about what his old "business" entails after the World War.[9] When, as Mary North Minghetti declares, "All people want is to have a good time" (319), Tommy's disregard for and control over other men can be turned to new advantages. "I've brutalized many men into shape but I wouldn't take a chance on half the number of women," he tells Nicole (298). Although one implication here is that he is entirely capable of bending Nicole to his will, the possibility remains that there may be no need to if she is already matched to him—morally and sensually if not yet economically. Their ostensibly demilitarized world nevertheless retains wartime features such as social displacement, sexual frustration and licentiousness, callous conduct, and territorial and material acquisitiveness. In such a time of continued flux, Tommy can scoff at "All this taming of women!" (298) because he has tamed or been tamed himself.[10] His transformation is incomplete and his remarks to and about Nicole are not without ambiguity and irony, but Nicole does invite his instincts, training, and power to rest on her. On Golding's yacht, "In her cherished presence Tommy Europeanized himself quickly" from the languages and manners of his foreign escapades (276). She provides a channel for his passionate nature, and eventually she offers him a shared home in the Villa Diana.

Tommy and Nicole are suited to each other not only because he opens up for her a new (or revisited) world based on instinct and amorality and, potentially, indifference, or because he will not treat her as a sick patient (Tavernier-Courbin 218–20), but also because he can be the "protector" (316) of the Warren global empire—a position for which he is well prepared through his command experience in colonial wars and in defense of imperial capitalism. Having waited for five years and acted out his frustrations through foreign military engagements, he at last acquires the granddaughter of a robber baron as his consort, a woman whose retinue when traveling requires a system of lists and numbered baggage trunks, "the equivalent to the system of a regimental supply officer who must think of the bellies and equipment of three thousand men" (265). These two highly competent, high-mannered, and sometimes explosive personalities may prove Dick Diver wrong in his admonition that they would merely "be new to each other" (315). Their adaptability characterizes them as strongly as their other qualities—Nicole in her escape from psychotherapy into a more independent adulthood and Tommy in his transformation from a peripatetic soldier into a married veteran. Although facing the new challenge of having to settle down to "l'amour de famille" (315), he has shown already that discipline and artifice may be combined successfully on the battlefield, so his future most likely holds further performances as sensual husband, business enforcer, and (according to several critics) neo-barbarian—though a domesticated one.[11]

Tommy's apparent success in reinventing himself in "the broken universe of the war's ending" (253) may indicate that a professional soldier's merciless attitude will run through the social realignments of the postwar era, yet the sternness in his regimen and ideas is balanced by the exoticism of his varied experience and the glimpses of vulnerability in his actions and feelings. Moreover, his presence in *Tender Is the Night* is weighted fairly evenly with that of Abe North, in the novel's narrative construction and thematic pattern, so that equal measure is given to Abe's sensitive morality, restorative comedy, and titanic defeat and to Tommy's survivor strength, abstemious control, and redirected energy. Ranged against them both is not Dick Diver's profligate empathy and professional misdirection but the unwarranted conceit, third-rate talent, and flimsy celebrity of McKisco and other representatives of a hollow future. The scandal-mongering Mrs. McKisco is the cause of the duel between her husband and Tommy, who defends honor and propriety from gossip and jealousy. In bullying Mrs. McKisco and later brutally criticizing Lady Caroline Sibly-Biers, he enforces the strong arm of civility over indiscretion and indecency. Unconcerned with such physical efforts to reestablish patriarchal authority, Abe North chooses the abstraction of comedy to serve his attack on philistine values and the kind of close-minded logic that creates war states and mass-production social conformity. Together the two war veterans present a complex reply to the real barbarians—those who conduct their lives as if the war meant nothing. Yet despite facing the war's challenge of continued violence and disruption, the men do not end up as nervous wrecks like Virginia Woolf's Septimus Smith, whose loss of feeling during the war leads to uncontrollable fear afterwards.[12] Instead, they are exceptional figures who can best be considered together but should not be oversimplified. Whether by embracing or rejecting their warrior status, they give bold performances on the uncertain stage of postwar European and American reconstruction. In that sense, Dick Diver's comment about Abe's unexpected reappearance in

Paris might be used as a summary of soldiers' unlikely survival in World War I and the veterans' influential roles in *Tender Is the Night*: "Popular but not probable" (112).

NOTES

1. The general reader may benefit from a brief note about some key features of F. Scott Fitzgerald's 1934 novel *Tender Is the Night* that are especially relevant to this essay, which focuses not on the main narrative strand of the novel—the marriage of Dick and Nicole Diver—but on important thematic and structural roles played by the Divers' two closest friends, the First World War combat veterans Abe North and Tommy Barban. The marriage originates during the war, after the wealthy Nicole Warren has been sent to Switzerland (traveling there aboard a U.S. Navy cruiser) for psychiatric treatment, where she falls in love with her young doctor, Dr. Diver. He takes over the sole care of Nicole during their marriage but eventually compromises his early ideals in the face of the overwhelming influence of the Warren family fortune, the increasing impact of modern consumer culture, and the postwar emphasis on hedonism and selfishness—all of which affect Dick's fragile hold on his own purpose and identity. Ranged against the failure of the marriage and the professional and social fall of Dick Diver are the stories of Abe North and Tommy Barban—the first of whom becomes a victim of alcohol and the second of whom becomes Nicole's new husband. How and why these two men arrive at those points, and what their status as veterans means to our understanding of this complex and powerful novel, are questions that this essay will explore.

2. Arthur Mizener, too, views Abe North as a "dramatic parallel" to Dick Diver (120). The real-life models of Abe North point to the complexity of the fictional character. The writer Ring W. Lardner Jr. and the playwright Charles MacArthur (the source for Abe's story of the waiter and the musical saw) were both heavy drinkers, but their sardonic humor and popular brilliance are more tellingly reflected in Abe's character. After Lardner's death, Fitzgerald wrote a tribute for the *New Republic* in which he noted his friend's "noble dignity" (qtd. in Bruccoli and Baughman 61–62; Le Vot 122–24, 214, 217).

3. The costume supports Judith Fetterley's view of Dick Diver as a feminized character, shown also in his efforts as a host and nursemaid. Moreover, she argues, "The negative attitude toward conventional masculinity is deeply embedded in the imaginative structure of *Tender Is the Night*" (222).

4. For a contrasting view of the trenches scene, see James H. Meredith, who argues: "In North's case, the war itself has traumatized him to the point that he can only see the dead. Like Egyptian hieroglyphics without the Rosetta Stone, North cannot read the landscape and know what it means beyond his personal pain" (191).

5. It remains a mystery, but Abe's role in *Tender Is the Night* may be revealed in some substitute anagrams for the game he refused to play. The letters that make up "Abe North" can be rearranged into (a) Nat B. Hero (Not be a hero), (b) Ban T. Hero (Ban the hero), and (c) Tan B. Hero (from his Riviera sojourn), as well as (d) The Baron (contrasting with Nicole's robber baron grandfather), (e) hate born (or vice versa, but either way connected to the war), and perhaps most appropriately (f) Be a thorn (maybe in the side of "Mr. S. Flesh," an American name spotted by Dick and Nicole in the *Paris Herald* [22]).

6. Jacqueline Tavernier-Courbin suggests that with his amoral sexuality Tommy provides Nicole with a guide to a "new pagan, primitive, and, at the same time, highly civilized world." She also notes the tendency of European critics to view Tommy in a more positive light than American critics do (229, 231–32, n. 11).

7. Cf. Abe North: "Tired of women's worlds. . . . My business is to tear them apart" (86).

8. Tavernier-Courbin, in a related context, argues that Nicole and Tommy tend to confront problems head on and do not naturally live in a world of illusion (218), but even for them the unnatural world of the moving picture has its allure and serves as both countermeasure and model for their own creations of selfhood. A similar conclusion might be applied to Dick Diver in his loss of illusions over Rosemary.

9. John Lucas's analysis of Tommy Barban as an absurd would-be hero is relevant to my argument here and above. He writes: "[T]here are no great causes for which he can fight. Tommy is an anachronism, a trained warrior stranded in the wrong age. . . . His military exploits, though seemingly heroic . . . are, at bottom, absurd. . . . And if Tommy is absurd in war he is also absurd in love" (98–99). While I partially accept his conclusion that the postwar reality that Tommy encounters is "the reduction of great themes to ineluctable pettiness, to a world of compromised possibilities" (100), my contention is that Tommy shows self-awareness of his absurd and at least outwardly anachronistic position as a hero and that he adapts himself to the modern circumstances of decaying ideals and underlying violence.

10. This perspective may help to reconcile such opposite critical views of Tommy Barban as those of Milton R. Stern and Jacqueline Tavernier-Courbin. Stern interprets Tommy's exclamation as supremely ironic, since "[w]hat he means by untamed women is limited entirely to sexual abandon" and he remains "the totally overmastering male . . . the conquering warrior" who defines Nicole exclusively in sexual terms (111–12). Tavernier-Courbin, on the other hand, sees Tommy as a sensual male, free from the constrictive morality exhibited by Dick Diver (218–19, 229).

11. For a sense of the variety of critical opinion that addresses the Barban-barbarian line of argument, see Gordon B. McConnell, Joan Kirkby, Arthur Mizener, and Milton R. Stern. McConnell writes, "When the affair [with Nicole] is consummated, Barban's sexual conquest embodies his barbaric aesthetic principles"

(107–8). Kirkby acknowledges that Tommy Barban is "an ambiguous figure": on the one hand, he is "a ruthless but necessary cleansing force. . . . However, in another sense, Barban could be seen as the barbarian that his name suggests" (166–67). Mizener confusingly calls him "a sophisticated and worldly barbarian of great charm" (105). More recently, Stern uses the term in his criticism: "Tommy is the barbarian dominator who belongs in the licentious post-war world and is Fitzgerald's prototype of the fascist" (112). My sympathies lie mainly with Kirkby's judgment, and the ambiguity that she notes is part of the hotel scene in which the first sexual encounter between Tommy and Nicole is followed by the interruption of two young women who want to wave to their departing sailor boyfriends. They are "young, thin and barbaric," and although Tommy politely allows them into the room, he and Nicole seem to make their exit very soon afterwards, thus complicating the association or disassociation between the new lovers and the young women's "barbaric" appearance. One interesting clue to interpretation may be found at the start of the paragraph in which that pertinent word appears: "Tommy saw a girl rush out upon the balcony below waving a napkin" (301)—perhaps a reminder that "the weakest person in the [Munich] café could have killed him with a flip of a knotted napkin" (205). If so, the young women and their behavior are more likely antithetical to his urbane sensibilities, and the common denominator of sexual intercourse among the pairs in the hotel scene does not necessarily imply that vulgarity results from following primitive passions. Yet having to coexist amid such common people and their pursuits is going to be the future that Nicole and Tommy will enter together.

12. Comparisons might also be made with the veterans depicted in Fitzgerald's short stories, particularly "May Day" (1920). Meredith notes: "Nearly every veteran involved in the plot ends up wounded or defeated in ways that flout the promise of peace. . . . [F]rom ensuring order, the war has merely brought its chaos to the home front" (176–77).

Works Cited

Bloom, Harold, ed. *Modern Critical Views: F. Scott Fitzgerald.* New York: Chelsea House, 1985.

Bruccoli, Matthew J., and Judith S. Baughman. *Reader's Companion to F. Scott Fitzgerald's* Tender Is the Night. Columbia: University of South Carolina Press, 1996.

Claridge, Henry, ed. *F. Scott Fitzgerald: Critical Assessments.* Vol. 3. Mountfield, East Sussex: Helm Information, 1991.

Doherty, William E. "*Tender Is the Night* and 'Ode to a Nightingale.'" Bloom 181–94.

Eksteins, Modris. *Rites of Spring: The Great War and the Birth of the Modern Age.* London: Bantam, 1989.

Fetterley, Judith. "Who Killed Dick Diver? The Sexual Politics of *Tender Is the Night*." Claridge 206–23.

Fitzgerald, F. Scott. *Tender Is the Night: A Romance*. Ed. Matthew J. Bruccoli. Everyman Library. London: J. M. Dent, 1996.

Fussell, Paul. *The Great War and Modern Memory*. London: Oxford University Press, 1975.

Gray, J. Glenn. *The Warriors: Reflections on Men in Battle*. 1959. New York: Harper and Row, 1973.

Howard, Michael. *The First World War*. Oxford: Oxford University Press, 2002.

Kennedy, J. Gerald, and Jackson R. Bryer, eds. *French Connections: Hemingway and Fitzgerald Abroad*. London: Macmillan, 1998.

Kirkby, Joan. "Spengler and Apocalyptic Typology in F. Scott Fitzgerald's *Tender Is the Night*." Claridge 153–69.

Le Vot, Andre. *F. Scott Fitzgerald: A Biography*. Trans. William Byron. Harmondsworth: Penguin, 1985.

Lucas, John. "In Praise of Scott Fitzgerald." Claridge 86–100.

McConnell, Gordon B. "Sane Crooks, Mad Puritans: Fitzgerald, Modernist Sociology, and Poor Material for a Socialist." *F. Scott Fitzgerald Review* 2 (2003): 85–115.

Meredith, James H. "Fitzgerald and War." *A Historical Guide to F. Scott Fitzgerald*. Ed. Kirk Curnutt. New York: Oxford University Press, 2004. 163–213.

Mizener, Arthur. "*Tender Is the Night*." Bloom 97–108.

Smith, Felipe. "The Figure on the Bed: Difference and American Destiny in *Tender Is the Night*." Kennedy and Bryer 187–213.

Stern, Milton R. "*Tender Is the Night* and American History." *The Cambridge Companion to F. Scott Fitzgerald*. Ed. Ruth Prigozy. Cambridge: Cambridge University Press, 2002. 95–117.

Tavernier-Courbin, Jacqueline. "The Influence of France on Nicole Diver's Recovery in *Tender Is the Night*." Kennedy and Bryer 215–32.

Woolf, Virginia. *Mrs Dalloway*. London: Hogarth, 1925.

CHAPTER THREE

Coming Home Defeated

*Soldiers and the Transition from War to Peace
in Post–World War II Japan*

BEATRICE TREFALT

Japan's recovery from its massive defeat in 1945 is often depicted as a story
of economic success. Unprecedented growth rates and vastly improved stan-
dards of living had by the 1960s rendered invisible much of the physical
damage of the war. But the postwar generation's prosperous upbringing did
not directly lead to the perceived "amnesia on war issues" for which Japan
is so famous among its former enemies. Even now, nearly sixty years after
the defeat, a sizable but admittedly declining percentage of the population
have experienced the war either as soldiers, as victims of the bombings of
the home front, or as widows or orphans of those fallen in battle. In fact, it
was not until the early 1970s that the first true postwar generation came of
age; throughout the 1950s and 1960s, the scars left by the war in the minds
of the Japanese people were still clearly visible even as the scars on the physical landscape were erased. Such scars in consciousness have remained tender throughout the postwar period, belying the widespread popular notion
that Japan has simply "forgotten" the war and highlighting the complex and
difficult process of transition from war to peace.

This process was particularly difficult for veterans of the Imperial
Army, the families of fallen soldiers, and those who had been prisoners of
war. An analysis of the integration of their experiences into the postwar nation allows us to understand better the extent and the nature of war legacies
and the difficult processes of reconciliation that accompany them. In Japan,
attitudes toward World War II veterans—as well as fallen soldiers—have remained highly ambivalent: former soldiers were, after all, the embodiment
of military forces not only defunct since 1945 but designated as bearing the

onus of war guilt during the Occupation and so reviled. The position of former soldiers with regard to war guilt was unclear: they could be portrayed either as victims of the Imperial Army and Navy or as complicit participants in Japan's aggressive war. The ambiguity of their relationship with the war effort has, in the postwar period, reflected the contested nature of memories of the war in general. This essay aims to clarify the factors that molded attitudes toward veterans, and the attitudes of the veterans themselves, in order to illuminate Japan's relationship to the war as it entered the second half of the twentieth century.

A number of scholars have recently traced the changing shape of memories of the war in the postwar period and have made important contributions to our understanding of the fluid and fragmented nature of memory.[1] None of them have, however, considered the nature of Imperial Army and Navy veterans' relationship to the postwar nation and to its social and cultural landscape. It is not my aim here to discuss the process by which pensions were allocated to the veterans or bereaved families, or the way in which bereaved families fought to have the sacrifice of their loved ones publicly recognized.[2] Rather, my aim is to illustrate Japanese soldiers' confrontation with defeat and with war guilt and the civilian population's confrontation with the soldiers' experience. After all, the defeat entailed the complete reformulation of the beliefs and ideas that had supported both soldiers and civilians during the war, and in that respect the integration of soldiers into a society at peace took quite a different path than in those nations enjoying victory. Japanese soldiers had left for the front as heroes; their image on their return was much more ambiguous.

This essay examines the return of Japanese soldiers in three distinct ways. First, it considers the attitudes of, as well as toward, prisoners of war. In the sense that all Japanese soldiers ended up being prisoners of war at the time of defeat, an exploration of the notion of capture in the Japanese context provides a useful point of departure. Second, it considers attitudes to the military in general, and to soldiers in particular, during the Occupation period, as well as the soldiers' responses to these attitudes. Third, it sketches briefly the recriminations of soldiers regarding the transmission of their experience after the period of high growth, when a generation that had not experienced the war reached adulthood.

In the West, the image of Japanese World War II soldiers is predominantly one of ruthless and dedicated fighters, imbued with a fanaticism that led them to commit unspeakable atrocities and to throw themselves into the fighting with complete disregard for their own lives, leading to hopeless and suicidal battles beyond the comprehension of their enemies (the battles of Guam in July 1944 and Okinawa in April 1945 are possibly the most famous, among countless examples). Indeed, the ratio of dead to captured in the Japanese Army was in inverse proportion to that of most Western armies involved in the Second World War. One author mentions figures of 175 dead to 1 captured among Japanese soldiers in places like Burma and New Guinea, compared with the general figure of 1 dead to 4 captured in Western armies.[3] It was this apparent selfless dedication to Japanese victory that in many circles earned Japanese forces the label of fanatics.[4] However, the notion of religious or political fanaticism is not particularly useful for understanding why soldiers died in such great numbers; nor does it provide a good basis for analyzing the problems faced by soldiers when they returned after the defeat. The experience of soldiers must be put in the context of prewar and wartime military training and doctrine.

Before the defeat, soldiers were held, publicly at least, in very high esteem. In theory, they were under the ultimate command of the emperor, a figure divine and inviolable, and this symbolic proximity to the emperor accorded the soldiers commensurate status. This high status was, however, predicated on a certain behavior, which the soldiers learnt during their training at the barracks and which the population understood through its own mobilization for wartime aims. If the population was to be dedicated, loyal, ready to die in the service of the nation, and frugal—relying on reserves of "spirit," as the war progressed, more than on physical goods—the soldiers were to be doubly so.

Absolute dedication, loyalty, and readiness to die in the service of the nation translated, in the soldiers' training, explicitly into the notion that they were not to surrender. The Field Service Code of January 15, 1941, contained the following lines: "Meet the expectations of your family and home community by making effort upon effort, always mindful of the honor of your name. If alive do not suffer the disgrace of becoming a prisoner; in death, do not leave behind a name soiled by misdeeds."[5]

Whereas in Western armies there is little stigma attached to being, or having been, a prisoner of war, the Japanese soldier had to win or fight to the death, according to the official ideology. If he failed to do so, suicide was his only allowable option. While the propaganda for soldiers stressed that this was part of timeless Japanese tradition and of the samurai ethic of Bushidō, the practice of no-surrender was in fact instituted only after the

Russo-Japanese War of 1904–5, and it was first widely publicized only in 1932.[6]

The experience of Japanese prisoners of war was fundamentally different from that of their Allied counterparts, not least because they were treated much better than those in the hands of their own army. (The often-brutal treatment of prisoners of war in Japanese hands is remembered with much bitterness in Southeast Asia and England, but particularly in Australia and New Zealand.)[7] The issue confronting Japanese prisoners of war was not the conditions in which they lived as prisoners of war, which were comparatively comfortable, but the fact that their own army had explicitly forbidden them to surrender. As loyal citizens and good soldiers, they should have killed themselves before, or at least upon, capture. Having become prisoners of war made them traitors.

It is obviously difficult to make sound generalizations on the degree of sincerity with which soldiers believed in the idea of shame of surrender. After all, with the defeat, some five million servicemen, of which slightly over three million were overseas, put their arms down and surrendered. While some did commit suicide in the wake of defeat, they were, on the whole, a very small minority. In fact, during the war many soldiers chose suicide rather than surrender not because they felt any shame but because they were afraid of how they would be treated by the enemy. In *Furyoki* (Diary of a Prisoner of War), the writer Ōka Shōhei points out that, had the army command had full confidence in the soldiers' belief in the shame of surrender, it would not have spread such detailed rumors about the way captured soldiers would be tortured and killed by Allied troops. It was, more than anything, the fear of a slow and agonizing death at the hands of the enemy, according to Ōka, that spurred many soldiers to commit suicide in the face of imminent capture.[8] Other sources also support the notion that Japanese soldiers had routinely been led to believe that they would be killed in the most horrible manner should they fall in enemy hands: according to a survey by the Allied Translator and Interpreter Service (a body attached to the Allied General Headquarters for the Southwest Pacific), dated April 4, 1944, 85 percent of soldiers had been convinced that they would be killed by Allied troops if captured. In any case, most of those captured were found unconscious or too ill to move.[9]

Even once they realized they were not going to be killed by the enemy, and even if they didn't particularly agree with the notion that they should not be able to live with the shame of their capture, a great percentage of prisoners of war considered that their status would stigmatize them in the future. According to the April 1944 Allied Translator and Interpreter Service Report, 76 percent of Japanese prisoners of war in the region expected to be punished or killed if they returned to Japan, precisely because they had let themselves be captured and had failed to commit suicide.[10] Even once Japan surrendered and it became clear that the military, under whose jurisdiction they would have been punished, was abolished and disbanded, many prisoners of war still expected to be discriminated against upon their return.

The attitudes of "new" prisoners of war (those who had surrendered after the defeat on the orders of their superiors) toward "old" prisoners of war (those who had been captured or had surrendered during the war) bore out these expectations. In the prison camps where all prisoners of war were now herded, there was a sharp distinction between "old" and "new." In his *Diary of a Prisoner of War*, Ōka recounts the kind of tensions that plagued the relationship between these two types of prisoners. He describes, in particular, how one of the "new" prisoners of war, who had surrendered with his entire unit after the end of the war, accused a group of "old," wartime prisoners of moral deficiency and lack of patriotism. In shrill tones, he asked the "old" prisoners how they dared to go on living and ordered them to kill themselves immediately. Interestingly, one of the "old" prisoners of war challenged the accusations of this "new" prisoner of war by raising the notion that there was, in fact, more honor attached to having been captured in battle. Those who had run away from battle and hidden in the hills were not as likely to be captured, he said, as those who had been fighting battles, had been hit by a bullet, and had been captured unconscious.[11] In this exchange, the "old" prisoner of war all but accused the one who had surrendered after the defeat of having run away from battle, whereas those who had been captured had not shied from the bullets. But there were also other ways of justifying the situation of those who had been captured, and a relatively common one was the use of the vocabulary of communism to describe soldiers as the downtrodden masses forced to serve the bourgeois classes, exemplified in this case by the hierarchy of the military. It is clear that some form of justification was required for those who had been captured during the war.

Despite these attempts at justification, few prisoners were not nervous about returning home. Ōka describes the worries plaguing a young prisoner of war from a small rural village who was considering moving to a big city upon his return. Having survived as a prisoner of war, he could not, he said, bear the accusing gaze of neighbors whose sons had died at the front.[12] Otis Cary, a member of the American Strategic Bombing Survey who had had some experience with Japanese prisoners of war, recalls a nervous joke, popular among prisoners, that detailed the precautions a returning prisoner might take before eventually showing himself in his hometown, let alone his neighborhood or his family home.[13]

The anxiety that prisoners of war felt about their return was not always justified. Ōka himself found on his return that "neither fathers who had lost sons, nor women who had lost husbands begrudged him the fact that he had survived."[14] Otis Cary wrote in late 1945 that there was "little feeling against prisoners of war in Japan": "as far as the people at home are concerned, everybody overseas now was a prisoner of war, and if their loved ones are among them and safe, all the better."[15]

Nevertheless, the prisoners' expectation that they would be hated if they returned led many to conceal for many years that they had been captured. Asada Teruhiko, for example, had been a prisoner of war at Cowra in New South Wales, a camp infamous for the ill-fated break-out attempt, on August 4, 1944, of 400 out of 2,223 Japanese inmates, in which 234 prisoners died and 108 were wounded. Asada reveals in his memoirs that although his family was overjoyed to have him back (a welcome that, to Asada, came as somewhat of a surprise and obviously a great relief) the family decided after discussion to tell the neighbors that Asada had been hiding in New Guinea, suggesting that it was less shameful to have been a straggler than a prisoner of war. Asada adds that "although there were those who regarded the war dead as having been fools, nevertheless . . . [there] lingered a certain amount of contempt for prisoners of war."[16]

Ōka himself tells his readers that surrendering was not, after all, as easy as people who had not experienced the war might think. He describes the difficulty of crossing the distance between the fighting units, avoiding detection from both sides, then having the signs of surrender recognized by the enemy, and ultimately having enough luck to encounter enemy troops willing to capture, rather than summarily kill, the approaching soldier.[17] Indeed, Ōka makes the point that he was lucky he wasn't holding a gun when his captors found him asleep in the jungle, or they might have shot him just to be on the safe side. Ōka recalls that it was said that American soldiers on Leyte shot corpses if they were holding weapons.[18]

Nevertheless, the stigma was not so easily dispelled, and the rancor that characterized the relationship between the "old" and the "new" prisoners of war in the prison camps following the defeat was slow to fade. According to a veteran of the battle of Guam, the Guam Veterans' Association was separated until the late 1960s into two distinct and antagonistic groups—"old" and "new" prisoners.[19]

Despite Cary's optimistic 1945 pronouncement that all prisoners of war were welcome home, the question of surrender and capture was thus still vexed many years later. It also arose in the early 1970s when two of the last stragglers returned to Japan, in 1972 and 1974 respectively. One of them, Yokoi Shōichi, had hidden in a cave on Guam for twenty-eight years. He had an inkling that the war was over, but, in his own words, he was ashamed to return home, having survived a battle where most of his comrades had died. The other, Onoda Hirō, had refused to believe that the war was over and, until convinced to surrender in 1974, had roamed the island of Lubang in the Philippines, securing it, in his own eyes, for the return of the Japanese Army.[20] With the return of these stragglers, the persistence of wartime attitudes and of their legacies was highlighted. For example, in 1974, Yokoi, who had run away from the enemy on Guam, was unfavorably compared with Onoda, who had "never" surrendered on Lubang, even though on his return two years earlier Yokoi himself had been hailed as a hero of sorts.[21] In another example, the author of a letter to the editor complained that Onoda would not receive adequate compensation, whereas others who had surrendered and become prisoners of war had received the pension. The letter's disgust with prisoners of war was palpable.[22] The decades that had passed since the war's end had thus only partly erased wartime understandings of valor.

The return of prisoners of war, and the stigma that led many of them to hide their identities, also had ramifications that went beyond their particular case. The end of any war brings with it the tallying of the dead and missing, a form of compensation or recognition for bereaved families, and often also drawn-out searches for the remains of war dead in battlefields— all necessary parts of the process of closure. In postwar Japan, closure was made particularly difficult by the no-surrender ethos of the Japanese Imperial Forces. The notion that being captured was shameful meant that many prisoners of war disguised their identity and their rank upon capture. Many successfully evaded recognition, and their fate remained unknown to their families. One of the prisoners of war who committed suicide during the failed 1944 breakout in the prison camp of Cowra in New South Wales had successfully hidden his identity, and it was not until the publication of a book on the incident in the late 1970s that members of his family, confronted with a photograph of his body hanging from the rafters of the camp kitchen, realized that he had died in captivity.[23]

The confusion regarding the fate of prisoners of war was also due to the fact that the Imperial Forces did not keep a tally of those who might have been captured. Even if the possibility that some soldiers had failed to adhere to instructions of the Field Service Code had occurred to the army and navy command, and even if it had been prepared to reveal to the population this alleged betrayal, the conditions of the battlefields made it impossible to account successfully for the fate of each soldier. In the harshest battlefields in New Guinea, Indonesia, the Philippines, and the Marianas, the disintegration of the organizational structure of the troops and the failure of supply lines from Japan meant that information on the death of soldiers in battle, or otherwise from starvation and disease, was neither reliable nor available. The Japanese government routinely sent out death notices that were later proven to have been premature. The significance of this practice in the wake of defeat was that many prisoners of war returned home to find their own graves and, more often than not, their wives remarried.[24] The psychological impact of the discovery of one's own public "death" was for some highly disturbing: in one famous incident in 1956, a man accused of a string of robberies claimed that he had turned to a life of crime after the shock of realizing, upon his return from the war in 1945, that officially he had died in the battle of Guadalcanal in 1942.[25] The expectation that soldiers had died in battles, rather than having run away and hidden, also informed the assumptions of officials in the Bureau of Repatriate Welfare, whose tallying of missing and dead tended to assume death rather than survival. This assumption was proven wrong over and over again, as "dead" soldiers returned home until the mid-1970s.[26]

In broader terms, the failure to account successfully for all soldiers prevented a sense of closure for many families. In 1972, the *Asahi shimbun* reported that some four hundred families were refusing the government's allowance for bereaved families because they refused to believe the government's assertion that their son or husband had died at the front.[27] There are numerous examples of aging fathers regularly scouring former battlefields in the Philippines, New Guinea, and Indonesia, searching for a son whose death notice they simply could not bring themselves to believe.[28] In this way, the return of prisoners of war, as well as that of many other soldiers mistakenly listed as dead, contributed to a sense of uncertainty regarding wartime losses. It also contributed strongly to a sense of distrust in the government's ability to account exactly for the lives lost at the front.

This is only one of the ways in which the situation of prisoners of war can enlighten us on the difficult process of putting to rest the legacies of the war. As Ōka points out in *Diary of a Prisoner of War*, all soldiers became prisoners of war after the defeat, and according to wartime propaganda none of them should have come home. Though the shock of defeat rendered wartime propaganda obsolete, the soldiers', or veterans' position in the postwar nation remained ambiguous because of the overlapping contradiction between wartime and postwar attitudes and because the soldiers had been part of an organization that was now reviled. Consequently, beyond the recriminations that surrounded the difficulty of accounting accurately for the dead, returning soldiers, their families, and the families of the war dead also had to deal with the integration of their experience and their loss into a nation now undergoing a tremendous change in leadership and self-image. The three million servicemen repatriated over the first three years following the defeat, including prisoners of war, returned home to the occupation of their country by Allied troops and to the Occupation forces' self-conscious attempts to remodel Japan in a democratic image. For returning soldiers, there would be long-lasting implications to the discussions, fostered and directed by the Occupation, regarding war guilt and the role of the "military" in Japan's aggressive expansion overseas.

As has been discussed in a number of recent works, the Occupation period witnessed the creation of a narrative of the prewar and wartime period that placed the blame for expansion squarely on the shoulders of the "military." Yoshida Yutaka, for example, argues that a coalition of Japanese elites and Allied Occupation officials reached a compromise on matters of war guilt for political reasons. War guilt, as publicly demonstrated during the Tokyo War Crimes Trials of 1946–48, was limited to members of the militarist wartime government (A-class war criminals), high-ranking officers (B-class war criminals), and members of the military forces who had committed war crimes (C-class war criminals).[29] John Dower has also discussed the ways in which the narrative of the war as espoused by the Occupation Forces precluded discussion of the war guilt of either the emperor or the population at large.[30] In a variety of subtle and not so subtle ways, the Occupation's re-education program attempted to convince the Japanese population that the "military" had been to blame for Japan's expansion, having hijacked the previously democratic Japanese government and having led the population into the quandary in which it now found itself.[31]

In the early months of the Occupation, when the Allied forces were still nervous about the eventual success of their mission, the equation of soldiers with the now publicly reviled military machine was made in a variety of ways. The Occupation forces strongly encouraged the Japanese media to publish reports on Japanese atrocities in China and Southeast Asia, and here the average soldier's complicity in war crimes was hardly ambiguous. On September 16, 1945, for example, the Supreme Commander of the Allied Powers issued a directive ordering the publication in all newspapers of an article describing the "rape of Manila" in February 1945. The impact on the population was enormous, and in one letter to the editors of the *Mainichi shimbun* published on October 7, 1945, the mother of a soldier asked that those who had committed atrocities be executed immediately—even if her son was among them.[32] The fact that demobilized soldiers were viewed as a potentially subversive force was also evident from the Occupation forces' directives that they must be discouraged from assembling in large numbers.[33] The bans put on public ceremonies of commemoration (such as the distribution of the white boxes containing the remains of the war dead) fostered a sense that there was nothing redeemable in what the military—even its lowliest soldiers—had done, as did the removal or at least the transformation of monuments that had glorified military figures and achievements.[34]

From being feted and honored at the time of their departure to the front, soldiers reported feeling neglected and despised at the time of their return. American commentators tended to explain the palpable disdain for demobilized soldiers as an extension of the disgust the population felt toward their wartime leaders in general. The social scientist Jules Henry explained in 1946 that Japanese people resented their own wartime leaders and the Japanese military organization more than they did the former enemy.[35] An article in the *Saturday Evening Post* of October 1949, entitled "Japs [*sic*] Hate Their Heroes," argued that the contempt that Japanese people felt toward their former leaders also extended to the repatriated soldiers: just as wartime propaganda was discredited, the soldiers who had embodied this propaganda were discredited.[36] Other observers agreed only in part: W. F. Warner argued in the same year that Japanese popular attitudes toward veterans contained admiration and traditional respect as well as contempt for their being part of the army that had betrayed Japan.[37]

Association with the former military forces was certainly not the only reason why soldiers were held in contempt in the early years of the Occupation. Pragmatic reasons, such as the shortages of food, housing, and employment that were plaguing the Japanese population after the defeat, forced many returned soldiers into begging or crime to survive. Returned soldiers were often associated with banditry and robbery or with the looting of military stores.[38] These crimes, however, further seemed to justify the notion that there had been nothing redeemable about the Imperial Forces.

In any case, the contrast between their departure to the front and their return was such that during the Occupation many embittered returned soldiers complained publicly in letters to the editor about the way they were treated.[39] This bitterness hardly abated in the decades that followed: survivors of suicide squadrons deplored that the former "heroes of the nation," the suicide pilots (*Tokkotai,* better known in the West as the Kamikaze), were often called, after the war, "special attack degenerates" or "Kamikaze fanatics."[40] Others mentioned in the 1980s how upsetting it was to hear their comrades' deaths described as "private" or "useless" deaths rather than as sacrifices dedicated to the nation.[41]

The early postwar years also witnessed constant and public accusations of officers and career soldiers in a way that seemed to dissociate the conscripts from the reviled military organization. As John Dower has shown, the publicized postwar murder of a former officer by men previously under his command encouraged other veterans to write about the cruelty of superiors and the maltreatment they had suffered as soldiers.[42] A number of lynchings were apparently the result of resentment toward officers.[43] Furthermore, according to Takahashi Saburō, toward the late 1940s the censorship of the Occupation period made publication of memoirs that condemned the war and war leaders particularly welcome. The publication of memoirs that contained criticism of high-ranking military commanders was encouraged.[44] Ōka Shōhei's *Furyoki* (Diary of a Prisoner of War), which first appeared in 1948, was followed in 1949 by *Kike wadatsumi no koe* (Listen to the Voices of the Sea), a collection of writings by students conscripted as soldiers and killed in the war, and by Takagi Toshirō's *Imphal,* in which the author condemned military leaders for their irresponsible actions in Burma, which in his view unnecessarily cost the lives of countless soldiers.[45]

Many of the memoirs and novels published by veterans in the wake of the defeat draw a sharp contrast between the lowly, conscripted private, often helplessly pushed along by events beyond his control, and cruel and sadistic officers spouting wartime propaganda. Ōka Shōhei's novel *Nobi* (1952, translated into English under the title *Fires on the Plain*) is a good example of the way the experience of the soldier was presented to the population. The central character is Private Tamura, who, abandoned by his own unit because of his illness, wanders through the battlefields of Leyte, tagging behind the remnants of the Japanese Army. Hunger, illness, and eventually his encounters with cannibalistic fellow soldiers accompany his descent into madness. The novel highlights throughout the irrationality of officers and their brutality toward their charges: in the first four pages of *Fires on the Plain*, we find Tamura's squad leader slapping him in the face, screaming because Tamura has failed to gain admission to the hospital and has come back to his unit—a unit that cannot even feed those soldiers well enough to forage for food. The squad leader tells Tamura to go back to the hospital, and, should he fail to gain admittance, to blow himself up with his hand grenade. He adds: "And look here, Private Tamura, try to cheer up! Remember—it's all for the Fatherland. To the very end I expect you to act like a true soldier of the Emperor."[46] In *Fires on the Plain*, the military and the war eventually turn normal human beings into murderers and cannibals. Ogawa Tetsuo's memoir *Terraced Hell* is another example of writing that attempted to convey to readers the inescapable madness that accompanied the disintegration of the Japanese Army in the Philippines.[47]

Throughout the 1950s, the best-selling war memoirs were those that emphasized the helplessness of low-ranking soldiers as they were forced to obey the irrational orders of their superiors. Such understandings of the experience of ordinary soldiers were also visible in the press: when, in 1956, four stragglers returned from the island of Mindoro, their attempt to be patriotic was compared favorably with the attempted suicide, in 1945, of wartime Prime Minister General Tōjō Hideki.[48] And years later, in 1972, there were veterans who found pride in publicly recounting that, during the war, they had merely pretended to believe the orders and admonitions of their officers: they distanced themselves from the organization of the Imperial Army by showing off how they had been "bad soldiers."[49] In a sense, the veterans that distanced themselves from the wartime military forces by insisting on their wartime cynicism were able to place their experience in the same conceptual framework as the broader population: their unwillingness to identify the war effort made them the victims of the army, just as the population was portrayed as the army's victim in the narrative of the war adopted during the Occupation.

Not all veterans, however, were willing to couch their experiences in such a way: they wanted to find in their experience more meaning than that of battles fought for the wrong reasons, for a military organization that had, in a sense, "hijacked" the nation. They were unwilling to accept that their patriotism during the war had been misplaced. They were angered with the dismissal of the death of their comrades as "private deaths" or "useless deaths" and of their own, often terrible experience as having ultimately endangered the nation rather than protected it. Similarly, a great proportion of bereaved families wanted the sacrifice of their son or husband recognized as valid. Such feelings underpinned the bitter disputes regarding the status of the Yasukuni Shrine: this commemorative monument was removed from the aegis of the state during the Occupation due to its religious nature, but it was not replaced, in the view of the Association of Bereaved Families, by a monument that publicly and unequivocally commemorated the sacrifice of ordinary soldiers in the war.[50] The status of the Yasukuni Shrine is in contention to this day, as evidenced by the uproar that greeted Prime Minister Koizumi Jun'ichirō's visit to the shrine two days before the anniversary of defeat on August 13, 2001. It highlights the difficulties faced by Japan in the process of postwar reconciliation within its own national borders, let alone at an international level.

Despite the long-running nature of disputes on commemoration and integration of soldiers' experience into postwar memory, the passing of generations has brought with it another set of recriminations. In Japan, as in many other countries, a seemingly insurmountable gap in worldviews and reference points has separated the generations that experienced the war and those that followed. And while, for the most part, the temporal and symbolic distance that separates contemporary Japan from its wartime counterpart has been viewed appreciatively, it has also brought with it a sense of loss.

This sense of loss was clearly visible at the time the last stragglers returned to Japan in the early to mid-1970s. While the mind-set that had supported these soldiers during their decades in hiding was foreign to the younger generation, many older people viewed it with nostalgia. They agreed that the period before and during the war had had its faults, but in their view it had, at least, produced people prepared to believe in something and to act selflessly. That generation they contrasted with a younger generation intent on self-gratification, the pursuit of leisure, and dedication to the acquisition of material goods. Furthermore, according to many older commentators, their hard work and their sacrifices had allowed the younger generation to enjoy the benefits of living in a prosperous nation. What the postwar nation had gained in material riches it had lost in spirit.[51]

Similar tensions are explored in postwar literature. Toyoko Yamasaki's novel *The Barren Zone* traces the return home of a prisoner of war who has spent eleven years in Siberia and his slow adjustment to postwar culture.

Written in 1976, Yamasaki's description of central character Iki's displacement in a nation now dedicated to economic growth resonates with the sentiments of spiritual emptiness raised by the return of stragglers only a few years before. Iki, a highly successful career soldier and strategist during the war, is captured by Soviet troops in Manchuria in 1945. Accused of war crimes and espionage, he remains in prison camps in Siberia until 1956. After his return to Japan, he spends a few months helping fellow returnees find work and eventually reluctantly accepts a position at a trading company, whose president sees in Iki's officer training an asset for the strategic development of his business. Iki's feelings of worthlessness—the skills he learned during the war he considers useless now—are often exacerbated by the realization that his experience as a soldier is beyond the comprehension of younger people and also outside their interest.[52] In Kōno Taeko's short story "Iron Fish," the protagonist's need to understand her fiancé's last moments prompts her to have herself locked in a museum overnight; there she spends the night in a replica of the manned torpedo in which her fiancé died during the war.[53]

The notion that the younger generation of Japanese is completely uninterested in the experiences of soldiers and that the wartime generation has, in fact, failed to transmit them in a valuable way continues to provoke comment. The writer and journalist Kawaichi Kōji, who was a child at the time of the defeat, has related his shock at seeing a begging maimed veteran on a street in Osaka in 1985. For Kawaichi, the realization that other passersby either failed to notice the veteran or ignored him pointedly was almost more shocking that the veteran's presence itself.[54] More recently, the controversial cartoonist Kobayashi Yoshinori, in his manga (cartoon) *Sensōron*, angrily draws the gulf separating his generation from that of his grandfather: the experiences of the wartime generation are lost forever as it dies off, leaving the younger generation with no antidote to their decadent pursuit of materialistic pleasures.[55]

In many ways, then, the return home of defeated soldiers has left postwar Japan with some irresolvable tensions. As we have seen here, the quandary in which prisoners of war found themselves at the end of the war resonated, more broadly, with the difficult integration of the experiences of all soldiers into postwar Japan, a nation whose very beginnings, during the Occupation, were built upon the rejection of the wartime military leadership. According to some bereaved families and veterans, sacrifices have gone unrecognized; according to others, the sacrifices should not have been made in the first place and must not be recognized lest they imply some kind of honor in Japan's wartime mission. The ambiguity of the soldiers' position has not been resolved, and their experiences are thus difficult to discuss. Japan's meteoric rise to economic power has further overshadowed the legacies of the war, making the wartime and postwar experience mutually unintelligible for Japanese of different generations.

These are some of the issues that have accompanied Japan's transition from war to peace in the wake of the surrender of August 15, 1945. They are not particularly unique: there are parallels in the way soldiers dealt with their lot in Germany after World War I and with the difficult process of reconciliation that has affected the position of Vietnam veterans in the United States and in Australia. The grounds for comparative research are fertile, and Japan's experience must not be neglected.

NOTES

1. James Orr, *The Victim as Hero: Ideologies of Peace and National Identity in Postwar Japan* (Honolulu: University of Hawaii Press, 2001); Yoshikuni Igarashi, *Bodies of Memory: Narratives of War in Postwar Japanese Culture, 1945–1970* (Princeton: Princeton University Press, 2000); Lisa Yoneyama, *Hiroshima Traces: Time, Space and the Dialectics of Memory* (Berkeley: University of California Press, 1999); John Dower, *Embracing Defeat: Japan in the Wake of World War II* (New York: W.W. Norton, 1999).

2. I have discussed the nature of commemoration in Beatrice Trefalt, "War, Commemoration and National Identity in Japan, 1868–1975," in *Nation and Nationalism in Japan,* ed. Sandra Wilson (London: RoutledgeCurzon, 2002), 115–35.

3. Ruth Benedict, *The Chrysanthemum and the Sword: Patterns of Japanese Culture* (Boston: Houghton Mifflin, 1946), 39. Benedict's calculations were based on American casualty estimates and are confirmed elsewhere; see *Allied Translator and Interpreter Service Report* no. 76 (February 7, 1945), Australian War Memorial, which estimated that in the Noemfoor and Sansapor battles (off the coast of Dutch New Guinea) only 133 Japanese soldiers and 642 Taiwanese soldiers were captured out of a force of 15,041 men in total.

4. John Dower has illustrated how the image of the Japanese soldier changed from a small and harmless monkey to an enormous and threatening gorilla as the Japanese advanced unchecked through Southeast Asia in the early months of 1942. See John Dower, *War without Mercy: Race and Power in the Pacific War* (New York: Pantheon Books, 1986), illustrations 4 and 10. See also Beatrice Trefalt, "Fanaticism, Japanese Soldiers and the Pacific War, 1937–1945," in *Fanaticism and Conflict in the Modern Age,* ed. Matthew Hughes and Gaynor Johnson (London: Frank Cass, 2005), 33–47.

5. Quoted in Haruko T. Cook and Theodore F. Cook, eds., *Japan at War: An Oral History* (New York: New Press, 1992), 264.

6. Saburō Ienaga, *Japan's Last War: World War II and the Japanese, 1931–1945* (Canberra: Australian National University Press, 1979), 49, 186. The first publicized case of a prisoner-of-war suicide is that of a certain Major Kuga, who had been taken, unconscious, by the Chinese during the Shanghai Incident of 1932 and who killed himself in a gesture of atonement immediately upon his release. He became a great national hero and was widely held up as an example of true patriotism and correct behavior. Louise Young, *Japan's Total Empire: Manchuria and the Culture of Wartime Imperialism* (Berkeley: University of California Press, 1998), 75–77.

7. See, for example, Hank Nelson, *Prisoners of War: Australians under Nippon* (Sydney: Australian Broadcasting Corporation, 1985).

8. Ōka Shōhei, *Furyoki* [Diary of a Prisoner of War] (Tokyo: Kuramoto, 1952), 353.

9. *Allied Translator and Interpreter Service Research Report* no. 76 (April 4, 1944), Australian War Memorial. This is not to say that there were no instances when Allied troops killed surrendering Japanese soldiers.

10. Ibid. The suicidal outbreaks at Japanese prisoner-of-war camps at Featherston in New Zealand and Cowra in New South Wales further underline the strong hold this doctrine had on a great proportion of Japanese soldiers. Charlotte Carr-Gregg, *Japanese Prisoners of War in Revolt: The Outbreaks at Featherston and Cowra during World War II* (Brisbane: University of Queensland Press, 1978).

11. Ōka, *Furyoki*, 363.

12. Ibid., 422.

13. "From Otis Cary in Tokyo to Don Keene in Tsingtao, November 25, 1945," in *From a Ruined Empire: Letters—Japan, China, Korea, 1945–1946*, ed. Otis Cary (Tokyo: Tuttle, 1984), 217.

14. Ōka, *Furyoki*, 422.

15. "From Otis Cary," 227.

16. Asada Teruhiko, *The Night of a Thousand Suicides: The Japanese Outbreak at Cowra*, trans. Ray Cowan (Sydney: Angus and Robertson, 1970), 23–124.

17. Ōka, *Furyoki*, 357.

18. Ibid., 358.

19. This veteran was interviewed in a weekly women's magazine after the discovery on Guam, in January 1972, of straggler Sergeant Yokoi Shōichi. *Shūkan josei jishin*, February 19, 1972, 53.

20. Beatrice Trefalt, *Japanese Army Stragglers and Memories of the War in Japan, 1950–1975* (London: RoutledgeCurzon, 2003).

21. See, for example, the comparative discussion of their merits in *Asahi shimbun*, March 11, 1974.

22. *Asahi shimbun*, March 12, 1972.

23. The book was Harry Gordon, *Die Like the Carp!* (Sydney: Cassell Australia, 1978). The story of his family's confrontation with the manner of his death is part

of the display on the Pacific War within the Museum of the Australian War Memorial.

24. Dower, *Embracing Defeat*, 60. Of the stragglers who returned from the island of Anatahan in 1951, five were confronted with the fact that their wives had remarried. *Asahi shimbun*, July 7, 1951.

25. *Nippon Times*, February 17, 1956; Trefalt, *Japanese Army Stragglers*, 33.

26. The last "straggler" was discovered in December 1974 hiding on the island of Morotai in Indonesia. Trefalt, *Japanese Army Stragglers*, 160–78.

27. *Asahi shimbun*, February 8, 1972.

28. See, for example, stories in the *Mainichi shimbun*, October 24, 1972; *Asahi shimbun*, October 21, 1972; *Shūkan bunshun*, November 13, 1972, 38–39.

29. Yoshida Yutaka, *Nihonjin no sensōkan: Rekishi no naka no henyō* (Tokyo: Iwanami Shoten, 1995).

30. Dower, *Embracing Defeat*, 449–54; Richard Minear, *Victor's Justice: The Tokyo War Crimes Trial* (Tokyo: Tuttle, 1972).

31. See, for example, Dower, *Embracing Defeat*, 247; Meirion Harries and Suzie Harries, *Sheathing the Sword: The Demilitarisation of Japan* (London: Hamish Hamilton, 1987), 66–68; Mark Gayn, *Japan Diary* (Tokyo: Tuttle, 1981), 6–7; Yoshida, *Nihonjin no sensōkan*, 31.

32. Dower, *Embracing Defeat*, 60; *Mainichi shimbun*, October 7, 1945, quoted in Kimura Takuji, "Shūsen chokugo no guntai to shakai: 'Kyūgunjin gurūpu' no keisei o megutte" [Army and Society in the Immediate Postwar: The Establishment of the "Ex-military Groups"] (MA thesis, Hitotsubashi University, 1997), 44.

33. Kōseishō engo kyoku (Ministry of Health and Welfare, Bureau of Social and Repatriate Welfare), *Engo gojūnen shi* [Fifty Years of Repatriate Welfare] (Tokyo: Gyōsei, 1997), 55–58.

34. William P. Woodard, *The Allied Occupation of Japan 1945–1952 and Japanese Religions* (Leiden: E. J. Brill, 1972), 148; Trefalt, "War, Commemoration."

35. Jules Henry, "Initial Reactions to the Americans," *Journal of Social Issues* 2 (August 1946): 20. See also Trefalt, *Japanese Army Stragglers*, 38.

36. Harold G. Noble, "Japs [sic] Hate their Heroes," *Saturday Evening Post*, October 12, 1949, 8–19, 143–44. See also Trefalt, *Japanese Army Stragglers*, 38–39.

37. W. F. Warner, "Repatriate Organisations in Japan," *Pacific Affairs* 22 (September 1949): 276. See also Trefalt, *Japanese Army Stragglers*, 39.

38. Hisashi Kubota mentions that in 1946 banditry and armed robbery were prevalent among returned servicemen. "Letter from Hisashi Kubota in Osaka to Don Keene in Tsingtao," in Cary, *From a Ruined Empire*, 194; Dower, *Embracing Defeat*, 59; Kimura, "Shūsen chokugo no guntai to shakai," 34.

39. Kimura, "Shūsen chokugo no guntai to shakai," 46; Dower, *Embracing Defeat*, 60.

40. Hagomoro Society of Kamikaze Divine Thunderbolt Corps Survivors, *The Cherry Blossom Squadrons: Born to Die* (Los Angeles: Ohara Publications, 1973), 58–59.

41. Nitta Mitsuko, "Eirei to senyūkai," in *Kyōdō kenkyū: Senyūkai*, ed. Takahashi Saburō (Tokyo: Tabata shoten, 1983), 222–24, quoted in Takahashi Saburō, "Senkimono o yomu" (Kyoto: Akademia, 1988), 149–52.

42. Dower, *Embracing Defeat*, 58–59.

43. Kimura, "Shūsen chokugo no guntai to shakai," 25.

44. Takahashi, "Senkimono," 36.

45. Nihon senbotsu gakusei shuki henshū iinkai, *Kike wadatsumi no koe* (Tokyo: Tōdai kyōdō kumiai shuppansha, 1949); Takagi Toshirō, *Imphal* (Tokyo: Yūkeisha, 1949).

46. Ōka Shōhei, *Fires on the Plain*, trans. Ivan Morris (Westport, CT: Greenwood Press, 1957), originally published as *Nobi* (Tokyo: Sōgensha, 1952), 6.

47. Ogawa Tetsuo, *Terraced Hell: A Japanese Memoir of Defeat and Death in Northern Luzon, Philippines* (Tokyo: Charles E. Tuttle, 1972).

48. *Shūkan sankei*, December 16, 1956, 4.

49. See, for example, the discussion by former veterans in *Shūkan shinchō*, February 12, 1972, 34–35, 38–39.

50. The problems of commemoration are discussed in detail in Trefalt, "War, Commemoration."

51. See, for example, Kusayanagi Daizō, "'Tennō no shitateya' Yokoi Shōichi" [Yokoi Shōichi, "The Emperor's Tailor"], *Bungei shunjū* 50 (April 1972): 242–54; see also comments in *Shūkan shinchō*, February 5, 1972, 117.

52. Toyoko Yamasaki, *The Barren Zone: A Novel*, trans. James T. Araki (London: Gollancz, 1985), 239.

53. Kôno Taeko, "Iron Fish," in *The Shōwa Anthology*, ed. Van C. Gessel and Tomone Matsumoto (Tokyo: Kodansha International, 1985), 362–74.

54. Kawaichi Kōji, *Saigo no senshisha: Rikugun ittōhei Kozuka Kin'shichi* [The Last War Dead: Private First Class Kozuka Kin'shichi] (Tokyo: Kawade shobō shinsha, 1986), 7–8.

55. Kobayashi Yoshinori, *Sensōron* (Tokyo: Gentōsha, 1998), 64.

CHAPTER FOUR

"Battle Dress to Sports Suit; Overalls to Frocks"

American and British Veterans Confront Demobilization, 1945–51

MARY ANNE SCHOFIELD

The human race has two outfits: a civilian suit and a uniform; two sets of

morals: civilian and military; two occupations: civilian and military. Both

setups require considerable orientation. It is just as hard to adjust a human

to military life as it is to adjust him to civilian life.

Morton Thompson, *How to Be a Civilian* (1946)

In his preface to *Writing after War,* John Limon ponders: "[W]hy, since war is ugly, does writing beautify it?" (4). It is a question to ask of literature written not only during the war but after it as well. Is postwar literature an effort to sanctify and find order in the chaos that has preceded it? Is it a palliative that attempts to find a meaning in the often unclear relationship between a war and its peace? Does the immediate postwar literature of the Second World War, that of 1945 to 1951, by American and British writers paint an unrealistic, fairytale version of the war and its aftermath? Or do the fictional and nonfictional accounts accurately represent the ways the war continued to affect people, both combatants and noncombatants, in the peace that followed it?

In the foreword to *The Evening Bulletin's Veteran's Guide* (1945) the editors write that the "termination of the war" is "a pretty tricky phrase, as no one has stated exactly what event will mark the war's official end. It is not the end of actual fighting nor formal surrender. . . . [I]t may be the signing of a peace treaty a couple of years after the last shot was fired. Your guess is as good as ours" (n.p.). These editors accurately summarize the difficulty of defining the boundaries of the post–Second World War period and by extension its literature. Here I examine two classes of texts from the period 1945 to 1951: (1) nonfiction books and articles on the returning veteran's transition to peacetime, written by governmental agencies, psychologists, and social workers, and (2) fiction written by men and women who were not in combat themselves but who probably had a friend or family member in the war. These texts have clearly specified audiences: the nonfiction is written primarily for the veteran, though it occasionally addresses those on the home front who are welcoming him back; the fiction is written primarily for a woman in his life, whether a mother, sister, wife, or sweetheart. Together they constitute a small but significant body of literature heretofore ignored by critics and scholars of the Second World War. I am not examining books written by the veterans themselves; their literature is self-referential, for they tell stories to themselves about themselves, and there is no place for a nonveteran audience. Nor am I studying literature written by and about disabled veterans, for it is also self-referential, with a mixed audience of veterans and their caregivers. Further, both these literatures have been previously studied. I am concerned only with works by nonveterans that target the veteran and home-front audience.

The nonfiction works primarily teach communication: the veteran must learn to speak civilian, and those on the home front must help him reconnect by learning to speak a patois of military and civilian. (After the immediate peace period of 1945–51, both narrators and auditors learn to speak the language of postwar disillusionment, but that is another study.) Nonfiction works give the returning veteran a literal and metaphoric lexicon to make his reentry into "Civvy Street" as easy as possible. Rather than addressing the long-term future—the usual concern of works by veterans themselves—they focus on short-term solutions to facilitate reentry. Morton Thompson, in his *How to Be a Civilian* (1946), suggests that the "quickest way anybody's found to get adjusted to life, liberty, and the pursuit of happiness, as a Civilian, is to keep in touch with some buddy who has also been discharged" (29); the two of them can speak the language of the soldier/veteran to each other as they relearn the language of the home front. Thompson provides a list "of frequently used Civilian words and phrases, together with their equivalent in the language of the service" (209). "Inside a month," he concludes, "you should be able to speak like a Civilian" (209) and, he leaves unstated but implied, be ready to function as a part of the civilian world once again. The fictional works for the home-front audience attempt to show this reintegration, but often they suggest that returning veterans and the women to whom they return have come to speak widely different languages that cannot easily be reconciled.

Thompson notes that female veterans—WACs, WAVEs, SPARs, and women Marines—do not pose the same reentry problems, for themselves or for their loved ones, that male soldiers do: "The principal thing most of the girls in khaki and blue seem to want to do is get out of those blitz britches and wear a hat with cherries on it. They've seen what they've seen and they've done what they've done and they've been where they've been, but women just naturally adjust better than men" (203). That is, they are more willing to return to prewar domestic roles and fantasies. In contrast, their counterparts at home, women who did not go into service, "are scurrying around asking everybody for advice on the problem of the returning soldier" (193); they do not return to the prewar fantasy as docilely.

When this literature addresses the women in the life of the returning soldier, it emphasizes their role of helping the man reintegrate into the world he left and providing a bridge back to a reassuring normalcy. For example, Arch Soutar, writing in the *Saturday Evening Post*, December 1944, asserts:

> You'd better forget about the "G.I. Joe" stuff when the door opens and your son or husband stands there with all his unexplored new problems and strange, perplexing fears. For that boy of yours is sick and tired of all this patronizing Joe business floating back to him from out of the States. From now on, he's going to have a sobering job on his hands merely changing back to the boy he used to be, a transition many times more difficult and painful than that of civilian-into-soldier, and a thousand times more disturbing emotionally, because he's all alone in this change-over. He's got to do this thing himself, without the comfort and moral support of a camp full of others like him. He must achieve this where everyone can watch him as he struggles to fall back into the pattern of normal civilian life again. (35)

Soutar continues: "You can encourage your own boy best by preparing yourself to make adjustments, by controlling your own emotions, by maintaining a calm, intelligent guard against his tantrums and periods of alternating elation and depression, by silently letting him understand that no matter what happens for a while, you are there and are his refuge" (38).

Writing in 1945, Kenneth Howard attempts to outline the terms on which the returning veteran and his wife can take up their long-disrupted relationship. "Reunion," he notes, "after a long separation such as war occasions, is very like getting married again. The difference is that there is the memory of past experiences to go on" (76). Earlier he has described how, in a satisfactory marriage, the new couple forms an "us" unit: "two individuals create something new in which both are involved, which adds to their individual and mutual strength and establishes for them a place in the community" (12). The returning veteran and his spouse who has acted independently during the war must take up the challenge of recreating the "us." According to Howard, "[T]he 'us' is like a fire, lit and tended by both partners, but obviously not identical with them. If either of them neglects it, it tends to go out. In return, it warms both of them and they naturally come to depend on it and each other for heat" (22). But the process of re-creating an "us" after the couple is reunited can be problematic. "The first stage of reunion, like that of marriage itself, is the stage of the honeymoon. . . . [The couple] should have a period in which to satisfy each other, to discharge the sexual tension, to renew their knowledge of each other and to see what changes have occurred" (77). "After the honeymoon comes the awakening. When the sexual need is temporarily satiated they come down to earth and once again begin to see each other as they really are" (82). Like others of this period who portray returning veterans' personal relationships, Howard attempts to guide couples' transition, providing a bridge between their dreams—the foxhole dreams of the combatant and the idyllic fancies of his wife or sweetheart—and the realities of the immediate postwar world.

Indeed, one could say that all of the literature of the immediate postwar period offers reentry lessons for both the war veteran and the home-front veterans; it constitutes a patriotic remarriage manual. While it maintains the prewar status quo, invoking a prelapsarian world, blindly ignoring many crucial changes experienced by both parties during the war, and functioning as a shelter from the harsh realities of reentry, it also tries to integrate the new man and the new woman created by the war with their prewar selves. Like a second honeymoon, it is about getting to know you—again.

While couples were apart, they were among the many Americans who "lived the war," in the words of the historian William Graebner, "as a series of dreams—dreams of idyllic reunions with loved ones long absent, of a world so productive as to abolish need altogether and open the way to a limitless leisure, of plentiful and meaningful work, of a blissful and harmonious domesticity" (42). Howard's book describes the veteran's implicit marriage pact: "We have to ask what it is that sustains him during separation, what is it that makes it worth while to sacrifice desire and practice self control. . . . The answer is . . . the value he places on his marriage and home and his place in it. At home, remember, he was the head of the household. He carried the burden of responsibility and accepted obligations. In return he got affection, comradeship, love, and the feeling of being wanted and of being important in his own little sphere" (44–45). The American dream of achieving success and prosperity through hard work and sacrifice is fulfilled and then enjoyed in the happy home.

This "golden thread" of the "American Dream" (Dodds 1), or, in British works, the British equivalent to that dream, is the controlling plot of both fiction and nonfiction that deals with returning veterans in this immediate postwar period. The ubiquitous romances continue the upbeat energy and dynamism of the immediate cessation of hostilities and the upbeat portrayal of the victorious and honorable veteran. Observing American literature, Harold Dodds notes in 1943: "We are not fighting for a new order. We are fighting for a world in which America can chart her future progress as a projection of the curve which her history has already plotted" (3). The literature of 1945 to 1951 plots just this curve. Both fiction and nonfiction writers attempt to counter the mental and geopolitical fragmentation that really occurs at a war's end by publishing, perhaps too hastily, but fascinatingly and importantly just because of that haste, documents that continue the heroic tone of the war. The voice of disillusionment, disenchantment, and disenfranchisement, which is the mark of the literature from the Korean Conflict and the Cold War, is heard only sparingly during this brief space between the wars. For a brief six-year period, the dream continued as all hailed the returning, conquering heroes.

The literature written from 1945 to 1951 is that of raw, untested peace; in it the war and its consequences are assimilated into preexisting patterns and standard tropes that are absorbed into the national consciousness as quickly as possible. It does not break new ground in fictional terms, nor does it offer much in-depth examination of postwar issues in the nonfiction. It is a literature of return—but a return to what and to whom is addressed only in terms of preexistent forms. These fictional and nonfictional accounts, both British and American, examine and recount the uneasy encounters between returning men and the women to whom they return. Some are written for the faithful Penelope as she anxiously awaits the return of her Ulysses, and others are given to the loyal Ulysses as he prepares to return to his Penelope. Both are tales of life after war with its conflicting public and private voices that are not modeled and modulated into one unified voice. There is clearly a need for a new hegemonic world order after the war, yet these texts do not provide it.

Is there a difference, then, between the "lived" reality of the returning veteran and the "narrated" reality? The iconography of this raw peace literature reverts to prewar narrative patterns and gender stereotypes. The displacement that is felt by both the veteran and the home-front dweller after the war is countered by an evocation of romantic, prelapsarian images of existence before the war. Mass Observation's long study *The Journey Home* examines just these continuing dreams, remarking that "[t]omorrow's public behavior patterns are molded in today's private fantasies" (7); "Civvy Street" becomes both the best dream and the worst nightmare of the returning veteran, who "longs for the comfort and warmth and personal affection of it after the cold, impersonal regimented life of forces or factory" (35). This fantasy of return, I conclude, is just that—a fantasy of a paradise that no longer exists. Coming out of uniform means more than moving from "battle dress to sports suit; overalls to frocks," Mass Observation notes; "If minds are to look willingly forward from sports suits to boiler suits, from frocks to maternity gowns, they must know that the future means something which is theirs to build" (102). Yet the fiction and the nonfiction do not offer a way to create that meaning. Instead, they rely on an established notion of the domestic paradise lauded in the popular romance genre of the period that "reinforces the stable family unit and home front that the veteran fought for" (Shuker-Haines 225); there is no paradigm presented beyond the nostalgic present moment of return, reunion, and retreat. As Sebastien Knowles comments, the prevalent postwar fantasy is "one of a return to the pre-war status-quo, modified only by such changes as will be necessary to prevent serious discontent" (18).

Morton Thompson best describes the fantasy-paradise that soldiers create when he remarks that time and distance build up the soldiers' dreams, "make them golden." "You'll get to thinking of home as the one perfect place in the world," he writes, "a place where nothing ever goes wrong, there is no graft and no politics and no gossip and no inequality, a world where everybody loves you and everything is just all right. Then, when you find home little changed from the place you left, you are hurt and you start screaming that everything's changed. As a matter of fact nothing's changed, much, except your dream ideas, which have to fit themselves to things as they were and as they are" (199–200). Mona Gardner, writing in the *Ladies Home Journal* of December 1945, explains the reality and its difference from the "dream" when she observes:

> Sweet unreal fantasy is an occupational disease with husband G.I. In his foxhole and on his time off, he literally feeds on rosy dreams of his dear, dear home. When it turns out to be the same old place, he's stunned and resentful. While he is romanticizing at a distance, Mrs. G.I. has probably been looking at the same holes in the screen, at the same leaky faucet, having squabbles with the grocer, but serenely dreaming of the day when Joe will come home and mend the screen, fix the faucet, mop the grocery shop up with the grocer, and bear her off to that little orange grove in California. (74)

While Thompson addresses Ulysses, Gardner addresses Penelope: "Everybody's talking about how to treat your soldier and help him reconvert to civilian life! Well, what about the wives? They've got a job of reconverting too. They've got to stop being independent and get used to having a full-time boss around the house.... Why doesn't somebody write one about how to behave toward a wife when she's reconverting into a clinging vine" (41). "Marriage counsel has become a necessary part of American life," Gardner continues. For "if returning G.I.s come home with the same definition of wife they went away with—and all indications confirm that they will—then there are rocks ahead for a vast number of marriages" (72).

Neither the male nor the female dream will be realized. The fiction and nonfiction of the period try to adjust the divergent visions before there is a World War III on the home front, and they do so by resorting to prewar, prelapsarian narrative patterns in which male and female visions of domestic life harmonize. Thus they respond to the divergence by avoiding it: they offer a band-aid, not a cure.

In 1941 Pearl S. Buck had a prescient view of the dilemma to be encountered in the postwar world. Writing *Of Men and Women*, she observes:

[E]very war sets women back a generation, and this in spite of industrial gains for them. . . . Psychologically and emotionally, war sets
women back in man's mind and in their own. For man comes home
from war a spoiled creature, and one too often weakened by self-pity
and conceit. He has had to be pampered and praised into considering
himself a hero so that he would be a hero, and everyday life is flat after
war, and his wife must go on with the pampering and praising or he
will feel unappreciated. (155)

By and large, the American nonfiction provides a how-to-pamper manual
for the returning veteran, and much, though not all, of the fiction at least
attempts to follow the same program by presenting a reassuring vision of
the nuclear, familial romance, which promises containment, and therefore
peace, to lull the anxieties of the immediate postwar Ulysses and his Penelope.

In Britain, fiction and nonfiction of the immediate postwar period exhibit much the same subjugation of the private voice of personal feeling and
experience to the public voice that champions a return to "normalcy." Gail
Braybon and Penny Summerfield argue that the majority of British women
found that the war "did them good in lots of ways," and J. B. Priestley says
that while older women wanted to return to hearth, home, and husband,
younger women wanted more. The enormous study conducted in Britain
by Mass Observation during and immediately after the war supports these
views. Servicewomen, the studies found, emphasized that the war experience had made them grow up. The same was true of women who worked as
civilians, who cited gains of becoming "better and more complete people,
losing the inhibitions of a secluded existence, understanding their common
social and physical, spiritual and corporeal humanity with others, gaining a
sense of national identity and acquiring a new gender identity" (21). Like
their American counterparts, British nonfictional and fictional accounts of
the war and its aftermath present, for both men and women, "heroic" stories of personal transformation that must be tempered by a return to a prewar status so that the after-war self can be viewed as a continuation of the
earlier self, thus avoiding the polarization that could result from the destabilized gender categories.

Because the American and British romances of the immediate postwar
were being produced rapidly to meet the need for postwar certainty and
dreams, they present women characters in rather stereotypic ways; the mes-

sage was more important than its mode of expression. In general, veterans' wives in the romances fall into the categories outlined by Mona Gardner in 1945: "A—she has tried on the family pants, become a completely functioning individual, and she loves it; B—she has reluctantly worn the family pants and can hardly wait to get them off; C—she has never acquired maturity because she has continued to live a little-girl relationship with parents; D—she is exaggeratedly feminine because she has been living a purely feminine routine with three or four other women" (41). And the popular romances objectify and present their female characters in these stereotypic roles in an effort to preserve the postwar dream.

The use of prewar narrative codes in this immediate postwar literature is reminiscent of William Wordsworth's nineteenth-century poetic techniques. In 1964 Geoffrey Hartmann explained that Wordsworth "look[ed] back in order to look forward" (29). Wordsworth began by retelling an event that had occurred in real time about which he had thought long and hard, and in the retelling he endowed the event with a symbolic meaning that heightened and strengthened the original encounter. A Wordsworth poem "is seen to be a reaction to this consciousness as well as its expression" (16), and "this consciousness blends at once and imperceptibly with a new state or rather motion of mind, *statis* being replaced by an evolving sense of *continuity*" (17, emphasis added).

In a similar way, the fiction and nonfiction of 1945 to 1951 revisit a romanticized home front. From clothes to food, from housing to sex, the soldier is led through a world half-remembered, a paradise seemingly lost. Treatises and pamphlets from the United Kingdom, like Kenneth Howard's *Sex Problems of the Returning Soldier* (1945), Mass Observation's *The Journey Home* (1944), the British Information Service's *Britain and the Veteran* (1945), Caroline Haslett's *Problems Have No Sex* (1949), and George Pratt's *Soldier to Civilian* (1944), and from the United States, like the U.S. War and Navy Department's *Going Back to Civilian Life* (1945), the U.S. War Department's *Welcome Home* (1944), *The Evening Bulletin's Veteran's Guide* (1945), Herbert Kupper's *Back to Life: The Emotional Adjustment of Our Veterans* (1945), John Mariano's *The Veteran and His Marriage* (1945), and Willard Waller's *The Veteran Comes Back* (1944), all demonstrate the need for a return to paradise. As Alice Ross Colver asks in her novel *Homecoming* (1945): "How would it look to them when they all came together again after these many months of separation? Would it seem good? Or strange? Would the confines of its walls be irksome or warmly enfolding? Would they be able to pick up the broken threads of their lives after their absences in war? Or wouldn't they? Would life go on as it had been, a close-knit, happy affair? Or was there no possible return to old ways and old days?" (9).

The answer is found in what Bridget Fowler labels "magical fictions," an apt descriptor of these texts. In *The Alienated Reader: Women and Romantic Literature in the Twentieth Century*, she argues that "we need to move beyond the traditional dichotomy between realism and ideology to focus on the demand for *magical fictions*. The specific use-value of the romance lies in its interweaving of images of 'civilization' and women's discontents, with the miraculous suspension of these alienating conditions. Enjoyment of the genre depends on an acceptance—however brief—of its conventions, hence the abandonment of the disenchanted, secularized perspective of modernity in the pursuit of a 'magical garden'" (91).

Because the immediate postwar years offered only fragmentation, incoherence, and disillusionment geopolitically, it is understandable that fiction writers and readers wanted to return to a unified, simplistic view to escape, if only briefly, the complexities of the postwar world. And the majority of the fiction written in America and Britain met this need. But even romances ended up expressing some of the discontent that the demands of the form would exclude. (This discontented voice would later become the primary voice of the Cold War fiction.) The supposedly utopian return to normalcy that romance writers espoused in their fictions when speaking in their public voice was undercut by a tension in the lives of their heroines; only begrudgingly do some of them provide the haven the returning veteran seeks. The heroine, because of her wartime work outside the home, now challenges the mysterious prerogatives of masculinity that the returning veteran brings with him. Though these novels, like the nonfiction guides for veterans, try to offer "magical fictions" of postwar life to their audiences, they do not entirely succeed.

A compelling metaphor for the dream of a paradisal postwar life is given in May Edginton's *Fruit of the Tree* (1947), published in Britain as *The Soldier and the Ladies*. Here the man's fantasy of what life will be like after the war is presented as a song: "All the sleeping men sang it in great low voices—the music of their world that was to be . . . the world of fecundity where all the men had laboured and suffered for came true; the rising of the sap again, the greening of the trees of life, the opening eyes of all the new children, the love of women not too strong or too busy, the great and simple rights of the men who had earned them with their all" (28).

Central to these romances' magical vision for both men and women is the creation of new life after the deaths of the war. John Stanbro, the protagonist's brother, wants to marry and have a son; he wants "to see creation go forward again" (57), but the woman he is in love with, Lesley West, is one of the career women of the war who must be reeducated to procreate. Jessica, back from serving in the women's armed forces and doing her duty, marries her longtime love, Lionel Ranger, and happily returns to the prewar domestic idyll. But although Edington's younger women fulfill their men's fantasy by returning to private life, her older heroines do not. Mother Millicent Stanbro, for example, moves into the public arena by joining the women's club lecture circuit and seeks a divorce from her husband, Patrick. She does not want to participate in his postwar dream, preferring instead to pursue a dream of her own. May Edginton's postwar paradise is ambiguous at best.

In *Please, No Paregoric!* (1946), Ethel Hueston rejects the "paregoric propaganda" (40) that is being marketed to both men and women in the immediate postwar years. Mother Wade, like Millicent Stanbro, joins the lecture circuit for the women's clubs, where women "learn to express themselves with force and precision so we might make ourselves felt in the community and the nation" (102). In both novels, the men return to what they fantasize will be a traditional home life, but, like the women, only a few succeed in living the fantasy.

The postwar fiction written by women relies heavily on the stereotypes of veterans' wives that nonfiction writers publicized, and confident romancers use the stereotypes only to question them. For example, in Alice Ross Colver's *Homecoming* we meet Bunny, the child bride (type C), who is unable to relate to, understand, or help her young veteran husband, Gerry; Joan, the Red Cross worker, who does not believe in healing the heart, her own or that of her husband, Keith, and who can only heal his body (type A); and Kathy, who reluctantly wears the pants while her husband is in the Pacific theater (type B). But the most important character is Ada, the mother of all three of these boys and wife of Philip. The end of the war brings her new life: "She looked as if she had come back to the end of one kind of life and were facing the beginning of another. A more exciting one" (118). She tells her husband that she wants a divorce. She will no longer pander to his male fantasy of home: "Home—where love dwelt and peace and beauty and understanding. . . . All through his war experience he had thought about it, idealizing it" (24). In her new life, Ada becomes a popular and respected speaker for women's clubs, lecturing and educating about women's new position in the postwar world: "Perhaps you do not fully realize what it is that we *have* given up," Ada says to her lecture audience of homemakers, wives, and mothers. "Let me remind you. We have abandoned the privilege and responsibility of being queens in our private lives. We had a throne— but we have left it for the arena. On the throne we ruled. In the arena we only—struggle" (174). But Alice Ross Colver cannot endorse such a total reversal of the magical romance. In the final pages of the novel, Ada tempers her message to the postwar woman:

> We modern women are paying too great a price for our modernity! We have won a Pyrrhic victory! We can't imitate or rival men in all the various walks of life and at the same time function as wives and women in the house! We lose everything that way because we don't succeed anywhere! We are dodging our destiny! We have got to sacrifice either our ambition or our peace of heart! We have got to choose! . . . Let us return, then, to an old and familiar role with a new and enlightened outlook. With all the knowledge and understanding we have gained by our adventure into the world, we have proved to the men what we set out to prove! Let us also prove to them what they—and we—have forgotten. That *from our homes* we can shape the thoughts and minds and spirits of the future leaders of mankind. (*Homecoming* 178–79)

The "return" is not easy; neither the war veteran nor the home-front veteran seems to learn the language of Civvy Street easily. In several novels, violence erupts because of characters' inability to blend their respective fantasies and languages. These novels could be described as dystopic romances.

In Maritta Wolff's *About Lyddy Thomas* (1947), the veteran, Ben, will not grant the divorce that his wife, the titular heroine of the novel, seeks. She married him before he left for the battlefront when she was only eighteen, and although the home-front war has caused her to grow up, the battlefront war has not resulted in a similar education for Ben. He wants his fantasy, and when Lyddy will not cooperate he threatens, rapes, and beats her. Ultimately, he is murdered by a delusional Italian woman, Mother Maciatto, who refuses to believe that her son won't return from the war and blames any man in uniform for his death.

Another dystopic romance is Clarissa Fairchild Cushman's *The Glass Barracks* (1950). Lee and John Farquoson begin postwar life in Vetsburg, the

Veteran's Housing Unit, which looks like "endless lines of endless barracks spreading out like the legs of a gigantic centipede joined with more barracks" (5). Living in this dismal setting saps the life from their postwar hopes; able neither to move backward to recapture their earlier dreams nor to move forward to create new ones, they are caught in the limbo of afterwar. As Lee remarks: "I've said to myself that in the future when we have more chance of space and privacy, then we'll live more graciously. I've been in a state of—we . . . I've endured, but I haven't enjoyed" (3).

Still another example of the dystopic romance, this one by a man, is Niven Busch's *Day of the Conquerors* (1946). Mark Gregory, a war correspondent, returns to San Francisco, to his wife, Corrine, and his son, Lorry, after having been kept alive in Saipan by his dreams of his American home that he found in magazine advertisements. He returns to a nightmare, and in one of the closing scenes of the novel the reader watches as Mark abandons the dream: "There was a place toward which they could have moved, if he'd let them—a place where a woman was standing . . . a woman, not a destroyer. . . . The woman was the future, waiting beyond conjecture for his mind and will and body at last to embrace her" (276). Mark proves unable to embrace that future, and the novel ends flatly with the abandonment of all romance, magic, and dreams. Busch's novel points the way to the large number of post-1951 fictions that will examine such disillusionment in detail.

Thus the veteran's dream of returning to an idealized memory of home and working toward a brighter future is at best ambiguously supported by the fiction of the period and in some instances is rejected entirely. The American Penelope seems to be less than happy with the return of her Ulysses and more than a little disenchanted with the postwar dream. In the British fiction of the same period, the characters seem to be content to be alive and participating, at whatever level, in the dream.

To conclude: the primary form of immediate postwar fiction is that of the romance because it reinforces the idea of the stable family and the continuity of home life that the veteran fought for, dreamed about, and supposedly returned to. The returning, alienated veteran has to be reintegrated into this domestic sphere; the violence of the war has proved to the male soldier the superiority of this domestic world, and he must become a part of it again. The central ideology, then, is reintegrating men into the postwar, primarily feminine domestic world and thereby regenerating them. As Mona Gardner observed in 1945, "In the army [the soldier] has gone through what doctors call regression of ego, funneling his many complex emotions to a simpler level. For the love of home, his wife and children, he has had to substitute buddy love, company love, and fear, fear, fear. It will take him two to three months to discard one set of instincts and acquire new ones" (72). Postwar romance novels argue that self-renewal and nonviolent regeneration is possible but certainly not in Gardner's short time frame.

Morton Thompson best sums it up in *How to Be a Civilian*, when he writes that "[p]eace is an interval between wars during which the military—which appears to mean every male on the planet at the time—gets out of uniform and tries to learn the temporary role of civilian" (x). The literature I have examined here is the interlude of street clothes in what is perhaps always a uniformed society.

Note

I would like to thank Phylis Wright, director of the Inter-Library Loan Department of Villanova University, and her invaluable staff for making this essay possible.

Works Cited

Primary Sources

Algren, Nelson. *The Man with the Golden Arm*. New York: Doubleday, 1949.

Baber, Ray E. "Marriage and the Family after the War." *Annals of the American Academy of Political and Social Science* 229 (Sept. 1943): 164–75.

Becker, Carl L. *How New Will the Better World Be? A Discussion of Post-War Reconstruction*. New York: Alfred A. Knopf, 1944.

Bellow, Saul. *Dangling Man*. New York: Vanguard Press, 1944.

Bolte, Charles G. *The New Veteran*. New York: Reynal and Hitchcock, 1945.

Bowker, Benjamin C. *Out of Uniform*. New York: Norton, 1946.

British Information Services. *Britain and the Veteran*. New York: Information Division, May 1945.

Buck, Pearl S. *Of Men and Women*. New York: John Day, 1941.

Busch, Niven. *Day of the Conquerors: A Novel*. New York: Harper and Brothers, 1946.

Carleton, Marjorie. *The Swan Sang Once*. New York: William Morrow, 1947.

Carson, Robert. *Stranger in Our Midst*. New York: G. P. Putnam's Sons, 1947.

Cartwright, Morse A. *Adult Adjustment*. New York: Institute of Adult Education, 1945.

Charles, Joan. *And the Hunter Home.* New York: Harper and Brothers, 1946.

Colver, Alice Ross. *Fourways.* Philadelphia: Macrae-Smith, 1944.

———. *Homecoming.* Philadelphia: Macrae-Smith, 1945.

Cushman, Clarissa Fairchild. *The Glass Barracks.* Boston: Little, Brown, 1950.

Davis, Clyde Brion. *The Stars Incline.* New York: Farrar and Rinehart, 1946.

Dodds, Harold W. *Out of This Nettle, Danger.* Princeton: Princeton University Press, 1943.

Dumas, Alexander G. *A Psychiatric Primer for the Veteran's Family and Friends.* Minneapolis: University of Minnesota Press, 1945.

Edgerton, Alanson H. *Readjustment or Revolution?* New York: McGraw-Hill, 1946.

Edginton, May. *Fruit of the Tree.* Philadelphia: Macrae-Smith, 1947.

Evening Bulletin. *The Evening Bulletin's Veteran's Guide.* Philadelphia: Bulletin, 1945.

Gardner, Mona. "Has Your Husband Come Home to the Right Woman?" *Ladies Home Journal* Dec. 1945: 41, 72, 74.

Goodman, Jack, ed. *While You Were Gone: A Report on Wartime Life in the United States.* New York: Simon and Schuster, 1944.

Habe, Hans. *Aftermath: A Novel.* New York: Viking Press, 1947.

Hargrove, Marion. *Something's Got to Give.* New York: Sloane, 1948.

Haslett, Caroline. *Problems Have No Sex.* London: Hodder and Stoughton, 1949.

Havinghurst, Robert J., et al. *The American Veteran Back Home.* London: Longmans, Green, 1951.

Helton, Roy. "The Inner Threat: Our Own Softness." *Harper's Magazine* Sept. 1940: 337–43.

Hill, Reuben. *Families under Stress: Adjustment to the Crises of War Separation and Reunion.* New York: Harper and Brothers, 1949.

Howard, Kenneth. *Sex Problems of the Returning Soldier.* Manchester: Sydney Pemberton, 1945.

Hueston, Ethel. *Please, No Paregoric!* Indianapolis: Bobbs-Merrill, 1946.

Kupper, Herbert I. *Back to Life: The Emotional Adjustment of Our Veterans.* New York: L. B. Fischer, 1945.

Lambert, Eric. *The Veterans.* London: Shakespeare Head, 1954.

Lundberg, Ferdinand, and Marynia F. Farnham. *Modern Woman: The Lost Sex.* New York: Harper and Brothers, 1947.

Mariano, John H. *The Veteran and His Marriage.* New York: Council on Marriage Relations, 1945.

Marquand, John P. *Repent in Haste.* Boston: Little, Brown, 1945.

Marshall, Marguerite Mooers. *Arms and the Girl.* New York: Triangle Books, 1943.

Mass Observation. *The Journey Home: A Report Prepared by Mass Observation for the Advertising Service Guild.* London: John Murray, 1944.

McDonagh, Edward C. "The Discharged Serviceman and His Family." *American Journal of Sociology* 51 (May 1946): 451–54.

Merrill, Francis E. *Social Problems on the Home Front: A Study of War-Time Influences*. New York: Harpers and Brothers, 1948.

Meserve, Nathaniel. *King of This Hill*. Garden City: Doubleday, 1947.

Miller, Helen Topping. *Candle in the Morning*. New York: D. Appleton-Century, 1947.

Nichols, Margaret. *Always with Me*. 1944. Philadelphia: Blakiston, 1945.

Nicoll, Mildred Robertson. *Family Post Bag*. London: Hodder and Stoughton, 1947.

Nivens, Allan. *This Is England Today*. New York: Charles Scribner's Sons, 1941.

Overton, Grace Sloan. *Marriage in War and Peace*. New York: Abingdon-Cokesbury Press, 1945.

Paterson, Dorothy. *The Family Woman and the Feminist*. London: William Heineman, 1945.

Peattie, Margaret Rhodes. *The Return*. New York: William Morrow, 1944.

Pratt, George K. *Soldier to Civilian*. London: Whittlesey House, 1944.

Priestley, J. B. *British Women Go to War*. London: Collins, n.d.

Robinson, Mabel Louise. *The Deepening Year*. Philadelphia: Westminster Press, 1950.

Rothery, Agnes. *Balm of Gilead*. New York: Dodd, Mead, 1946.

Schrag, Otto. *Sons of the Morning*. Garden City: Doubleday, Doran, 1945.

Seifert, Elizabeth. *Homecoming*. New York: Dodd, Mead, 1950.

Soutar, Arch. "Home Coming Isn't Easy." *Saturday Evening Post* 16 Dec. 1944: 35–36, 38.

Sturgis, Robert. *Hidden Season*. New York: M. S. Mill, 1946.

Thirkell, Angela. *Peace Breaks Out*. 1947. New York: Pyramid Books, 1972.

Thompson, Morton. *How to Be a Civilian*. New York: Doubleday, 1946.

U.S. War and Navy Departments. *Going Back to Civilian Life*. Washington, DC: Government Printing Office, 1945.

U.S. War Department. *Welcome Home*. Washington, DC: Government Printing Office, 1944.

Vance, Ethel. *Winter Meeting*. Boston: Little, Brown, 1946.

Waller, Willard. *The Veteran Comes Back*. New York: Dryden Press, 1944.

Wolff, Maritta. *About Lyddy Thomas*. New York: Random House, 1947.

Secondary Sources

Anderson, Karen. *Wartime Women: Sex Roles, Family Relations, and the Status of Women during World War II*. Westport, CT: Greenwood Press, 1981.

Baker, Niamh. *Happily Ever After? Women's Fiction in Postwar Britain, 1945–60*. New York: St. Martin's Press, 1989.

Bartlett, C. J. *A History of Postwar Britain, 1945–1974*. London: Longman, 1977.

Bergonzi, Bernard. *Wartime and Aftermath: English Literature and Its Background, 1939–1960*. New York: Oxford University Press, 1993.

Bragdon, Elizabeth, ed. *Women Today: Their Conflicts, Their Frustrations and Their Fulfillments*. Indianapolis: Bobbs-Merrill, 1953.

Bragg, Melvyn. *The Soldier's Return*. London: Hodder and Stoughton, 1999.

Braybon, Gail, and Penny Summerfield. *Out of the Cage: Women's Experiences in Two World Wars*. London: Pandora Press, 1987.

Bremmer, Robert H., and Gary W. Reichard, eds. *Reshaping America: Society and Institutions, 1945–1960*. Columbus: Ohio State University Press, 1982.

Calder, Angus, and Dorothy Sheridan, eds. *Speak for Yourself: A Mass-Observation Anthology, 1937–1949*. London: Jonathan Cape, 1984.

Cole, Harold. "Home from the Wars: The Popular Press Views the Veteran Problem, 1944–1948." *North Dakota Quarterly* 46.3 (1978): 41–61.

Davies, Alistair, and Alan Sinfield, eds. *British Culture of the Postwar: An Introduction to Literature and Society, 1945–1999*. London: Routledge, 2000.

Deutsch, James. "Coming Home from 'the Good War': World War II Veterans as Depicted in American Film and Fiction." PhD diss., George Washington University, 1991.

Duchen, Claire, and Irene Bandhauer-Schoffman, eds. *When the War Was Over: Women, War and Peace in Europe, 1940–1956*. London: Leicester Press, 2000.

Eisinger, Chester E. *Fiction of the Forties*. Chicago: University of Chicago Press, 1963.

Fowler, Bridget. *The Alienated Reader: Women and Romantic Literature in the Twentieth Century*. New York: Harvester Wheatsheaf, 1991.

Gasiorek, Andrzej. *Post-War British Fiction: Realism and After*. London: Hodder Headline Group, 1995.

Graebner, William. *The Age of Doubt: American Thought and Culture in the 1940s*. Boston: Twayne, 1991.

Hartmann, Geoffrey H. *Wordsworth's Poetry, 1878–1814*. New Haven: Yale University Press, 1964.

Hartmann, Susan M. "Prescriptions for Penelope: Literature on Women's Obligations to Returning World War II Veterans." *Women's Studies* 5 (1978): 223–39.

Honey, Maureen. *Creating Rosie the Riveter: Class, Gender, and Propaganda during World War II*. Amherst: University of Massachusetts Press, 1984.

Hurd, Geoff, ed. *National Fictions: World War II in British Films and Television*. London: BFI Publishing, 1984.

Ivie, Rachel L., Cynthia Gimbel, and Glen H. Elder Jr. "Military Experience and Attitudes in Later Life: Contextual Influences across Forty Years." *Journal of Political and Military Sociology* 19 (1991): 101–17.

Jones, Peter G. *War and the Novelist: Appraising the American War Novel*. Columbia: University of Missouri Press, 1976.

Klein, Holger, ed. *The Second World War in Fiction*. London: Macmillan, 1984.

Knowles, Sebastian D. G. *A Purgatorial Flame: Seven British Writers in the Second World War*. Philadelphia: University of Pennsylvania Press, 1990.

Lewis, Jane. *Women in England, 1870–1950*. Brighton: Wheatsheaf Books, 1984.

Limon, John. *Writing after War: American War Fiction from Realism to Postmodernism*. New York: Oxford University Press, 1994.

Little, Roger D., and J. Eric Fredland. "Veteran Status, Earnings, and Race." *Armed Forces and Society* 5.2 (1979): 244–60.

Modell, John, and Duane Steffey. "Waging War and Marriage: Military Service and Family Formation, 1940–1950." *Journal of Family History* 13.2 (1988): 195–218.

Morgan, David, and Mary Evans. *The Battle for Britain: Citizenship and Ideology in the Second World War*. London: Routledge, 1993.

Philips, Deborah, and Ian Haywood. *Brave New Causes: Women in British Postwar Fictions*. London: Leicester University Press, 1998.

Piette, Adam. *Imagination at War: British Fiction and Poetry, 1939–1945*. Basingstoke: Macmillan, 1995.

Shuker-Haines, Timothy Maxwell. "Home Is the Hunter: Representations of Returning World War II Veterans and the Reconstruction of Masculinity, 1944–1951." PhD diss., University of Michigan, 1994.

Sinfield, Alan. *Literature, Politics, and Culture in Postwar Britain*. Berkeley: University of California Press, 1989.

———, ed. *Society and Literature, 1945–1970*. New York: Holmes and Meier, 1983.

Smith, Malcolm. *Britain and 1940: History, Myth and Popular Memory*. London: Routledge, 2000.

Stevenson, Randall. *The British Novel since the Thirties: An Introduction*. London: Batsford, 1986.

Swindells, Julia. "Coming Home to Heaven: Manpower and Myth in 1944 Britain." *Women's History Review* 4.2 (1995): 223–34.

Townsend, Colin, and Eileen Townsend. *War Wives: A Second World War Anthology*. London: Grafton Books, 1989.

Turner, Barry, and Tony Rennell. *When Daddy Came Home: How Family Life Changed Forever in 1945*. London: Pimlico, 1995.

Virden, Jenel. *Good-bye, Piccadilly: British War Brides in America*. Urbana: University of Illinois Press, 1996.

Waldmeir, Joseph J. *American Novels of the Second World War*. Paris: Mouton, 1969.

Westbrook, Robert B. "'I Want a Girl, Just Like the Girl That Married Harry James': American Women and the Problem of Political Obligation in World War II." *American Quarterly* 42 (Dec. 1990): 587–614.

Wicks, Ben. *Welcome Home: True Stories of Soldiers Returning from World War II*. London: Bloomsbury, 1991.

Wilson, Elizabeth. *Only Halfway to Paradise: Women in Postwar Britain, 1945–1968*. London: Tavistock, 1980.

Wisniewski, Jacek. *Mars and the Muse: Attitudes to War and Peace in Twentieth Century English Literature*. Warsaw: Wydawnictna Uniwersytetu Warszaskiego, 1990.

CHAPTER FIVE

"When All the Wars Are Over"

The Utopian Impulses of Toni Morrison's Postwar Fiction

JENNIFER TERRY

In her sixth novel, *Jazz*, Toni Morrison captures a particular moment of optimism, of "modernity," in her depiction of 1920s New York. Describing "the City . . . when all the wars are over and there will never be another one," the narrator exclaims, "Here comes the new. . . . History is over, you all, and everything's ahead at last" (7). The protagonist, Joe Trace, recalls his own jubilation and pride at marching alongside black troops returned to Harlem from World War I: "[I]n 1919 . . . I walked all the way . . . with the three six nine . . . because the War had come and gone and the colored troops of the three six nine that fought it made me so proud it split my heart in two" (129).[1] This hopeful vision of the postwar future raises issues of how for African Americans military service can be tied up with concerns about "Americanness," with proving manhood, patriotism, and bravery and therefore asserting belonging. The black claim to citizenship (felt to have been earned through sacrifices made for the nation), however, remained problematic after the war. For *Jazz* also details the East St. Louis rioting that involved discharged and "disgruntled veterans who had fought in all-colored units . . . and came home to white violence more intense than when they enlisted and, unlike the battles they fought in Europe, stateside fighting was pitiless and totally without honor" (57). The proud return from World War I was thus often accompanied for black soldiers by disillusionment and disappointment at the inequality and violent oppression still in operation at home, the lack of political agency unchanged by their efforts overseas on behalf of America and democracy.[2]

Bearing such considerations in mind, I wish to argue that war and its aftermath are central to the conception of Morrison's 1998 novel, *Paradise*.

Indeed, *Paradise* was originally going to be entitled *War*.[3] Exploring aspects of the text to which this title would have drawn explicit attention, I interrogate what military service means for African Americans, the definitions of "home" that emerge from experiences of combat overseas, and Morrison's depiction of the rhetoric and repercussions of war through the embattled stance taken by the all-black town of Ruby. For, according to Carolyn Denard, Morrison "places at center stage men who embrace violence" (80). My essay proposes that *Paradise* delineates the corruption of a utopian vision that, although engendered by postwar dispossession, itself becomes oppressive and eventually and inevitably leads to further aggression. Here an African American community that defines itself against the rest of America comes to emulate and rehearse the structures and recourse to violence of the dominant culture.

Male departure to and return from war is a pattern of movement that shapes Ruby's story. The town's history is situated according to participation in the two World Wars and the following conflicts in Asia, and much of the narrative present is overshadowed by not only the civil rights struggle but also the Vietnam War. Once troop desegregation begins in Korea, military service brings exposure to the interracial contact that is increasingly viewed as corruptive by the founding fathers of Ruby. Yet, in apparent opposition to the community's wish to isolate itself from the dissolute world around it, from other populations both white and black, combat with the national armed forces is still regarded as commendable, as formative. It remains somehow bound up with proving fortitude and manhood, with the patriarchs' self-righteous defense of the place they have "cut . . . out of mud" for themselves in this land (6).

As I will explore later, going away to war crystallizes particular ideas of home and community. And the veterans' postwar vision for Ruby leads to an attack on outsiders. Indeed, the terms of the "protection" of the town from external threat echo the codes of national fortress building. Hence I suggest that, although Morrison's text fails to present an explicit critique of American militarism and imperialism despite a focus on the era of Vietnam, attempts to engage indirectly with such dynamics can be identified in her narrative. Above all, violence erodes the hope described in *Jazz* of a time "when all the wars are over."

The long history of African American service in the U.S. military involves segregation, subordination, and overlooked contributions. In the early twentieth century, fighting in the First World War offered black soldiers fresh hope of earning a place, and correspondingly more rights, as citizens in modern American society. Yet as *Jazz* depicts, such ambitions often met with violent white backlash and governmental hostility or indifference during the postwar period. The contradictions of racially segregated forces fighting for "American" ideals of democratic equality and freedom became acutely evident during World War II, a conflict in which the Allies defined themselves against a supremacist enemy practicing racial persecution and removing civil liberties. Yet "[i]n the years following World War II, a wave of violence swept the South as African American veterans returned home" (Dudziak 23). The Vietnam War brought full military desegregation, but the draft was biased against the economically disadvantaged, black casualties were disproportionately higher than white ones, and racial tensions within American forces erupted at such moments as the assassination of Martin Luther King.[4]

The narrative of *Paradise* is littered with references to military service, and past American conflicts are frequently invoked. In 1949, when naming their town, the men of the community, nearly all ex-soldiers, make suggestions connected to the Second World War: "Pacific veterans liked Guam, others Inchon. Those who fought in Europe kept coming up with names only the children enjoyed pronouncing" (17). Elsewhere brief mention is made of a "Purple Heart" and "army-issue tents" (10). Steward Morgan's sense of "home" is defined in terms of the ranch "where his American flag flew on holidays; where his honorable discharge papers were framed," and military training is seen as a testing ground, as the sphere in which the town leaders proved themselves as young men (88). The narrative of Ruby's past is oriented by U.S. conflicts: Reverend Cary "was not among the first families, so his arrival was associated not with World War II, but with Korea" (204). And allusion is made to the prosperity, the "War money," that international hostilities engender for Americans (107). The novel is also, however, threaded through with the losses and deaths caused by war. One ex-soldier remembers "military crosses spread for miles," and some female characters have been left widowed by men who died in "Europe or Korea or someplace" (154, 199). All of these references work to establish a historical model of service in the military, of departure and return, honor and bereavement. Such themes are key to both the envisioning and the collapse of this "dreamtown" (5).

The narrative present of *Paradise* covers a period extending from 1968 to 1976, and in most of the many character perspectives provided there is some allusion to the war being conducted in Vietnam.[5] These details situate the town's story and constantly remind the reader of the United States' controversial part in this conflict. For example, in the account of Mavis's flight from domestic violence, mention is made of her "killed-in-action brothers" and "the checks in two brown government envelopes" that after their deaths were sent to her mother (32). In addition, one of the hitchhikers that Mavis picks up while on the run "talked for thirty-two miles . . . about the owners of the six dog tags that hung from her neck. Boys in her high school or whom she had known in junior high. . . . All dead or missing" (34). Such Vietnam casualties, although evident only from understated references, from gaps and silences, echo through the chapters of *Paradise*. Later Mavis drops off another two girls at a cemetery where "[l]ines of cars necklaced the entrance. . . . [They] thanked Mavis and got out, running a little to join a set of graveside mourners. . . . What she thought were military students turned out to be real soldiers—but young, so young, and as fresh-looking as the headstones they stood before" (34). This minor episode suggests the tragedy of the many lives lost in Vietnam, the numerous fresh grave markers, the youth of the boy soldiers and of the girls hitchhiking to bury and mourn their male peers. In 1974 even Reverend Misner wonders, "Had the times finally gotten to him? . . . Had the long, unintelligible war infected him? Behaving like a dormant virus in blossom now that it was coming to a raggedy close? Everybody on his high school football team died in that war. Eleven broad-backed boys. They were the ones he had looked up to, wanted to be like. Was he just now gagging at their futile death?" (160). This undercurrent of commentary on the losses of Vietnam flows through the text, although the politics of the war are not confronted head on. Indeed, Misner's description of a wasted generation, of the war as unintelligible and futile, is as overt as Morrison's criticism gets.[6]

Among the townspeople Jeff Fleetwood is a serviceman whose grievances with the Veteran's Administration on his return from Vietnam include his four severely disabled children whose condition he blames on the war (58, 156). As Justine Tally observes, "Jeff's complaint before the Administration is never specified, but the fact that he is ignored . . . may point to the government's reluctance to admit that exposure to Agent Orange causes malformation in off-spring" (27). While this veteran's sense of frustration manifests itself in violent rage, other community members are haunted by loss. Soane Morgan's narrative tells of her sons, Scout and Easter, who were killed within two weeks of each other: "Babies. One nineteen, the other twenty-one. How proud and happy she was when they enlisted; she had actively encouraged them to do so. . . . Like a fool she believed her sons would be safe. . . . Now she had four unopened letters mailed in 1968" (100–101). Soane is left mourning the deaths of both her children, punishing herself for the pride and joy she experienced at their enlistment, too scared to open their last letters home. Her husband, "like most of the Morgans, had seen action, which is to say live death. . . . He knew that bodies did not lie down; that most often they flew apart and that what had been shipped to them in those boxes . . . was a collection of parts that weighed half of what a nineteen-year-old would" (112). Deacon is filled with helpless anger at the thought of his sons being "[b]uried in a bag like kittens" (106). The pain of their loss is amplified by his own knowledge of the horror of wartime death, the violent rending of the body that takes place, and the partiality of the corpses that were sent back to Ruby. In this explicit confrontation with the likely condition of Scout and Easter's remains, notions of bravery and honor collapse into abject grief, even shame.

This conflict, it appears, prompts neither a parade celebrating the return of courageous black veterans nor a white backlash against such soldiers. Vietnam instead looms like a specter over the narrative present. Despite frustration and hurt like that of Deacon discussed above, *Paradise* does not really engage critically with the controversial involvement of American forces in eastern Asia. Nor does Morrison's narrative raise issues of the draft or of the objections preoccupying the black public figures who spoke out against the war at the time. Muhammad Ali's televised comments about his refusal to go to Vietnam provide just one example of African American protest at the United States' imperialist forays against nonwhites elsewhere in the world: "They want me to go to Vietnam to shoot some black folks that never lynched me, never called me nigger, never assassinated my leaders" (qtd. in Maycock 23). Before his death Martin Luther King also damned American foreign policy, charging the U.S. government with being "the greatest purveyor of violence in the world today" (qtd. in Maycock 23). The failure to acknowledge such questioning of militarism is remiss in *Paradise*. The novel sketches the domestic strife of the civil rights struggle but does not place it next to the violent repression that African Americans were being asked to participate in alongside whites overseas. In the dynamics of the narrative, however, an exploration of aggression as a reaction to difference, and of supremacist positioning, does take place. Although Morrison's depiction of the war sidesteps much of the political debate surrounding Vietnam, issues of militarism, defense, belonging, and "othering" are tackled indirectly in the story of the town of Ruby.

This story begins in 1890 when, disappointed by the failures of Reconstruction, a group of ex-slaves from Louisiana and Mississippi sets off to find a new home in the American West.[7] The freedmen eventually reach the aptly named settlement of Fairly, a black town that is being built by light-skinned African Americans in Oklahoma. The newcomers, however, are turned away, dismissed, perhaps for their poverty, more likely for their dark skin, so they move on and set up a town called Haven for themselves. The painful memory of being excluded by fellow blacks, named the Disallowing, shapes the ex-slaves into "a tight band of wayfarers bound by the enormity of what had happened to them" (189).[8] Fairly's rejection causes them to choose self-sufficiency and isolation: in fact, "Everything anybody wanted to know about the citizens of Haven . . . lay in the ramifications of that one rebuff out of many" (189). And when later generations see this settlement fail, a group of World War II veterans try to repeat their forefathers' project by moving further West and founding a new community called Ruby. The entrenched position they adopt, however, eventually comes to betray the original vision.[9]

The America that faces these veterans on being discharged is little more receptive than that which met the First World War soldiers described in *Jazz*:

> The rejection, which they called the Disallowing, was a burn whose scar tissue was numb by 1949, wasn't it? Oh, no. Those that survived that particular war came right back home, saw what had become of Haven, heard about the missing testicles of other colored soldiers; about medals being torn off by gangs of rednecks and Sons of the Confederacy—and recognized the Disallowing, Part Two. It would have been like watching a parade banner that said WAR-WEARY SOLDIERS! NOT WELCOME HOME! So they did it again. And just as the original wayfarers never sought another colored townsite after being cold-shouldered at the first, this generation joined no organization, fought no civil battle. They consolidated the 8-rock blood and, haughty as ever, moved farther west. (194)

For African American servicemen the return home to the United States meant coming back to violence rather than gratitude, humiliation rather than pride. The greeting the Haven veterans receive from white society causes them to attempt to replicate what the ex-slaves did following Fairly's contemptuous dismissal. Rather than combating the Jim Crow laws of their segregated and unjust nation by joining forces with civil rights campaigners, the patriarchs of Ruby opt for separatism, placing as much distance as they can between their homes and other communities (both white and black). Faced with the erosion of Haven by migration, poverty, and white encroachment, the veterans see a "dwindling postwar future" (16). Threatened by "unmonitored and seething" violence, a world "where your children were sport, your women quarry . . . where every cluster of whitemen looked like a posse," they opt to protect their families by removing them beyond the rest of society (16).[10] And "like the ex-slaves who knew what came first, the ex-soldiers . . . headed not for . . . Saint Louis, Houston, Langston, or Chicago, but deeper into Oklahoma, as far as they could climb from the grovel contaminating the town their grandfathers had made" (16). Against the dominant flow of African American migration, the community goes further west onto land purchased with pooled discharge pay (so echoing the earlier movement of European American pioneers).[11]

The new patriarchs feel that they are repeating their forefathers' choices, yet the inflexibility with which they adopt laws of exclusion perhaps means that the spirit of their community's previous way of life is lost. This male generation's service in the armed forces has crystallized, but also frozen, their ideas of home and, in particular, of the desirable conduct of women. Their memories become idealized while they are away, and with their decision to move deeper into isolation the veterans don a mantle of superiority, of independence but also pride, scorning all those outside their haven.[12] Indeed, I argue that the ex-soldiers assume a rigidity of attitude and an ethnic absolutism not found in the tales of their predecessors.[13] As Cyrus Patell observes, "Built in opposition both to the white culture and to the other black communities that once shunned its inhabitants, Ruby's communitarianism nevertheless organizes itself around conceptions of racial purity and patriarchal authority" (139).

The servicemen were accompanied through the Second World War by their vision of home: "Loving what Haven had been—the idea of it and its reach—they carried that devotion, gentling and nursing it from Bataan to Guam, from Iwo Jima to Stuttgart" (6). And having romanticized the community, once discharged and disappointed, the ex-soldiers seek to recreate Haven as they pictured it. This is illustrated by their attitude toward food: "Back from the war, [the] men were hungry for down-home food, but dreaming of it for three years had raised their expectations, exaggerated the possibilities of lard making biscuits lighter than snow, the responsibility sharp cheese took on in hominy. . . . Steward remembered everything differently. Shouldn't the clove be down in the tissue, not just sitting on top of the ham? And the chicken-fried steak—Vidalia onions or Spanish?" (81). Such musings may appear insignificant, yet they demonstrate one effect of military service. Dreaming of "down-home food" for three years causes Steward Morgan to idealize, fetishize, the culinary production of the townswomen. On his return the real meals cooked for him thus cannot meet his expectations. Steward remembers things differently, and this influences not only his criticism of food but also the perception he has of the community. His absence "exaggerated the possibilities," meaning that Haven, and then Ruby, can't live up to his vision.

The Morgan twins' ideas of community can be traced back to their childhood memory of a tour of black towns made by the men of Haven. In a prosperous settlement they saw "nineteen Negro ladies arrange themselves on the steps of the town hall" (109). These "refined" black women posing for a photograph captivated the boys with their "slender feet . . . in thin leather shoes" and waists "not much bigger than their necks" (109). They "preened" in white and yellow dresses and their voices were "musical . . . low, full of delight" (109). The scene remains a vivid recollection for the brothers even after the war: "Deek's image of the nineteen summertime ladies was unlike the photographer's. His remembrance was pastel colored and eternal" (110). This exemplifies the idealized notion of black womanhood that the Morgans cherish. The memory is a celebration of the grace and beauty of the women, but it also constitutes a frozen vision against which the patriarchs hold up everything else. The "Negro ladies," both respectable and attractive, become paragons of what the twins think black women should be. Deacon's picture is as static as the photographer's, acknowledging only the part of the posers' lives presented on this one occasion. Still this image of womanhood shapes the leaders' conception of Ruby: "Quiet white and yellow houses full of industry; and in them were elegant black women at useful tasks; orderly cupboards minus surfeit or miserliness; linen laundered and ironed to perfection; good meat seasoned and ready for roasting" (111). This idealized view of domesticity links the pastel Negro ladies with the town's orderly white and yellow homes. Black women are associated with an iconography akin to that of the nineteenth-century "angel in the house," a gender construction involving both the idolization and regulation of female behavior conventionally pertaining to white bourgeois women. This version of acceptable and desirable femininity, described by John Duvall as a "cult of true black womanhood," comes to define the patriarchs' notion of the whole community (and, as will be demonstrated, of what threatens it) (142).[14] Indeed, Steward sees it as "the vision that carried him and his brother through a war, that imbued their marriages and strengthened their efforts to build a town where the vision could flourish" (279).[15]

The utopia of Ruby is conceived as a place where black women are safe to walk at night. Unlike elsewhere in the United States, here the townswomen can wander at will, knowing that there is no white threat, that "[n]othing for ninety miles around [thinks they are] prey" (8).[16] This is in some senses a very positive assertion. The notion of the town as an enclave of security, however, comes to have further implications. As Patell writes, "This is a patriarch's view of women's freedom" (183). To defend their families, to preserve their image of Negro ladies, the ex-soldiers set themselves up in the role of guardsmen. The town is described as "free and protected," yet this picture is dependent on exclusion, obedience, and conformity (8). When there is dissent about the meaning of the communal oven, when young people want change in the 1970s, this is perceived as a threat to the New Fathers' vision.[17] Hence the progressive Reverend Misner condemns Ruby as "some fortress you . . . built up and have to keep everybody locked in or out" (213). And the patriarchs' zealous safeguarding of the town eventually leads to an aggressive attack on defenseless women, the very figures the Old Fathers wanted to prevent from falling prey to white men. To the veterans "Ruby represents the best of all possible worlds for women, but clearly Morrison exposes . . . the central unacknowledged contradiction of the male communal narrative that authorizes the hunting of women in the name of protecting womanhood" (Duvall 143).

The climactic assault on the neighboring community known as the Convent (once a Catholic boarding school, now an informal women's refuge) is anticipated by earlier acts of exclusion. Because the dark-skinned founding families of Haven rejected outsiders, marrying only each other, the descendents of the town are a "[b]lue black people, tall and graceful" (193). They describe themselves as "eight-rock, a deep deep level in the coal mines," locating in their pure blackness a sense of racial superiority (193). Military service is the one sanctioned activity that unavoidably brings town members into contact with other communities, and during World War II Roger Best met and courted a light-skinned African American woman. On being discharged he sent for the girl who had had his child during the war, planning to take her with him to Ruby, yet she was greeted with scorn: "Only Steward had the gall to say out loud, 'He's bringing along the dung we leaving behind.' Dovey shushed him. . . . Fairy DuPres cursed him. . . . But they were just women, and what they said was easily ignored by good brave men on their way to Paradise" (201–2). The insularity and hostility toward difference of those whose ancestors were disallowed mean that they condemn a mother and her baby (figures they elsewhere claim to protect). The patriarchs see Roger's bride as an agent of contamination, as someone who threatens the purity of their community, and he is thereafter despised "for marrying . . . a wife of racial tampering" (197). The "good brave men" choose exclusion rather than inclusion. Fearing a dilution of eight-rock blood, the town leaders exhibit arrogant ethnic absolutism and later refuse to help when the outsider dies in childbirth. This move is repeated when, on his return from service in Vietnam, Menus Jury is persuaded not to marry a "sandy-haired girl from Virginia" (195). His seniors "said she was more like a fast woman than a bride," and he "[c]hose . . . to submit to his father's rule" (278). The patriarchs' laws to preserve their paradise hence involve, not only the protection of community, but also the rejection of persons with any racial variation. Infiltration, even by fellow blacks with some legacy of white blood, is perceived as detracting from the vision of Ruby that they cherish.[18]

The contact with racial difference (and therefore anxiety about miscegenation) brought about by experience in the military is illustrated in one further narrative episode. Here, however, the consternation at "mixing" is induced not by women but by the violence of warfare. Tied up with Deacon Morgan's rage that his sons have to be buried in bags because of their dismembered and incomplete condition is a fear that white body parts might have been mixed in with their own because they belonged to integrated units.[19] His need to know if all the parts are black again points to the town's preoccupation with "racial consistency," to one of the reasons for the attack on the heterogeneous household of the Convent (112).

Before launching a violent assault the patriarchs demonize their female neighbors: "The women in the Convent were . . . a flaunting parody of the nineteen Negro ladies of [Steward] and his brother's youthful memory and perfect understanding. They were the degradation of that moment they'd shared of sunlit skin and verbena" (297). The Morgan twins' perception of the runaway and refugee women clearly places them in opposition to their recollections of iconic femininity and the vision held for Ruby. With their "streetwalkers' clothes and whores' appetites" members of the Convent household form a "new obscene breed of female" that blasphemes against the veterans' sacred notion of womanhood (297). When the order of things starts to unravel in Ruby, when dissent is voiced and change creeps in, the founders of the town turn to a group of outsiders for someone to blame, painting them as unnatural women, contaminants polluting their other- wise wholesome community.[20] Indeed, Steward sees his neighbors as "a per- manent threat to his cherished view of himself" (279).

The patriarchs, gathered at the Oven in a war cabinet, label the women "sluts" for their independent and ungodly way of life (276).[21] They twist the sanctuary that the Convent has offered to various troubled townspeople into a malevolent force of corruption. The women are condemned in terms of gender; lacking men, their household must be immoral, but there is also a racial element to their demonization. Although readers are not told which, one of the Convent inhabitants is white, three others are black, and Connie, from South America, appears to be of mixed race.[22] The racially composite female community hence goes against all of the eight-rocks' sensibilities about segregation and arouses their fears of being tainted: "If they stayed to themselves, that'd be something. But they don't. . . . Drawing folks out there like flies to shit and everybody who goes near them is maimed somehow" (276). The phrase "[d]rawing folks out there like flies to shit" echoes Stew- ard's vicious condemnation of Roger's wife, "the dung we leaving behind," and the perceived threat is that such "mess" will penetrate and disease the town (201, 276).[23]

The patriarchs' rhetoric "others" the women, most of whom they have lived alongside for years, so that they may blame and attack them: "When the men spoke of the ruination that was upon them—how Ruby was chang- ing in intolerable ways—they did not think to fix it by extending a hand in fellowship. . . . They mapped defense instead and honed evidence for its need" (275).[24] The ex-soldiers perceive the Convent women as enemies and gather proof to justify their intended violence. Convinced of their rectitude and duty, "[l]ike bootcamp recruits, like invaders preparing for slaughter, they [met] to rave, to heat the blood or turn it icicle cold the better to exe- cute the mission" (280). Chillingly, the veterans of Ruby act as if engaged in a military exercise, readying themselves for combat. Indeed, the twins' "single-minded" attitude before a household of unarmed neighbors is linked to their frame of mind when joining up for service in World War II (12). And after the men have shot down the woman who greets them at the

Convent door, "[f]ondling their weapons, feeling suddenly . . . young and good they are reminded that guns are more than decoration, intimidation or comfort. They are meant" (285). "The New Fathers . . . are animated—warm with perspiration and the nocturnal odor of righteousness. . . . God at their side, [they] take aim. For Ruby" (18). Exhilarated and self-righteous, they proceed to mow down the remaining women, who run "like panicked does" from those who hunt them in the name of their town (and, in the case of Deacon and Steward, also their sister, "Ruby. That sweet, modest laughing girl whom [they] . . . had protected all their lives") (18, 113). The men's ruthless determination on a mission of aggression, their zeal for a violent purge of the "filth" seeping into their homes, of course stands in stark contrast to the idealized image of a community where no one is thought of as prey.[25]

The story of Elder Morgan's return from fighting in World War I can perhaps illuminate how the vision of Ruby has been corrupted, how the New Fathers have become what they once opposed. In 1919 the twins' older brother disembarked at a port near New York City and, taking a walk around, "saw two men arguing with a woman": "From her clothes . . . he guessed she was a streetwalking woman, and registering contempt for her trade, he felt at first a connection with the shouting men. Suddenly one of the men smashed the woman in her face with his fist. . . . Just as suddenly the scene slid from everyday color to black and white. . . . The two whitemen turned away from the unconscious Negro woman sprawled on the pavement" (94). Elder intervened, fighting the white men, but when the police were called he fled. His account reveals an attitude markedly different from that of those attacking the Convent in 1976. Initially the soldier empathized with the men rebuking a prostitute, yet when they assaulted her the scene became racialized, involving "whitemen" and a "Negro woman." Elder's physical confrontation of whites was a very dangerous act for a uniformed African American at the time. And he thus ran, knowing the consequences if he awaited the law. Perhaps the poignancy and message of this story, however, lie not in the intervention of the black veteran but in the way he memorializes it.

Elder does not demonize the woman in New York; instead, he berates himself for abandoning her: "He never got the sight of that whiteman's fist in that colored woman's face out of his mind. Whatever he felt about her trade, he thought about her, prayed for her until the end of his life. . . . He didn't excuse himself for running . . . and didn't expect God to cut him any slack for it" (94–95). When his wife repairs his uniform (the symbol of his service for his country) he tells her to "remove the stitches, to let . . . the buttons hang or remain missing" (94). He puts his bloodstained handkerchief away with his two medals, commemorating not his bravery in battle nor his pride as a black soldier, but the scene on his return from war illustrating the racial violence and oppression of the nation for which he has been fighting. Later Elder is buried as he wished, "in the uniform with its rips on display," in memory of the assaulted woman and what he views as his own failure to see the intervention through (94). Subsequent perspectives offer insight into how attitudes have hardened in Ruby: "Steward liked that story, but it unnerved him to know it was based on the defense of . . . a whore. He did not sympathize with the whitemen, but he could see their point, could even feel the adrenaline, imagining the fist was his own" (95). Steward is disturbed by his brother taking the part of a so-called streetwalker; he instead aligns himself with the censure and contempt exhibited by the white men. The step from Steward's visualizing of his own attack on the prostitute in this story to the actual offensive against a group of condemned women in the Convent is not all that great. This Morgan sees no contradiction in simultaneous adoration of Negro ladies and hatred for the female outsiders. Elder perhaps would have.[26]

According to Morrison, *Paradise* asks, "How do fierce, revolutionary, moral people lose it and become destructive, static, preformed—exactly what they were running from?" ("Paradise Found" 78). The assault on the Convent represents the final stage of the perversion of the original dream of Haven that is suggested by this question. Although the men claim to be protecting Ruby from contamination, the fact that the Oven, symbol of the founding ethos of the community, shifts and skews during their mission surely indicates that the idea of the black town has been betrayed. Indeed, after the attack Deacon feels "remorse . . . at having become what the Old Fathers cursed: the kind of man who set himself up to judge, rout and even destroy the needy, the defenseless, the different" (302). This realization of the role he has played highlights how the Ruby patriarchs have assumed the righteousness of those who enacted the original Disallowing and the supremacist rhetoric of the white oppressor.

The vision of an all-black town in the West as a promised land, held first by ex-slaves, then by veterans facing a bleak postwar future, goes horribly awry. The eight-rocks who relocate to Ruby believe strict separatism will solve all their problems. But in fact their new world is marred by repressive gender definitions and increasingly authoritarian government in the face of dissent: "They think they are protecting their wives and children, when in fact they are maiming them" (306). Patriarchal and high-minded leaders demonize and scapegoat a neighboring female community, becoming mirrors of what their forefathers sought to leave behind. This culminates in a violent offensive as the ex-soldiers try to wipe out the difference perceived to threaten their haven. Through such developments *Paradise* explores how a previously persecuted group can become like their historical oppressors and how African America occupies a space within (and without) the value systems of white America: "They think they have outfoxed the whiteman when in fact they imitate him" (306). It is this alignment of communities that explains why, despite their choice of isolation, the men of Ruby serve in the U.S. military. For the call to enlist and protect your nation appeals to the very same principles that the townsmen live by: defense of the space claimed as home, cultural superiority, manly fortitude, civic duty, and vigilance against those who bring group identity into question.

Using Ruby and its disallowance of "others," a "hard-won heaven defined only by the absence of the unsaved, the unworthy and the strange," Morrison's novel examines how units of belonging, paradises, are shaped (306). The utopian vision of the founding fathers is betrayed when their male descendents become destructive, fixed in beliefs that bear a disturbing resemblance to dominant national ideology. The patriarchs' entrenched position as guardsmen of a narrowly conceived version of domestic and community life, their inability, "deafened by the roar of [their] own history," to accept change, causes the dream to implode (306). Morrison hence explores what happens when difference and fear of contamination are used to justify aggression, when "home" is delineated in terms of exclusion and conformity. In this dynamic do we perhaps find the critique lacking in the text's depiction of Vietnam? As already discussed, the author fails to engage directly with the politics of American militarism. Yet *Paradise* is littered with the losses and ramifications felt by an African American community as a result of U.S. conflicts, and in the allegorical tale of the town of Ruby and its neighbors some larger issues are grappled with. The campaign of maligning and then obliterating the Convent women comes, above all, to reveal the danger of assuming an imperialist position and the devastating effect of violence enacted along such lines. In the end "[*Paradise*'s] projection of a social utopia" can be seen to "arise from its confrontation with and reversal of the male-dominated [racially absolute] bourgeois social model" (Willis 107).[27]

NOTES

1. The 369th Regiment was an all-black unit of American soldiers assigned in World War I to fight with French troops. For their bravery they were dubbed the Harlem Hellfighters.

2. In 1995 Morrison discussed the postwar violence that faced such veterans: "World War I—like all the other wars—called black men to serve. . . . They fought for the country that lynched them, and when they came back and wore their uniforms in many parts of the country, they were again lynched. There were a lot of emasculations. . . . People were snatched out of houses and burned, killed, or maimed. So the violence was particularly nasty after the war" ("Interview with Angels Carabi" 40). In *Song of Solomon* the character of Reverend Cooper has "a knot the size of a walnut . . . behind his ear" from when white Philadelphians objected to the attendance of black soldiers at an Armistice Day parade (233). In the fracas caused by whites throwing rocks, the police ran down the uniformed veterans with horses, the hoof of one causing Reverend Cooper's permanent bodily disfigurement. In addition, many African American servicemen were mentally scarred by their experiences on the battlefields of World War I. Morrison explores this in her second novel, *Sula*, through the character of Shadrack, who is left "[b]lasted and permanently astonished by the events of 1917" (7). In 1920 Shadrack returns to occupy a marginalized position in his hometown, "[t]wenty-two years old, weak, hot, frightened, not daring to acknowledge the fact that he didn't even know who or what he was . . . with no past, no language, no tribe, no source, no address book . . . no pocket handkerchief . . . no can opener, no faded postcard, no soap, no key, no tobacco pouch, no soiled underwear and nothing nothing nothing to do" (12).

3. Apparently the title was changed because Knopf feared it might put off Morrison fans. While publicizing the book the author has commented, "I'm still not convinced they were right" ("This Side of Paradise").

4. The Vietnam veteran Arthur E. "Gene" Woodley Jr. explains in Wallace Terry's recording of oral accounts from African American servicemen, *Bloods*, that "I didn't ask no questions about the war, I thought Communism was spreading, and as an American citizen, it was my part to do as much as I could to defeat the Communist from coming here. . . . And I thought the only way I could possibly make it out of the ghetto, was to be the best soldier I possibly could" (238–39). This commentary reveals economic deprivation to have been a catalyst for young black men to join the military in search of a way out (and "up"). It also exposes the influence of state-sponsored propaganda and an association between citizenship and armed service. Today the U.S. military advertises itself as one of the most integrated institutions of the nation, yet this arguably demonstrates only the racial prejudice and economic inequality still so prevalent elsewhere in American society. While for some service in the armed forces is still seen as "proof" of citizenship, it is important to acknowledge contemporary debates about how such participation might be

complicit in America's oppression of nonwhites elsewhere in the world. For useful studies of citizenship as inflected by race, class, and gender, see Torres, Mirón, and Inda, as well as Orleck's discussion of Evelyn Nakano Glenn and Alice Kesseler-Harris.

5. *Paradise* is made up of nine chapters or books, each headed by the name of a female character from either the town or the Convent. Within each chapter, however, Morrison employs multiple narrative focalizers.

6. Making a similar point, Tally writes, "The war and its decimation of the young black male population permeates *Paradise* even though it never makes a frontal appearance: there are repeated references to dogtags, body bags, funerals. . . . Like the Civil War in *Beloved* and World War I in *Jazz*, the Vietnam War in *Paradise* is an ever-present given. Unlike the Civil War, which liberated the slaves, and World War I, which gave blacks new hope that, having performed so well in battle and having been so well-accepted in Europe, they could no longer be denied full citizenship in the U.S, the Vietnam War reaffirmed the conviction that African American males were being used again as so much cannon fodder; fully 60% of the names on the Vietnam War memorial are those of blacks" (26).

7. Commenting on this era Morrison notes, "During Reconstruction, which occurred after 1865, two things happened. First, there was a lot of migration of black people. They built towns, and in some places—particularly the West—they were very well organized and prosperous. There were over 100 black towns in Oklahoma, with their own banks, schools, and churches. . . . But there was also a huge backlash during Reconstruction. Blacks were attacked by white people, including the business community, because they were making a lot of money, were self-sufficient, and were on land that other people wanted. Then the lynchings began to increase. So there was a combination of dashed hopes of freedom after the [Civil] war and some successes" ("Interview with Angels Carabi" 40). In an article published shortly after *Paradise* Julian Borger examines one of the surviving black-run communities of the West. Rentiesville "is one of the last of Oklahoma's black pioneer towns, the defiant stump of a forgotten but remarkable project. The dream was for the towns to merge together into a black state—a utopia, where freed slaves and their families could till the land and build a new society free from white discrimination, with a new-found self-confidence born of emancipation and the triumphant black role in the Civil War" (2). "War veterans and the families of ex-slaves fleeing the rising tide of post-reconstruction racism congregated [in Oklahoma], and founded a total of 27 black-run towns, a dozen of which are still on the map" (3). This history has obvious resonances with Morrison's exploration in *Paradise*.

8. Discussing the genesis of her novel, Morrison explains, "I read a lot of newspapers about the people who went to Oklahoma. About soliciting people to settle Black towns. . . . And I got interested in one little sentence . . . 'Come prepared or not at all.' It encouraged people to come with a year or two or three of supplies or money, so that if things didn't go right they would be able to take care of themselves. And the newspaper articles indicated how many people came with fifteen thousand dol-

lars and so on, but there was a little paragraph about two caravans of Black people who got to Boley or Langston, or one of those towns, and were turned away. . . . So I thought about what it must feel like to make that trek, and be turned away by some Black people. . . . So I've taken that route—these people just go somewhere else. They're determined to make it, and they do. But it makes them very isolationist. . . . They're very separatist people" ("Blacks, Modernism" 11–12).

9. "Most of [those black towns] disappeared, but I'm going to project one that moved away from the collapse of an original black town. . . . They went from being very rebellious, to being progressive, to stability. Then they got compromised and reactionary and were unable to adjust to new things happening" ("Interview with Angels Carabi" 43).

10. Oklahoma has a long history of racial violence. In the novel it is described as "a state shaped like a gun," and, as Morrison notes, it is also home to Tulsa, where in 1921 the government first bombed its own citizens from the air, attacking a black neighborhood for sheltering a fugitive (*Paradise* 16) (see "Interview with Angels Carabi" 40).

11. In following this frontier model, heading not toward the traditional African American promised land of the North but west, the people of Ruby and their utopian hopes are perhaps symbolically aligned with dominant national mythologies. Interestingly, a group of escaped slaves also go west at the very end of Sherley Anne Williams's 1986 novel *Dessa Rose*.

12. Morrison observes, "Many of these people think of themselves as Chosen and exceptional . . . and the question becomes, 'If you are chosen, does that not also require you to exclude other people?' The basis of being selected is the rejection of others, and paradise itself is a gated place" ("Conversation with Toni Morrison").

13. I borrow Paul Gilroy's term *ethnic absolutism*.

14. Hence here the "African-American men's sense of identity parallels that of the patriarchal structures of middle-class white culture" (Duvall 142).

15. This accords with Angelika Bammer's commentary on utopias imagined by men: "[W]omen are not absent in male fantasies of utopia. On the contrary, they are central. Often when utopia is invoked, a vision of woman appears as if the two were metaphorically interchangeable. . . . From the perspective of male fantasies, the role of women has not been to change the world, but to inspire men to change it. Thus women abound in men's utopias as projections of men's desires; as authors of their own texts, they are rarely to be found" (14).

16. "[Ruby] neither had nor needed a jail. . . . A sleepless woman could always rise from her bed . . . and sit on the steps in the moonlight. And if she felt like it she could walk out the yard and on down the road. No lamp and no fear. . . . She could stroll as slowly as she liked, think of food preparations, war, of family things. . . . On out, beyond the limits of town, because nothing at the edge thought she was prey" (8–9). Central to the conception of Haven was its communal core, a shared necessity, meeting place, and landmark bearing the founding fathers' inscription, "a huge,

flawlessly designed Oven that both nourished them and monumentalised what they had done" (6–7). In 1949 the veterans reconstruct this oven in Ruby to pay homage to the vision of their ancestors. The Oven has a particular significance, however, in terms of the protection of women. This arises from a history of subjugation in America that meant many black women suffered sexual exploitation by white men. Originally the landmark of the Oven was built to celebrate the fact that the towns-women had escaped vulnerability to such abuse. In Oklahoma none of them would have to work in white houses and "[i]t was that thinking that made a community 'kitchen' so agreeable" (99). Yet by the time of the move to Ruby the Oven is no longer a functional cooking device or a sign of communal living. It has become only a monument to the safety that the New Fathers believe they provide for their women-folk. Indeed, some fear that it has become a "shrine" (103).

17. "The virulent arguments over the exact wording and meaning of the motto on the Oven are a sign of how desperate the town fathers are to control the town's official narrative: they conceive of the oven as a place for conversation but not de-bate, a place to share accepted narratives but not to propose new counternarratives" (Patell 181).

18. According to Duvall, "Haven and Ruby stand as displaced representations of early American exceptionalism; if the white American male's freedom was en-hanced by the presence of the enslaved racial other . . . something strangely similar occurs in *Paradise*. For Ruby's men, their exceptionalism and sense of freedom lies in their genetically pure African heritage unsullied by any drop of white blood" (144).

19. "Easter and Scout were in integrated units . . . [but] whatever was missing, the parts were all of black men—which was a courtesy and a rule the medics tried hard to apply for fear of adding white thighs and feet to a black head. . . . [Deacon] did not want [Soane] even to imagine the single question he put. . . . Are all the parts black? Meaning, if not, get rid of the white pieces" (112).

20. As Mantel points out, "The fears of the community displace themselves upon a group of strangers, living symbolically outside its walls" (26).

21. "Before those heifers came to town this was a peaceable kingdom. . . . These here sluts out there by themselves never step foot in a church. . . . They don't need men and they don't need God" (276).

22. Morrison deliberately obscures racial identity in *Paradise*, frustrating the reader's expectations by not saying whether it is Mavis, Gigi, Pallas, or Seneca who is white. She discusses "withholding racial markers . . . so that the reader knew every-thing, or almost everything, about the characters, their interior lives, their past, their faults, their strengths, except that one small piece of information which was their race. . . . [I]t was a way of saying that race is the least important piece of infor-mation we have about another person" ("Transcript"). This perhaps relates to a simi-lar experiment in a much earlier piece of writing, her short story "Recitatif."

23. One of the female elders of Ruby overhears the attackers preparing them-selves with such rhetoric and muses, "[s]o . . . the fangs and the tail are somewhere

else. Out yonder all slithery in a house full of women. Not women locked safely away from men; but worse, women who chose themselves for company, which is to say not a convent but a coven" (276). Lone DuPres hence perceives the way in which the men's discourse projects all evil onto the outsiders.

24. Morrison explains, "They would triumph because they would do the rejecting—the second generation. I don't think that was true of the first generation in . . . Haven." But by the 1970s "tolerance had turned to anger and defence, because they were really threatened, not so much by the women, but by what was happening inside that town. They had no means to deal with post-war veterans and communicable sexual diseases and abortion, and all of these things were sort of seeping into this very clean, very pristine town" ("Conversation with Toni Morrison").

25. Morrison suggests, "It was important that the men of the town were thinking how much they loved women as they went to assault the women in the convent. . . . Their mothers, their sisters. . . . Because they really believed that their role was the protection of women and children. So they couldn't possibly be misogynists. But what does frighten them is the idea of women who don't need men. . . . Of course what's really going on is that the town can't handle some of the contemporary problems . . . Vietnam veterans returning, women being restless" ("Black Pearls" 2).

26. Tally writes, "Women for the men of Ruby fall into two categories: the angel of the house and the worthless whore. Much as Steward admires . . . Elder's intervention on the part of a black woman insulted by white men, it bothers him that the woman in question was a streetwalker, as if that somehow made her less worthy of help from an attack" (76–77).

27. I refer in part here to the narrative projection or afterlife that concludes the novel in defiance of patriarchal violence. Willis, although writing prior to the publication of Paradise, identifies at least some of the utopian impulses delineated in Morrison's fiction.

Works Cited

Bammer, Angelika. *Partial Visions: Feminism and Utopianism in the 1970s*. London: Routledge, 1991.

Bent, Geoffrey. "Less Than Divine: Toni Morrison's *Paradise*." *Southern Review* 35.1 (1999): 145–49.

Borger, Julian. "Paradise Lost." *Guardian* 6 Oct. 1998: 2–3.

Bouson, Brooks J. *Quiet as It's Kept: Shame, Trauma, and Race in the Novels of Toni Morrison*. Albany: State University of New York Press, 2000.

Brandt, Nat. *Harlem at War: The Black Experience in World War Two*. Syracuse: Syracuse University Press, 1996.

Cliff, Michelle. "Great Migrations." *Village Voice* 27 Jan. 1998: 85–86.

Denard, Carolyn. "Paradise." *Ms.* 8.5 (1998): 80.

Dudziak, Mary L. *Cold War Civil Rights: Race and the Image of American Democracy*. Princeton: Princeton University Press, 2000.

Duvall, John N. *The Identifying Fictions of Toni Morrison: Modernist Authenticity and Postmodern Blackness*. New York: Palgrave, 2000.

Franklin, John Hope, and Alfred A. Moss Jr. *From Slavery to Freedom: A History of African Americans*. New York: McGraw-Hill, 1994.

Gates, David. "Trouble in Paradise." *Newsweek* 12 Jan. 1998: 62.

Gilroy, Paul. *The Black Atlantic: Modernity and Double Consciousness*. London: Verso, 1993.

Gray, Paul. "Paradise Found." *Time* 19 Jan. 1998: 62–68.

Kakutani, Michiko. "Worthy Women, Unredeemable Men." *New York Times* Jan. 1998: E8.

Klinghoffer, David. "Black Madonna." *National Review* 9 Feb. 1998: 30–32.

Leonard, John. "Shooting Women." *Nation* 26 Jan. 1998: 25–29.

Mantel, Hilary. "No Disco, No TV, No Diner, No Adultery." *Literary Review* Apr. 1998: 26–27.

Matus, Jill. *Toni Morrison*. Manchester: Manchester University Press, 1998.

Maycock, James. "War within War." *Guardian Weekend* 15 Sept. 2001: 20–28.

Morrison, Toni. "Black Pearls." With Katharine Viner. *Guardian* 24 Mar. 1998: 2–5.

———. "Blacks, Modernism, and the American South: An Interview with Toni Morrison." With Carolyn Denard. *Studies in the Literary Imagination* 31.2 (1998): 1–16.

———. "A Conversation with Toni Morrison." 1998. 21 Apr. 2001 <www.borders.com/features/ab99013.html>.

———. "Home." *The House That Race Built*. Ed. Wahneema Lubiano. New York: Vintage Books, 1998. 3–12.

———. "Interview with Angels Carabi." *Belles Lettres* 10.2 (1995): 40–43.

———. *Jazz*. London: Picador, 1992.

———. "Morrison's Slice of Paradise." With Deirdre Donahue. 8 Jan. 1998. 21 Apr. 2001 <www.ustoday.com/life/enter/books/b128.htm>.

———. *Paradise*. London: Chatto and Windus, 1998.

———. "Paradise Found: A Talk with Toni Morrison." With A. J. Verdelle. *Essence* 28.10 (1998): 78–80.

———. "Recitatif." *Call and Response: The Riverside Anthology of the African-American Literary Tradition*. Ed. Patricia Liggins Hill and Bernard W. Bell. Boston: Houghton Mifflin, 1998. 1776–86.

———. "The Roots of Paradise." *Economist* 6 June 1998. 10 Sept. 1999 <www.economist.com/archive/view.cgi>.

———. *Song of Solomon*. London: Vintage, 1998.

———. *Sula*. London: Vintage, 1998.

———. "This Side of Paradise." With Anna Mulrine. 19 Jan. 1998. 21 Apr. 2001 <www.usnews.com/usnews/issue/980119/19new.htm>.

————. "Transcript." 21 Jan. 1998. 24 Apr. 2001 <www.time.com/time/community/transcripts/chattr012198.html>.

Mullen, Robert W. *Blacks in America's Wars: The Shift in Attitudes from the Revolutionary War to Vietnam.* New York: Monad Press, 1973.

Nalty, Bernard C. *Strength for the Fight: A History of Black Americans in the Military.* New York: Free Press, 1986.

Orleck, Annelise. "Gender, Race, and Citizenship Rights: New Views of an Ambivalent History." *Feminist Studies* 29.1 (2003): 85–102.

Patell, Cyrus R. K. *Negative Liberties: Morrison, Pynchon, and the Problem of Liberal Ideology.* Durham: Duke University Press, 2001.

Shockley, Evelyn E. "Paradise." *African American Review* 33.4 (1999): 718–19.

Smith, Dinitia. "Toni Morrison's Mix of Tragedy, Domesticity and Folklore." *New York Times* 8 Jan. 1998: E1.

Tally, Justine. *Paradise Reconsidered: Toni Morrison's (Hi)stories and Truths.* FORECAAST 2. Hamburg: Lit Verlag, 1999.

Terry, Wallace. *Bloods: An Oral History of the Vietnam War by Black Veterans.* New York: Ballantine Books, 1984.

Torres, Rodolfo D., Louis F. Mirón, and Jonathan Xavier Inda. *Race, Identity and Citizenship: A Reader.* Oxford: Blackwell, 1999.

Walter, Natasha. "How Paradise Was Lost." *Guardian* 26 Mar. 1998: 12–13.

Williams, Sherley Anne. *Dessa Rose.* London: Virago, 1986.

Willis, Susan. *Specifying: Black Women Writing the American Experience.* Madison: University of Wisconsin Press, 1987.

Wood, James. "The Color Purple." *New Republic* 2 March 1998: 29–32.

Wood, Michael. "Sensations of Loss." *The Aesthetics of Toni Morrison: Speaking the Unspeakable.* Ed. Marc C. Conner. Jackson: University of Mississippi Press, 2000. 13–24.

Wynn, Neil A. *The Afro-American and the Second World War.* Rev. ed. New York: Holmes and Meier, 1993.

PART TWO

RECONCILIATION

CHAPTER SIX

Searching for Peace

John Dryden's Troilus and Cressida or Truth Found too Late

JANET DAWSON

Shakespeare turned the well-known medieval versions of the doomed love of Troilus and Cressida into the play *Troilus and Cressida* early in the first decade of the seventeenth century, probably around 1602, according to most critics. He set the play in the seventh year of the Trojan War, at the point where the fatigued Greeks are becoming discontented after a long and fruitless siege of the city of Troy. The physical and moral stagnation that pervades the actions and attitudes of Greeks and Trojans alike, the diminution of their heroic stature, the loss of the original sense of purpose in the war and, finally, the ignominious slaughter of Hector in the final act all portray a world that is unmistakably in decline. The permanence of war, of accelerated violence and an absence of systems, ground rules, or procedures for mediating individual conflicts or redressing injustice, takes the participants to the verge of chaos. Ulysses apprehends this universal disorder in act 1, scene 3, as a situation in which not only is natural law violated in specific cases, as when brute force prevails over right or sons kill their fathers, but the constitutive principles of justice themselves have been lost from sight. The prospect in the final scene of a fresh cycle of revenge denies the audience access to the kind of self-knowledge and learning necessary to tragic closure. The generic title *problem play* summarizes the discomfort that the discordant discourses of cynical exploitation and amorality have provoked in succeeding generations of readers, theatergoers, and critics.[1]

John Dryden's rather lesser-known Restoration version, *Troilus and Cressida or Truth Found too Late* (1679), the subject of this essay, retains most of the explicit and implicit themes of his predecessor's version—civil disobedience, treason, poor decision making, betrayal and friendship, intrigues and factions, indeed, the general representation of a world on the verge of collapse. However, in the process of rewriting and reordering it, Dryden situates his play in the penultimate year of the war and incorporates an unmistakably Hobbesian purpose in the final call to obedience to a single sovereign that Ulysses elicits from the victorious Greek army and that prevents chaos. Dryden also uses the Trojans to convert the play into a tragedy with which the audience can identify.[2]

Dryden was writing for a Restoration audience following the conclusion of the civil war and the restoration of the monarchy. I argue that he used the Greeks and Trojans to draw instructive parallels with recent English history, which, as he saw it, would avoid the mistakes of the past by embracing the need for change without humiliating those who had been defeated. The portrayal of disorder in Dryden's play can be read as pointing to the need for democratic institutions that are based on freedom and that uphold the rule of law rather than private and arbitrary violence.

The first part of this essay reads Dryden's play in light of Thomas Hobbes's influential theory of commonwealth, set out in *Leviathan* (1651), a theory of obedience and absolute sovereignty that Dryden must have approved, given that he casts the Greeks as the undisputed victors at the end of the play. The second part considers Dryden's portrayal of the Trojans as the blameworthy victims of their internal weaknesses, both political and moral, and of an incoherent philosophy. The Trojans, an inverted mirror image of the Greeks, are limited by their failure to adapt the principles of sovereignty and obedience to new circumstances until it is too late. At the same time, the Trojans provide the mainspring of the tragic action. The mood of tragedy is entirely missing if the focus of attention is exclusively Greek. Dryden goes beyond Shakespeare's implicit reflections on the waste of military destruction and beyond Hobbes's insistence on absolute obedience and discipline by using the new, somewhat sentimentalized framework of reconciliation and self-sacrifice to accommodate, without rancor, familiar values such as fidelity, filial obedience, friendship, and brotherly love.

Indispensable to the question of postwar peacemaking is the subject of the third part of the essay, which relates the philosophy of Hobbes, in the aftermath of civil war, to the context of 1679, when Dryden rewrote Shakespeare's play about the tragedy of the Trojans. The Trojan fighting force, equated explicitly by Dryden with the "old Britons," is completely wiped out in the final scene of his play, an outcome somewhat at odds with that expected from the prologue, which claims to show that "Trojan valour did the

Greek excell" (*Troilus* Prol. 32). The "old Britons" were those who had been responsible for and had emerged chastened from the upheavals of the chaotic two-decade interregnum between the Long Parliament of 1640, under Charles I, and the restoration to the throne of England in 1660 of Charles II. In 1679, the complex of problems that had led to civil war had still not been resolved effectively. That year's events included the moment of anti-Catholic hysteria and public disorder known as the Popish Plot. The exclusion crisis of the early 1680s gave way to the tyranny of James II, but in December 1688, just when it looked as if England might face another civil war, the Protestant Prince of Orange was invited to rule. He was proclaimed King William III in February 1689. The tenure of the Crown became conditional, and the liberty of the subject and the power of Parliament were secured against the power of the Crown.

Dryden's version of *Troilus and Cressida* keeps the two historical moments of the interregnum and the Popish Plot in mind. The internal divisions characterizing the general English social and political scene of the seventeenth century and the call to obedience at the end of Dryden's play can be read together as a rallying cry to Restoration Englishmen under Charles II to avoid the errors of the past and mark a new path for the future, following the Greek example.

Dryden's dramatic treatment contextualizes Thomas Hobbes's principles of commonwealth as a model of good government, at war or in peace. The Greeks adopt the principles of sovereignty and obedience and are transformed from disorganized warlords in such a way that we can only conclude Dryden approved of their example. The war is ended and an alternative to endless violence is presented. One of the major differences between Dryden's version of *Troilus and Cressida* and Shakespeare's is the absence of the dynamic of revenge at the end of the play.

The theoretical formulation of *Leviathan* had a very practical aim: to offer a reasoned way out of the permanent state of war and conflict that had blighted all aspects of English life for over a hundred years, with the result that war and peace had ceased to be distinguishable. In the 1640s, these upheavals had included civil war and the execution of the king. D. H. Pennington's essay "Political Debate and Thomas Hobbes" lists the "few inescapable questions" that had dominated English political life for more than a century: "Who should hold power in the organized community? When was it justifiable to overthrow by force an established government? And why should the citizen who had disobeyed one government obey the next one?"

(303). Disputes about the rights and duties of rulers and subjects were nothing new; there had always been rebellions and factions at court as well as riots and violence in public life. These, however, ceased to be regarded as abstractions in light of the events of the 1640s. Civil war and "ideas that questioned the whole order of society, the destruction of the monarchy, the House of Lords, and the Church—all this would have seemed inconceivable until it happened," concludes Pennington (303). *Leviathan,* as political philosophy, does not instruct its readers in detail how to end a specific war, nor does it comprehensively prescribe for peace. What it sets out to do is to lay the theoretical foundations for lasting peace and the rule of law.

Hobbes gives special attention to two issues: sovereignty in the English state and dissidence in the church. The political quarrel between King Charles I and the Scots arose in 1637 when the king tried to impose the Anglican service on Presbyterian Scotland, a move that led to riots in the Presbyterian Church, the signing of the National Covenant, and the raising of an army to defend the church. By 1640, the army had occupied the northern borders of England. Local opposition to the king spread, was made manifest politically in the Long Parliament of 1640, and escalated into an armed conflict in 1642. The violent overthrow of the government, the execution of the king, new institutions, rule by dictator, and finally the restoration of the monarchy all succeeded each other in the space of twenty years.

Hobbes's major interest is the question of sovereignty, but this question is not referred to any church authority; indeed, Hobbes makes it clear that he distrusts all forms of ecclesiastical authority. He links human consciousness directly to civil power rather than scholastic doctrine. His concept of natural law is that man is motivated by selfishness and must use his reason to preserve himself from pain.

The first part of *Leviathan,* "Of Man," is an extended reflection on the condition of mankind. The natural propensity of man is one of subjection to passion and material self-interest, and the human condition, accordingly, is one of permanent war.[3] Dryden shows Greeks and Trojans alike as victims of the same malaise. Yves Charles Zarka points out that Hobbes understands "war" both as a specific instance of international conflict and as the permanent condition in which interpersonal relationships lead inevitably to conflict. The proposition of self-interest forms the premise for "Of Commonwealth," a vision of a covenant form of government by means of which men can live in peace and material well-being and avoid lapsing into the natural condition of war.

Hobbes envisions a commonwealth as a political unit similar to the Roman *civitas*, and he formally defines it in chapter 17 as "that great Leviathan . . . One Person, of whose Acts a great Multitude, by mutuall Covenants one with another, have made themselves every one the Author, to the end he may use the strength and means of them all, as he shall think expedient, for their Peace and Common Defence" (228). The two basic political requirements are, first, the choice of a single sovereign (which may be a democratic assembly, an aristocratic assembly, or a single man, such as a monarch) who will provide for and defend the security of every subject and, second, the unqualified obedience of those subjects. The unity of covenant is a process of authorization, not just "consent" or "agreement," and is expressed thus: "I authorize and give up my Right of Governing my selfe to this Man, or to this Assembly of men, on this condition, that thou give up thy right to him, and Authorize all his Actions in like manner" (227).

Since the sovereign provides for security and defense, all power and resources should be centrally concentrated. This concentration of power is better, in Hobbes's view, than any excesses that may result from it. In exchange for security, the subject obeys his sovereign representative. Subjects cannot lawfully change their representative on the basis of any previously existing covenant or be obedient to any other sovereign. The need for concentration of power in a single central locus with unity of command has a corollary: all dissent, disobedience, depositions, factions, conspiracies, and cabals are unlawful because those involved represent, at most, only part of an assembly and do not have full authorization.

Hobbes makes it quite clear that a confederated state power (such as the Greek army), a family (such as the Trojan dynasty), and a nation-state may all look very similar to a commonwealth—if they are ruled by a patriarchal sovereign, for example. This feature alone, as the Trojans amply demonstrate, does not confer the essential strength and security of a commonwealth. The key is the covenant: "But yet a Family is not properly a Common-wealth; unlesse it be of that power by its own number . . . as not to be subdued without the hazard of war. For where a number of men are manifestly too weak to defend themselves united, every one may use his own reason in time of danger, to save his own life, either by flight, or by submission to the enemy, as hee shall think best" (Hobbes 257).

The Greeks in Dryden's play are a confederate army, headed by King Agamemnon. They have been besieging Troy for nine years with little success. Their ostensible mission is to recover Helen, captured by the Trojans and now the mistress of Paris inside Troy. This task is hindered by internal divisions and acts of disobedience. By means of a rationally calculated set of maneuvers, spearheaded by the loyal Ulysses, the final scene, when the Trojans are conclusively overcome, appears to justify the superiority of sovereignty and obedience as principles of government.

The Greek situation is largely seen from the point of view of the Greek military leaders—Agamemnon, Ulysses, Nestor, Menelaus, and Diomedes—who gather in the opening scene to discuss their lack of progress in the war. They quickly identify their major problem as the rebellion of their champion warrior, Achilles. Acts of disrespect and insubordination have already created divisions in the ranks, and Agamemnon's chief advisers, Nestor and Ulysses, fear further splits. Agamemnon concludes the scene as a sovereign should by ordering Nestor and Ulysses to stop the disintegration: "To you we leave the care: / You who cou'd show whence the distemper springs, / Must vindicate the Dignity of Kings" (*Troilus* 1.1).[4] The "Dignity of Kings" looks like the Hobbesian ideal of submission to a single sovereign as the basis of collective security.

The tactics employed to restore the dignity of the office of the king are the concern of the foremost Greek princes for the rest of the play. Dryden completes what are merely hints in Shakespeare's *Troilus and Cressida* by using Ulysses to mastermind a multipart strategy with contingency plans. As a result of a suggestion that includes the sacrifice of Patroclus, the strategy concludes with the military operation that leads to the successful defeat of the Trojans. Most of it, though, has a political and psychological component, especially the "divide and rule" strategy that will prevent the popular Achilles from associating with his friend Ajax and drawing the soldiers' support away from the king. Even Thersites, Ajax's cynical slave, whom Ulysses calls "a Species, differing from mankinde," is drawn into the overall plan (2.3). Ulysses anticipates Thersites' resentment toward his master, Ajax, who has humiliated him and weaves it into the "divide and rule" strategy to good effect.

The expedience of the Greeks in knowingly sending Patroclus to his death and their view that Thersites is not worthy of being treated as a human being remind us that some segments of the population still lack freedom and human rights. However, we must suppose that Dryden approved of this harsh application of the spirit and techniques of Hobbes, since in the final triumphalist speech of the play Ulysses looks forward to peace—"Now peacefull order has resum'd the reynes, / Old time looks young, and Nature seems renew'd"—and acclaims the sovereign with "Hayl Agamemnon! truly Victor now!" (5.2). He then restates the Greeks' original problems— envy, pride, factious nobles, and the confusion of public good with private interest—as a salutary warning to the assembled army before pointing up the moral in the final couplet: "Then since from homebred Factions ruine springs, / Let Subjects learn obedience to their Kings" (5.2). Here we note that obedience is assumed to be "learned," part of the process of authoriza- tion by which individuals, out of patriotic duty, come to respect the office of king rather than an inalienable allegiance to a divinely appointed person.

The twin principles of Hobbes's commonwealth—absolute sovereignty and obedience—are advocated explicitly to the audience as the new consti- tutional arrangement, a notion of representation that in theory makes pos- sible a transition from the natural condition of civil war, which exists when many individuals live with no state to govern and protect them, to a peace- ful collective stability where the sovereign authority protects his subjects while respecting the individual instinct for self-preservation. The suppos- edly original injustice, though, understood to be the abduction of Helen, is not mentioned.

Ulysses' reasoned strategic planning has converted the Greeks from a disorganized and disobedient collection of men into a single unit under one sovereign leader, irrespective of whether we think this is good for the long- term collective welfare. The Greeks, however, are basically a military unit, functioning here only on the battlefield. The Trojans are interesting as a government, an aristocratic dynasty organized along patriarchal lines, and we see them at war and as a civil unit.

The Trojans represent a counterpoint to the Greeks. Imprisoned within the city walls, they have resisted attack for nine years, but their depleted military strength depends solely on Hector, the king's eldest son. Disobedi- ence and disunity are not initially visible in the way that they are in the Greek camp, but internal disorder and philosophical incoherence prove ultimately to be the Trojans' downfall because these flaws determine the course of the war and remain unrecognized until it is too late. In Hobbes's terms, they stem from the fact that the Trojans are not organized as a com- monwealth; even as a patriarchal society they are inconsistent. The charac- teristics of their internal disorder include a preoccupation with pleasures of the flesh rather than public affairs, a lack of willingness to negotiate terms with the Greeks when the opportunity presents itself, and a preoccupation with self-image rather than a realistic assessment of their situation. Troy lacks properly organized decision makers who can rationally discuss, in the context of this war, real causes, ends, and means that are the concern of everyone or who can handle diverse points of view without lapsing into emotional language and spurious arguments that flatter the personal prestige of a few elite figures. Deep-seated structural changes mainly affecting family roles cut across the traditionally understood concepts of patriarchal authority and filial obedience. When the questions of obedience and authority converge in the love affair between Troilus and Cressida, the tragic potential of the drama starts to emerge.

There are many illustrations of the weaknesses and follies of the Trojans. Until act 4, scene 1, when Cressida is exchanged for Antenor, the chief members of the court seem to be carrying on life as usual: a life of luxury, self-indulgence, and, in the case of Hector, fantasy combats in chivalric register. The tone is set in act 1, scene 2, when Troilus claims, without embarrassment, that he is too weakened by love for Cressida, who has not yet become his lover, to go out and fight—"Why should I fight without the Trojan Walls, / Who, without fighting, am ore'thrown within"—and some lines later declares that he is "weaker than a Woman's tear" (1.2). In a comment to Pandarus in act 1, scene 2, Cressida refers to Troilus as a "sneaking fellow," the image of a soldier who tries to preserve his own life by avoiding danger. He is not an obedient subject who places himself at the service of the commonwealth.

Similarly, Paris spends more time with his mistress, Helen, than on state affairs. This view endorses history, but there are also allusions to effeminacy, as when Priam describes Paris as "Like one besotted on effeminate joys" (2.1). This view provides a mirror image of Troilus's own self-description and vividly describes the culture of the court. Love provides the tragic potential in Troy, but the concept is initially that of a private affair of greater importance than state business. The 1679 audience of the play would undoubtedly have made the connection between the Trojan court and that of Charles II.

As the play wears on, it becomes clear that, although self-discipline and obedience might look like suitable remedies for the manifest ills of the Trojans, Dryden wishes to emphasize that what the Trojans need most is to be reconstituted as a commonwealth. The court of King Priam is a family dynasty, whose first working principle is the maintenance of honor and prestige. The atmosphere of self-indulgence and complacency in which the war unfolds obscures characters' recognition of whether actions spring from obedience, loyalty, or wisdom. The first major scene to show both the undermining of traditional authority and the failures in decision making is act 2, scene 1: the council meeting held to formulate a response to a peace proposal that has arrived from the Greeks. This is not the first peace proposal, apparently, to have been received from the Greeks, but it may serve to bring the war to an end, provided the Trojans return Helen. Priam recognizes that Troy is in a precarious position, but instead of taking the appropriate decision himself, as he should, he defers to Hector, Aeneas, and Troilus. After a debate, whose real subjects are honor and prestige, the proposal is rejected.

Hector, speaking first, advocates letting Helen go, first on the grounds that she is not worth the blood that has been spilt and then using the moral argument that "if this Hellen be anothers wife, / The Morall laws of Nature and of Nations / Speak loud she be restor'd" (2.1). Aeneas and Troilus refuse to relinquish Helen. Troilus, who previously had not wanted to fight for Troy, asks whether "fears and reasons [are] fit to be consider'd / When a King's Fame is question'd" and declares that it would be "unmanly theft / When we have taken what we fear to keep!" He finishes by declaring Helen "a subject of renoun and honour" (2.1).

Honor is the word that gains Hector's support with no further debate. Helen ceases to be an expensive hostage and becomes, in Hector's words, "a cause on which our Trojan honour / And common reputation will depend" (2.1). In a reversal of logic, keeping Helen in Troy is justified as "honourable" because to give her back would be an admission that the Trojans had acted dishonorably in the first place when they captured her. The peace proposal is rejected, and Troilus makes his escape, saying, "I have business" (2.1)—business that turns out to be a tryst with Cressida. Hector concludes: "A woman on my Life: ev'n so it happens, / Religion, state affairs, whater'es the theme / It ends in women still" (2.1).

This scene is quickly followed by another, absent in Shakespeare's play, that is dominated by Hector's wife, Andromache. She too defends the honor of war—but not with Helen as its object. The first part of Andromache's message concerns a request from her son, Astyanax, who is not on stage, that Hector should challenge the Greeks and teach them a lesson.

The Trojans have apparently become blind to the fact that the Greeks are actually occupying their land, and Astyanax, the young son of Hector and Andromache, reminds them that this basic Hobbesian reason of material self-preservation is a good reason to attack the Greeks: "to prove they

do not well to burn our fields; / And keep us coop'd like prisners in a Town"
(2.1). Hector is impressed by his son's sense of honor: "What sparks of honour / Fly from this child!" (2.1), and he himself repeats the reason:

> Is not that Country ours? Those fruitfull Fields
> Wash'd by yon Silver flood, are they not ours?
> Which of these haughty Grecians, dares to think
> He can keep Hector prisner here in Troy?
>
> (2.1)

Greek aggression does not, however, lead the Trojans to draw up a coherent plan of action; instead, it leads to a personal challenge from Hector
aimed at enhancing his personal honor. Priam is unenthusiastic. If Hector
were to die, not only would there be no one to instruct Astyanax in the skills
of war, but Troy would lose the main guarantor of its safety. Hector is not
just a soldier; he is a symbolic leader. "If Hector only were a private Man,"
says Priam, "This wou'd be courage, but in him 'tis madness / The generall
safety on your life depends" (2.1). Aeneas also agrees with Priam on the
grounds that, while the Greeks have reserves if Ajax or Achilles should lose,
the Trojans have nobody to replace Hector.

Hector listens to this exposition of the problem but objects that his father has not mentioned the main argument for obedience, the very name of
"father":

> Alas, my Father!
> You have not drawn one reason from your self,
> But publick safety, and my Sons green years:
> In this neglecting that main argument
> Trust me you chide my filiall piety:
> As if I cou'd be won from my resolves
> By Troy, or by my Son, or any name
> More dear to me than yours.
>
> (2.1)

This speech marks the distinction between patriarchy and sovereignty
referred to earlier. The term *publick safety* recalls the Hobbesian notion of
material security that the sovereign covenants to supply and preserve, either in person or through his authorized public representatives, in return

for the obedience of the commonwealth. In his speech Hector implicitly recognizes the possibility of a covenant and acknowledges that, if he has been authorized to protect the Trojan people, he is no longer free to act on his own initiative without breaking that covenant. The point Hector actually makes, however, is that Priam has offered all possible arguments except the key one: father. Public safety, implicitly, is a minor argument. Had Hector regarded Priam as his sovereign rather than his father and acted as a subject rather than a son, he would have no option other than to obey his command. On the other hand, although Priam speaks for public safety (which he calls "generall safety"), he does not do what public safety and sovereignty require, namely, explicitly prevent the combat. There is, therefore, a failure of authority.

This question is complicated further when Priam invites Andromache to speak, asking, "Have you no right in Hector, as a wife?" (2.1). This is a question that patriarchy and sovereignty alike require that she answer in a way that supports Priam's evident will. Instead, she inverts the rules of gender and hierarchy by supporting her husband and providing a rationale for his proposed challenge, based on the idea that conflict enhances her own worth:

> I would be worthy to be Hectors wife:
> And had I been a Man, as my Soul's one
> I had aspir'd a nobler name, his friend.
> How I love Hector, (need I say I love him?)
> I am not but in him:
> But when I see him arming for his Honour,
> His Country and his Gods, that martial fire
> That mounts his courage, kindles ev'n to me:
> And when the Trojan Matrons wait him out
> With pray'rs, and meet with blessings his return;
> The pride of Virtue, beats within my breast,
> To wipe away the sweat and dust of War:
> And dress my Heroe, glorious in his wounds.
>
> (2.1)

The speech seems rhetorically conventional. Andromache wants to be worthy of Hector as his wife, and the business of war becomes a signifying practice when he has returned home and she is dressing his wounds. She regards bloodshed not as wasting a life but as conferring on her a virtue and status that she otherwise would not have. Her identity derives from her husband: "I am not but in him." Hector is presented as a combination of Roman soldier, one who fights courageously for his honor, his country, and his gods (the word *matron* picks up on the virtue of the high-born Roman wife), and chivalrous knight, though Andromache describes his combat as being for her rather than for a courtly mistress.

Andromache specifically dissociates the combat from any "cause so black as Hellens rape" by making herself both cause and prize of the proposed combat: "but when you fight for Honour *and for me,* / Then let our equal Gods behold an Act, / They may not blush to crown" (2.1, emphasis added). The noble cause, in other words, is reflected glory, no better and no worse, perhaps, than any other in the repertoire of causes touted so far for this war. She successfully presses her husband to issue a challenge, a risky enterprise in which loss would spell defeat for all Trojans but victory would honor only her. Hector is flattered by this speech and reacts by acknowledging her exemplary masculinity: "Come to my Arms thou manlier Virtue come; / Thou better Name than wife! Wou'd'st thou not blush / To hug a coward thus?" (2.1).

In act 5, scene 1, Andromache influences Hector again, this time dissuading him from fighting on the basis of a nightmare she has had. When Troilus finds out that Hector has been persuaded not to fight, he launches into a sarcastic diatribe against superstition and the intervention of priests in royal affairs. Dryden appears to make Andromache's influence a negative one, since Hector submits to his wife rather than to his father, his king, or what we would call common sense. From Hobbes's point of view, she would be seen as injecting passion into a situation calling for reason and undermining the unity of command necessary to sovereignty.

This long scene is interesting in providing a critique of some of the issues that obstruct peacemaking or fail to put an end to bloody conflict even when opportunities to do so present themselves. First, not everybody stands to gain by ending this war. The most obvious case here is Andromache. Second, the basically informal exchange of the points of view of a handful of people has serious defects. Most notably, opinions are neither presented to a wider audience nor subjected to a process of debate that sets out causes, consequences, previous errors, or the value of particular courses of action, past, present, or future. Each speaker represents only himself, and there is not even a process of negotiation. Emotive language and appeals to the prestige and glory of individuals, rather than attention to the adequacy of the reasoning or the justice of the cause, determine the outcome. Post hoc rationalizations reiterate fallacies. Dialogue and the search for common ground are forestalled because the Trojans fail to identify the key criteria of justice in Troy and because, as seems the case here, they do not want to talk. In addition to the chaos that Shakespeare feared arose from the failure to identify the constitutive principles of justice, Dryden pinpoints overdependence on the senses and passions rather than reason.

The speech in which Andromache incites Hector to war makes a curious reference to friendship: Andromache says she wants to be a worthy wife but would much rather be Hector's "friend." The speech does not clarify its allusion to friendship, except to exalt the names of "friend" and "wife" above that of "mistress" and to defend male courage. The figure of the friend, however, is instrumental in act 3, scene 2, a scene of private rancor and reconciliation between the brothers Hector and Troilus that provides an opportunity to partly problematize the masculine roles of: "man," "friend," "private and public person," and "brother." It is crucial to the tragic outcome in the sense that it anticipates the sacrifice and loss inherent in the final act, showing, in part, why they are necessary, but concludes on a conciliatory note of friendship. The possibility of friendship is absent from Shakespeare.

In this scene, Hector arrives to break the news to Troilus that Cressida, now the latter's lover, is to be sent to the Greek camp in exchange for the hostage Antenor. This decision has been taken at a separate meeting, which the audience does not see, and at which, it learns later, Troilus was not present because was been busy making love. To prepare Troilus for the bad news and to minimize both his anticipated fiery temper and any temptation to "grieve beyond a man" (3.2), Hector emphasizes their fraternal relationship. He does this four times before stating the content of his message. On one occasion, the word *brother* is accompanied by that of *friend*: "I thought a friend and Brother best might tell it" (3.2). Troilus undertakes to control himself with manly restraint, assuring Hector, "I will not rage" and "I won'not be a woman" (3.2).

In the previous scene, Troilus advocated a course of action (retaining Helen in Troy) that would defend "a King's fame" (3.1). Now, when the interest is more personal, he changes his mind, and this apparently forces Hector to change his view of the situation confronting them all. Forgetting the "King's fame," he refuses to give up his lover. Hector tries to negotiate on behalf of the common good: the sacrifice may be personally worse for

Troilus, but "for the general state, / . . . all our common safety, . . . depends / On freed Anthenors wisdome" (3.2).[5] He explicitly sets the question of security, as well as the king's fame, against the loss of a mistress:

> If parting from a Mistriss can procure
> A Nations happiness, show me that Prince,
> Who dares to trust his future fame so farr
> To stand the shock of Annals, blotted thus,
> He sold his Country for a woman's love?
>
> (3.2)

Troilus is not convinced, and their argument shifts briefly to a topic not yet mentioned but fundamental to any relationship concerning kings or leaders: those for whom the relationship exists, the subjects, here the public. Troilus dismisses the public as "the Lees of vulgar slaves" and declares that "the publique sum" is made up of "Millions of such Cyphers" (3.2). When Hector points out that "Our Father has decreed it [Cressida's exchange]" (3.2), Troilus's indifference causes Hector to exclaim "How! No matter Troylus? / A King and father's will!" (3.2). As far as Troilus is concerned, the decree is "unjust," and he says peevishly: "Then you'r no more my friend," to which Hector retorts, "Go to, you are a boy" (3.2).

The remainder of the scene turns on the breaking and restoring of friendship. Troilus brings together the terms of betrayal, brotherhood, and friendship by calling Hector "a traytor to thy Brother / . . . / Nay more, thy friend: but friend's a Sacred name, / Which none but brave and honest men shou'd wear" (3.2). This insult, however, is turned against him when Hector declares impatiently, "All this ye Gods, / And for the Daughter of a fugitive / A Traytor to his Country!" and concludes by calling Cressida "common" (3.2). The comment devalues Cressida, just as Troilus has devalued both king and subjects. It also indicates another turn in the line of argument noted in act 2, scene 1, due to changing criteria and the use of emotional language. When Troilus unfavorably compares Andromache's chastity to Cressida's, this is too much for Hector, who walks off, claiming that his brother has spurned his "friendly counsel" and raging, "Ungrateful as thou art: hereafter use / The name of Brother; but of friend no more" (3.2).

Troilus comes to his senses, recognizing that he has condemned himself by losing his temper after he promised not to. This recognition marks the beginning of reconciliation that brings the brothers to a renewed and stronger appreciation of friendship and brotherhood in a common cause: all three elements of friendship, brotherhood, and the common cause are important. Troilus laments his three losses: of a woman, a brother (Troilus assumes the role of elder brother to be that of protector), and a friend:

> For I have lost (oh what have I not lost!)
> The fairest, dearest, kindest of her Sex,
> And lost her ev'n by him, by him, ye Gods,
> Who only cou'd, and only shou'd protect me!
> And if I had a joy beyond that love,
> A friend, have lost him too.
>
> (3.2)

Hector does not interpret this as just a sentimental speech about a lady, since the first thing he notes is the value Troilus attributes to friendship: "Speak that again: / (For I cou'd hear it ever) / . . . / Saidst thou not a friend!" (3.2). Rapprochement is facilitated by Hector's realization that words spoken under duress often bear little relation to what is in the heart or the mind and that being human inevitably generates emotional stress. When Troilus says, "You told me I must call you friend no more," Hector responds that he did not mean what he said: "Alas! It is the use of human frailty / To fly to worst extremities with those / To whom we most are kind" (3.2).

Reconciliation is effected by Hector, who offers terms of peace to his brother: he confirms that he neither accuses nor blames him but attributes "the wild disorderly account / Of all thy words and deeds on that mad passion [love]" (3.2), and he gives credence to Troilus's feelings by offering to break the agreement or, failing that, to fight to redeem Cressida. Troilus, in turn, responds generously by advising Hector to do neither, since Hector's fault would then be greater than his own. He concludes: "That you have pitied me is my reward" (3.2). Hector's concluding remarks to the third act are a paean to victorious friendship: "And heaven and earth this testimony yield, / That Friendship never gain'd a nobler field" (3.2).

Dryden notes in his essay "Grounds of Criticism in Tragedy" that one of the features of tragedy is the function of "exciting of pity and terror in us" (16), and one of the functions of this scene is to mark the tragic potential of Troilus. Troilus's comment to Hector "That you have pitied me is my reward" not only indicates renewed friendship but, through the reference to pity, signals to the audience that Troilus is being prepared for his role as tragic hero. Henceforth, Troilus is slowly transformed from a coward, controlled by his passions, to someone whose very suffering raises him to tragic dignity, which, in the final scene, includes even heroism.

Hobbes's principles of commonwealth seem to provide a plausible framework for civil security but include no mechanisms for terminating conflict. He intends the use of reason to prevent war. However, human frailty, emotion, personal aggrandizement, and ulterior motives have played a large part, at a collective level, in escalating the prospect of violence. The more intimate exchange between Hector and Troilus serves as a counterweight to the preceding warmongering by recognizing that humans do often react heatedly in matters of importance to them. The two parties successfully abort their heated dispute, which could have gone further, by avoiding as far as possible recriminations and humiliation and by acknowledging sympathetically the concerns of the other. Reconciliation and the tragic mode provide appropriate endings. All the male Trojans of fighting age will die, but extinction of a dynasty is not the tragic point. Dryden makes the lovers, Troilus and Cressida, the focus of tragic suffering. They die having seen the truth and acquired knowledge, but, as the play's subtitle indicates, it is "Truth Found Too Late."

The case of Cressida is more complex, since her fate is to supply obedience in a context where sovereignty and protection are absent or, at best, ambiguous. Hobbes had provided exceptions to the universal rule of obedience; Dryden's Cressida turns out to be an example who turns these exceptions into paradox. The rules of obedience that Hobbes framed for men do not clearly apply to her, and she emerges as a figure who stands neither outside war nor in peace. Once she has been taken to the Greek camp, to whom should she be obedient? Custom dictates loyalty to king, father, and husband in exchange for their protection. According to Hobbes, a prisoner of war is one of only four cases in which a subject is free to disobey the sovereign, since the covenant lasts only as long as the power by which the sovereign is able to protect his subjects,[6] and that condition patently fails if one has become a prisoner. A captive, on the other hand, may ask for quarter or attempt to run away. By asking for quarter, the captive simply defers the wrath of the victor. He who has been granted quarter "hath not his life given, but deferred till farther deliberation; for it is not an yeelding on condition of life, but to discretion" (Hobbes 256). Nor does having one's life spared entail that the victor automatically accepts any act of submission or any proposal involving offers of ransom or services as a servant or slave. Hobbes highlights the inherently disadvantageous bargaining position of the captured soldier without making it clear whether the prisoner of war and the captive are one person or two. In many circumstances, such as war, the captive and the prisoner of war coincide, since both are males taken in the course of fighting. There are no specific norms for females in Hobbes's vision of the commonwealth.

When Cressida arrives in the Greek camp, her status, whether that of "hostage," "prisoner-of-war," or "captive," is unclear. The king took away his protection by decreeing that she be exchanged for the more valuable Antenor, so she is hardly a captive. Only males qualify as prisoners of war, so she cannot "legally" disobey.

Cressida might try running away, although escape seems unrealistic since she has nowhere to go and, as a woman, nobody to protect her: She could try to bargain for her life, but she lacks any skill useful to the Greeks. Eventually she is forced by her father, Calchas, to offer her body, this being, as he says, the only option that will prevent him from being "treated like a slave and scorn'd, / My self in hated bonds a Captive held" (5.2).

The major problem of obedience to Calchas is that he is a traitor to Troy and therefore subject to opprobrium. When Aeneas discovers that Cressida is to be offered for Antenor, his reaction is "What! Has the King resolv'd to gratifie / That Traytor Calchas; who forsook his Country, / And turn'd to them, by giving up this pledge?" (3.2), which also implies that the deal may have been partly engineered by the father. Dryden makes Calchas a more important focus of attention than Shakespeare does, not just because he is a traitor, and ipso facto disobedient or disloyal to the king, but because he is a superstitious priest. Calchas, like Andromache, is a target for the anticlerical sentiments of Troilus.

On two occasions Calchas, the father, commands his daughter. The first is shortly after Cressida arrives in the camp, when Calchas is feeling nostalgic for Troy: "I have a womans longing to return / But yet which way, without your ayd I know not" (4.2). (It may seem incredible that Calchas would contemplate returning to Troy, where he is reviled as a traitor, but he is portrayed as someone who can act on a whim without considering the implications.) In the Greek camp, both father and daughter are under the protection of the military leader Diomedes, and although Calchas appears to have formulated no clear plan of escape, he feels that Diomedes' evident attraction to Cressida can be turned to their advantage. Therefore he instructs his daughter to "dissemble love to Diomede" (4.2). Since Diomedes "can never be deceiv'd, / But by strong Arts and blandishments of love," Cressida's performance must be convincing. But Cressida objects to this: "How can I answer this to love and Troilus?" (4.2). For her such dissembling verges on infidelity, given that she has pledged faith to Troilus earlier in the play (3.2). Calchas nevertheless overrides Cressida's objections of conscience and suggests that she must give Diomedes Troilus's ring to prevent Diomedes from suspecting that she already has a lover in Troy.

Cressida's dilemma is a matter of conscience: how to reconcile faithfulness to Troilus with obedience to a father. Dryden leaves the antagonism to priests and superstition implicit in the play. In 1679, however, the anticlerical sentiments suggested would have been interpreted by the audience in the context of the political crisis in which the claims of the Royalist Tories, defending the absolute hereditary rights of the Crown, opposed the Whigs, often dissenting Puritans, who supported parliamentarism and wanted freedom of conscience and worship. The competing claims of obedience and conscience bring out the complexity, not so much of different interests (which can be solved by bargaining), as of worldview, where the different parties are generally unwilling to cede ground without losing face or coherence.

When Troilus comes to the Greek camp to look for Cressida and witnesses what he believes to be Cressida's betrayal of him with Diomedes, he seeks out Diomedes to fight him to the death. Calchas, on learning Troilus's intent, is alarmed because, as he tells his daughter, both he and she are under the protection of Diomedes, and if Diomedes dies, "We lose not only a Protector here, / But are debard all future means of flight."[7] Therefore, Calchas gives his daughter another command: she must find Troilus and do what she can to prevent him from killing Diomedes. Cressida does indeed go out in search of Troilus, but she has her own motives for doing so: fearing that Troilus will be killed, she feels remorse for her duplicity and wants only to explain herself to him and show him that her infidelity was not what it seemed. As she tells her father, "I'le be justify'd or dye" (5.2).

In the case of Cressida's faithfulness to Troilus, the scenario is complicated by the fact that Troilus is not her husband, although she thinks of him as such. During Pandarus's initial efforts to bring the pair together, Cressida made her uncle promise beforehand to let her marry Troilus (Pandarus is her guardian in the absence of Calchas). The fact that marriage is understood to have been promised and that rings have been exchanged expresses her intention to be faithful and creates a context in which she can think of herself as obedient to a husband. Indeed, when Cressida was first informed that she had to join her father, she already thought of Troilus as her family: "I have no touch of birth; no spark of Nature: / No kinn, no blood, no life;

nothing so near me / As my dear Troilus" (4.1). As was the case with the friendship between Hector and Troilus, fidelity represents a value that must be upheld. Cressida cannot, therefore, obey her father without suppressing her conscience, since she is betraying someone to whom she has pledged her love, and she cannot obey her conscience without being disobedient to her father. The sentimental interest of the play is Dryden's means of exploiting the tragic resolution of these dilemmas because it offers the only potential for reconciliation.

Cressida is a tragic type, neither villainess nor perfectly virtuous. In his essay "The Grounds of Criticism in Tragedy" Dryden dismissed Shakespeare's play as tragedy on the grounds that the tragic lovers remained alive, and he stipulated that "it is necessary that the hero of a play be not a villain, that is, the characters which ought to move our pity have virtuous inclinations, and degrees of morall goodness in them" (16). Making Cressida tragic involves transforming her from a semicourtesan into something resembling a woman of virtue. Dryden goes to some lengths to ensure that the audience sees Cressida in a different light from her traditional portrayal as the faithless lover. Perhaps we can evaluate his success in this task by comparing his Cressida with that of his literary forebears: Shakespeare, who made his leading lady responsible for the world's ills, and Henryson, who punished her with leprosy.

Dryden initially presents Cressida as beautiful and flirtatious. She has grown up in and around the luxury-loving Trojan court and cannot be untainted by her surroundings. The affair with Troilus begins as a carnal one, a game in which she plays hard to get, and she seems destined to become a femme fatale, like Helen before her. However, Dryden tones down more salacious scenes in accordance with decorum. The scene in Shakespeare's play that performs in full the enthusiastic reception given Cressida by the presumably sex-starved Greeks is reduced in Dryden's version to a short verbal report by Pandarus. Similarly, her betrayal of Troilus is accompanied by the cogent reason of self-preservation, and its performance is edited.

In a more positive vein, Dryden emphasizes Cressida's various tendencies toward virtue. After the lovers have sworn to be faithful to each other, Cressida anticipates the tragic finale by expressing suffering: "O those who do not know what parting is / Can never learn to dye" (*Troilus* 4.1). Suicide, of course, is the conclusive proof of her virtue for Troilus. Furthermore, in a curious scene with Calchas that probes the psychology of exile, father receives daughter with apparent delight, spiced with nostalgia for Troy:

O, what a blessing is a vertuous child!
Thou hast reclaim'd my mind, and calm'd my passions
Of anger and revenge: my love to Troy
Revives within me, and my lost Tyara
No more disturbs my mind

(4.2)

What the "lost Tyara" refers to and the reason for the anger are not explained. The speech, though, bears the trace of a King Lear who has passed
from madness to a calmer frame of mind. Cressida, projected accordingly
into the role of Cordelia, becomes a virtuous child. It might be objected that
Cressida had no choice other than to rejoin her father, but Calchas's words
provide the audience with an opportunity to see virtue in Cressida. All her
subsequent actions are acts of obedience, first to her father, then to Troilus.
In the tragic denouement, when Diomedes produces Troilus's ring as "evidence" that she has been untrue, she calls Diomedes' behavior "unexam-
pled, frontlesse, impudence" before kneeling in submission to Troilus, whom
she addresses as "my only Lord" (5.2).

The fatal stabbing causes Troilus to believe her, and the lovers are briefly
reconciled before she dies. Cressida dies happy knowing that she was finally
believed. Troilus, left alive, is torn between pity and despair: pity for Cressida's sacrificial act, which invites, in the audience, the corresponding reaction of tragic pity; and despair, which leads him to place his sword to his
own breast. Catching sight of Diomedes and hearing the latter mocking his
"vain credulity," he is motivated to fight a last battle in which, according to
the stage directions, "All the Trojans dye upon the place, Troilus last" (5.2).

Greek success in "putting an end" to the particular war cannot be read
in any other way than as a call for unification and absolute obedience
around a strong sovereign. In 1679, Dryden had every reason to think that
absolute obedience and absolute rule were necessary to prevent the many
religious and political contradictions evident in the way England was gov-
erned, and already creating civil disorder in London, from becoming a
new civil war. This reason would be strengthened by another one: in 1679,
Dryden held posts in the court of historiographer and poet laureate. He
would have felt the pressing need to uphold the authority of the king against
civil disobedience and simultaneously to quiet the public's fears.

When Charles II was restored to the throne in May 1660 after Commonwealth rule, both he and the people of England seemed to have learned

the value of moderation. In April 1660, in the Declaration of Breda, Charles had announced his intention to rule with a parliamentary government and to grant an amnesty to his political opponents. However, despite his desire to forget the traumatic years between 1642 and 1660, the issue of sovereignty had still not been resolved. His first Royalist parliament insisted on royal prerogative. Then, when, contrary to Charles's declarations at Breda, the supremacy of the Church of England was restored, complete with bishops, one immediate consequence was the persecution of dissenters and nonconformists, rather than the promised amnesty.

The king's extravagance coupled with the inability of Parliament to manage English finances led to a secret alliance with Louis XIV in Roman Catholic France. This alliance, in 1672, sparked a war with England's commercial and colonial rivals in the Netherlands. The negative effect of the French alliance, together with the effect of Charles's attempts to rule without limitations, was intensified by enactment of the anti-Catholic Test Acts. Events came to a head in 1678 with the Popish Plot.

The Popish Plot provided details of a fictitious Roman Catholic plot to murder Charles II. Titus Oates, the principal informer and conspirator, swore that the plan was to replace Charles with his unpopular Roman Catholic brother, James, Duke of York. In addition to the climate of hostility and suspicion evidenced by the many cabals, conspiracies, and factions that already existed, the plot fomented a new terror. By 1679, this terror was at its height, with disorder in the streets.

The Hobbesian state of war between individuals can be overcome by instituting a basically judicial political order designed to prevent the exchange of verbal and visual signs from degenerating into war. Peace, as Hobbes understands it, means, not the suppression of disagreement or controversy, but the mediation of conflict by law rather than acts of private violence (the latter being the outcome in Shakespeare's version of the play). Dryden makes the same point against private acts of violence in *All for Love,* his 1678 version of Shakespeare's *Anthony and Cleopatra.* One of Restoration theater's major departures from Shakespearean drama is to emphasize that the world can no longer absorb acts of personal revenge.

This reading alone, however, does not explain the sympathy that Dryden must have intended his audience to feel for the plight of the lovers and the Trojans in general. Nor, given the many interlocking political and religious issues, would absolute rule prove, in reality, to be a good model in the decade following 1679, when the rule of James II became despotic.

When the hysteria of the Popish Plot had abated, the outcome was to attempt, in the early 1680s, to exclude James from the line of succession, while the different religious and political viewpoints were gradually consolidated into two political parties, still with opposing interests: the Whigs and Tories. However, this stability was only apparent. The end of Charles's reign and that of James II afterwards were both absolutist and marked by terror. Further bloodshed was prevented, in the latter part of 1688, only by the invitation to the Protestant Dutchman William of Orange to rule Great Britain and by the imposition of constitutional limits on the Crown.

Dryden's tragic affection for the Trojans is distinct from his admiration of the Greeks. Patriarchy, representing the unity of the family and its continuity in time as the basic element of society, was crumbling, with resulting confusion and undermining of functional roles. Act 2 tends to attribute collective problems to women as objects and subjects. Act 3, by contrast, concentrates on male roles, revising the meaning of masculinity in this situation of great stress but without glorifying war, endorsing revenge, or justifying self-pity. All previous arguments between Hector and Troilus about obedience and blood ties are defused with reference to the concept of friendship (a horizontal rather than vertical relationship, emphasizing the attribute of sympathetic understanding).

In his essay "Individualism and the Mystery of the Social Self," Wayne Booth coins the word *philiation,* a word that combines the blood relationship of the Latin *filius* ("son") and the Greek *philia* ("love," "friendship," "liking," "attachment"). It is of interest in the present work because of the link Booth makes between philiation and Aristotle's discussion of various types of friendships, which include "every genuine tie—of love, of club membership, of family, of responsibility to slaves or masters, of patriotism—even of business relations" (81). These philiations make life tolerable and rewarding.

"Friendship" or "philiation" makes sense in the cultures of Troy and of England in 1679, structured traditionally around families and networks of siblings and cousins, with few, if any, serious binding alternatives, political or affective. The Trojan dynasty fails to recognize the need for renewal until tragedy can be the only outcome. Successful reconciliations take place twice, both of them at a sentimental rather than a political level, and this helps redeem the sense of loss and waste. Cressida's suicide may be seen as the outcome of personal despair when her few options have been exhausted; but she also draws attention to values—of fidelity and friendship—that cannot be enforced but that bind people together and make life tolerable and rewarding.

The connection between 1679 London and Troy is not fortuitous: London had long been referred to as New Troy.[8] Many in the theater audience had lived through the fraternal enmity of the civil war. Where history had made "brothers" sworn enemies on the basis of religious or political differences, a "friend" might conceivably offer a new and positive departure (a philiation) in the weakening family networks of late-seventeenth-century England. Perhaps from this standpoint we can understand why the Trojans fight valiantly at the end of Dryden's *Troilus and Cressida* but nevertheless all die.

R. J. Kaufmann comments in his essay on the poetics of tragedy in *All for Love* that "[t]ragic writing is a cultural and not merely a personal enterprise and through its fierce disputes insights accumulate which are part of a national heritage" (88). Among these insights was what Kaufmann called Dryden's "divided vision," a "hybrid of disenchanted political realism and romantic nostalgia" (89). This divided vision sees human imperfections at the same time as "human greatness actively transforming its world." In this play, "Dryden does not deny heroism so much as he embalms it, memorializes it in the form of terminal tragedy. His heroic [and tragic] stage is a museum of vital feelings honored lest they be forgotten but securely preserved from present use" (89).

It might seem to be stretching language to refer to a return to peace in the context of Troy, or of seventeenth-century England, given that the end of the Civil War certainly was not the end of conflict; Dryden wrote his play, after all, in the 1670s, the turbulent time of the Popish Plot, which revived antagonisms that the Civil War had never entirely laid to rest. The war lingers on in memory and in its effects: Dryden discusses it in his attached prefaces, and Hobbes, in *Leviathan,* tries to theorize ending war as somehow breaking the chain of nature, in which man's behavior on the basis of self-interest leads to acts of aggression and counterattacks. Both Dryden and Hobbes project the possibility of a lasting peace without forgetting what everyone has lived through. *Troilus and Cressida* was designed to keep alive the memory of war without glorifying or justifying war, and it ends up being a dramatic testimony to war's futility.

Constructing war/peace as a binary category makes it a game with winners and losers in which the winner takes all. But in Dryden's play, though the war is shown to have horrific effects on the losing Trojan side, some Trojans recognize or derive benefits from it: Andromache's sense of self is fed by the battlefield heroism of her husband, and Hector needs to test and prove his prowess in order to stimulate his own sense of worth.

Further, while Dryden admires the Greeks, "winners" of the war in both reality and the play, for their relative efficiency and rationalism, he intends his audience to feel for the defeated but stupid Trojans (who, for the 1679 audience are not a remote "them" but a nostalgic part of "us"). One of Dryden's purposes was to use the play to bring everyone into its embrace. The war is not presented as a winner-takes-all situation: even the "winners" know they have lost their innocence, and even the enemy is shown in some ways that can engage the audience's sympathy and respect.

The major problem with Hobbes's philosophy and Dryden's drama is that, although both are written with close knowledge and experience of war in mind, the theoretical underpinning envisages a final objective, peace, as its opposite ideal state rather than a workable strategy. As so much of recent history can inform the twenty-first-century reader, "not being at war" does not necessarily entail "being at peace" or the permanent disappearance of war and conflict. *Peacekeeping* is perhaps a better term that avoids the dangers of idealism. The commonwealth model of covenanted sovereignty and obedience functions when the covenant is remembered and respected but fails in practice when the covenant is forgotten. Oppression, acts of humiliation and reprisals, token parliamentarism, blind conformism, injustice, and intolerance are just some of the obvious manifestations of failure.

We cannot legislate against conflict or against different voices with different points of view, some of which may appear irreconcilable. The decision-making apparatus of Troy points forward to what, perhaps, was felt to be missing in England in 1679: public rather than private powers whose functions are, first, to debate rationally the nature of collective representation, justice, and security, defining the limits of freedom of all, and, second, to debate and react to events that could change that principled framework.

What is absent in Troy, and what the insistence on obedience tends to obstruct, is the concept of freedom with its concomitant rights and obligations, understood as belonging to everyone and not restricted by the imposition of religious or moral codes. Otherwise, treason and dissidence come to amount to the same thing. The emphasis on rationality of procedure presupposes, not that sentiments are bad per se, but that the resolution of conflicts concerning injustices requires reference to causes, ends, and means rather than strategies based on the mood of a single person or deference to the whim of a persuasive personality.

Another element that is wholly absent from this play is the concept of the public as subject. The period of peace that Ulysses looks forward to in the closing lines remains in the future. The covenant is assumed to have been made but is not seen. Nor does the audience see Thersites transformed from a slave and "a Species, differing from mankinde" to a subject. Troilus refers to the public with contempt, and the entire Trojan army is wiped out, with only history to guide us as to what happens to the Trojan people. This play does not address the return to peace from the perspective of the subject.

An additional problematic, assuming that the public (or masses) have become subjects, might concern the public management of people organized by what the philosopher Peter Sloterdijk would call horizontal power, in gatherings that may merge spontaneously from people's being in close proximity, without any linkage to a controlling leader. If obedience no longer signifies respectful submission, what is the effect on relations between horizontal and vertical powers, and how does a government responsible for public safety manage large groups of people, which may behave spontaneously and unpredictably (as in the case of what would be in Hobbes's time described by the notion of "the mob" or "public disorder")?

My framework here for addressing issues concerning the return to peace draws on models of democratic freedom in which the highest value is ongoing debate and reflection about collective identity and purpose, as opposed to ideal solutions to the latest particular problem. "Democracy," "freedom," "obedience," "peace," "war," "friendship," "honor" and "glory" are all abstract concepts whose richness and power tend to be underappreciated until seen in operation. In this context, the performing arts not only remember war or discuss peace but are able to bring out the power and contradictions of language and their effect on successful communication. This prompts a last reflection about language itself.

It is almost axiomatic to think of falsehoods and distortion as typical in the discourses of war and of the prewar periods, which use words to manipulate or deceive people; to sweeten reality, supporting and confirming the ideas of an established order and avoiding unpleasant realities; and to confuse fantasy and reality. This essay has mentioned a number of them. Such discourses abound, particularly, when worldviews collide and are not amenable to negotiation or dialogue. Recognition that reality is not so simple as to accommodate only one point of view, that words are spoken and deeds committed in haste, and not always for the pure motives attributed to them, is the first step toward reconciliation in *Troilus and Cressida*.

One of the crucial tasks, perhaps, facing those primarily responsible for managing the phase of a return to peace ought to be a reexamination of the language and symbols used in the preceding war: those concepts of

broad scope, such as "obedience," "honor," and "justice," whose many connotations and uses exacerbated conflict or led to breakdown in communication. Thus notions of obedience such as submission, loyalty, faithfulness,
conformism, patriotism, and consent to authority can be examined without
the pressure of a highly charged conflictive environment to dictate a single
meaning in a single context. We owe it to the principle of respect for difference and the definition of freedom to understand what people think they
are fighting for.

NOTES

1. For a complete summary of literary critical responses to Shakespeare's
play, including the coining of the term *problem play* by Frederick Boas in 1896, see
Martin.

2. Dryden's *Troilus and Cressida* has received little critical attention. However,
for a general but relevant discussion of Dryden's concept of tragedy that applies to
Troilus and Cressida, see Kaufmann.

3. For an extended discussion of Hobbes's theory of war, see Zarka, ch. 6, "De
La Guerra," 139–58, and for a discussion of his theory of the state, see ch. 9, "Del Es-
tado," 213–25.

4. The Summers edition of John Dryden's *Troilus and Cressida or Truth Found
too Late* contains no line numbers. As the scenes are rather long, only act and scene
division are cited.

5. Note also that Antenor is seen as the answer to the "common safety" of
Troy.

6. See Hobbes, ch. 20.

7. Once again, Dryden signals the ambiguity of the political status of father
and daughter in the Greek camp, which is only heightened by Calchas's unreliability
as a reporter: if Diomedes is indeed their protector they are his subjects and cannot
ethically run away, whereas if he is their captor they are his prisoners and it would
make no sense for them to turn to him for help.

8. London was known as "Troia Nova," or New Troy, because of a legend that
after the Trojan War Aeneas led a party of Trojans to Britain and that his great-
grandson, Brutus, founded London and called it Troia Nova.

WORKS CITED

Booth, Wayne C. "Individualism and the Mystery of the Social Self; or, Does Am-
    nesty Have a Leg to Stand On?" *Freedom and Interpretation: The Oxford Am-
    nesty Lectures 1992.* Ed. Barbara Johnson. New York: Basic Books, 1993.

Dryden, John. *All for Love*. Ed. N. J. Andrew. New Mermaids. London: Ernst Benn, 1975.

———. "The Grounds of Criticism in Tragedy." 1679. Preface to *Troilus and Cressida*. *The Dramatic Works*. Ed. Montague Summers. Vol. 3. New York: Gordian Press, 1963.

———. *Troilus and Cressida or Truth Found too Late*. 1679. *The Dramatic Works*. Ed. Montague Summers. Vol. 3. New York: Gordian Press, 1963.

Hobbes, Thomas. *Leviathan*. Ed. C. B. MacPherson. 1651. Harmondsworth: Penguin, 1968.

Kaufmann, R. J. "On the Poetics of Terminal Tragedy: Dryden's *All for Love*." *Dryden: A Collection of Critical Essays*. Ed. Bernard N. Schilling. Englewood Cliffs, NJ: Prentice Hall, 1963. 86–94.

Martin, Priscilla, ed. *Troilus and Cressida: A Casebook*. London: Macmillan, 1976.

Pennington, D. H. "Political Debate and Thomas Hobbes." *From Donne to Marvell: The New English Guide to English Literature*. Ed Boris Ford. Rev. ed. Vol. 3. Harmondsworth: Penguin, 1990. 303–16.

Shakespeare, William. *Anthony and Cleopatra*. Ed. Michael Neill. World's Classics. Oxford: Oxford University Press, 1994.

———. *Troilus and Cressida*. Ed. Alice Walker. New Shakespeare. Cambridge: Cambridge University Press, 1969.

Zarka, Yves Charles. *Hobbes y el pensamiento político moderno*. Trans. Luisa Medrano. Barcelona: Herder, 1997.

CHAPTER SEVEN

Romances of Reconstruction

The Postwar Marriage Plot in Rebecca Harding Davis
and John William De Forest

DON DINGLEDINE

As Nina Silber illustrates in *The Romance of Reunion*, stories of southern women and northern men falling in love and uniting in marriage captured the popular American imagination in the immediate post–Civil War era. Silber's classic study expertly identifies "the beauty of this standard plot device" for a nation struggling with the return to peace after a long and bloody civil conflict: "Relying on accepted cultural stereotypes of women's emotional but submissive nature, . . . authors allowed northern audiences to reconcile themselves with a South that could never really threaten the North, to ally themselves with a 'rebel element' that offered mainly a flirtatious defiance of Union principles. In this way, real sectional antagonisms could now be displaced and defused by promoting harmony with these coquettes of the confederacy" (115).

The problem with this romantic vision of sectional reunion is clear: the romance of reunion skirted unresolved issues of race and rights that, long after the Civil War, continue to haunt America. To be sure, the romance of reunion's emphasis on (white) "harmony" through old-fashioned gender stereotypes and without a hint of forward-looking social reform was one key to its popularity. Fortunately, another romance—and a more promising road to true and lasting peace for *all* citizens—also captured the American imagination following the Civil War.

The dominance of stories such as those Silber describes has effectively overshadowed alternatives to and variations on the stock romance plot in the post–Civil War era, but the emancipation of four million African American slaves inspired many Americans—white and black, male and female—to envision the return to peace in radically new ways as well. With the onset of Reconstruction, as the historian Eric Foner notes, "the foundations of public life were thrown open for discussion" (278). Novelists joined politicians in the debate. In 1867, for example, the year control of Reconstruction shifted from the conservative President Andrew Johnson to Radical Republicans in Congress, William Wells Brown and Lydia Maria Child each offered a unique romance of America's future after emancipation and the end of sectional conflict. Brown added four new chapters to what would be the fourth and final version of a novel he first published in 1853 as *Clotel; or, The President's Daughter. A Narrative of Slave Life in the United States.* Whereas each of the novel's three earlier incarnations ends with its protagonists living as fugitive slaves in Europe, the 1867 version brings them back to the United States at the outbreak of the Civil War. Straying from the pattern of happy couplings that close the romance of reunion, *Clotelle; or, The Colored Heroine. A Tale of the Southern States* stakes a claim to African American citizenship and patriotism by having the hero enlist in the U.S. Colored Troops and die valiantly for his country; after her husband's death, Clotelle lives peacefully on the very plantation where she was once enslaved, having purchased the land and established a freedman's school on it when the plantation is confiscated and sold at auction by the federal government.[1] Unlike Brown's, Lydia Maria Child's vision of peace after the Civil War in *A Romance of the Republic* maintains the basic outline Silber identifies, ending with not one but three romantic unions. Like Brown, however, Child imagines a radically reconstructed nation. The three happy couplings that end Child's novel do not simply reunite white North and white South but bridge racial divides as well: each of the three unions is interracial.[2]

The examples of Brown and Child do not challenge Silber's thesis as much as they expand it, suggesting what is gained by shifting attention to read stories of courtship and marriage not just as romances of reunion but also as romances of Reconstruction. Seen from this vantage point, what these gendered romances say, directly or indirectly, about the future of a people whose emancipation was the cornerstone of America's Reconstruction becomes a central concern. To test this claim, I want to look closely at Rebecca Harding Davis's *Waiting for the Verdict*, another novel published in 1867, the first year of Radical Reconstruction, and another that rewrites the dominant narrative Silber identifies to make reconstruction of the old order essential to the nation's peaceful and lasting reunion. With Davis's novel as a point of comparison, I will then examine John William De Forest's *Miss*

Ravenel's Conversion from Secession to Loyalty, also published in 1867, which fits Silber's thesis to the letter (although it does not receive extended treatment in *The Romance of Reunion*). Reading De Forest's romance of reunion as a reaction against the romance of Reconstruction exposes the unstable foundation of inequality and oppression—of women and African Americans both—on which peace is constructed in the romance of reunion.

Waiting for the Verdict is a romance of Reconstruction and a reconstruction of romance. In it, Davis consciously explores how discourses of race and gender overlap in the back-to-peace period through the stories of three couples: Rosslyn Burley, a white northern abolitionist born in poverty, and Garrick Randolph, a slaveholding white southern aristocrat; Margaret Conrad (Garrick's cousin) and John Broderip, a mulatto surgeon passing for white; and Nathan and Anny, escaped slaves searching for each other against the backdrop of war. My focus here is on the union of Rosslyn and Garrick, which alters the popular plot Silber identifies in several ways. In Davis, for example, the man represents the South and the woman the North. More important, whereas antebellum mythologies of race and gender go unchallenged in the romances Silber examines, the courtship of Rosslyn Burley and Garrick Randolph suggests that the reunion of North and South depends on the revision of these mythologies. The success of this coupling hinges on the man's ideological reconstruction.

From the moment Davis introduces Garrick Randolph, she emphasizes how his outlook has been shaped by the southern plantation, a sheltered world of privilege, leisure, and the chivalric romance. This slaveholder enters the war not to defend his region or right to own slaves but with the hope of living up to a vague ideal of heroism: when the body of a Union spy turns up on his land, Garrick rises "chivalrously" to the challenge and takes up the dead man's mission. Garrick's cousin Margaret calls his impulsive action "a fool-hardy bit of Quixotism" (41). "All of Randolph's thoughts ran formally like sentences in books," Davis writes, "and sounded to him generally, as if some one else had spoken them" (49). Davis's concern is not with the difference between "real life" and a life of books as much as the difference between a new literary realism, or the book in hand as she conceived it, and the romance tradition ingrained in American culture.[3] One of the most haunting images in *Waiting for the Verdict* suggests what is at stake—for nations at war as well as for nations remembering war as they return to peace—in this struggle between competing modes of discourse. As Garrick travels north on the Ohio River with Rosslyn Burley, the river's flow comes to symbolize the relentless motions of war: "Steamers met them unceasingly, with waving banners, triumphant music, laden to the water's edge with men hurrying to the battlefield; other boats swept silently before them, and in their wake, filled with gaunt-eyed spectres from the fever hospitals, or maimed wrecks of men going home to die" (71–72). Dreams of glory and heroism in battle give way to the reality of suffering and death, but such sights are not enough to make Davis's would-be hero disavow his romantic ideals.

Garrick does not engage in physical combat on the battlefield, but the "sentences" flowing from his mind repeatedly clash with both the narrator's and Rosslyn's perspectives. In one evocative scene, Rosslyn shows Garrick a sketch of a packing crate being opened at a station for the Underground Railroad. Inside is the bent body of a slave who has died in a daring attempt to escape bondage; drawn with "wonderful power," the sketch "told the whole history of a man who had starved and toiled to the end of the long voyage, and died in sight of land" (68–70). Yet Garrick Randolph cannot see the reality of the scene before him.[4] The slaveholder's mind conjures up images of his own "fat, lazy negroes at home," and he scoffs at the drawing, branding it inflammatory abolitionist "fiction." "But this is true," Rosslyn counters.

Although Rosslyn's revelation that she is the drawing's artist momentarily unnerves Garrick, it does not discourage his romantic interpretation of either the sketch or its creator, and he simply cannot comprehend how she could have rendered this scene with "the strength, the purpose, the passion of a man" (70). Angered by his incredulity, Rosslyn exclaims that she has "had the ugly fact" of slavery "'in my hands—in my hands'—holding them out as if to shake some clinging stain from them." Gazing at the hands uplifted before him, Garrick's eyes "only noted the rose flush in their palms, and their nervous, slight grace" (69). "There is room, there, you see, for another figure," Rosslyn tells him. "That was I." All Garrick can do is look at her sketch and say, "I am sorry to frame you *even in fancy*, Miss Burley, in a scene like this" (68–69, emphasis added). He then proceeds to reframe her according to her white body, just as he reframes the slave she has drawn according to his ideal image of the black body—"his fat, lazy negroes at home."

Waiting for the Verdict deconstructs the mythologies of the planter class by positioning Garrick in relation to women and African Americans in ways his culture's narratives, and his mind as molded by those narratives, work to preclude. As soon as Garrick takes up the dead spy's mission, the novel deflates his ideas of heroism and his prejudices of race and gender by having Pitt, a slave, and then Rosslyn, a white female, rescue him from the brink of death. In both instances the irony is lost on Garrick. Still, these experiences initiate his reconstruction and, just as important, invite readers to engage the politics of representation at a time when the nation was struggling with its own reconstruction.

While Davis's realism records women's roles in the war—Rosslyn is active in relief work, she crosses into Confederate territory in her work for the Underground Railroad, and she acts as a Union spy—Garrick is busy writing his own narratives in which the male is active and the female passive. Rosslyn saves Garrick's life at the risk of her own, but as their romance blossoms, this is how his imagination figures their meeting: "he had put his hand on the white dove which he would have lured to his breast"; "It was as if the one white lily of the world had waited for him to pluck and hide its sweetness in his breast" (146, 289). (Garrick Randolph appears to be in the wrong novel; as we shall see, Davis's unreconstructed white male and De Forest's white lily—Lillie Ravenel—would make a happy couple.)

Davis's realism challenges the traditional war narrative's reliance on the exceptional white male as hero. By privileging his place in society, such stories deny the significance of what Davis called the "commonplace" American—women, blacks, the working class, and even the affluent but imperfect and unheroic white male, as Garrick turns out to be. By constantly contrasting the reality she depicts with that scripted by Garrick's mind, Davis emphasizes how his self-image as an active, dominant, self-reliant individual is enabled by the misrepresentation of others. Setting himself at the center of history's busy flow, he sets white women above it and blacks below it. Their dependence on white males is naturalized and perpetuated, and their contributions to history go unrecorded.

Davis was writing this novel for serialization when America was in transition, trying to make sense of the Civil War and the nation it created.[5] As Silber shows, and as an analysis of De Forest's novel will illustrate, the war was already being rewritten in ways resembling the narratives scripted by Garrick Randolph's mind.[6] By the end of the century the nation's memory was shaped largely by the romance of the Lost Cause: a nostalgia for the antebellum plantation; an erasure of the brutal realities experienced in slavery and in war; the disappearance of the slave, as both cause and participant, from the Civil War; and the removal of white women from the "contamination" of war and social reform. If Garrick's response to Rosslyn's drawing dramatizes the way American culture, in both the North and the South, would erase the slave's suffering from history, absolving the nation of its postwar responsibilities to African Americans, then his reconstruction mirrors Davis's hope that a new literary realism might stave off the romance that ultimately overtook the popular imagination.

Davis's couple weds *before* their happy ending. To Garrick's imagination it is an unexpected turn of events: "only now," his uneasy mind intuits on his wedding day, "had the curtain risen and the play begun," with "all that had gone on before . . . not but the prologue" (317). The story that unfolds after Garrick and Rosslyn's marriage suggests that the permanent or "happy" reunion of North and South will demand ongoing social reform. From the perspective of African Americans both free and enslaved, after all, did a prewar state of peace to which America might return in 1865 ever truly exist? In this sense, the novel's titular premise of "waiting" is progressive, especially when read against Andrew Johnson's veto of the Reconstruction Act, which asserted that the work of Reconstruction was complete and the verdict was in. Garrick's growing sense of guilt over betraying a slave named Hugh in the final days of the war argues otherwise. When he learned that Hugh possessed a will disinheriting Garrick's father, and therefore Garrick, the slaveholder sentenced the feeble old man to certain death by donating him to the Confederate government. Back home with Rosslyn after the war, however, Garrick slowly starts to think of Hugh as a man; he agrees to assist Nathan, Hugh's son, to find his father.

Garrick Randolph's mental reconstruction brings him into historical Reconstruction. During his journey through the postwar South, Garrick is startled to find himself echoing his wife's radical opinions, "for which he had lectured her sharply the very day before he left." Even the way he speaks changes: "Travelling with Nathan, he did not use the arrogant tone habitual to him before he married." "It was impossible," the narrator explains, "to feel in the same way to a chattel whom you could trade for a mare and filly, and the man who would probably poll his vote with you at the next election." Garrick is unaware of the change, but "Nat was keenly conscious of the difference" (435). And for the first time in the novel, Davis records the suffering caused by racism through Garrick's point of view. Garrick witnesses the South's return not to peace but to a new form of warfare with the Ku Klux Klan and to a new form of slavery with the rise of sharecropping. By titling the chapter in which these events occur "Chivalry's Harvest," Davis suggests the nation's obligation to confront and redress the consequences of its past actions. When his stay in one community is disrupted by the murder of a freedman's teacher, Garrick finally plays not an imagined but a real role in history by adopting the victim's daughter. Asked about his wife's likely reaction, Garrick replies without pause: Rosslyn's "hearth and heart would take in all the orphans of the world." That hearth, Davis suggests, promises to be a truly peaceful one. With the two partners bound by a common ethic of social responsibility and justice, their union is solid.

The postwar marriage plot as Davis reconstructs it encourages readers to imagine the return to peace in progressive ways. It must be acknowledged, however, that the final vision of a reconstructed America in *Waiting for the Verdict* is not as forward-looking as we might wish. Davis, recall, explores America's post–Civil War future not just through the relationship of Garrick Randolph and Rosslyn Burley but also through the stories of two other couples. Nathan is reunited with Anny and their young son Tom; the future appears to bode well for this family of former slaves as they set up house on land owned by Rosslyn. Nevertheless, the novel's closing image of two separate and self-contained households, one white and one black, stands in stark contrast to the racially mixed families with which Lydia Maria Child closes *A Romance of the Republic*. The limited scope of Davis's vision, which seems to anticipate Jim Crow segregation, is especially clear when we consider how easy it would have been to have Rosslyn and Garrick adopt a black child rather than (or in addition to) a white one. Even more troubling is the fate of John Broderip and Margaret Conrad: soon after the mulatto's racial identity is revealed, he dies in battle, and it is suggested that Margaret Conrad never actually loved Broderip but fell in love, *through* him, with his white double.

As disappointing as it is, Davis's clumsy attempt to preserve "natural" boundaries between black and white in the final pages of *Waiting for the Verdict* is not nearly as conservative and reactionary as the natural order established by John William De Forest. Ironically, however, the happy ending of De Forest's romance is, in a sense, the interracial coupling from which Davis backs away. *Miss Ravenel's Conversion from Secession to Loyalty* explores America's return to peace after the Civil War through Lillie Ravenel's courtship by two suitors, John Carter, of southern descent, and Edward Colburne, a northerner. This romantic triangle, I believe, is as much a struggle over the freed black body as it is a struggle for the hand of the white woman. As Alice Jardine suggests male writers often do, De Forest appears to be using the symbol of the white female body to work out the concerns of the dominant culture, in this case the racial hierarchies threatened by emancipation and Radical Reconstruction. Ultimately, the union of the white hero with a woman who—discursively, at least—is both white and black is not the cause for alarm, for in this romance the white man remains dominant.

Through Lillie Ravenel, women are associated not simply with the South, as Silber's thesis suggests, but also with the southern system of slavery. Her father's sole motive for becoming a slave owner was to finance her lavish tastes. His outspoken defense of the Union, however, drives them north at the start of the war. In Dr. Ravenel's analysis, the distinction between southern slave owner and slave, between civilized and savage, has blurred: white southerners "have fed on the poor blacks," he explains, "until they can't abide a man who isn't a cannibal" (8). He labels the South's uprising an "Ashantee rebellion." The feminine South becomes Africa, and secession a slave rebellion.

"Now Miss Ravenel was a rebel," De Forest informs his readers. "Like all young people and almost all women she was strictly local, narrowly geographical in her feelings and opinions. She was colored by the soil in which she had germinated and been nurtured" (10). Although her father refuses to turn cannibal, blackness lingers on Lillie's tongue. When she defends the region that has "colored" her, this supporter of an "Ashantee rebellion" slips into "Ashantee English," in this instance "right nice." "[C]oloring to her temples" when her father admonishes her for this linguistic impropriety, Lillie explains: "'I must be allowed to use those Ashantee phrases once in a while. . . . We learn them from our old maumas; that is, you know, our nice old black nurses'" (11).

The implications of Lillie Ravenel's rhetorical blackness for the novel's vision of postwar race relations suggest themselves in De Forest's descriptions of female sexual desire. Both Lillie's father and the novel's narrator express their preference for Colburne as suitor; Lillie's instincts draw her to Carter, however, as when she and her father witness the departure of his regiment:

> How superb in Lillie's eyes was the Colonel, though his face was grim
> and his voice harsh with arbitrary power. She liked him for his bronze
> color, his monstrous mustache. . . . How much prouder of him was she
> because she was a little afraid of him, than if he had seemed one whom

she might govern! Presently a brilliant blush rose like a sunrise upon her countenance. Carter had caught sight of them and was approaching. A wave of his hand and a stare of his imperious eye drove away the flock of negroes who had crowded their lookout. (193)

Carter's ability to control the "flock of negroes" around him gives him the advantage over Colburne, Lillie's northern suitor, as well as over Lillie: "[S]he was afraid of him, and yet could not bear to be away from him for a moment. He had such an authority over her—his look and voice and touch so tyrannized her emotions that he was an object of something like terror; and yet the sense of his domination was so sweet that she could not wish it to be less, but desired with her whole beating brain and heart that it might evermore increase" (225). Once married, Lillie insists on calling her husband "Mr. Carter," which "seemed to express her respect for this man, her husband, her master" (226). As soon as the couple sets up house, readers see Lillie "slaving for" Mr. Carter, "tiring herself out for his dear sake" (234).

"A woman is only happy when she is the slave, body and soul, of some man," a character explains to John Carter. "She is happy just in proportion to her obedience and self-sacrifice. Then only she is aware of her full nature" (352). The message is the same, but such observations typically come from the narrator, who makes pronouncement after pronouncement concerning the "true" nature of women; on nearly every page readers encounter such phrases as "no woman likes" and "especially a woman." After another description of Lillie's deep-rooted attraction to the slave plantation, for instance, the narrator turns to the reader: "Let us not be too severe upon the barbarian beliefs of this civilized young lady. For some reason which I shall not trouble myself to discover, all women love aristocracies" (156).

Again, discourses of race and gender overlap in the back-to-peace period, and the language of biological determinism De Forest weaves almost obsessively around Lillie Ravenel is strikingly similar to that found in arguments justifying slavery before the war and sharecropping after, as well as in arguments against Radical Reconstruction and explanations for its "failure." If women and Africans are inevitably enslaved by nature, then the limits of Reconstruction are predetermined. The growth of Lillie Ravenel's character is driven by her two marriages, her "conversion" from Miss to Mrs. With her first husband she discovers her need to be mastered. Equally disturbing, if we read John Carter as the slave's southern master,[7] is how Lillie's relationship with him brings her to what the narrator calls "the culminating point in her womanhood: higher than Baby it was impossible for her to go." "Lillie Reaches the Apotheosis of Womanhood" is the title of this chapter in her conversion, which opens: "Woman is more intimately and irresponsibly a child of Nature than man." It is difficult not to see the freed slave as the subject of the sentences that follow, which are disturbingly violent in their insistence on the need for control, the necessity of suffering, and the logic of respecting Nature's limits:

> She comes oftener, more completely, and more evidently under the power of influences which she can neither direct nor resist, and which make use of her without consulting her inclination. Her part then is passive obedience and uncomplaining suffering, while through her the ends of life are accomplished. She has no choice but to accept her beneficent martyrdom. . . . At the same time, a loving spirit is given to her, so that she is consoled in her own anguish, and does not seriously desire that the cup may pass from her before she has drunk it to the dregs. She has the patience of the lower animals and of inanimate nature, ennobled by a heavenly joy of self-sacrifice, a divine pleasure in suffering for those whom she loves. (372)

De Forest's narrator adamantly confirms the advice a character gives Carter when, as quoted above, she too yokes a woman's happiness irrevocably to her "obedience" and "self-sacrifice." Only when a woman becomes "the slave, body and soul, of some man" is she "relieved from prison and permitted the joy of expansion," the advice continues. "It is a seeming paradox, but it is solemnly true" (352).

The happy ending of De Forest's romance suggests that his novel's insight into power dynamics and the nature of suffering is intended for the would-be white philanthropist—personified here by the abolitionist Edward Colburne—as much as it is for African Americans dissatisfied with the tentative, partial nature of freedom and peace in the post–Civil War period. Like the slave, Lillie loses her southern master in the war. Nature dictates that she cannot remain masterless for long, however, and Colburne succeeds in winning Lillie's hand the second time around, in part because she has learned her proper place under her first husband.[8] The war also teaches Lillie's northern suitor a lesson important to winning his southern bride, it seems. A letter he writes from the battlefield contains a passage "worth copying," De Forest's narrator explains, "because it bears some relation to the grand reconstruction experiment of the Doctor." Lillie's father returns South to experiment with educating his former slaves and paying them for their labor, but his findings are similar to Colburne's, whose first-hand experience with African Americans in the war leads him to doubt the possibility of civilizing them and "inducing them to work": "I am as much of an Abolitionist as ever," he confesses, "but not so much of a 'nigger-worshipper.' I don't know but that I shall yet become an advocate of slavery" (251).[9] Colburne's conversion, complementing as it does that of his soon-to-be wife, suggests a flawed and problematic reunion, one that essentially re-inscribes the very hierarchies and inequalities that led up to the Civil War.

De Forest's flawed vision of a bright future for Colburne in America's postwar economy as well as with Lillie Ravenel is encoded, perhaps, in the name of this mineralogist's son: "Coal Burn" evokes industry, blackness, and the exploitation of "natural" resources. Discussing Colburne's financial prospects with his daughter's suitor, Dr. Ravenel utters another gendered version of postemancipation racial discourse: "[T]he greatest difficulty which man has overcome in climbing the heights of civilization is the fact that he has had to tote women on his shoulders." The white man's burden herself overhears these words and admonishes her father, objecting not to the content of his advice but to his diction, for "tote" is another example of the "Ashantee English" Dr. Ravenel usually reprimands his daughter for using. "I thought you never used negro phrases, Papa," Lillie interjects (466).

To address the hopes and concerns of a nation in the process of return-ing to peace, both Rebecca Harding Davis and John William De Forest turned to the immediate past, to the problem of American slavery and the war that ended it. As Davis dramatizes in the struggle between stories gen-erated by Garrick Randolph's mind and those sketched by Rosslyn Burley, our view of the past—what we remember and how we remember it—shapes our actions in the present as well as our hopes for the future. With this in mind, a comparative analysis of *Waiting for the Verdict* and *Miss Ravenel's Conversion from Secession to Loyalty* would be incomplete without consid-ering their contrasting histories in the American literary canon. Davis's progressive vision of the nation's return to peace after the Civil War was es-sentially erased from American cultural memory for more than a century after its original publication, a fate shared by the similarly forward-looking postwar visions of William Wells Brown's *Clotelle* and Lydia Maria Child's *A Romance of the Republic*. De Forest's attempt to naturalize a reunion based on the continued oppression and exploitation of women and African Americans, on the other hand, was championed for its "down-to-earth, anti-chivalrous accuracy" and for "rescu[ing] war from heroics and sexual relations from sentimentality" (Stone 87; Wilson 688).[10] "Miss Ravenel stands alone, the first realistic heroine in American fiction," Gordon S. Haight proclaimed when De Forest's novel was reissued in 1955 (xvii). As recently as 1995, *The Cambridge Companion to American Realism and Naturalism* offered a chronology in which De Forest published *Miss Ravenel's Conversion* and "Alfred Nobel perfects dynamite" in 1867 but in which the publication of *Waiting for the Verdict, Clotelle*, or *A Romance of the Republic* in the same year was not mentioned (Pizer ix). At stake here is not simply which texts we decide to preserve but the cultural paradigms that privilege some texts while erasing others, and how traditional paradigms have limited the issues and concerns at the heart of our literary canons. The resulting "impoverishment of our literature," as Carolyn L. Karcher describes it, "has had the effect of inhibiting our very capacity to imagine, let alone create, alternatives to white supremacy, male dominance, and a perpetual state of war with other peoples" (Introduction xxxviii). Volumes such as *Back to Peace* play an essential role in the search for alternatives, especially if the readiness of nations to go to war diminishes as we gain a deeper understanding of the return to peace.

Notes

I would like to thank Carolyn L. Karcher, Sharon M. Harris, Rodney D. Olsen, and Julie Russo for their insightful comments on earlier drafts of this essay.

1. This practice, which promised a true and lasting restructuring of the southern social order, was unfortunately short-lived, with most land remaining in the hands of former slaveholders (to whom in some cases it was returned by federal mandate).

2. For an excellent analysis of *A Romance of the Republic*, see Karcher, *First Woman in the Republic*.

3. On Davis's contributions to the development of American literary realism, see Harris and Pfaelzer.

4. Davis is making a revisionary allusion to Henry "Box" Brown, who escaped slavery in a small box carried by rail to a Philadelphia depot. The details of her revision are telling: Davis turns a successful escape into an unsuccessful one, a heroic episode into a tragic one, and a subject into an object. I thank Carolyn L. Karcher for suggesting these implications of Rosslyn's sketch. Pfaelzer observes that in the engravings that appeared in the *Galaxy* with Davis's novel, the only nonmulatto African American depicted is the dead slave, "and that from the back" (145).

5. *Waiting for the Verdict*'s thirteen-installment serialization in the *Galaxy* began in the magazine's February 15, 1867, issue; it appeared in book form later the same year.

6. As Pfaelzer reads it, "Davis's portrait of the slaveowner Randolph serves as an allusion to the northern reader, well-intended but ambivalent and uninformed" (144).

7. Although he lives in the North and fights for the Union, Carter's ancestry is southern: "[N]o family in Virginia boasted a purer strain of old Colonial blue blood than the Carters." Professing his love of plantation life, he admits that "if I could have done everything that I fancied, I should have become a sugar planter" (22–23).

8. "In such matters," De Forest's narrator philosophizes while Lillie Ravenel contemplates Edward Colburne's marriage proposal, "a woman can do little more than sit still while others transact her history. She was under the spell: it was not she who would control her own fate: it was Mr. Colburne" (475).

9. This is how De Forest depicts the actions of one group of slaves when their master flees during the war: They "came upon the house like locusts of destruction, broke down its doors, shattered its windows, plundered it from parlor to garret, drank themselves drunk on the venerable treasures of the wine closet, and diverted themselves with soiling the carpets, breaking the chairs, ripping up the sofas, and defacing the family portraits" (233).

10. "Under the emerging criteria of literary realism," Young argues, "women's interest in writing about war represented a flagrant violation of gender norms; war novels, like war itself, were ostensibly a matter for men. Male jeremiads about women's Civil War fiction angrily and anxiously defended these boundaries, repeatedly constructing the Civil War as a literary battlefront under assault by armies of inferior but powerful women." Young cites gendered appraisals of *Miss Ravenel's Conversion from Secession to Loyalty* and its fate in the marketplace by William Dean Howells and De Forest himself (7–8).

Works Cited

Brown, William Wells. *Clotelle; or, The Colored Heroine. A Tale of the Southern States*. Boston: Lee and Shepard, 1867.

Child, Lydia Maria. *A Romance of the Republic*. 1867. Lexington: University Press of Kentucky, 1997.

Davis, Rebecca Harding. *Waiting for the Verdict*. 1867. Ed. Donald Dingledine. Albany, NY: NCUP, 1995.

De Forest, John William. *Miss Ravenel's Conversion from Secession to Loyalty*. 1867. Ed. Gordon S. Haight. New York: Holt, Rinehart, and Winston, 1955.

Foner, Eric. *Reconstruction: America's Unfinished Revolution, 1863–1877*. New York: Harper and Row, 1988.

Haight, Gordon S. Introduction. *Miss Ravenel's Conversion from Secession to Loyalty.* By John William De Forest. New York: Holt, Rinehart, and Winston, 1955. v–xx.

Harris, Sharon M. *Rebecca Harding Davis and American Realism.* Philadelphia: University of Pennsylvania Press, 1991.

Jardine, Alice A. *Gynesis: Configurations of Woman and Modernity.* Ithaca: Cornell University Press, 1985.

Karcher, Carolyn L. *The First Woman in the Republic: A Cultural Biography of Lydia Maria Child.* Durham: Duke University Press, 1994.

———. Introduction. *Hobomok and Other Writings on Indians.* By Lydia Maria Child. New Brunswick: Rutgers University Press, 1986. ix–xxxviii.

Pfaelzer, Jean. *Parlor Radical: Rebecca Harding Davis and the Origins of American Social Realism.* Pittsburgh: University of Pittsburgh Press, 1996.

Pizer, Donald, ed. *The Cambridge Companion to American Realism and Naturalism, Howells to London.* Cambridge: Cambridge University Press, 1995.

Silber, Nina. *The Romance of Reunion: Northerners and the South, 1865–1900.* Chapel Hill: University of North Carolina Press, 1993.

Stone, Albert E., Jr. "Best Novel of the Civil War." *American Heritage* June 1962: 84–88.

Wilson, Edmund. *Patriotic Gore: Studies in the Literature of the American Civil War.* 1962. New York: Norton, 1994.

Young, Elizabeth. *Disarming the Nation: Women's Writing and the American Civil War.* Chicago: University of Chicago Press, 1999.

CHAPTER EIGHT

The Unpleasantness at the Chandrapore Club, and the Mayapore Club, and the Jummapur Club

Forster, Scott, and Stoppard and the End of Empire

LAURIE KAPLAN

And everyone at the Club was very friendly, going out of their way to

explain that although they didn't go in much for poetry, they had nothing

against it, so that was all right, dinner was soup, boiled fish, lamb cutlets,

sherry trifle and sardines on toast, and it beats me how we're getting away

with it, darling, I wouldn't trust some of them to run the Hackney *Empire.*

Well, it's all going to end. That's official. I heard it from the horse's mouth—

Flora Crewe, in *Indian Ink*, by Tom Stoppard

In the aftermath of the Great War, the peace of the 1920s and 1930s brought about a peculiar crisis of identity for the British in India. For some Anglo-Indians, a vision of imperial permanence obscured the realities of the Indian political and social landscape, and their sense of complacency seemed a remnant of the nineteenth-century spirit of empire. "The war to end all wars had taken place," the secretary to the governor of Bombay commented, and the general feeling was that "there was not going to be any [more] war, there was not going to be any recession, everything in the garden was lovely and we carried on in India the rather golden tradition we'd learnt at Oxford" (Symington and Symington 2/1).[1] But postwar India was not Oxford, and the colony was showing signs of imminent fracture from Mother England. In the time of peace between the wars, class and race distinctions, ideas about gender and the position of women in the public sphere, even the dominance of the British Empire—all these certainties seemed to be in flux. The peace, in fact, destabilized assumptions and relationships that had seemed so permanent.

From the catastrophes of Mons, Gallipoli, Verdun, the Somme, and Passchendaele a new worldview emerged, one that reached India with the returning soldiers of the British and Indian armies and thereby challenged the established codes of racial segregation. In tacit support of King and Empire, Indian officers had received the King's Commission, worn the King's uniform, and spoken the King's English. Side by side, officers and soldiers of the Indian and British armies had fought in the trenches, and on the battlefields the Indian armies proved themselves brave, efficient, committed to duty, and worthy of the King's Commission. Returning "home" to India from their war postings, the British officers found that they were more like their Indian counterparts in their codes of service and duty than they were different and that they had more in common with these "brother officers" than with their own wives and families who had stayed in India or gone to England for the duration of the war. One British officer described this war-forged phenomenon as simple fact: "[W]e were a family and there is no other word to express our relationship" (Wood and Wood 2/7).

A concept mystical and sacred to warriors, the bond of brother officer to brother officer was strong and compelling. When enlightened British officers interceded to gain access to the clubs for their Indian "brothers," they were first met with resistance, but that resistance vanished when they threatened to withdraw their own troops from membership or their polo ponies from use by the club members. The power of the British officers in effecting a change in a club's constitution, bylaws, and eligibility codes was monumental (Chatterjee 2/5). When the British officers began to demand that their brother officers be admitted to membership, admission of Indian officers with the King's Commission could not be denied by the club functionaries (Vira 2/3). "The British Empire almost split on the subject of Indian membership of clubs," Major-General Wood asserts in an interview about the end of the Raj, and the "'Indianization' of both the civil and military services" helped to bring down the color bar when it was challenged (qtd. in Allen 114).

It is therefore revealing that although the British officers and sahibs tried to break the color bar, the women of the Raj seemed to hold fast to the segregated space that the club offered. The wives who had stayed behind in India throughout the war held entrenched ideas about rank, status, and social hierarchy in the outposts of the empire, and they resisted transformation of the clubs that served as their social space. Some critics describe the "cruel" behaviors of British women toward Indians. Benita Parry, for example, cites "that particular brand of brutality which flourished amongst British females replanted in the colonies" (184). "Coarsened" by lives of "unearned privilege," women in India assumed that they were part of a superior race and "simply did not see [Indians] as human" (78, 184). In the cultural fortress of the British club, women of the Raj fought off new ideas about race and gender relations and "suppressed their intellectual curiosity" (Parry 273). The club remained a corner of a foreign field that was forever imperial England.

The postwar process of integration of the historically segregated clubs mirrors the complexity of the Independence movement itself. To admit Indians into the rarefied circle of membership in English clubs would be to suggest that "'Englishness' may be an acquired characteristic, a matter of culture, not color" (Gorra 2). At risk for the British was their idea of their own cultural identity, their sense of hierarchy and power, their concept of ceremony and ritual in exile; at risk for the Indians was their dignity in the face of prejudice and what Paul Scott calls the "studied insult" and the "social rebuff" (*Jewel* 167–68), their discomfort in seeming to condone the social power of the English, and their own cultural identity, which they would appear to give up if they were to conform to the rules and regulations of the imperialists.

In literary works that focus on the interwar years, the private clubs, emblematic of the idea of empire and the colonial experience in India, carry the weight of British values in transition. The literary image of the club is iconic: membership suggests codes of English gentlemanly and ladylike conduct; the architecture conjures images of graciousness, stability, and permanence; the rooms convey the social distance and exclusivity of a superior caste. The clubs stand, in literature as well as in fact, as microcosms of the transforming state. E. M. Forster, Paul Scott, and Tom Stoppard are

British writers who have analyzed the symbol of the club and its meaning in the Indian landscape. Forster's *Passage to India*, Scott's multivolume *Raj Quartet*, and Stoppard's play *Indian Ink* examine how cultural and social networks hold the Raj together even when it is beginning to dismantle itself. Each writer spent part of his life in India: Forster first traveled to India in 1912 and then returned to work as secretary to the Maharaja of Dewas; Scott served in the British Army in India during World War II and subsequently returned after the war ended; Stoppard, who had been born in Czechoslovakia and then lived in Singapore before it fell to the Japanese, grew up in India before moving to England as a young adult. The authors use the iconography of the club and the formality of its codes to dissect an arrogant society too sure of its imperial power and its hierarchical position to notice that things are changing around it. Although an essence of nostalgia or sentimentality infuses these literary works—nostalgia not for the Raj, but rather, it seems, for the culture, the people, and the landscape of India— they reveal the ugly tensions, prejudices, and discriminatory values that shaped the time of peace between the wars.

The transition to integrated clubs posed complicated problems in a society where segregation by class, rank, occupation, gender, and race had been meticulously observed for generations. Gentlemen's clubs were by their very nature stodgy and representational: they signified "English life all over again: nothing strange, nothing exotic, nothing new or original" (Vira 2/3). Usually the clubs were "owned by [their] members and restricted in membership" in terms of occupation, rank, and class (Allen 258). Men had to be elected by the other members; they had to conform to written and unwritten codes of behavior. The members supported the club through subscriptions, and in return the club offered the British gentleman and his guests a convivial meeting place, a library of sorts, playing fields for tennis, golf, and polo, and a social arena where civilian and military families could mix and dance and play cards. Limited as it was to perhaps two or three or four British couples at one small civil station like Chandrapore *(A Passage to India)* or Mayapore *(The Raj Quartet)* or Jummapur *(Indian Ink)*, and confined by rules proscribing any real mix of race and class, Anglo-Indian club life was often unrelentingly dull, monotonous, and repetitious. In a description that replicates the literary representations of club life, Iris Portal, the daughter of a provincial governor and the wife of an Indian Army officer, recollects that "we were a small community continually re-meeting each other" (3/26).

Membership lists from clubs in the years between the wars reveal the composition of the clubs' societies. By the early 1930s, integration of the membership had become a fact. A partial List of Members at the Allahabad Club in October, 1934, for example, reveals that "few Indians and fewer women" were members (Allen 112–13). Paul Scott's *The Jewel in the Crown* provides a glimpse into the Gymkhana Club's administrative history when Mr. Srinivasan, who served as the first Indian secretary of the club (from 1947 to 1950), shows his English companion the membership book for the years 1939–45:

> If you look through the pages you will see the signatures of one or two Indian members. But they were of course all officers who held the King-Emperor's commission. . . . The committee were in rather a quandary when King's commissioned Indian officers first began to show up in Mayapore. It was always accepted that any officer on the station should automatically become a member. Indeed it was compulsory for him to pay his subscription whether he ever entered the place or not. And you could not keep him out if he was an Indian because that would have been to insult the King's uniform. (179)

Major-General Wood offers the following example of club integration when his battalion was sent from the hill station in Jakarta to Dacca (Bangladesh):

> There was a club, a[n] . . . entirely civilian membership as there was no garrison in Dacca, and 25 British Officers appeared. . . . But with us was an Indian King's Commissioned Officer, a Sikh. . . . [T]he local civilians came to our Commanding Officer and said they were terribly sorry, they were in a very awkward position, but the rules [of] the Club were absolutely adamant that nobody . . . except a British member could join. . . . [T]hey therefore much regretted that the Indian Officer serving with us would not be eligible as a member. My Commanding Officer, very rightly and very promptly, said in that case no officer of my regiment can be a member of your club. Lt. Rujinara Singh holds His Majesty's Commission and he will be a member or none of us will. . . . [T]he Dacca Club . . . could not refuse club membership to their defenders, and they yielded without question. (Wood and Wood 2/4–2/5)

Paul Scott recapitulates this scene in *The Jewel in the Crown*. Mr. Srinivasan recounts the quasi-mythical story of the Viceroy Lord Willingdon, who founded his own club in Bombay "in a fit of rage because the Indian guests he invited—in ignorance—to a private banquet at the Royal Yacht club were turned away from the doors in their Rolls-Royces" (172). Mr. Srinivasan's story suggests, perhaps, that powerful men in the larger cities could act on their new ideas about integration; they did not have to wait for the minor functionaries of the small clubs in remote civil stations to open the doors of the clubs to nonwhites.

Tom Stoppard in *Indian Ink* provides a look at a club in a small Native State where segregation is still a fact of membership in the period between the wars. Set in two locales and two time periods—1930 (India) and the 1980s (England and India)—this play takes up the themes of "Indianization," equality, accommodation, and change. When, as assistant to the resident magistrate, Captain Durance offers an honorary membership in the Jummapur Club to Flora Crewe, a poet visiting from England, and escorts her to the Saturday night dinner dance, the scene is set for cultural comedy. "There are not so many British here so we tend to mix more," he tells her (52). "With the Indians?" she asks. "No. In India proper, I mean *our* India," he replies, "there'd be two or three Clubs. The box-wallahs would have their own and the government people would stick together, you know how it is—and the Army . . ." The idea of "mixing" at the club means that British Army and British civilians interact. Indeed, the members of the Jummapur Club believe that they have lowered the membership bar: they include not only British civilians but BOR (British Other Ranks) as well.

In *The Jewel in the Crown*, Mr. Srinivasan, who functions as Scott's commentator on imperial history, relates how World War II generated another kind of problem with "mixing," but his focus is both racial and class bound:

> It wasn't until the war began and the station began to fill up not only with a larger number of Indian King's commissioned officers but also with English officers holding emergency commissions that the committee actually had to pass a *rule*. . . . [T]he new officers were not only holders of temporary commissions but tended to be temporary in themselves, I mean liable to posting at almost any time. And of course among them there were likely to be men called up from all walks of civilian life, men of the type who, well, wouldn't be at home in the

atmosphere of the club. And so for once the committee found themselves thinking of ways of keeping out some of their own countrymen
as well as Indians. We, who were not eligible, watched all this from the
sidelines with great interest. (180)

Scott's panoramic social comedy, set in the last years of the Raj, re-
verses the imperial gaze: the Indians see how the exclusionary codes of the
British clubs can be turned against the not-quite-pukka British soldiers. As
Michael Gorra points out, "Scott had a Balzacian delight in describing the
rules that allowed the Raj to function as a social machine" (33). The rules,
the etiquette, and the protocol become "the wheels and gears that run a club
or a regimental mess" and maintain the aura of superiority.

In *Indian Ink*, Tom Stoppard gives Flora, the outsider—and a woman—
an opportunity to express not only her confusion about the rigid rules
guarding club membership but also her thinly veiled disgust at the exclu-
sions. Flora reflects attitudes like those expressed by Daphne Manners and
Sarah Leighton in *The Raj Quartet*; these women stand in direct opposition
not only to Forster's Adela Quested and the other ladies of the Chandrapore
Club set but also to the women of the Mayapore Club. Flora, Daphne, and
Sarah all like India and the Indian people. Flora intuitively understands her
ambiguous place as "a carnival float representing Empire—or, depending
how you look at it, the Subjugation of the Indian People" (4), but she also
asserts that "it's not for me to apologize for the Raj" (35). She even accuses
the cautious artist Nirad Das of "*deserv[ing]* the bloody Empire" (43) for
kowtowing to the idea of British artistic superiority.

Stoppard's critique of racial segregation forms part of the subtext of the
play, and he shows the absurdity of the exclusionary/inclusionary membership rules. When Durance tells Flora about one of the "Juniors"—that is, an
Indian officer who serves as second in service to the resident magistrate—
he also forecasts the effect of "I-zation," the codeword, as he explains to
Flora, for

Durance: Indianization. It's all over, you know. We have Indian officers
in the Regiment now. My fellow Junior here is Indian, too, terribly nice
chap—he's ICS, passed the exam, did his year at Cambridge, learned
polo and knives-and-forks, and here he is, a pukkah sahib in the Indian
Civil Service.
Flora: Is he here?

Durance: At the Club? No, he can't come into the Club.
Flora: Oh. (53)

What is obvious to both Flora and Durance is the fact that the "acquired" Englishness of this young officer undercuts what Gorra identifies as "the belief in an absolute distinction between England and India, in a racialized model of cultural identity and authenticity" (3). By the time the Jummapur Club opens to Indians, Captain Durance is dead, "killed at Kohima in March 1944 when British and Indian troops halted the advance of the Japanese forces" (78). Flora is dead too and buried in India.

Forster began writing *A Passage to India* before the Great War, and the book was published in 1924, in a period of peace that was also a period of Anglo-Indian social unrest. "Mosque," the first section of the novel, opens with a view of Chandrapore and its environs, the landmarks of which are iconographic. The signifiers of empire are the oval Maidan, the hospital, the railway station, the "little civil station," the gardens that turn Chandrapore into "a tropical pleasance washed by a noble river," and the "red-brick club" (4–5). The second chapter of "Mosque" shows Dr. Aziz's circumscribed places in the Indian and British social hierarchy and the lack of dignity accorded him by British men and women. The third part of the triptych provides a split setting: spiritual space (the mosque) and social space (the club). Here Dr. Aziz adumbrates one of the exclusionary social codes: "Indians," he tells Mrs. Moore when she apologizes for not inviting him to accompany her from the holy Indian space to the socially consecrated British space, "are not allowed into the Chandrapore Club even as guests" (21–22).

Forster provides only a vague description of the Chandrapore Club, but the implicit solidity of the "red-brick" building is symbolic. Serving as an immutable setting for British diversions, a center of English society, and the locus of regulated, "civilized" behavior for a displaced race, the Chandrapore Club exudes universal messages about the codes of imperial deportment. It is part of Forster's satire, therefore, to bring the reader into the club just as the British are letting down their hair and enacting the frothy comedy *Cousin Kate.* Since the focus here is the dignity of the actors (especially the dignity of the women), the "[w]indows were barred, lest the servants should see their mem-sahibs acting" (22). The absurdity of the whole scene is ratcheted up a notch by the formality of the evening's closing rituals: "[T]he amateur orchestra played the National Anthem. Conversation and billiards stopped, faces stiffened. It was the Anthem of the Army of Occupation. It reminded every member of the club that he or she was British and in exile" (24). The ironic proximity of these two dramatic enterprises—the silliness of the light comedy fusing with the emotional tenor of the anthem—suggests the instability of the space: the club resonates with comic as well as nationalistic potential, with sentimental reminders of England and empire, and with images of white solidarity, all of which haunt the rest of the novel.

The terseness of Forster's description of the red-brick club suggests an entrenched, recognizable, and permanent social order. Beetling on the brow of the hill, the club, an imperial icon, seems architecturally indiscreet. David Cannadine notes that throughout the empire many of the ubiquitous gentlemen's clubs of the nineteenth century "[were] constructed in Scottish Baronial or Gothic Revival style redolent of history, antiquity, hierarchy and tradition" (34), but the Chandrapore Club, in its very vagueness and generality, its lack of particularity, refers, perhaps, to the mid-Victorian stodginess of Victorian England—even suggesting a place like Coketown in Dickens's *Hard Times*. Gorra points out that the lack of "any trace of contemporary reference made Forster's Raj seem incapable of change, and in consequence *A Passage to India* appears to float in time" (29). While the historical connotations are broad and ambivalent, the Chandrapore Club is obviously linked through its evocative red bricks to the British historical past and the glory days of the imperialistic vision.

"Caves," the second section of *A Passage to India*, begins and ends with scenes at the club. The circular structure of "Caves," with the ill-starred visit to the mystical Marabar Hills and the tragic return to Chandrapore, serves as a comment on the British experience in India. Not only does this section of the novel focus on the disastrous results of "mixing," but it also serves to replay in miniature the journey out, the incursion "up the country," and the return home.

As "Caves" begins, Miss Quested sits on the upper verandah of the club, and her view includes the hills that "look romantic in certain lights and at suitable distances" (138). Because Miss Quested can appreciate a view only when it is at a distance, she initiates the tragic consequences that Forster sees as the result of premature cultural mixing. She is overheard expressing regret that the outing to the Marabar Caves that Dr. Aziz promised to arrange has never materialized. Making a sweeping generalization—

"Indians seem rather forgetful"—she racializes her opinions. Passed along by one of the servants at the club to Dr. Aziz, her comments "accreted emotion" (139), and the echoes of discontent that spread outward from the Chandrapore Club must gather for a final bellow. It is therefore apt that at the end of this middle section, after the debacle at the Marabar Caves, after the trial, and after Miss Quested has departed for England, the British of Chandrapore once again collect themselves at the club. This pattern also replicates circular movement—but the "return" here shows how the social net has disintegrated in the wake of the "rape" and the trial. Post-tragedy, the club draws the British together as a group, but the community is depleted, and the remaining British officials seem conscious that their identity has changed.

Fielding's requested "official appearance" at the Chandrapore Club turns out to be a final performance in aid of imperialism. Fielding attends "the grim little function," but he finds that the "skeletons of hospitality rattled. . . . [T]he more the club changed, the more it promised to be the same thing" (306–7). The "new"-ness of some of the members signals transitions, but as Fielding leaves the club and walks past the mosque—reversing Mrs. Moore's journey from the mosque to the club—he reflects on the fact that "the more modern the country gets, the worse'll be the crash." His return to England shortly after this unpleasant scene at the club underscores the spirit of recrimination that has infected the British community.

Forster dramatizes the thesis that the cross-cultural friendships that ground the novel are premature in this postwar period. "Alas," Dr. Aziz tells Mrs. Moore's son, "the two nations cannot be friends" (349). Nature seems to agree: "'No, not yet,' and the sky said, 'No, not there'" (362). As Benita Parry notes, "[T]he last pages of A Passage to India [are] thick with symbols and omens of reconciliation, fertilization and salvation, and of their opposites, divisions, death and annihilated human hopes" (316). It would take another war to shift the relative spaces inhabited by the Europeans and the Indians.

The clubs depicted in British novels and plays that are set during the period between World War I and Independence provide a vivid backdrop for dramatizations of social transition, and the clubs' trappings generate an iconography replete with conflicting meanings for both the imperialist and the colonized. The drama involves the ways club members' prewar consciousness of their own elevated position in the social hierarchy gives way in the postwar period of peace to social and political insecurity. With war as the catalyst for change, the club symbolizes the transformation of Raj into a meritocracy and later into a democracy. Although the native soldiers "earned" their equality of status earned through war service and meticulous attention to duty, not every British subject in India would agree that "earning" a position was enough to warrant membership in a closed society. Paul Scott's Mr. Srinivasan is canny enough to acknowledge that "[a]n Indian who sought and obtained a commission knew what problems he was likely to encounter" (*Jewel* 180) when he tried to join a club, and even if an officer holding the King's Commission could not be blackballed, the unpleasantness that emanated from the membership might be enough to keep him away.

Forster's Chandrapore Club, Stoppard's Jummapur Club, and Scott's Mayapore Club evoke a sense of claustrophobia and conformity, but the clubs also symbolize social attainment. In literature, the exclusive clubs provide spaces where histories—public and private, personal and political—collide and where the comic, nationalistic, patronizing, snobbish, and cruel overlap. The little worlds of the clubs mirror the narrow minds of the one-dimensional members—"men and women burdened by massive social pressures and crippled by tight emotional restraints" (Parry 273–74). The regulated spaces of the clubs offer protection against the exoticism and sensuality of India itself. Characters go to lengths to avoid compromising positions that could result in gossip—and everyone gossips. In an interview collected in *Plain Tales from the Raj*, Lady Rosamund Lawrence, the wife of an ICS district officer and governor, commented on the endemic nature of gossip in a circumscribed community where "somebody's wife [was] going after somebody's husband, or vice versa" (10). Note that in *A Passage to India* Ronny Heaslop and Adela Quested conform to the community's expectations about correct behavior as they go to extraordinary lengths to avoid gossip. Similarly, in *Indian Ink*, Durance remains very conscious of the way gossip can affect his career: as they sit on the verandah of the club, Durance cautions Flora, "We'll have to go inside in a minute if no one comes out." He conforms to club rules because "[t]here's nothing to do here except gossip" (53). Since Flora's reputation has preceded her—she is, after all, a poet—Durance deems it necessary to be extra careful about what the ladies inside the club might think.

Literary representations of scenes in the British clubs in India seem timeless, to the extent that Paul Scott's *Raj Quartet* and Stoppard's *Indian Ink* depict social evenings that nearly replicate Forster's in their specifics as well as their peculiarities. Rigid rules safeguard club members against the unknown, against the fear that India itself arouses in them (Parry 279). If in prewar India the clubs were venues for graphic racial and class-bound insults and for rejection based on race and class, in the postwar world the clubs test characters' acceptance of new realities, and the snubs become more insidious.

One of the new realities is the position of women. As Margaret Mac-Millan says in *Women of the Raj*, "When the Club first began to assume a central position, in the nineteenth century, women were not allowed to use it except on special occasions. By the twentieth century, however, most had capitulated and accepted women as members, a recognition perhaps of their role in supporting the Raj" (52). The memsahibs—the ladies of the Raj—are credited by some social historians as being "remembered with praise, sympathy, and only a little censure" (Hubel 53–54); they seem to be "emblems of stability" to some contemporary critics. But perhaps "emblems of stability" carries retrogressive implications. To novelists like E. M. Forster and Paul Scott, for example, it is primarily the women who abide by old traditions of the empire: in club settings, women are rude, snobbish, class-bound, peremptory, and bitter about the changes they cannot control. It is as though in the peaceful period between the wars the women have little to do except gossip and meddle in others' affairs.

Hence, with Flora, Daphne, and Sarah as obvious exceptions to the rule, women and their attitudes toward the "natives" and "real India" are often shown in literary works as increasingly negative and destructive. Dr. Aziz agrees with his friends' generalization "that all Englishwomen are haughty and venal" (9); Durance tells Flora, "I'll tell you where it all went wrong with us and India. It was the Suez Canal. It let the women in. . . . When you had to sail round the Cape this was a man's country and we mucked in with the natives. The memsahibs put a stop to that. The memsahib won't muck in, won't even be alone in a room with an Indian" (56). And Paul Scott's depiction of women in the post-Independence era is perhaps most disturbing in its implication of prejudice and bitterness:

The women have plump, mottled arms, and wear sleeveless cotton shifts. Without the knitted cardigans you feel they would put on at home of an evening over these summer dresses they have a peeled, boiled look. They are young. They sit together—opposite their husbands—an act of involuntary segregation that by now is probably

becoming familiar to the Indians as they get used to a new race of sahibs and memsahibs from Stevenage and Luton but may still puzzle
them when they recollect how critical the old style British were of the
Indian habit keeping men and women so well separated that a mixed
party was almost more than an English host and hostess could bear to
contemplate. (*Jewel* 173)

In subtle and not-so-subtle ways, Forster, Scott, and Stoppard also ne-
gate these views of women's intransigence. Characters like Mrs. Moore in *A
Passage to India*, Daphne Manners and Sarah Layton in *The Jewel in the
Crown*, and Flora in *Indian Ink* violate not only social codes but also, in
some cases, sexual taboos.

Transformation of the Anglo-Indian clubs from private domains to more
democratic venues thus symbolizes the end of the Great War and imperial
domination, and integration of the clubs serves to underscore the idea (if
not the reality) of post–World War II peaceful co-existence and brotherhood of men. In *The Jewel in the Crown,* the first book of *The Raj Quartet,*
Paul Scott devotes part 4 to "An Evening at the Club," a chapter that becomes a nonlinear projection and recapitulation of the theme of integration
and racial mixing that structures the whole quartet of novels. This chapter
provides a scathing critique of British attitudes toward India and Indians.
The nonlinear progression of the text allows Scott the freedom to excavate
the symbol of the club in terms of codes of behavior, prejudices, biases, and
new ideas that run concurrently with the transformation of the country
from colonial dependence to Independence. Scott's *Quartet* spans the interwar period, but the novels focus more specifically on life in India during
and after World War II, on the making of the peace, on the final negotiations for Independence, and on post-Independence social confusion.

In "An Evening at the Club," Scott splits the time frame into two parts,
1942 and 1964, using the past—the "old"—to contrast with images of the
"new":

Between Banyanganj and Mayapore there are to be found the modern
labour-saving, white-washed, concrete homes of the *new* British colony, and then, closer in to the town still, the *old* British-Indian Electrical factory, *newly* extended but still controlled by British capital. From

the British-Indian Electrical the traveler who knew Mayapore in the *old* days and came in by air would find himself on more familiar ground as he passed in succession, the red-brick Mayapore Technical College which was founded and endowed by Sir Nello Chatterjee, and the cream-stucco Government Higher School.

Going from the cantonment bazaar which is still the fashionable shopping centre of Mayapore, along the Mahatma Gandhi road, once styled Victoria road, the traveler will pass the main police barracks on his left and then, on his right, the Court House. . . . Beyond the chummery, on both sides of the road, there are other bungalows whose style and look of spaciousness mark them also as relics of the British days. . . . If you turn left, that is to say west, and travel along Club road you arrive eventually at the Gymkhana. Both the club and hospital buildings can be seen distantly from the T-junction of the *old* Victoria, Hospital and Club roads. And it is along Club road, facing the maidan, that the bungalow of the Deputy Commissioner is still to be found, in walled, arboreal seclusion. (161–62; emphasis added)

Exploring a landscape and signage that has changed radically while it has hardly changed at all, Scott emphasizes how "British" India itself has adapted to, but has never really accepted the implications of, the peace. As the chapter progresses, the English narrator fixes his gaze on the inhabitants of the landscape, on an "Indian middle class" strolling out and enjoying

the comparative cool of the evening. . . . There is a hush, a sense emanating from those taking the air of their—well, yes, a sense of their what? Of their self-consciousness at having overstepped some ancient, invisible mark? Or is this a sense conveyed only to an Englishman, as a result of his residual awareness of a racial privilege now officially extinct, so that, borne clubwards at the invitation of a Brahmin lawyer, on a Saturday evening, driven by a Muslim chauffeur in the company of a Rajput lady, through the quickly fading light that holds lovely old Mayapore suspended between the day and the dark, bereft of responsibility and therefore of any sense of dignity . . . caught up by his own people's history and the thrust of a current that simply would not wait for them wholly to comprehend its force, he may then sentimentally recall, in passing, that the maidan was once sacrosanct to the Civil and Military, and respond, fleetingly, to the tug of a vague generalized regret that the maidan no longer looks as it did once, when at this time of day it was empty of all but a few late riders cantering homewards. (162–63)

Scott evokes the past and the present, and there is an aura here of historical troubles. On the way to the club, the car passes through iconic civic spaces or by symbolic imperial monuments—the police barracks, the courthouse, the hospital, and, eventually, the Gymkhana Club. Scott's irony gains momentum as he delicately describes the cricket, the flower show on the maidan, and, finally, the elite lounge bar at the club, where Lady Chatterjee and her English guest feel oppressed by the snobbish and racially charged atmosphere. It is 1964, and the young white members of the club do not want to "mix" with the Indians or see the "real India." The room is redolent with resentment.

In the post–World War II/post-Independence world of *The Raj Quartet*, Scott's classic club, with its verandahs and views, attitudinizing and snubs, shows how little this interior space has changed since Forster's memsahibs acted out *Cousin Kate* or since Mr. Fielding fled in disgust from the Chandrapore Club. But the extended scope of these interrelated novels also allows Scott the freedom to anatomize microscopically not only the architectural space but also the public and private characters and their places in imperial history. Perusing the lounge bar of the Gymkhana Club, the English narrator finds the club appallingly retrogressive: "The servants still wear white turbans beribboned to match the wide sashes that nip in the waists of their knee-length white coats. White trousers flap baggily above their bare brown feet, and stir old memories of padding docile service" (*Jewel* 165). The narrator is perfectly aware of the rudeness and incivility with which the English "ladies," "for want of simple politeness," allow "*lacunae*" to develop and to engulf Lady Chatterjee and her English companion. "There is nothing so inwardly clear as social rebuff—" the narrator notes, "a rebuff which in this case is also directed at the stranger because he has arrived with one Indian as the guest of another" (168).

The dining room of the club, with its "absence of beef, the omnipresence of mutton" (172), resonates with implicit commentary about the history of imperialism in India:

It is a square room, with a black and white tiled floor, and walls paneled in oak to shoulder height, and white-washed above. Three square pillars, similarly paneled to the same height, support the ceiling at apparently random but presumable strategic points. There are something like a score of tables, some round, some rectangular, each with its white starched cloth, its electro-plated cutlery and condiment tray, its mitred napkins, its slim chromium flower vase holding a couple of asters, its glass jug filled with water and protected by a weighted muslin cover. There is a large Tudor-style fireplace whose black cavity is partly hidden by a framed tapestry screen. Above the fireplace there is a portrait of Mr. Nehru looking serene in a perplexed sort of way. One can assume that when Daphne Manners dined here the frame contained a coloured likeness of George VI wearing a similar expression. (173–74)

Scott's detailing technique includes a subversive particularity of description: if for Forster the general suggests the specific, for Scott the specific reveals the universal. The dining room of the club in Mayapore is the dining room of all clubs; the mixture of pride and prejudice displayed by the members is redolent of the racial attitudes displayed by members of other clubs. Scott's explicitness highlights the "black and white" of the tiles and the "white-wash" of the walls and seems to suggest racial overtones in the construction of the rooms. His subsequent description of the swimming pool at the club is devastating in its implications: the pool, Mr. Srinivasan points out, "is seldom used because it is open to all and neither race seems particularly to fancy the idea of using it when it can't be guaranteed that the person last using it was clean. There is a story that two or three years ago an Englishman emptied all the chamber pots from the ablution cubicles into it" (174). Four pages later Mr. Srinivasan completes this story. He reveals that the English "horseplay" also included the "making of a little Diwali, a parody of our festival lights. So they got hold of some candles and stuck them into the pots and lighted them and set them afloat" (178). Scott allows Mr. Srinivasan's eloquence to stand as an indictment of English boorishness, of imperial racism.

Paul Scott excavates with exquisite precision the whole texture of a hyphenated society perched on the edge of enormous changes. From the first mention of "the club" on the first page of the *Quartet*, from the first mention of "rape" on that same page, Anglo-India simmers in tensions arising from clashes of race, class, occupation, and gender. In 1964, the year the unnamed English visitor is taken by Lady Chatterjee to meet with Mr. Srinivasan at the Gymkhana Club, in a period of peace years after the chaos of Independence and the horrors of Partition, the British in India have been marginalized. In the integrated clubs, however, the British still snub the Indian members; they barely contain their race-consciousness, and they indulge in destructive "horseplay" that mocks the Indians' spiritual life.

Like Scott, Tom Stoppard uses a split time frame to develop his critique of imperial and colonial attitudes.[2] Stoppard sets part of *Indian Ink* at the Jummapur Club in 1930, but to point up the ways things have changed/not changed in the microcosm of the club he allows 1930 to meld into the 1980s, a period of relative peace compared with the 1990s, when racial tensions flared in England and in India (Burton 227). As the scenes merge, the new dramatic situation reflects the past. It is half a century later, and Pike, an American, and Dilip, an Indian, are locked in a kind of postcolonial foxtrot. The two young men, both university professors, have gone to Dilip's club—the same Jummapur Club—where Pike, boorish and provincial, discovers that the dress codes of the past still hold in the present. Dilip is "smartly dressed in a jacket and tie" (48), but Pike, who is underdressed for the dining room, must borrow a jacket and a tie or be turned away at the door. Dilip manages to find a jacket for Pike—"The jacket is a faded beige gabardine with metal buttons, the skimpy jacket of a servant. On the breast, however, not instantly apparent, is a short strip of grimy campaign ribbons"; the tie, however, "is tip-top, Jummapur Cricket Club" (49). Dilip must act as Pike's guide, supervising the socially clumsy American and explaining the codes of correct behavior. Pike's ridiculous outfit is matched by his own outrageous behavior—for example, later in the play Pike asks the Rajah of Jummapur if "*Namaste*" is his "Christian name"; "I am not Christian," the Rajah replies, "I was just saying goodbye" (66)—but the situational irony is deepened by Dilip's announcement that he has borrowed the jacket from "an Old Soldier," a "Subadar, B Company, 6th Rajputana Rifles," who is now "in charge of supervising the cloakroom" (50).

Obviously comfortable with the trappings of the Raj, Dilip has become an inheritor of the past. He feels perfectly at home at the Jummapur Club: "*this* was the place in the old days when the palace was still the private residence of the rajah," he tells Pike excitedly (51). But it is the Old Soldier who brings this examination of the British club full circle. Mr. Ram Sunil Singh was a small boy in 1930 when he worked as Flora's "punkah wallah." He served with distinction in World War II—Dilip points out to Pike that Mr. Ram Sunil Singh has earned the 1939–45 service ribbon and the Burma Star. By the 1980s, however, Mr. Ram Sunil Singh "is without one leg. He has no sons. He has three daughters, two of them unmarried and to marry the

third he sold his army pension and secured for himself a job which is clean-
ing toilets. Tomorrow . . . [w]e can take a cup of tea together on the *maidan*
and talk of old times" (50). This spiral of descent may suggest one of Stoppard's themes: the post-Independence world offers few rewards for the servants of the empire, for the men who had earned the King's Commission
and had worn the King's uniform.

Interviewed about the integration of clubs in the period between the
wars, Raj Chatterjee, a manager with Imperial Tobacco India, described
the elite Peshawar Club as "the last bastion of British club life," yet even the
membership committee of the Peshawar Club could be persuaded that "integration" was in their own interest:

> It just would not take Indians. . . . Then came to Peshawar a Cavalry
> Regiment, and I think it was the 7th Light Cavalry. Rather an odd Col-
> onel. A man called Julian de Wilton. And he said "Look, either you take
> my Indian Officers or my British Officers will not join your club." So
> they ignored him. . . . [The Colonel said] "Alright then. You will not
> have my horses for your Vale Hunt," which was really the mainstay of
> the Peshawar Club. . . . So they hurriedly called a meeting, an extraor-
> dinary general meeting, and they changed the constitution or bylaw or
> whatever it is, and that was that. Indians started coming in. Oddly
> enough, thirty years later Julian de Wilton's son, Geoffrey de Wilton,
> was my assistant the last year of my service with the [Imperial Tobacco]
> company. (2/5)

Admission of the brother officers into the clubs in the years of peace
following the Great War was the thin edge of the wedge—the prelude to Independence. India had lost 680,000 men in the trenches of the 1914–18 European conflict; in the two decades that followed, Indians began to fill the
ranks of both the civil service and the officer corps (Collins and Lapierre
19). It seems fitting, then, that in August 1947, in preparation for Partition
and the end of the Raj, the Imperial Delhi Gymkhana Club—"an institution
that once had been one of the most privileged sanctuaries of India's British
rulers"—was the scene of what Larry Collins and Dominique Lapierre describe as the "most touching farewell of all" (288). "The Officers of the
Armed Forces of the Dominion of India" invited as their guests for a final
evening of nostalgia "the Officers of the Armed Forces of the Dominion of
Pakistan": "With their well-trimmed moustaches, their Sam Browne belts,

their British uniforms and the rows of decorations they had won risking their lives in the service of India's British rulers, the men mingling under the lantern chains all seemed to have been pressed from the same mould" (288). At the end of the evening, before the singing of "Auld Lang Syne," Brigadier Cariappa said au revoir to the mixed gathering of Moslems and Hindus collected together in the grand ballroom: "We have been brothers. We will always remain brothers. And we shall never forget the great years we have lived together" (289).

With the declaration of Indian Independence in 1947, with the consequent partition of India, and with the withdrawal of the British from the empire they had inhabited for centuries—a withdrawal that seemed terribly abrupt, even though the idea of "quit India" had been uppermost in the minds of the Anglo-Indians for decades—the postcolonial period of integration and reconciliation became even more complex and unstable. The end of the Raj brought indescribable religious and cultural violence to the former colony. Paul Scott describes vividly the political and social tension accompanying the fall of the Raj on the first page of *The Jewel in the Crown*: the centuries of subjugation of the Indian people coupled with the radical new ideas permeating the modern consciousness in the interwar period exploded with "the spectacle of two nations"—India and England—"in violent opposition, not for the first time nor as yet for the last because they were then still locked in an imperial embrace of such long standing and subtlety it was no longer possible for them to know whether they hated or loved one another, or what it was that held them together and seemed to have confused the image of their separate destinies" (3).

NOTES

1. This interview transcript is included in the oral archive "Plain Tales from the Raj." The audiotapes are held by the Imperial War Museum, London. For the transcribed materials from this source I have corrected misspellings and edited out the verbal tics (e.g., "er") that the typist has included in the transcriptions.

2. Correlations between Scott's *Quartet* and Stoppard's radio play *In the Native State* and the stage play *Indian Ink* have been noted by other critics. In "India, Inc.?" Antoinette Burton writes: "Critics writing about the play rushed to pigeon-hole it as a Stoppardesque equivalent of *The Jewel in the Crown*, and so to reiterate what were, by the time the BBC aired *In the Native State* in 1991, the familiar lineaments of the Raj nostalgia syndrome. Stoppard was as aware of the appetite the British public

displayed for rehearsals of the Raj's glory as he was of the fact that the subject was in danger of exhausting its appeal" (226).

Works Cited

Allen, Charles, ed. *Plain Tales from the Raj: Images of British India in the Twentieth Century*. 1975. Calcutta: Rupa, 1992. A selection from the complete tapes and transcripts of the BBC recording series.

Burton, Antoinette. "India, Inc.? Nostalgia, Memory and the Empire of Things." *British Culture and the End of Empire*. Ed. Stuart Ward. Manchester: Manchester University Press, 2001.

Cannadine, David. *Ornamentalism: How the British Saw Their Empire*. London: Penguin, 2001.

Chatterjee, Raj. Interview. "Plain Tales from the Raj," cat. no. IWM 004914/04.

Collins, Larry, and Dominique Lapierre. *Freedom at Midnight*. 1975. London: Harper-Collins, 1982.

Forster, E. M. *A Passage to India*. 1924. San Diego: Harcourt Brace, 1984.

Gorra, Michael. *After Empire: Scott, Naipaul, Rushdie*. Chicago: University of Chicago Press, 1997.

Hubel, Teresa. *Whose India?* Durham: Duke University Press, 1996.

Lawrence, Lady (Rosamund). Interview. "Plain Tales from the Raj," cat. no. IWM 004938/83.

MacMillan, Margaret. *Women of the Raj*. 1988. London: Thames and Hudson, 1996.

Parry, Benita. *Delusions and Discoveries: Studies on India in the British Imagination, 1880–1930*. Berkeley: University of California Press, 1972.

"Plain Tales from the Raj." Interviews conducted by Charles Allen et al. and recorded by the British Broadcasting Corporation. Oral archive, cassette tapes and transcripts, 1972–74. Imperial War Museum, London. Accompanying catalog of holdings, *Plain Tales from the Raj: A Catalogue of the BBC Recordings* (London: India Office Library and Records, 1981).

Portal, Iris. Interview. "Plain Tales from the Raj," cat. no. IWM 004952/07.

Scott, Paul. *The Jewel in the Crown*. Vol. 1 of *The Raj Quartet*. 1976. Chicago: University of Chicago Press, 1998.

———. *The Raj Quartet*. 1976. Chicago: University of Chicago Press, 1998.

Stoppard, Tom. *Indian Ink*. London: Faber and Faber, 1995.

Symington, David, and Anne Ellen Symington. Interview. "Plain Tales from the Raj," cat. no. IWM 004963/05.

Vira, Dharma. Interview. "Plain Tales from the Raj," cat. no. IWM 004965/03.

Wood, George, and Mary Wood. Interview. "Plain Tales from the Raj," cat. no. IWM 004972/08.

CHAPTER NINE

Community and Harmony in Charlotte Eilenberg's Post-Holocaust Play *The Lucky Ones*

CLAIRE TYLEE

A map of the world that does not include Utopia is not worth even glancing at.

Oscar Wilde, *The Soul of Man under Socialism*

At the end of the twentieth century, Britain celebrated the fiftieth anniversary of VE Day (the end of World War II in Europe in 1945), and in 2002 the Queen's Golden Jubilee, fifty years since her accession. It is ironic that this public nationalism should, rather than uniting the nation, reinforce a sense of alienation for many Britons.[1] Charlotte Eilenberg's debut play *The Lucky Ones*, premiered in London in 2002, chose to recall a different set of anniversaries, one that stressed sources of conflict both within Britain and between Britain and other parts of the world. In 1968, when the play opens, thirty years after Kristallnacht and British efforts to save European Jewish children through the Kindertransport scheme,[2] Britain faced another influx of refugees fleeing a tyrant, this time Kenyan Asians (to be shortly followed by Ugandan Asians). In that year Enoch Powell's notorious anti-immigration speech "Rivers of Blood" triggered a furious debate about British national identity, racial prejudice, and refugees.[3] Eilenberg specifically recalls that controversy, at a time when it was flaring again over asylum seekers from Afghanistan. Her play raises to the surface the anti-German prejudice fostered by so much twentieth-century British culture—literary, dramatic, cinematic, musical—to the detriment of the descendants of the very prewar refugees Britain had already rescued.

Most of Britain's major artists have been involved in the production of enduring texts concerning the two world wars, alongside the more ephemeral output of popular culture and reinforced by officially sponsored works. These texts, which help promote an ideology of national identity, continue not only to entertain but also to indoctrinate. The power of such wartime propaganda and stereotyping, particularly as perpetuated through films, has tended to ossify ideas and attitudes, fifty or even seventy-five years later, that are incompatible with racial harmony and peace between nations. Even postwar films continue to demonize the German enemy. *The Great Escape* has become a reference point in contemporary British culture, as witness its playful adaptation, *The Chicken Run*, and countless advertisements. As I prepared this chapter, *The Guns of Navarone* was broadcast on prime-time television (9:00 p.m. on a Saturday evening on Carlton).[4] These films show the British as impossibly heroic and the Germans as cold, ruthless, and cruel. In literature, the portrayal of Germans needs to move forward from the one-dimensional sadism of Lawrence's Prussian officer, the animal greed of Mansfield's German boardinghouse guests, the cunning of Buchan's spies, and the unscrupulousness of Greene's invaders in "Went the Day Well?"[5] Not only do such characterizations reinforce attitudes of automatic suspicion, loathing, and hostility, but the cultural detritus forms a crust over the pain and desire that should inspire us to passionately renew life.

In recent years the generation born after World War II has challenged inherited British culture. By rewriting the nation's history from new perspectives, young authors have problematized issues of patriotism and national identity, highlighting the complex patterning of the social fabric. English heroic stereotypes of the stiff upper lip and the jolly Tommy, with their racist essentialism, have been mercilessly mocked by plays such as *Oh What a Lovely War* and television series such as *Blackadder* and *Fawlty Towers*.[6] More seriously, a new evaluation of cultural hybridity has developed—for instance, among dramatists with roots in Northern Ireland, the Asian subcontinent, and the Caribbean who refuse to subsume British under "English."[7] In particular, this has resulted in several plays by Jewish-British women writers that have publicly exposed personal dilemmas about identity, loyalty, and responsibility. Among them are dramas by Sue Frumin, Diane Samuels, and Julia Pascal. In this essay I examine and set against these the new play by Charlotte Eilenberg, *The Lucky Ones*.[8] Eilenberg challenges the taken-for-granted opposition between being British and being German that the earlier plays tend to accentuate, and she reveals the longing such opposition may deny. Her play accords with the analysis in two turn-of-the-century novels by other British writers of European Jewish descent, Anita Brookner and Linda Grant. Together with Brookner's *Visitors* (1997) and Grant's *Still Here* (2002), Eilenberg's *The Lucky Ones* calls for a reassessment of Germany's emotional legacy to Britain and looks hopefully forward.

Eilenberg's play received extensive critical coverage, with reviews in both daily and weekly papers.[9] There was wide agreement that the play was "commendable" and "extremely promising," being "remarkable," "impressive," and "powerful." The only voice of dissent came from Rhoda Koenig in the *Independent*. She traced what she saw as a deep problem with the play (its static, diffuse, and sketchy character) to its autobiographical source: "[W]hat [Eilenberg] has created is not so much a drama as a reminiscence." As several critics noted, the foreword to the published text of the play reveals that Eilenberg's father was a Jewish refugee from Nazi Berlin, yet her mother was an English Gentile and Charlotte and her brother were raised in West London. So the play is hardly a documentary, but it does arise out of her own background. This was generally seen to be a source of the play's "accuracy and sensitivity," the details of the refugee milieu apparently all ringing "exquisitely true" (John Gross in the *Sunday Times*).

There was praise for the play's dialogue, characterization, and emotional tension, despite its being perceived as structurally flawed: the plot, although gripping and full of surprise, was found to be contrived, schematic, and "none too plausible," with a "mind-boggling" twist (Benedict Nightingale in the *Times*). Although the critics kept to the unspoken pact of not revealing the secret at the end of act 2, they strongly disagreed with each other about the ending. Aleks Sierz of *What's On* found the final scene "perhaps unnecessary," and Michael Billington of the *Guardian* thought the revelation "makes nonsense" of Leo's ferocity. Whereas Alistair Macaulay of the *Financial Times* found the final scene "the most surprising of all, and the most touching" and Jane Edwardes in *Time Out* described it as "a most moving flashback" in a play written with sympathy yet "without ever being sentimental," Nicholas de Jong in the *Evening Standard* found the ironic secret "sentimental," its revelation one of the structural flaws in the play. On the whole, though, the play was judged to be strong and "intelligent" (Kate Bassett, *Independent on Sunday*), a "complex, ruthless, compassionate play"

(John Peter, *Sunday Times*) that displayed "emotional and intellectual integrity" (Sierz) and a "refusal to lapse into bogusly comforting sentimentality" (Charles Spence, *Daily Telegraph*). Above all, as John Nathan observed in *Jewish Chronicle*, "[W]eighty themes are handled with an admirable light touch."

In my view, the London critics were too literal-minded and conventional. They expected to find the surface historical realism of the "well-made play," which was precisely what Eilenberg was challenging.[10] I find the structure of the play innovative. As I shall try to demonstrate, it not only enables Eilenberg to challenge (British) patriarchal values by the feminist aesthetic of "writing beyond the ending" but also draws on mythical patterns to deal afresh with what Nathan called "the still festering sore of post-Holocaust guilt and reparation" *(Jewish Chronicle)*. Far from being "unnecessary," the final scene is the courageous heart of the play.

Like the earlier plays by Jewish women mentioned above, *The Lucky Ones* arises from the situation of Jews who fled the Continent and sought refuge in England in the 1930s. However, despite covering a thirty-year period on stage, it does not display Britain just before or during the war, as do the other plays. Nor is it concerned with anatomizing differences between the native English and the newcomers, revealing racism and insularity to which the incomers must adapt or perish. Nor, most importantly, is its primary focus on one female protagonist and her relationships with other women. Its main characters are four *Kinder,* Jewish children rescued from Berlin just before the war and now settled in London: two married couples, Leo and Ottilie Black and Anna and Bruno Mosenthal, who between them have a son, Daniel Black, and a daughter, Beth Mosenthal. The two families are related because Leo and Anna are brother and sister, originally Blumenstein. The four members of the wartime generation, proud to be British, are forced to reevaluate their situation by an encounter with another German uprooted from Berlin, Lisa, who has come to Britain only after the war. She is younger than they are, childless, and married to an Englishman. She is not Jewish; moreover, her wealthy father probably benefited from the dispossession of German-Jewish refugees. Although the play deals with generational conflicts that are widely recognizable, it also invites its audience to believe in an illicit affair that develops between Lisa Schnee and Leo Black and endures secretly for thirty years across the political and ethnic divide, "against the odds." What does Eilenberg achieve by this plot, in the shadow of the Holocaust and the spectral rise of the New Right?

Recent British plays have dealt with war by portraying it as the uncanny underside to peace, through plots haunted by the ghost of a British soldier. He is the figure of the killer who must be abjected or sublimated from the civil society but who remains the unspoken reminder of the violent deaths society is founded upon. Such plays are ironic rejoinders to remembrance ceremonies and war memorials: "they shall not grow old . . . to the end they remain." The unforgettable figure embodies ambiguity, heroic in sacrifice yet degraded by spilt blood. Impossibly, he materializes to be "seen" by the audience in reproachful relation with the living, unable himself to rest in peace despite the peace his wretchedness enabled.[11] However, these plays differ from plays that attempt to deal with a different legacy of war dead, not dead soldiers but dead civilians. Most British plays about the Holocaust are haunted by places and events that are not shown on stage. There are American and Continental plays actually set in the camps (*Playing for Time, Bent, Cannibals*), but the nearest most British plays come is the model ghetto of Teresienstadt. The drama of the places of extermination takes place offstage (in *Copenhagen, Dreams of Anne Frank, Laughter*); the degradation is not seen but present by its absence, the taken-for-granted horror that determines all else. In the plays by Frumin (*The Housetrample*) and Samuels (*Kindertransport*) the figure of a camp survivor appalls the girl who escaped; in Pascal's own production of *Teresa*, Teresa, who did not survive, is played by an actress who did and who confronts the audience with her own survival.[12] But the camp conditions are not represented on stage, and the dead do not return.

Nevertheless, in real life Jews are haunted by the brutal past, as recent family memoirs and autobiographies by women have demonstrated. Such books as Ann Karpf's *The War After*, Lisa Appignanesi's *Losing the Dead*, and Louise Kehoe's *In This Dark House* are testimonies to a trauma transmitted across the generations.[13]

However, *The Lucky Ones* is haunted, not by the repressed abject, as are these other war works, but by its obverse: repressed desire. It arises not from waking nightmare but from wishful daydreaming. And the place where the fantasy of desire can be imaginatively lived out and fulfilled is eventually shown on stage in the final scene. It is a play that shows a melancholy underlying everyday life, a disquiet that comes not from the trauma of degraded death but from the dream of lost living happiness. It is not, like so much Jewish writing, concerned with how to live with the memory of traumatic experience; it is concerned with regaining the lost object of desire, with creating a magical space where the imagination can play freely, where obligations can be evaded and the desires prohibited by the real social world can be indulged and enjoyed. That utopian space, which is the true subject of the drama, means different things to different characters.

For its first three-quarters, the play is concerned with the difficulties and obstacles that constrain happiness and fulfillment. It begins like a play by Alan Ayckbourn, a social comedy set in the garden of a prosaic suburban house in North London in 1968, where people come and go through the French windows or sit in deck chairs on the lawn, eating al fresco, reading newspapers, or playing bridge. This convincing visual masquerade is put into question aurally by the faintly foreign accents and the German words interspersed in an overheard phone conversation; Wagner's Ring Cycle is being played. That it is a masquerade is emphasized by Ottilie's appearance dressed in a secondhand fashion frock purchased in a charity shop. These may be the "Lucky Ones" of the title, those who escaped Nazi Germany, but their lives are somehow not a picnic. This may look like a traditional English social comedy, dealing with forbidden sexuality and rebellious children in tones of restrained politeness and using the audience's laughter to license some outspokenness, especially at the funeral in act 2. But it is not farcical. The discomfort runs far deeper than the dissonance between sound and sight, between glaring appearance and underlying reality. As late as 1998, Anna says: "Do you know the one thing I really hate? It's that I've been here for over sixty years and I still have such a strong accent" (86). This is a home in which no one feels really at home.

The awkwardness is enacted not only by the characters' slightly unnatural English speech and disagreements over the correct choice of expression or by Anna Mosenthal's defensiveness at enjoying Wagner, "that bloody racket," as described by Bruno, who is almost a parody of "an English officer and a gentleman."[14] It is manifested in the hypercritical exasperation shown toward the children by their fathers, which results in tension between all four parents. The husbands are particularly tetchy and complaining. Argumentatively Bruno agrees with Enoch Powell's "Rivers of Blood" speech: "Why-the-hell should Britain allow in every Tom, Dick and Harry who wants to come here" (2).[15] The general discomfort is symbolized by Bruno's amputated leg, a war wound that still gives him pain. He was crippled while serving with the British Army in Kenya. Although the pain is worsening, he irritably refuses to claim his due compensation. The character who is most conscious of being ill at ease with himself is Leo. His last lines in the play include the troubled query: "How can we live with our-selves?" (95). He feels in "limboland": "A Britisher with a funny accent, and I can't go home" (40). It is Leo who triggers the plot of the play by deciding to sell the country cottage that he and Bruno bought fifteen years before, partly with money from Leo's father, Willy. And it is Leo who provokes an argument with the other three, first by deciding to sidestep the estate agent and make a hugely inflated profit from a chance buyer, Lisa Pendry, and then, when he discovers her to have been born Lisa Schnee, German but not Jewish, by setting an outrageous condition on the sale.

Regarding her father as one of those who "profited from the blood of the Jewish people" (36), he requires Lisa to apologize for the "silence and complicity of the German people" (37) over the murder of six million Jews. Refusing to admit that she is "dirty by association" (37), she leaves, and the others argue over Leo's ultimatum. It becomes clear that they are united in resentful anxiety, an anxiety that, however hard the wives try, cannot be dis-pelled because its sources lie in a past that cannot be changed. They can never be perfect enough to justify their own survival when so many per-ished; nor can there ever be adequate reparation for what they have lost. Bullied and emotionally blackmailed by Willy, they have inherited an im-possible burden of need and obligation, and they transmit it to the next generation.

The dream cottage in the country represents their wish that their life could be different, that they could jointly "put down roots" in England and provide a new inheritance for their children. The decision to sell seems to be an admission that the wish has failed: "it wasn't practical" (3), Bruno judges. It was fun to play and relax there at the beginning of their marriages when the children were small, but after fifteen years it needs repairs, and none of them goes there any more. Yet it was the place where all of them, in their own ways, were at peace with themselves and happy. As Beth re-members it years later, she was never again so happy as when she went hop-ping through the woods for hours, shouting, "Who's got energy? Me, me, me" (63).

Set in the New Forest, the cottage draws mythical significance from En-glish culture, not least because the forest recalls the Forest of Arden in *As You Like It*, the wood in *A Midsummer Night's Dream*, *Under Milk Wood*, Sherwood Forest, and the *Children of the New Forest*.[16] From the beginning of the play, the cottage sounds like an enchanted place outside the law. Yet it is not simply the make-believe Wendy House of the Never Never Land where we are free of parents and need never grow up; by the end of the play, it has been revealed as the place of adult sexual transgression and transformation. As foreshadowed in act 1 by the implicit "under the greenwood tree" allusion of its forest location, in the final scene the cottage becomes the setting for the traditional tale of magical change. Although a contemporary audience is unlikely to know of Arthur Pinero's play *The Enchanted Cottage*, some may remember the 1945 film based on it.[17] In that story, a scarred war veteran and his plain wife escape from society to a remote cottage where they are transfigured in each other's eyes by their mutual love.

Beyond the universal fairytale overtones of romantic metamorphosis, or the subliminal mythical significance of the forest, to which a British audience can respond with deep sympathy (a sympathy that counteracts any antipathy that may be aroused by the marked German-English accents), the cottage has a personal significance for each of the Blacks (if not for the prosaic Bruno). The first indication of this is given by Anna Mosenthal (née Black) early in the play. In a shy revelation that Bruno calls "romantic nonsense," she admits that the view across the meadows always took her back to her childhood in Wannsee. "Wannsee! Wannsee, without the See" (3), responds Bruno. The most poignant indication of the cottage's personal significance is given by Ottilie, the youngest of the four, who remembers leaving Berlin by Kindertransport at the age of thirteen: "I never saw my parents ever again" (52). She recalls standing on the balcony at Anna's house in Wannsee when she was about eight, holding her mother's hand to look out over the lake. She says, "I try to remember her, who she was, whether she got on with my father or not, and where I come from, and who I am. I've no idea. [*Upset.*] I've no idea" (19). Anna disputes whether it would have been Wannsee or Westerland auf Sylt. There is no way of resolving this: "Who's to say?" Although they would not have known in 1968, Wannsee was, of *[Eilenberg]* course, where in 1942 Hitler's accomplices signed the so-called Wannsee *[knows]* Protocol, the plan for the Final Solution of the Problem of the Jews.[18] But if one theme of Eilenberg's play is that the past guiltily infects the present, her play also presents the hope that memories innocent of what was to happen can resurrect our happiness.

Act 2 of *The Lucky Ones* begins thirty years later on the day of Leo's funeral. Ottilie and Bruno are already dead, and Beth and Daniel have grown up. Born and brought up in London, their English is fluent and there is no trace of the masquerade. They are now in their early middle age, both single and with a child each that they don't see. In another scene of recriminations we discover that Daniel feels Leo poisoned his life, just as Willy poisoned Leo's, by forcing him to carry "the burden of history on his shoulders." As Beth and Daniel sit with Anna in her garden, Lisa turns up, in an ironic re-play of the first act, to offer the cottage back to the family as a gift: "It is still a magical place just as you remember it," she assures Anna. Lisa did per-form the impossible: she went back to Leo to apologize and signed the con-tract. It is now that her secret thirty-year affair with Leo is uncovered: "thirty years sleeping with the bloody enemy" as Daniel puts it (in an unwit-ting echo of Leo's mockery of Willy, twenty years before). In the face of An-na's fury Lisa explains that she and Leo had needed to be together because they both felt outsiders. Chronologically the play ends there in 1998, with Daniel, Beth, Anna, and Lisa sitting together in Anna's back garden, emo-tionally drained and contemplating their lives.

The last scene of the play flashes back twenty years to show Lisa and Leo lovingly together at the cottage. It is the day of Daniel's wedding, to which Leo has not been invited. The lovers bicker and make up, jokingly disagreeing about the relative merits of Goethe and Heine, the German poet and the German-Jewish poet who had to convert in order to publish. Leo is in his typical state of anxiety over a double bind he perceives himself to be in with regard to the wedding. He is brought to relax by Lisa. She gently recites to him Goethe's poem "*Uber allen Gipfeln / Ist Ruh*": "Calm lies over the hilltops." This is the Second Night-Wanderer's Song, which is a response to the First Night-Wanderer's Song: "I am weary of it all." "*Was soll all der Schmerz und Lust?*" (What is the sense of all this pain and joy?) Lisa is, by implication, the *susser Friede* (the sweet peace) Leo has longed for. He repeats affectionately after her, "*Kaum einem Hauch*" (scarcely a breath of air).[19] Here is German spoken happily and lovingly on the English stage, not extracted nor translated, but simply integrated into their intercourse as the adequate expression of deep feeling. The play ends with the two of them sit-ting together in the cottage garden, toasting to the future of the "lucky ones" of the next generation.

The desire that fuels the play is revealed more openly in Linda Grant's novel *Still Here*, which also confronts the legacy presented to a generation of Jewish children born in Britain by a mother who was a German refugee of the Kindertransport.[20] In this case, Lotte Rebick (née Dorf) is from Dres-den but is now living in Liverpool, married to the grandson of Russian-Polish escapees from the Krishniev massacres. Lotte bequeaths to her daugh-ter and son, Alix and Sam, not only love but sorrow and regret. Although her parents also escaped to Britain, she never regained what she lost before the age of fourteen: her home with her family (117–18). In Grant's novel the physical legacy of a derelict factory behind the Iron Curtain stands for the impossibility of gaining true reparation for the "golden lost realm of [emotional] affluence and status" that was "brutally eradicated by racial theory" (123). What Lotte lost was not only familiar objects but also her "country and its culture, whose writers and composers she had been taught to consider hers also; and her language," which she occasionally uses in endearments to the children, "*Einschlafen, mein Liebling*" (6). Despite her rage at being dispossessed, she does not return to Dresden but instead makes excursions down to London. There she can "satisfy in herself a hunger to be German once more. German at a concert in the Wigmore Hall. German standing in front of a Dürer at the National Gallery. German in the consumption of a Black Forest gateau in a teashop in the Cromwell Road" (119). Her bitterness is less at material loss than at exile from cultural opulence and the right to revel in it: "[S]he was in exile, always in exile" (131). As Alix recognizes, despite the intolerance Lotte met in Liverpool, particularly from Jews, "[S]he couldn't get the German out of herself; didn't want to, why should she? She wanted to reclaim that part of herself she had to suppress all those years, the German that was hiding in her" (132).

Lotte has had to repress her Germanness because of the prejudice of the English around her, Jews included. Leo has had to repress his Germanness because of his father's bitterness. Bruno describes Willy as "eaten up with anger and resentment. You daren't even say a word of German in his presence for fear of being thrown out" (42). The critic Benedict Nightingale called him "an obsessed, embittered monster."[21] A similar state of mind to Willy's is analyzed in Anita Brookner's novel *Visitors* (1997),[22] where the elderly grandmother Kitty, another German-Jewish emigré, is seen as monstrous in her will to manipulate and dominate others. Brookner accords her the same understanding that Eilenberg accords to Leo's bullying of Daniel. In the novel, Thea, "a typical English widow" (128) who was the non-Jewish wife of Kitty's cousin comes to recognize that she provided a "safe haven" for Henry (220)—perhaps in the way that Lisa did for Leo. Henry's family, although distanced from exile, suffered from a kind of homesickness. They were in need of security, "fearing abandonment or dispossession" (220). Kitty's husband realizes that "that will of hers," "always criticizing, demanding, calling to account" (164), actually drove her son away. Thea sees that in fact "others took flight" in the face of Kitty's neediness, the need "for love, for comfort, for support, for reassurance" (210) that Kitty has in common with Henry. In the novel, Thea discovers her own sense of alienation, fear, and need. She finally tries to meet the need in Kitty by a change in herself. In the play, Lisa makes an even greater gesture toward Leo. In act 2 she recounts to Daniel, Beth, and Anna how, prompted by Leo's accusation, she did investigate her own complicity in the Nazi past. This might seem less credible if we did not also have, for instance, Christa Wolf's public acknowledgment of her generation's complicity in her fictionalized autobiography, *A Model Childhood* (1976).

In the play, Beth is the one who immediately understands Lisa's claim that what she and Leo had in common was a sense of unbelonging: "I don't even feel British. I don't feel part of it any more than you do, Lisa. I'm lost, left out, on the edge of it all" (83).[23] Beth has tried to assuage her own alienation by bringing up her son in the Jewish religion. (The older generation of Blumensteins were christened and lived as assimilated Germans, but that didn't save them from the Nuremburg Laws.) By contrast, Daniel's marriage to an Arab is his version of Oedipal rebellion, like Leo's against Willy: "sleeping with the enemy." The problem of whether to espouse Jewish identity, and especially of how to accomplish this after the Holocaust in a country distinct from Israel, is a constant anxiety in Anglo-Jewish literature, as in life. The play raises that issue in conjunction with the parallel dilemma of how to be German after the enormities of World War II. If, in *Still Here*, Wigmore Hall is a place where Lotte can indulge her hidden German identity, in *The Lucky Ones* the cottage in the New Forest enables Lisa and Leo to meet their mutual desire to rise above intolerance and bitterness and to reclaim a taint-free Germanness, free of their parents' imposed burdens. Eilenberg does not leave this resolution at the safe level of aesthetic distance such as is offered by a concert recital of German lieder staged in evening dress at Wigmore Hall. In *The Lucky Ones*, German culture is pared back to the intimacy of gratified lovers, one in a formal suit embracing the other naked beneath a dressing gown.

But the play does not stop at profane love. A Freudian interpretation would suggest that the original lost object of desire is the mother, our first "home." While Leo and Bruno reverted to boyhood at the cottage, Anna and Ottilie played at being their mothers, cooking. As we have seen, the view over the meadows from the kitchen window is a view associated with their mothers. Because the mothers died in the camps, that association has a special value. If Lisa casually calls the view "sacred" to Anna, we see that the place is more seriously holy to Leo. Leo's woodshed is a sanctum that no one is allowed to enter. As Daniel discovers when he trespasses, Leo keeps there the framed photos of his and Ottilie's mothers in a kind of shrine.

When Lisa agrees to have Leo's ashes scattered at the cottage that she wants to donate to Daniel, she is offering an inheritance that has more than material value. Daniel as an adult finally recognizes what he has missed—"What I could have had . . ." (86)—and he cries for a whole lost world of loving acceptance. We see that world in the final scene. Through the complex imaginative poetry of drama, Eilenberg has revealed, behind the harsh, bullying *Vaterland* that dominates British stereotypes of German culture, the lost, succoring feminine culture that is eclipsed by war and propaganda.

Eilenberg's play takes the great risk of embarrassing or alienating her audience by dealing openly with matters that many people (like Anna) believe "are better left unsaid." She breaks down defenses by means of humor.[24] Using Daniel's typically Jewish jokes, she outfaces what is pejoratively defined in the play as the "Hampstead Mafia" that constituted her first audience, and she uses Leo's mimicry to mock Willy's burdensome nagging. Then, with the dream cottage, she opens up that desirable "third space" where everything can be said, everything accepted, in a magical embrace where needs not only are not castrated (as Leo says to Bruno) but are welcomed and passionately met. That may seem utopian. But it is important that Eilenberg does not use any nonrealist conventions to display this dream. The only sense of heightened reality stems from the recitation of German poetry, which signifies the mutual harmony between the lovers. This recalls the ending of Christina Reid's antiwar play about the troubles in Northern Ireland, *My Name, Shall I Tell You My Name,* a plea to reenact the First World War Christmas Truce in No Man's Land, where the soldiers from each side actually did smoke each other's cigarettes and play football together, singing the same hymns in different languages. That is already a powerful myth in British culture, recalled on stage in *Oh What a Lovely War,* where the German soldiers sing "Heilige Nacht" and the British audience hears "All is calm, all is bright."[25] Eilenberg and Reid offer a seemingly impossible dream of reconciliation that we have to have a mad faith in and take risks to achieve.

But Eilenberg has gone further. Although all the characters foreground the problems they find in naturalizing as English despite their British citizenship, arguing over whether they only *were* or still *are* Berliners because of having originally come from there, the play not only poses difficult questions about the inheritance of the British and German pasts but asks those questions from within the problematic area of Jewish identity. Lisa criticizes Leo for keeping her "invisible"—that is, for symbolically keeping his German connections hidden—but Eilenberg's play is unusual in being set in the heart of an assimilated Jewish family, rendering their Jewish identity open to view. Although all the characters are "from Berlin" originally, in the play the (British-German) Jews form the dominant group against which Lisa, the Gentile, is the outsider. The debates take place not against a putatively anti-Semitic wider culture but among the Jews themselves. "The Jew" is not an odd one out; Jews in their diversity, mocking Jewish stereotypes, are the taken-for-granted bedrock of the play. The debates are not resolved (and the situation for the third generation, Jacob and Tareq, is not satisfactory), but the complex narrative structure of the play suggests that Leo and Lisa's legacy may lessen the burden for the next generation.

This is not only because their own processes of reconciliation are clearly healthy and their secret liaison is finally revealed. It is also because the very form of Leo's funeral takes on a new meaning in the light of the play as a whole. Daniel, his nearest male relative, does not say Kaddish according to Jewish custom, yet Leo has a funeral at which a rabbi and friends are present. His choice of music is significant. It creates that hybrid third space of an eclectic new European culture, in which Jewish folk memory and the English pastoral tradition are mingled with German idealism and Italian operatic passion, overriding fascist concepts of "purity":

> *Daniel:* Yes, some Klezmer folky stuff, erm . . . "the Lark Ascending" . . . then a bit of Wagnerian fascism, some bombastic ghastly shite from *The Ring*, God, I remember that booming our through most of my childhood, oh yes, and the best bit, that famous love duet from *La Traviata* . . .
> *Lisa:* "sempre Libra" *[sic]*. (65)

This indicates the hybrid cultural heritage that Eilenberg's play suggests we all have a right to, even a nostalgic longing for. If much of British culture aims to construct narratives of the imagined *national* community that comes together in time of war, as Benedict Anderson argues in *Imagined Communities*,[26] then *The Lucky Ones* can be seen as a gesture toward the imagined *European* community constructed and continually reestablished by peace treaties and dreams of harmony.

NOTES

1. See, for instance, Anne Karpf's *The War After: Living with the Holocaust* (London: Heinemann, 1996).

2. An account of this scheme is given in Bertha Leverton and Schmuel Lowensohn, eds., *I Came Alone: The Stories of the Kindertransports* (Sussex: Book Guild, 1990).

3. A discussion of the speech, made April 20, 1968, and of Powell's political influence over the ensuing debate is to be found in Patrick Cosgrave, *The Lives of Enoch Powell* (London: Bodley Head, 1989), ch. 11, especially 246–50.

4. *The Great Escape*, dir John Sturges (U.S., Alpha, 1962; *The Guns of Navarone*, dir. J. Lee Thompson (G.B., Columbia, 1961); *The Chicken Run*, dir. Peter Lord and Nick Park (U.S., Universal Studios, 2000).

5. See D. H. Lawrence, "The Prussian Officer," in *The Prussian Officer* (1914); Katherine Mansfield, *In a German Pension* (1911); and John Buchan, *The Thirty-Nine Steps* (1915). Graham Greene's story "Went the Day Well?" was used for the film *Went the Day Well?* (in the United States, *Forty-Eight Hours*), dir. Albert Cavalcanti (G.B., Ealing, 1942). Miss Kilman in Virginia Woolf's *Mrs. Dalloway* (1925) is none too pleasant either.

6. The scripts for *Blackadder* were published in book form: Richard Curtus and Ben Elton, *Blackadder Goes Forth*, in *Blackadder: The Whole Damn Dynasty* (London: Michael Joseph, 1998). Both television series are frequently rebroadcast and are available on video. Theatre Workshop's *Oh What a Lovely War* (London: Methuen, 1964) was adapted to film and video and is frequently shown on television.

7. They include plays and playwrights such as *A Jamaican Airman Foresees His Death* by Fred D'Aguiar; Winsome Pinnock's *A Hero's Farewell*, in *Six Plays by Black and Asian Women Writers*, ed. Katija George (London: Aurora, 1996), and Christina Reid's *My Name, Shall I Tell You My Name*, in *War Plays by Women*, ed. Claire M Tylee (London: Routledge, 1999).

8. This was first produced at the Hampstead Theatre, London, in April 2002. Its brief first run, April 22–June 1, was extended for a fortnight, but the play did not transfer to the West End. It has been published as Charlotte Eilenberg, *The Lucky Ones* (London: Methuen, 2002), with a foreword by the author. Page references in the text are to this edition.

9. The reviews have been collected and republished in *Theatre Record*, April 9–22, 2002, 491–94. All the following quotations are from that source.

10. The introduction to the student edition of Caryl Churchill's play *Top Girls*, ed. Bill Naismith (London: Methuen, 1991), contains her remarks about traditional dramatic structure and her need, as a woman, to find a new form (xxii). The temporal structure of *Top Girls*, the plot of which also revolves around a sexual secret, demonstrates the ironic effectiveness of ending with a flashback scene—and no one has criticized *that* construction as "flawed."

11. These plays include Louise Page's *Salonika*, Peter Whelan's *Accrington Pals*, Frank MacGuinness's *Observe the Sons of Ulster*, and Caryl Churchill's *Cloud Nine* and can be regarded in a tradition with Noel Coward's *Post-Mortem*, Gwen John's *Peakland Wakes,* and others. For bibliographical details of these and other war plays,

see Claire M Tylee, ed., *War Plays by Women* (London: Routledge, 1999), 10–11, 224–25.

12. See Sue Frumin, *The Housetrample*, in *Lesbian Plays: Two*, ed. Jill Davis (London: Methuen, 1989); Julia Pascal, *Teresa*, in *The Holocaust Trilogy* (London: Oberon, 2000); and Diane Samuels, *Kindertransport* (London: Nick Hern, 1995). For details of the other Holocaust plays, see Alvin Goldfarb, "Select Bibliography of Holocaust Plays, 1933–1997," in *Staging the Holocaust: The Shoah in Drama and Performance*, ed. Claude Schumacher (Cambridge: Cambridge University Press, 1998), 298–334.

13. See Lisa Appignanesi, *Losing the Dead: A Family Memoir* (London: Chatto, 1999); Ann Karpf, *The War After: Living with the Holocaust* (London: Heinemann, 1996); Louise Kehoe *In This Dark House: A Memoir* (New York: Schocken, 1995).

14. For a discussion of this phenomenon among emigré Jews, see Ian Baruma, "Churchill's Cigar," *Granta* 65 (Spring 1999): 327–43. Historical studies of German-Jewish refugees in Britain include Marion Berghahn, *German-Jewish Refugees in England: The Ambiguities of Assimilation* (Basingstoke: Macmillan, 1984), republished as *Continental Britain: German-Jewish Refugees from Nazi Germany* (Oxford: Berg, 1988); Bernard Wasserstein, *Britain and the Jews of Europe, 1939–45* (London: Leicester University Press, 1999); Tony Kushner, *The Holocaust and the Liberal Imagination* (Oxford: Blackwell, 1994).

15. See note 3 above.

16. Apart from plays by Shakespeare, the references are to the traditional legends of Robin Hood, set in Sherwood Forest, Nottingham; to Dylan Thomas's radio play *Under Milk Wood* (1953); and to Frederick Marryat's children's adventure tale, *Children of the New Forest* (1847). These exciting forests are very different from the threatening places of the tales by the Brothers Grimm.

17. See Arthur Wing Pinero, *The Enchanted Cottage: A Fable in Three Acts* (London: Heinemann, 1921). The 1945 film *The Enchanted Cottage*, dir John Cromwell (U.S., RKO), followed a silent version of the same title, made in 1921.

18. See, for instance, ch. 11, 229–43, of Richard Breitman's *The Architect of Genocide: Himmler and the Final Solution* (London: Bodley Head, 1991).

19. These poems by Johann Wolfgang von Goethe can be found in *The Penguin Book of German Verse*, ed. Leonard Forster (Harmondsworth: Penguin, 1959), 207–8. The translations I have given are my own.

20. Linda Grant, *Still Here* (London: Little, Brown, 2002); page references in the text are taken from this edition.

21. *Theatre Record*, April 2002, 492. These are not the only literary works by British women writers about Jewish refugees from Nazi Europe, and the "embittered monster" is a recurrent trope. Other novels by women that figure Kindertransport-ees include Bernice Rubens's *Madame Sousatzka* (London: Eyre and Spottiswoode, 1962); Lore Segal, *Other People's Houses* (New York: Harcourt, 1964); Judith Kerr, *The Other Way Round* (London: Collins, 1975); Gillian Tindall, *To the City* (London:

Hutchinson, 1987); Anita Brookner, *Latecomers* (London: Cape, 1988); Elaine Feinstein, *Mother's Girl* (London: Hutchinson, 1988); Anita Desai, *Baumgartner's Bombay* (London: Heinemann, 1988); Zina Rohane, *The Sandbeetle* (London: Hodder and Stoughton, 1993); they also figure in short stories such as Ruth Fainlight's "Another Survivor" (1978), in *Dr Clock's Last Case and Other Stories* (London: Virago, 1994), 74–90; Esther Woolfson's "Rosh Hashanah," in *Flamingo Scottish Short Stories 1995*, ed. Tom Adair (London: Flamingo, 1995), 182–209; and Elaine Feinstein's "Christmas in Berlin," in *The Slow Mirror and Other Stories,* ed. Sonja Lynden and Sylvia Paskin (Nottingham: Five Leaves, 1996), 39–46. The monster appears in the works by Rubens, Fainlight, and Woolfson and also figures in Diane Samuels's play *Kindertransport.*

22. Anita Brookner, *The Visitors* (London: Cape, 1997). Page references in the text are to this edition.

23. Eilenberg makes clear in the foreword to her play that this sense of alienation is autobiographical.

24. When I saw the play at Hampstead Theatre in June 2002, among a mainly Jewish audience, Daniel's Israel jokes were met by a moment of stunned disbelief followed by uproarious laughter.

25. Any self-indulgent tendency to sentimentality by a British audience is undercut when the British soldiers respond with a lewd version of "tidings of Comfort and Joy." Theatre Workshop, *Oh What a Lovely War* (London: Methuen, 1964), 48–53.

26. Benedict Anderson, *Imagined Communities: Reflections on the Origin and Spread of Nationalism* (London: Verso, 1991).

CHAPTER TEN

Vietnamese Exile Writers

Displacement, Identity, the Past, and the Future

RENNY CHRISTOPHER

In my book *The Viet Nam War/The American War: Images and Representations in Euro-American and Vietnamese Exile Narratives,* I argue that so far works by Vietnamese American writers have been more properly defined as exile narratives than as immigrant narratives because of their focus on the writers' pasts in Viet Nam rather than on their experiences of assimilation in America. These works have also had a didactic quality, teaching U.S. audiences about Vietnamese culture, and have presented a clear preference on the part of the writers for their home country. Two books by writers of a younger generation, Nguyen Qui Duc's *Where the Ashes Are: The Odyssey of a Vietnamese Family* and Jade Ngoc Quang Huynh's *South Wind Changing,* could be defined as works of both exile literature and immigrant literature in their construction. They address the lingering impact of the war on the writers' families and on their country of origin and their adopted country. Duc focuses both on his own past in Viet Nam and on his family's experiences there after he fled to the United States in 1975, but he also focuses on his own experiences in becoming an American, experiences that are partially determined by his Vietnamese identity. Huynh, while he sets the bulk of his narrative in Viet Nam, focuses on his time in reeducation camp and exhibits relatively little nostalgia for Viet Nam; for him, politics overcomes culture, and since the Socialist Republic of Viet Nam is not the Viet Nam he wants, he turns instead toward the United States and American culture.

I have argued that Vietnamese exile representations are focused on cultural negotiations, on the process of becoming bicultural. This process isn't the same as assimilating, which is leaving behind one's culture of origin. This biculturality is one of the important ways in which Vietnamese American literature differs from much of Asian American literature. Vietnamese exile authors, while becoming "American," have insisted on remaining Vietnamese. The struggle to remain bicultural, to bring Vietnamese culture to America, in such a way that culture transcends national boundaries, is a theme that has run through most Vietnamese American literature. Duc's and Huynh's narratives differ from narratives by older writers in that the narrators describe much more of a struggle to maintain their Vietnamese identity. This is particularly the case for Duc, partially because he was very young when he left Viet Nam and partially because he wants to forge ties with the Socialist Republic of Viet Nam, a desire that his family does not share. These new, younger writers, born in the late 1950s, are making a step from exile literature into immigrant literature, which is to make one step from war into peace.

Bicultural identity and cultural fusion are not easy or painless to achieve, especially when, as for Vietnamese American writers, they are the result of the aftermath of a war that has made these writers and their families refugees. Andrew Lam writes in an article in the *Nation* of the experience of exile:

> Sometimes I go to a Vietnamese restaurant in San Francisco's Tenderloin district. I sit and stare at two wooden clocks hanging on the wall. The left one is carved in the shape of the voluptuous S: the map of Vietnam. The one on the right is hewed in the shape of a deformed tooth: the map of America. Ticktock, ticktock. They run at different times. Ticktock, ticktock. I was born a Vietnamese. Ticktock, ticktock. I am reborn an American. Ticktock, ticktock. I am of one soul. Ticktock, ticktock. Two hearts. (726)

Lam's "one soul . . . two hearts" might serve as a description of what biculturality is; his phrase echoes W. E. B. DuBois's description of African Americans feeling "twoness . . . two warring ideals in one dark body" (215). Lam's choice of metaphor for the shape of the two clocks/countries reveals that his affection still lies with Viet Nam and that he is uneasy in America. Duc and Huynh both end their narratives feeling uneasy in both cultures, particularly Duc, who feels at home only in a place that exists solely in his memory.

One of the results of this bicultural stance and the lingering nostalgia for home is that Vietnamese American authors have tended to write more about life in Viet Nam than about their experience of the assimilation process in America. They are interested in bringing their culture of origin into the American context of their exile. Exile is a common phenomenon in the twentieth century, and the exile author is an increasingly common figure. Edward Said calls this "the age of the refugee, the displaced person, mass immigration" (qtd. in Kaplan 30).

The question of literature in exile is also at issue in the Vietnamese-language exile press. Whether to term the Vietnamese-language literature produced by refugee writers exile literature is a topic of contention. This debate reflects how this war has not ended in the hearts and minds of many of those who were displaced by it. In an article that appeared in translation in the Australian *Journal of Vietnamese Studies*, Nguyen Hung Quoc addresses the question. Some writers whose main focus is anticommunism dislike the term *exile literature* because it sounds sad and "pitiful." They prefer to constitute themselves as the "authentic" contemporary Vietnamese literature and to call the communist writers in the Socialist Republic of Viet Nam the "exile" writers. Quoc dismisses this rather absurd claim but seeks to define what exile literature is:

> Living abroad and writing do not make a writer someone in exile: the pro-communist writers who are living abroad are not writers in exile. The feeling of being astray in his own country, by itself, is not enough to make a writer an author in exile. . . . It may be necessary to distinguish a writer in exile from a literature in exile. We may have writers in exile but not a literature in exile. When we speak of a literature in exile we envisage an activity which includes many aspects: authors and readers in exile, and their relationships through the media in their country of asylum. . . . [W]e can extract three conditions in the making of a literature in exile: (i) there must be authors in exile; (ii) there must be readers in exile; and (iii) they must be able to create a literary activity of their own, independent of the current literature in their country of origin. (26)

The Vietnamese-language exile writers are creating such a literature as Quoc describes, and those writers continue to focus on the lasting effects of the war. The English-language exile writers are not only writers in exile as Quoc defines but also writers attempting to bridge the gap between their pasts, their current lives as exiles, and the lives of English-language readers of their countries of refuge; building these bridges serves as a way of transforming war into peace. They stand in perhaps an even more lonely place by so doing, but they also prefigure future generations whose first language will be English, and who may think of themselves as exiles politically, but who will be at home in the West culturally. In the meantime, the current generation of exile writers, no matter which language they choose to publish in, are focused largely on Viet Nam, the past, and the war.

Nguyen Qui Duc brings both forms of literature together in *Where the Ashes Are* by bringing his father's prisoner-of-war (POW) narrative, published in the United States in Vietnamese, into his narrative. Duc makes his book the story of his family rather than purely his own story. In alternating chapters he traces his own experiences, those of his mother, who stayed behind in Viet Nam to wait for his father's release, and the story of his father's twelve-year imprisonment, for which Duc summarizes and quotes from his father's memoir, *Anh Sang va Bong Toi* (Light and Darkness), published by An Nghe Press in 1990. Duc, then, is one of the bridge builders, looking toward peace but still carrying, narratively, the burden of war.

Where the Ashes Are resembles other works of Vietnamese American literature in that it seeks to bring together a diverse community of readers, specifically to bring Euro-American readers into a Vietnamese American cultural reality. The book is dedicated to "the memory of my sister Dieu-Quynh, and to you." It is Dieu-Quynh's ashes that are referred to in the title of the book; the dedication brings together Dieu-Quynh—who never saw America but whose ashes rest here now—with her family and the American readers of the book, the "you" of the dedication.

The book begins with "A Note on Vietnamese Names," in which Duc explains Vietnamese naming conventions, which are complicated for monolingual English readers.[1] The book is printed with diacritics on all the Vietnamese names, and Duc writes all names Vietnamese style, including *Ha Noi* and *Sai Gon*. This marks a new trend in U.S. publishing, which has previously seldom printed diacritics and which has usually adopted the French colonial spelling *Vietnam*. By following this convention, Duc and his publisher are bringing English-language readers into Vietnamese culture, thus taking a bicultural rather than assimilationist stance.

Duc spends a substantial portion of his narrative detailing his family's life in Viet Nam, as most exile writers do. He begins his family's story with Tet Mau Thanh (the Tet Offensive of 1968), the event that sets their eventual exile in motion. His father, the deputy province governor, is taken prisoner

during the occupation of Hue, where the family is visiting Duc's grand-
parents for the holiday. Duc is at this time a boy of nine. He, his mother, and
two sisters will not see his father again for many years.

The family is from a very privileged class. Duc's grandfather was a man-
darin; "his own grandfather had been a regent through the reigns of three
young kings. Forced to sign a peace treaty with the French in 1884, my
great-great-grandfather had been cursed by history" (23). His mother's family also comes from the highest class. "Her family had always been respected as one that produced scholars—never anyone with the least bit of
interest in business or aptitude for it. Somehow in the dark days of socialism she found she had the acumen to make a living" (105–6). The family's
class status influences which side of the war they will be on—the losing
side, as it will turn out.

Duc grows up in a house full of servants, whom he calls "Uncle" and
"Auntie," and whose children he plays with. His older brother Dinh goes to
Bowling Green University in 1967, and his sister Dieu-Ha later joins Dinh in
the United States. The Nguyen family is fairly insulated from the war until
Duc's father becomes deputy governor in 1967 and they move from Da Lat
to Da Nang. Duc grows up with the cosmopolitanism typical of upper-class
Vietnamese families. After his father is taken prisoner, he whiles away time
reading his father's books. "I learned about Richard Milhouse Nixon, Pablo
Picasso, and Mao Tse Tung, as well as the poetry of Baudelaire and the philosophy of Voltaire and Rousseau" (32). Duc expects cosmopolitanism from
his readers as well, including lines of untranslated French in the narrative
(81). In this, also, he is in line with the majority of exile writers, the writers
of the older generation.

After two chapters told from his own point of view, he switches to his
father's point of view, drawing from his father's memoir. His father's story is
a very typical POW narrative, recounting first a long period of travel, when
he and other prisoners, including two Americans, were walked up the Ho
Chi Minh Trail, then a five-year period in solitary confinement, followed by
a six-year period during which other prisoners were gradually released but
he was held on and on for "reeducation." Duc devotes a large section of his
book to his father's narrative, thus keeping a large part of the focus of the
book on Viet Nam and the war. The elder man, during his solitary confinement, composed and memorized poetry, which he wrote down after his release and included in his memoir. Duc reproduces the poems at length;
except for these poems, his father's narrative reads very much like many

U.S. POW narratives in its depiction of the deprivations of prison life and the unbending, grim, and unimaginative demeanor of the guards. By bringing his father's narrative into his book, Duc allows U.S. readers to see the commonalities between American soldiers and POWs and their Vietnamese allies. This communality is something that has been recognized far too infrequently in Euro-American narratives and commentaries on the war.

Duc also devotes chapters to his mother's story. She has stayed behind after 1975 to wait for her husband's release. Her circumstances have worsened, though she always seems to have relatives who have resources, so that after she loses her job as principal of a girls' lycée she never really has to work but only pretends to work selling soup on the street so that she will not be hassled by the authorities. "Public security men once came to search my mother's house for hidden gold and stayed for an hour . . . but came up empty-handed. . . . They had not looked inside the pot of rice sitting on the brick stove in the kitchen" (100). Duc thus celebrates his mother's skills as a survivor in harsh wartime circumstances.

After eleven years, Duc's mother and father are reunited in Viet Nam when she is finally informed of what prison he's in and is allowed to visit. Shortly after, their mentally ill daughter, Dieu-Quynh, dies of kidney disease. The following year, Duc's father is finally released. Duc narrates these experiences as part of his own story—he does not separate himself from them narratively, although he was separated physically. In Vietnamese fashion his story is his family's story, a view that contrasts with the American ideology of individuality.

Duc intercuts his own experience as a refugee with the chapters detailing his father's and mother's stories. He leaves Viet Nam in 1975 at the age of sixteen, leaving his mother and his sister Dieu-Quynh behind to wait for his father's release. When he and other relatives get on the boat that will carry them out of Viet Nam, he is "suddenly aware that we had been on the losing side and now were ignominiously deserting our homeland and our ancestors. Images of my mother and sister swirled in my head. My chest and stomach burned with shame" (86). This response is very much a refugee's, rather than an immigrant's, response to departure for the new land.

When he arrives in America to live with his brother, he faces serious cultural dislocations, and it is here that his book takes on the character of immigrant literature, detailing his process of assimilation. His brother looks like an American to him, and his brother's Euro-American wife, Becky, presents a difficulty for him. "I couldn't bring myself to say her first name.

She was my elder, and in Vietnamese, I would have had to precede her name with the word Chi, 'Older Sister'" (138–39). Duc's brother Dinh has assimilated and succeeded in America. He has a red BMW, a house in the suburbs, a blonde wife, and a son. Even his ideas about "the war back home were strangely enhanced but also sanitized by television" (146). Dinh has become not a refugee but an immigrant. Dinh even suggests at one point that Duc should join the marines, unaware of the irony of what he suggests. "I didn't tell him I had seen a few marines in Viet Nam. Dinh hadn't seen the young girls thrown off their bicycles when marines reached down from their passing trucks to yank their hats away. He hadn't seen the masses of olive green steel transporting marines on the streets of Hue and Da Nang, or seen what they did in countless villages, firing mortars and burning huts" (150). Dinh has seen the war through American eyes, that is, through television, while Duc has seen it from the perspective of the occupied people and not of the occupying army that brutalizes enemy and ally alike.

Duc initially doesn't like U.S. culture, from the time he encounters it at a dance club in Guam while he's in transit. But he tries to reconcile the two cultures by finding similarities. When he goes looking for a job he reflects, "I had long heard about the value Americans placed on independence and self-sufficiency. Now, living in their midst, I wanted desperately to prove that I could be self-sufficient. The Vietnamese too value independence; millions had died defending it. Though foreigners often marvel at the acceptance by the Vietnamese of their prescribed roles within extended families, self-reliance is also cherished" (145). Duc is looking for a way to fit into U.S. culture by reaching for resources from his Vietnamese cultural background.

But he can't come to feel at home in America. The suburb his brother lives in drives him crazy. "For me the lawns began to stand for all that was sterile and uniform and conformist in America" (148). He heads for Canada, but because of his visa status he isn't supposed to leave the United States, so he goes with a friend to Washington, D.C., instead. He ends up working at a fast-food place in Alexandria, Virginia, and despite his dislike of America does begin to assimilate, although he tries to stay within the immigrant community, where he can speak Vietnamese and eat Vietnamese food. He feels very uncomfortable in the high school he attends. "I could not get used to the American habit of complaining about one's parents. . . . Even as I adopted their ways, I observed my friends through Vietnamese eyes" (158). He is pulled culturally in two directions, and that split, that competition for his soul, will remain with him permanently, his legacy as a war refugee who, unlike his brother, will not leave the past behind but will carry it with him, willing, as he is, to carry that pain in order to create a richer cultural experience.

In 1979 he becomes a social worker in San Jose. "I never questioned the fact that I was helping create instant Asian ghettoes and a massive bottom-rung work force serving the electronics industry. I didn't quite believe in the American Dream I was prescribing for the refugees, but enough of those I aided did eventually succeed" (162). The ambivalence he feels is most clearly shown when he finally applies for U.S. citizenship. When the examiner asks him questions about the Constitution, he gives answers out of panic and ignorance that the examiner takes to be jokes. When asked who takes over for the president, Duc answers "Alexander Haig," and the examiner passes him, saying, "You're really funny" (163). But for Duc, his split identity isn't really funny at all.

He becomes a social worker at Galang relocation camp, which processed over one hundred thousand refugees in the course of four years. Duc is happy to be helping Vietnamese people, but again he feels his own dividedness. "The refugees watched me because I looked like them and spoke their language but did not live their lives. . . . I was watching myself as well, a man transformed from a Vietnamese to an American, to a Vietnamese again" (197). In contact with Vietnamese outside America he has to face the degree of assimilation he has unknowingly undergone: "I believed that I retained in my most profound self a Vietnamese way of thinking, but outwardly I no longer acted Vietnamese. After a while the refugees' words added up to convince me how much I had changed" (198). He has become, to some extent, an American, taken on values that set him apart from the refugees. But at the same time he remains too much culturally Vietnamese to be truly American. He carries with him the legacy of war in his divided self.

When he returns to the United States to meet his parents, who have finally succeeded in leaving Viet Nam, he is racked with self-doubt. "I had earlier failed to set myself on the path of becoming the gentleman-scholar that was the aristocratic ideal of my family. Now I was prepared to abandon my Confucian duty to ease the later years of my elders" (209). He's filled with a sense of shame over his ambitions (he wants to go to London to accept a job offer from the BBC). When he meets his parents at the airport, his father's cosmopolitanism and worldliness put him at ease; the first thing his father asks is how Jesse Jackson's campaign is doing. In fact, his father copes with America better than Duc has—he immediately finds a job as a translator. When Duc asks him apprehensively how he'll get to work, his father matter-of-factly replies, "I'll take the M line to the Powell Street station" (212). For a man who has spent eleven years in reeducation camp, several of those in solitary confinement, navigating in San Francisco is no problem.

For Duc's father life in America is not difficult or fraught with dilemmas of identity. An old man already when he arrives, he knows very surely who he is in a way that Duc, arriving in America at sixteen, did not know. Duc's father writes and publishes in Vietnamese, knowing that his audience is the Vietnamese exile community, and he lives at peace in America, with no desire to return to Viet Nam, because the Socialist Republic of Viet Nam is not the Viet Nam he would wish to live in. He is truly an exile rather than an immigrant, and Duc, the immigrant, is stunned by his father's easy adjustment. "[M]y parents came to appreciate American society. Whereas I stubbornly lamented the impersonal, work-dominated, materialistic way of life, the impossibility of continued close friendships, the hypocritical government, the racial discrimination. My parents were always willing to overlook America's faults" (215). Yet Duc is much more American than they, wanting to follow his individual ambition rather than carry out his duty to his family. Once again, he suffers from the divided self that is his legacy of the war and his refugee/immigrant experience.

Duc does go to London but stays only two years. He decides to return to San Francisco when his father cries as Duc is leaving after being home for a visit. Duc has never seen his father cry before, and Duc's *hieu*, filial piety, reasserts itself. But before he leaves London he meets there his future wife, Gillian Anderson. All three of the Nguyen family siblings outmarry, something that seems perfectly acceptable to the parents, whose cosmopolitan attitude can encompass much cross-cultural communication while remaining rooted in an unconflicted Vietnamese identity.

There's an interesting tension in the book between what seem to be the political attitudes of Duc's father and mother and the attitudes that seem to be his own. He often reports incidents from his childhood in a way that reflects the prejudices of his upper-class Southern Vietnamese, anticommunist family, yet especially toward the end of the book it becomes clear that Duc himself is not particularly anticommunist. "Twice a week my mother and my uncle Anh-Anh and his wife trotted off to political training sessions" (100). The sarcastic tone seems to come from his mother's description of the event rather than his own feelings, just as the tone of the chapters detailing his father's experiences as a prisoner seems to come from his father's memoir. For example, in one of his father's chapters he writes, "Progressive ideas had not improved things. The equality of men and women, for example, had somehow robbed the women my father met of their femininity and characteristically Vietnamese graciousness" (112–13). Duc doesn't comment on his father's old-fashioned attitude; he simply reports it. In this way Duc acts almost as a ventriloquist for a story that he is only marginally part of, both in its events and in its ideology. In this way, in his fidelity to his parents' stories, he is attempting to fulfill his role as filial son, a role that he worries about fulfilling adequately because of the ways he has been changed by his sojourn in America. Ironically, he both does (by inclusion of his parents' story) and does not (through the creation of his own hybrid identity) fulfill that filial duty in the creation of his book.

His own attitudes emerge during the recounting of his own story. While reflecting on how bland he finds life in America, he thinks, "Oddly, I never blamed 'the Communists' for robbing me of my homeland. I had once feared them as ruthless enemies, but somehow I could never hate them" (147). When Duc's parents arrive in the United States, within a month he starts having political debates with them, which he feels very bad about. "I came to accept that for my parents, Viet Nam had been destroyed by cruel men blinded by Communist propaganda. For me, however, Viet Nam still existed: it was the place that held my cultural roots, my childhood. It was my homeland" (214).

Because of this feeling, Duc arranges to go to Viet Nam with a TV crew to film a documentary about his return. His parents warn him not to go, that he will be arrested, but he is determined. In Viet Nam, he is greeted as a stranger. Several people make remarks about how "fat" he is, a fat, pale American in contrast to the skinny, dark Vietnamese. His physical change marks his cultural change. His Vietnamese family criticize him for not living with and supporting his parents. He is also shocked by how his own modest American means look like extreme luxury next to the poverty of the Socialist Republic. He uses shoes lined up next to a doorway to symbolize this contrast. "My white canvas sneakers looked obscenely opulent next to the seven pairs of ragged flip-flops" when he visits family members (225).

He wants to feel comfortable in Viet Nam. "My exile was ending, and I strained to spot a familiar face on the streets. I wanted to be home" (229).

But the feeling does not come easily, if it comes at all. When he meets with old friends he is made "uncomfortable hearing about what [they] had been through after the fall of the South" (236) because he will be returning to the comforts of America. When a friend asks, "What do you think of your old home, fat man?" he has no answer (242).

He ultimately finds that his "home" exists only in memory, and his memory is continually thwarted by current reality. In Hue he finds the city to be short of material goods and "short of its old charm, also" (245), meaning that it is not the city he has cherished in his memory during his years of "exile." When he visits Ha Noi, a place he has never been to before, he finds that "Oddly, [it] felt like home" (256). He finds in Ha Noi the charm that he did not find in Hue. This is because it fits his imaginary picture of Viet Nam better than his actual old home does. After his return he writes that he misses home, but he can't quite define where home is for him. He writes of memories, rather than realities, of Da Nang and Da Lat, and of Ha Noi, "a city that now occupies a beloved space in my memory, or rather my heart" (260). Although "Viet Nam is still the place I call home," it is not his true home that the word *home* now conjures up for him. He is living in the liminal space of the permanent exile.

He admits that "my notions of my homeland are romanticized" (262) and says he has largely become an American, and his way of life would not fit in Viet Nam. He describes the liminal space he occupies as a quagmire, and he dreams, quite unrealistically, of raising his children in Viet Nam, completely failing to address the fact that his children will be only half Vietnamese, which will make them outsiders to Viet Nam even more than he is as an assimilated American.

One of the tasks that Duc performs in Viet Nam is to reclaim his sister Dieu-Quynh's ashes. He reflects that his other living relatives might leave Viet Nam and also live in exile. "We'd live there for ten, twelve, fifteen years, perhaps the rest of our lives. But some of us had to come back for the things we had left behind: our childhood home—the place, as the Vietnamese say, where our umbilical cords were cut. We would come back changed, but we would come back, for a loved one, and her ashes" (229). He concludes that "[w]here the ashes are, one should make that home" (264), thus proclaiming that family, not land, is what makes for cultural identity. His sister's ashes, along with the rest of his family, are in the United States, in San Francisco, now. But try as he might, the ashes can't quite bring him home. His home remains elusive, his identity suspended between that of immigrant and that of exile.

Jade Ngoc Quang Huynh's narrative, *South Wind Changing*, is less complex and less interesting than Duc's narrative, but it converges with Duc's in some interesting ways. Huynh's narrative focuses on his time in Viet Nam but is written from a much more assimilated perspective than Duc's, although this is not transparent in the narrative; it becomes clear only when Huynh's narrative is read in the context of other works such as Duc's.

One feature that sets Huynh's narrative apart from exile narratives by an older generation of writers is that although more than three-quarters of the book is set in Viet Nam it shows little nostalgia for the country and almost none of the features that are so prominent in other narratives, such as descriptions of Vietnamese foods, landscapes, and cultural traditions.[2] Huynh spends only the first fifty pages of the book on his first eighteen years in Viet Nam, then devotes the bulk of the book to the year he spent in a reeducation camp. Thus the picture of Viet Nam that emerges is not an idyllic, nostalgic, or positive one. There is also remarkably little about Huynh's large family in the book. Unlike Duc, who wrestles with *hieu* (filial piety) and *on* (moral debt) (Jamieson 16), Huynh seems to have assimilated to American individualism even before leaving Viet Nam. He wrestles with *on* at one point when he is in a position to escape from the labor camp, endangering the wounded guard who has been very friendly with him, but for Huynh individual liberty always wins out over every other personal or political consideration.

Huynh begins, "I was crying as I came into the world in 1957. . . . No one could have known, then, how much of my life was to be a continuation of these tears" (3). Huynh's is the most self-pitying of Vietnamese exile narratives, more than those of Nguyen Ngoc Ngan and Tran Tri Vu, who spent far more time in reeducation camps than did Huynh. His opening seems to place the book into a typically Vietnamese narrative style: "My story begins at the beginning of the nineteenth century, during the time my great grandfather, named Khoa, came to the newly settled rice-growing region of Vietnam" (3). What Huynh leaves out of this history is that the "newly settled" region of the Mekong Delta is actually the newly conquered region, where the expanding Vietnamese nation has pushed out the Khmer kingdom. Later in his narrative he says, "Vietnam and Cambodia had been enemies since the beginning of recorded history," as if the antagonism were mutual, rather than Cambodia being a victim of Vietnamese expansionism (56). The book overall lacks political and historical analysis to an extent that is very unusual among Vietnamese narratives and much more typical of American ones. Huynh was remarkably untouched by the war as a youth, and he seems to have only a shallow grasp of the politics of his home country. His anticommunism is uninformed, contrasting with the more sophisticated and conflicted positions Duc expresses in his narrative.

At one point Huynh makes the claim that "since [the communists] have taken over the south they have killed more of us than they did during the war" (202), which is untrue. He also blames the communists for Viet Nam's becoming "one of the poorest nations in the world" (203) and says that "when the northern government had taken over from the business-people, many sorts of [international] trade had come to a halt" (253), without ever mentioning the U.S. trade embargo (not lifted until 1994) and its effect on Viet Nam's postwar poverty. In this, again, Huynh's book is much more typical of an American point of view than a Vietnamese one.

The degree to which he was untouched by the war is remarkable. He describes a rather bucolic childhood on his wealthy father's farm until the Tet Offensive of 1968, which appears to be his first real contact with the war.[3] He writes, "I hated them for destroying my sleep" (10), indicating his real naïveté about the nature of the fighting. He's slightly wounded, and his sister kills herself because "she did not like guns and bullets, she did not like rockets and bombs and she did not want to be a victim or a witness to destruction" (19). Huynh admires his sister's act but seems largely untouched by it.

There are some odd elements of Huynh's narrative that cast doubt on the authenticity of some of the experiences he is reporting. He writes that helicopters sprayed a powder over his family's rice field. "It looked red to me but people said it looked orange. . . . [E]very time they sprayed, the leaves curled up on the plants and the trees died. The powder dropped down and dissolved into the river, stream, and creek. We drank the water daily" (19). I suppose he's suggesting that this is Agent Orange being sprayed, but Agent Orange is neither orange nor a powder (it is named after the color of the stripe on the barrel it was contained in).

After describing the Tet Offensive of 1968, he writes no more about the war except "The war continued on and off like a chronic disease. At night the VC controlled the village and during the day the Southern Government controlled it. We were trapped in the middle as victims" (20), yet he gives little sense of that victimization. Instead, he spends several pages describing a thwarted romance and exhibits his class prejudice when the woman he has been courting accepts an arranged marriage with a man whom Huynh scornfully refers to as "an uneducated peasant" (43). His only word on politics is "I didn't like either faction" (21). His rather simplistic analysis is "[A]ll the Vietnamese politicians are opportunists, more than Nationalists or anything else. Vietnam is a nation for the Vietnamese, but both the northern and southern governments import foreign theories and foreign weapons to try to increase their own power" (26–27). This nonpartisan cynicism is unusual among Vietnamese American writers. Huynh's individualism, through which he experiences the war mainly as an inconvenience to himself, fits the pattern of U.S. narratives much more than the pattern of Vietnamese exile narratives.

Huynh's best friend, Hanh, encourages him to pursue his education so he can become a leader of his country, but Huynh's ambitions are more personal, and he remains sufficiently untouched by the war that he can say, in 1975, when he takes the university entrance exams, "It seemed there would be a wonderful future ahead of me whatever I chose," whether law, medicine, or literature (32). Of course, no such future awaits him because, after the communist victory, his family fares badly. His father, a wealthy landowner, barely escapes being executed, and all of his brothers are placed in reeducation camps. Huynh is allowed to return to the university but is eventually picked up and sent to a labor camp, where he spends a terrible year. He escapes when he accompanies a wounded guard to a hospital. He lives with a friend's family, on forged papers, and makes two unsuccessful attempts to escape the country by boat until, on his third, he is successful. He and one brother make it to a refugee camp in Thailand.

After almost a year in the refugee camp he emigrates to the United States, where his oldest brother, a pilot in the Army of the Republic of Viet Nam whom he has believed to be dead, is living. Huynh arrives in the United States without English skills or job skills. At first he lives with his brother in Corinth, Mississippi, but he can't find much of a job there, so he becomes a true American, hitting the road looking for opportunity, moving "like a gypsy from place to place" (290). He wonders what his family would think of him, but he goes ahead. The search takes him first to San Jose, California, then to Bennington, Vermont, where he gets a scholarship to attend Bennington College. That is where he stops his narrative, although in actuality he went on to Brown University, where he earned an MFA.

He voices his ambition to a counselor in Bennington: "'I want to be a Vietnamese novelist,' I answered with all of my heart" (299). But Huynh is not in a position to become a "Vietnamese novelist": his education is in English, he is in the process of assimilating into American culture, and he identifies with the characters in Tolstoy's *War and Peace* (303). What Huynh may become is a Vietnamese American novelist, working to build a bridge between his two cultures, someone, like Duc, poised between refugee and immigrant, carrying the legacy of the war but writing to build bridges to peace. He ends his book with a picture of himself sitting in the sunshine on the Bennington campus, watching a butterfly, firmly placed in America, yet thinking of his scattered family—nine of his siblings living as refugees in the United States, his parents and two brothers still in Viet Nam. His last thoughts in the book are of his mother and the sufferings of her life. "How can I describe that life in words?" he asks (305). If he does, they will necessarily be words that translate between worlds.

A younger generation of Vietnamese Americans are carrying on that translation project, not in the form of narrative, but in the more linguistically and culturally embedded form of poetry. Works of poetry by Vietnamese American writers are just beginning to emerge. Truong Tran is a recent recipient of an MFA from San Francisco State University; he published his first volume of poetry in 2002. Christian Nguyen Langworthy is another poet of the same generation. Langworthy exemplifies those whose lives bridge cultures and those who carry the legacy of the war with them in body as well as mind. The son of a Vietnamese prostitute and an unknown GI father, he was adopted by an American family in 1975, when he was eight. He went through Army Reserve Officer Training Corps, served as a lieutenant in the U.S. Army Infantry, and received an MFA from Columbia. His chapbook *The Geography of War* (Cooper House, 1995) distills his own experience and memories into hard-edged poems.

The "geography of war," for Langworthy, is, in graphic form, the geography of Viet Nam. His concrete poem shows us where the war and his memories of it take place, and also the distance at which he now views them, declaring to himself that he is safe:

you realize you
walk on a two-
way
mirror through
which the dead can-
not
leap
back
(11)

In "Landing Zone" he writes of the perspective that American soldiers did not have: he describes soldiers emerging from helicopters that "descending flaunt / their rhythms" (14). But "They are unaware / we boys are watching, fascinated / by the weapons of war" (14).

The boys' fascination is shaped not only by their real-life experiences with war in their own land but also by American movies they've seen. In "The Game," the Vietnamese boys play cowboys and Indians on the streets of DaNang. The poem is fully aware of the irony of this game and ends with this stanza:

> The others shoot, the last Indian dies,
> and there is young Josie Wales—
> standing tall and still alive,
> breathing in gunsmoke,
> smelling burnt powder, and imagining
> certain victory and irrefutable
> defeat.
>
> (15)

The reference is to a Clint Eastwood movie where Eastwood plays a southerner whose family has been wiped out by Union troops during the Civil War; Langworthy refers, then, to an American movie hero who (at least from his own point of view) has had his land invaded by the same army that invaded Langworthy's land (and that Langworthy himself later joined, adding a layer of irony), and for whom a victory can be accomplished only in the context of loss.

Langworthy's poetry also alludes to the position of Amerasian orphans in the Socialist Republic of Viet Nam in "In This Country Revised," and "Mango." Several U.S. poets, John Balaban and Yusef Komunyakaa among them, have written poems about the experiences of Amerasians. This is the first that I know of by an Amerasian to appear in print.

> You go on living though
> unrecognized by your neighbor
> and you live by being dead,
> by not knowing your father's
> names which should be your own: Hanson, Baker, Jefferson, Mathers
>
> (17)

The line "you live by being dead" represents the paradox Langworthy incorporates into all his poems. Also, can it be coincidence that he chooses the name Mathers—as in Jerry Mathers, the Beaver?

In "Mango," Langworthy writes,

> You remember
> your father in his pressed uniform,
> the face of an American soldier,
> followed by countless others who
> handed you gum, and patted your shoulder
> . . . someone sees your face, and spits at the dust.
> They know who you are. They have a name for
> your kind, you child of the dust
>
> (27)

The child can make no connection to the procession of "fathers" who visit his mother and also no connection to his neighbors, for whom his face marks him as a product of that disapproved-of liaison.

In "Even as I Lie Pretending to Sleep," Langworthy records the experience of a boy whose mother works as a prostitute:

> and even as your son pretends to sleep
> his eyelids, closed, could never be dams
> against the tide and flow of tears
> when in the hours those men revisited
>
> (21)

And in "Woman under the Needle" he describes a "healing" ritual involving drawing blood with needles, then juxtaposes a second stanza:

> that soldier
> who felt ful-
> filled stood
> outside your
> open wound
> and closed the
> scab of door
> and smoked his

cigarette,
satisfied with
bleeding you
     (23)

He ends the book with the poignant "Dream of Silent Dreams," a poem
about haunting:

memories that haunt this house of mine—
to watch my dreams like films without color,
these voices blare from another time:
"When you leave this place forever,
remember me," my mother said.
"Remember me," my sister pleaded,
and silent dreams are far and near.
                    (37)

Langworthy has remembered and, in presenting *The Geography of War,* has
asked us not only to remember with him but to see anew through his eyes.

This is in effect what all of the writers of the refugee generations are
doing; by carrying the war, the past, into the present in narrative and verse,
Nguyen Qui Duc, Jade Ngoc Quang Huynh, and Christian Nguyen Langworthy represent a transitional period in Vietnamese American literature.
Poised between exile literature and immigrant literature, they are making
way for future generations of American-born Vietnamese writers who will
write out of a primary identity as Americans, but Americans with a strong
relationship to the American War in Viet Nam that is both similar to and
different from the relationship of non–Vietnamese Americans to that war,
a war whose memory U.S. culture as a whole seems unable to leave behind.

Notes

1. I have followed Vietnamese name conventions for Nguyen Qui Duc, who
prints his name Vietnamese style, with family name first and given name last. Because there are very few family names, it is the normal custom to refer to people by
title (if they have one) and given name; hence my reference to him as Duc. With
writers who use U.S. name conventions, turning the order around so that family

name comes last, as with Jade Ngoc Quang Huynh, I follow the U.S. custom of referring to them by family name.

2. See Christopher, ch. 2, for an extended discussion of these themes.

3. An interesting point of contrast between Duc and Huynh is that Duc calls it Tet Mau Thanh, its Vietnamese designation, while Huynh calls it the Tet Offensive, its U.S. designation.

WORKS CITED

Balaban, John. *Locusts at the End of Summer: New and Selected Poems.* Port Townsend, WA: Copper Canyon Press, 1997.

Christopher, Renny. *The Viet Nam War/The American War: Images and Representations in Euro-American and Vietnamese Exile Narratives.* Amherst: University of Massachusetts Press, 1995.

DuBois, W. E. B. *The Souls of Black Folk. Three Negro Classics.* New York: Avon, 1965.

Huynh, Jade Ngoc Quang. *South Wind Changing.* Minneapolis: Graywolf, 1994.

Jamieson, Neil. *Understanding Vietnam.* Berkeley: University of California Press, 1995.

Kaplan, Caren. "The Poetics of Displacement: Exile, Immigration, and Travel in Contemporary Autobiographical Writing." PhD diss., University of California, Santa Cruz, 1987.

Komunyakaa, Yusef. "Dui Boi, Dust of Life." *Dien Cai Dau.* Middletown, CT: Wesleyan University Press, 1988.

Lam, Andrew. "My Vietnam, My America." *Nation* 10 Dec. 1990: 724–26.

Langworthy, Christian Nguyen. *The Geography of War.* Oklahoma City: Cooper House, 1995.

Nguyen Hung Quoc. "The Vietnamese Literature in Exile." *Journal of Vietnamese Studies* 5 (1992): 24–34.

Nguyen Ngoc Ngan, with E. E. Richey. *The Will of Heaven: One Vietnamese and the End of His World.* New York: Dutton, 1982.

Nguyen Qui Duc. *Where the Ashes Are: The Odyssey of a Vietnamese Family.* New York: Addison Wesley, 1994.

Tran Tri Vu. *Lost Years: My 1,632 Days in Vietnamese Reeducation Camps.* Indochina Research Monographs No. 3. Berkeley, CA: Institute of East Asian Studies, 1988.

Tran, Truong. *Dust and Conscience.* Berkeley, CA: Apogee Press, 2002.

WARS WITHIN PEACE

CHAPTER ELEVEN

Seeing the War through Cut-off Triangles

H.D. and Gertrude Stein

KATHY J. PHILLIPS

H.D.'s short story "Ear-Ring" (1936) and Gertrude Stein's short play *An Exercise in Analysis* (1917) flit over the surface of small talk at socialite gatherings, where guests studiously avoid mentioning World War I yet seem to think of nothing else. This paradox is reflected in an overt theme of double vision, seeing and not seeing at the same time. Nevertheless, if characters try to deny the war, the texts themselves do not; they use a deliberately indirect style to explore both the war's traumatizing effects and its possible liberations. In fact, H.D.'s story contains a remarkably succinct manifesto for a new kind of art that could take account of a distressing fragmentation, yet at the same time fruitfully use fragments to question the war. Modeled on cubism in painting, this literature of "cut-off triangles" would interject "time-in-time"—or historical context—back into the aesthetic pleasures of "time-out-of-time," in a collage of odd juxtapositions (H.D. 105–6). Meanwhile, Stein's play glues together exploded fragments of conversation in cubistic arrangements even more "cut-off" and bizarre than H.D.'s.[1] Although modernists are often accused of escaping from social causality into a realm of pure art, H.D.'s associative stream of consciousness and Stein's disjointed "nonsense" jostle together specific, concrete references to the war in ways that suggest new lines of analysis.

These works by noncombatants provide an important complement to literature about World War I by combatants. Even when disillusioned, writing veterans often replace empty words like *honor* and *duty* with the newly meaningful word *camaraderie,* which somehow makes the war seem all right again. Moreover, veterans' focus on the sufferings of buddies gives little sense of the reasons why governments are requiring such slaughter or of the wider impact of the war on civilians. By contrast, H.D's story and Stein's play offer through their small talk a surprisingly large view of important postwar effects: (1) a sense of falling into a frightening whirlpool; (2) a scramble by governments and companies for territories and raw materials, perhaps leading to the replacement of democracy by plutocracy; (3) an unsettling of gender definitions and sexual arrangements; and (4) a revolution in art.

H.D. (pseudonym for Hilda Doolittle) characterizes the aftermath of World War I as "War dizziness," a fear that physical buildings as well as social structures, people as well as beliefs, have collapsed and could go on collapsing: "Everything in the world had gone down, in a vortex of babeltongues, long since. This [hotel dining room in Greece] was a whirl-pool in a backwash" (95–96). The vertigo that the main character, Madelon Thorp, experiences as a tourist only reflects, in miniature, a much more widespread postwar disorientation, "where everything might, at any moment, slip over the edge of nothing into nowhere" (95).

Caught within the general whirling, Madelon and her peers scramble to "Hold on to something" (95). At first Madelon clutches at the apparent order of numbers, repeating like a mantra the digits of the year, 1-9-2-0, or counting the reassuring appearances, three nights running, of a woman wearing diamond earrings (92). Although the expensive earrings may be "shriek-marks" that materialize the anguish of the woman's companion, a Russian refugee salvaging movable riches, they serve Madelon as quieter "paper-weights, set at two corners of the billowing fabric of her perception of this ball-room" (92). However, Madelon's harmless sequences of numbers, with their illusion of rationality, soon merge with the more ruthless logic of the account book, as flush war profiteers have "got it down to dollars and diamonds" (99). Sleek investors join refugees who have just lost most of their fortunes in placing their hopes of security in tangible objects: jewels and especially the oil wells of the American petroleum magnate who sits just beyond the White Russian exiles.

As the investors look hopefully ahead, they blot out unpleasant topics, including the sufferings of the war, the possible Allied prolongation of those sufferings to secure territory, and the role of profit in allowing new wars. But because those issues still nag at consciousness, H.D's story insists on a theme of seeing and not seeing at the same time, of not mentioning things while still somehow harping on them. An "unwritten pact," a "social law," decrees that "heads, self-consciously and a shade too indifferently, did not turn" toward the expensive diamonds, yet everyone follows their entrance minutely (92–93). Similarly, no one brings up the pains of the war, yet they hover unspoken in the room. Madelon is *Mrs.* Thorpe, but Archie Rowe, not her husband, accompanies her after the war. Is she a widow? Has the war driven the couple apart irreconcilably—as it did H.D. herself and Richard Aldington (Tate 169)? The story briefly hints at Madelon's personal losses through a bitter-sounding reference to a time "pre-war. Pre merry-widow" (96), with no explanation whether death or a gulf between the experiences of civilian and soldier has parted her from her husband.

If Madelon perceives that the oil and diamonds form part of a quest for stability within the general unmooring brought about by war, she also finds these anchors unsatisfactory. For one thing, she silently blames the powerful men among the dinner guests for the ugliness and exploitation of their entrepreneurship. The chatter of the Standard Oil magnate "bored into the thick Balkan air like one of his own steam-drills," producing aridity and "destruction" along with petroleum (97). After the war, it gradually dawned on the participants that imperial control of Mesopotamian and Persian oil had edged its way into European policy as a "first-class British [and French] war aim" (Yergin 188). Moreover, the postwar, explicit goal of Standard Oil of New Jersey was "to be interested in every producing area no matter in what country it is situated"; the U.S. government, which only ten years before had worried about an oil monopoly, now backed the oilmen's megalomaniac aims (Yergin 195, 199). In H.D.'s story, Madelon foresees that the willingness to use force to gain oil will continue into the future. She hears the voice of the American magnate blast into the "air, laden with cross-currents and counter-currents of diplomatic suavity, like a truck piled high with dynamite, veering suddenly into a *mardi-gras* carnival" (97).

Trying to avoid the ruthless materialism of those who chase "dollars and diamonds" down through the whirlpool set spinning by the war, Madelon seeks a different anchor, this time hoping for a support in art. She reminds herself that the notes of a violin and the columns of the Parthenon "still cut patterns in . . . human consciousness, now murky with din and battle" (103). Looking to orderly art as the only solace that "vied, in clarity, with debit and credit," Madelon thinks that art will somehow provide a secure foothold to move beyond the muck left by war and the scramble for raw materials (103).

In her optimism, Madelon sounds very much like the Cambridge academics F. R. Leavis and Q. D. Leavis, who, by the early 1930s, declared English literature "*the* supremely civilizing pursuit" (Eagleton 31). British participation in World War I led to a contradictory attitude toward art. On the one hand, the war fostered nationalist pride, a desire to promote "national" literature as a boost to patriotism. On the other hand, the war produced a "spiritual hungering," which some artists thought nonjingoistic poetry might fill better than words like *patriotism* and *duty* (Eagleton 30). Yet when the Leavises offered "rich," "complex," and "mature" art to counter the same commercialism that bothers Madelon, the academics' vagueness and their nostalgia for an idealized seventeenth-century rural life allowed literature buffs to "survive" postwar industrial society rather than "transform" it, as Terry Eagleton persuasively objects (33, 36). Madelon too looks to an idealized, long-ago world and vaguely credits "patterns" in art with revivifying power (H.D. 103).

Interestingly, H.D. comes to some of the same political dissatisfactions with art as Eagleton does, for she has Madelon perceive that the blithe patterning that was supposed to heal postwar traumas produces its own maladies. Although Madelon is trying to leave behind the chaos left by the oilman's mechanical steam-drill by turning to ordered art, she remains disappointed. If she replaces concrete objects with concrete patterns, the focus on concrete surface may still deny human values, objectify people, and hush up a more abstract analysis, including the crucial explanations for the war. Madelon herself begins to objectify people and empty them of complexity, by shrinking her companion Archie to two flattened sides of a silhouette, out of a "second-rate" Egyptian collection, and by disdaining the woman in diamonds as "a marble cast . . . done in inferior marble" (102, 93). People turn into art, and art turns into just another commodity. As Franco Moretti sardonically points out, when modernists from the surrealists to T. S. Eliot call for the random, incongruous juxtaposition of concrete objects, "an umbrella and a sewing machine meeting on an anatomical table," the effect looks very much like the strange but evocative juxtapositions in a department store display or the new realm of advertising (340). Enjoying art for art's sake uncomfortably resembles buying an item for buying's sake.

Yet here again H.D. anticipates Moretti's warnings about equalized, aesthetically valued objects or pretty words stripped of their connections to social causes. For H.D. has Madelon abandon her beloved, traditional art of violin and Parthenon, which she initially extols as something safely stabilized out of time, and start recommending instead a new art, which Madelon calls "cut-off triangles . . . superimposed" (105). Self-consciously modeled on cubism in painting, this new cubist literature would nevertheless go beyond anything possible in oils by interjecting "time-in-time"—or historical context—back into aesthetically distanced "time-out-of-time" (106). Within the resulting collage, she discovers (along with contemporary Virginia Woolf) precisely those historical and social links that Eagleton and Moretti thought missing from any modernist program (Phillips xii–xxix).

This new literature of cut-off triangles that H.D. calls for had, in fact, already been written by Stein. In *An Exercise in Analysis,* Stein too conjures up a socialite setting: a party, or at least a tête-à-tête, where two speakers plan future soirées or deliver a scathing postmortem on recent guests. The war is, of course, still going on in 1917, though Stein's speakers seem at first glance to ignore it even more resolutely than H.D.'s tourists. Behind the characters, however, Stein is very aware of some changes the war has already brought about, which will certainly persist after hostilities end. Paralleling the odd vision that enables H.D.'s travelers to simultaneously obsess over and blot out disturbing topics (like the ostentatious display of wealth and the role of war in making widows), a motif in Stein's play includes both seeing and not seeing the war. On the very first page, someone warns, "Do not see soldiers ahead they swim," but the next speaker replies, "So they do" (119). While the first voice cautions against seeing (because the men swim in the nude? because they inhabit restricted military areas, which one should at least pretend not to notice?), the speech instead alerts the listener—and us—to the soldiers' presence.

Given this specific introduction of a military ambience on the first page, the title and the first five lines (alternating with erratic scene labels) can be read as a commentary about the effects of the war on people and art:

AN EXERCISE IN ANALYSIS

A Play

I have given up analysis.
Act II
Splendid profit.
Act III
I have paid my debt to humanity.

Act III

Hurry.

Act IV

Climb. In climbing do not be contented.

(119)

The claim to have given up analysis registers a wartime sense that prewar meanings and frames have shattered, a mood corresponding to Madelon's "War dizziness" (95). While Stein's first line, "I have given up analysis," flatly contradicts the title, this beginning does not so much cancel the title as announce a new, paradoxical art that has given up direct, explicit analysis of the war but still pursues an indirect and implicit analysis through suggestive, multivalenced non sequiturs. For example, the second line, "Splendid profit," may mean that writer and reader metaphorically profit in giving up analysis, gaining the pleasures of wordplay, or the line may mean that the war has bestowed a more literal "Splendid profit" on a few investors because of certain commodities, like the oil that looms in H.D.'s story or the image of "rubber" that surges up in Stein's play (122).

Still in a military context, Stein's third line, "I have paid my debt to humanity," sounds like a tag a soldier might utter, perhaps in response to a patriotic journalist, treating the soldier as someone who pays out effort and suffering at someone else's behest, as opposed to someone who sells, for himself, like the Standard Oil man. Yet if this third line can be imagined as spoken by a serviceman who feels satisfaction in duty, the next injunction, "Hurry," and the warning "Climb. In climbing do not be contented" pick up the restlessness that characterizes most veterans. Whether these speakers attempt mountain climbing or social climbing, they face resistance, not the contentment in duty done or the reverence from an appreciative community that recruits may hope for but that veterans seldom experience. These five cryptic lines, then, glancingly touch on the war. Although brief, the glances take in a wide field of war: its economic motive in "profit," its reliance on sweeping propaganda phrases like "debt to humanity," the hurrying on of civilians (during and after war) who may prefer not to weigh up losses and lessons, and a shattering of belief in rationality and analysis.

Just as H.D.'s Madelon shakily tries to hold on to reason through the spell of "War dizziness" by repeating the digits of the year, Stein registers— and then spoofs—this need for order by obsessively numbering and labeling the lines of the play. *An Exercise in Analysis* divides into many "Parts" (up to LX, in its short, twenty-page length), and each part subdivides into

"Acts" (up to VI). Humorously, however, almost none of the acts extend be-yond a single line. The plan skips some numbers altogether, while others stutter on more than once. When an "Act III" follows another "Act III," Stein disingenuously offers a kind of "Take 2," to amend any mistakes, or simply to admit openly that all this numbering is folly, no more effective in recon-structing a stable world after the Great War than the "debit and credit" of Standard Oil (H.D. 103). Of course, those tidy entries in a ledger not only ineffectually stave off chaos but also, perhaps, require periodic wars, whereas Stein's wild proliferation of scenes rollicks along much more harmlessly.

Knowing that enumeration and direct evaluation, using all the old ter-minology of "Big Words" like *honor* and *duty* (Hynes 296), no longer carry credibility because of the war, H.D. and Stein turn to indirection, in the self-conscious literary programs they call "cut-off triangles" or analysis/no analy-sis. In such literature, "Everything seems unrelated yet diametrically related, as you slant one facet of a diamond into another set of values" (H.D. 106). H.D. slants facets of ancient Greece and modern America into each other to come up with insights on commodities and warmaking and gender, while the snippets of dialogue that Stein slants into each other evaluate war and sexuality as well as war and gender.

Initially, Madelon protests that no trick could "link Sparta up with oil-wells and the Hellespont with steam-drills," yet once she has incongruously set them side by side, the juxtaposition teaches her that she has erroneously idealized both ancient Greece and modern America (98). As she cubisti-cally crowds together the words "Xerxes—Salamas *[sic]*—Woodrow Wil-son" and "the United States of Pericles," she sketches a new view that reveals Athenian democracy to be less innocent and American democracy more suspect than she had thought (98, 100). That is, Greece may have occupied the moral high ground by defeating the invading Persians under Xerxes at Salamis, but Athens under Pericles soon invaded other Greek cities and pursued its own empire. Pericles boasted a democracy, but Athens defeated other cities not by vote but by force.

When H.D. then slants Woodrow Wilson into this illuminating dia-mond, she sees that he too, like Pericles, may be advertising a democracy not entirely true. Madelon asks tentatively, "Liberty? Wasn't that just the thing that had held the show together?" (99). Her question marks cast doubt on liberty as the main motive for the Allies, as the word *show* (soldiers' slang for horrendous bombardments) does double duty by suggesting the theatrical façade of propaganda. Although President Wilson loudly proclaimed that the Allies fought World War I to "make the world safe for democracy" and ensure "self-determination of peoples," once he got to the Versailles Conference in 1919 (the year before H.D. sets her story), Wilson allowed the Allies to retain their vast colonies, acquire Germany's overseas territory, and carve up the Middle East into equally imperial "mandates" (Winter and Baggett 352–53). Within these mandates, European—and American—oil companies could now call the shots. Madelon listens to the oil magnate explain "Greek etymology," which she feels "applied equally to Woodrow Wilson and to Pericles"; the lesson proceeds from "autocracy" to "democracy" to "plutocracy" (99–100). Both Athens in the Peloponnesian War and America after World War I stand revealed as imperial, with their goals not liberty but plutocratic rule (now by oil companies), and with their means not democracy but militarism. After all, the man whom Madelon calls "Petroleum" constantly sits shadowed by "the military attaché from Washington" (94).

Both Pericles and Wilson, then, betray democracy for power. Madelon also discovers that both ancient Greece and the modern Allies further transgress democracy by devaluing women, who cannot vote or make their own decisions. When the name *Mavrodaphne* for a wine reminds her of the ancient story of Daphne, Archie does not agree that the status of women merits any attention: "O, old '*daphne*,' he dismissed it" (100). According to a Greek myth (as retold by Latin Ovid), Apollo chases Daphne for sex, and after she prefers to be turned into a tree rather than submit to rape the god still molests her branches. To make wreaths for military captains, Apollo appropriates Daphne's laurel as the "sign of all I own" (Ovid 46).

This ancient ownership of women has not, in Madelon's opinion, ended in the twentieth century, for the very first words of H.D.'s "Ear-Ring" bluntly assert that "Someone had bought her with two diamonds" (92). Although this reference to a mistress may seem to focus on private affairs, H.D. draws the whole story of public plutocracy—acquiring territory for the sake of oil and jewels—out of an initial glimpse of women as property. As the historian Gerda Lerner will later argue, ancient societies may have first conceived the idea that they could exploit slaves from the oppression of women (77). Among the classical Greeks, Aristotle declared that male slaves could "apprehend" but not "have" rationality, a distinction that he had already codified to limit women (Lerner 209). By the time the nineteenth-century European imperial powers competed with each other in a rivalry that certainly contributed to the Great War, colonizers were still calling the Orient "feminine," meaning "passive," "silent," and "supine," as a means of justifying control (Said 138). While H.D. does not discursively analyze any of these links between gender and power, she graphically shows us the Standard Oil and military entourage revolving around a commodified and controlled woman.[2]

Just as Madelon grows weary of Archie's autocratic style, which will "go on impressing himself" while modern Daphnes remain confined to their trees (101), Stein's characters put up with the accommodations that still-dominant men can exact from women: "We do not allow Mr. Douglas to be contradicted here. We do not desire that he should feel himself beginning to be about to be wrong" (121). Nevertheless, while H.D. diagnoses the postwar attitudes toward women as scarcely improved over those of the ancient Greeks, Stein's speakers seem more cheerfully empowered to topple or at least ignore some of the old patterns for both sex and gender. When the anonymous voices in the play comment hopefully, "You said you would not be married. / Plenty of space to put things together," they imply both new physical space and new conceptual space to put partners of the same sex in the same bed (127). As suggested by this play as well as other World War I literature, such as Radclyffe Hall's "Miss Ogilvy Finds Herself," Kay Boyle's "Count Lothar's Heart," Helen Zenna Smith's *Not So Quiet*, and Rose Allatini's *Despised and Rejected*, the war may have contributed to clearing that space by throwing men together in trenches or protests and women together in support work. The greater range of types met, the greater intimacy of the contact, and the intensified need to taste life while it lasted may have enabled people to realize, perhaps for the first time, that their own same-sex desires were not a unique, personal quirk. In Stein's play, the sight of soldiers swimming leads to the conclusion "She was settled for it. For life. For me," as if her lack of response to the unusual, war-provided glimpse of nude men had made a woman recognize her real attraction to other women (120–21). Stein's speakers then exult, "Can you come together," repeating the line five times in a row, suggesting meanings on a gamut from coming over for a visit to sharing an orgasm (137). These speakers avoid the contemporary, medically tinged vocabulary for homosexuality by summing up their new life together, in part encouraged by the war, in the simplest possible words: "What is the name of the bedding. / It is different" (137).

These new sexual arrangements also entail questions about gender definitions, which are in turn tied to military propaganda. One interesting sequence in Stein's play circles around an elusive "bird," along with elusive concepts of "mannish" and "womanish":

Do not tell me about birds.
What is a bird.
We have suffered.
I can cure anything.
So can most fishes.
And birds.
And water-fowl.
There is plenty to blame. The introductions.
Waiting.
And memory.
Please be mannish.
Please do.
Please do be a sailor.
Please be womanish.
A bird.
There are many parts to the bird.
She knows.

(130–31)

According to turn-of-the-century notions of "sexual inversion," homo-sexual men must be "feminine"—that is, imbued with some trait construed as feminine, such as deference or musical appreciation. Lesbians must be "mannish," construed as bold. Sexologist Havelock Ellis, for instance, sur-prised to detect no "trace of a beard or a moustache" in his "cases" of ho-mosexual women, still claims to find in them the "brusque, energetic move-ments . . . the direct speech . . . the masculine straightforwardness and sense of honor . . . [that] suggest the underlying abnormality to a keen observer" (96–97). Defining "masculine" as athletic, frank, and honorable, Ellis per-mits only heterosexual men and lesbians into the domain of bold speech and action before demoting the women again, from honor into abnormality. With such gender constructions in place, it is no wonder that an active, ver-bal woman—like Stein herself—may have preferred the label *mannish* to claim her mind as well as her sexuality.

At the same time, Stein's own relationship with Alice Toklas "swerved perilously close to perpetuating the social conventions of the Victorian bourgeois marriage" (Stimpson 5). Yet if the speakers in the play can no more than Stein entirely cast off words like *mannish* and *womanish,* the characters deploy these terms with some fluidity. Is a sailor mannish? Are two sailors sleeping together doubly mannish (flouting Ellis, who thought that both men would be feminine)? If we imagine two women speaking here, does one ask for a husband's command and the other offer a wife's helpfulness? Or is one listener silently smiling while the other partner asks in turn for qualities that she has been trained to think of as mannish or womanish? While Catharine Stimpson usefully cautions that "to destabilize is not to eradicate" an inherited sex-gender system (11), Stein's two characters wildly play on the word *bird*, which could mean, according to the *Dictionary of Sexual Slang*, "woman" *or* "penis" *or* "female genitals" (Richter 20). With terms so congenially flitting everywhere, maybe the sexes do not after all differ as radically as the sexologists—or military propagandists—liked to think.

Stein's play jostles the military assumption that sailors and soldiers have cornered more mannishness than civilian men and that servicemen derive their coveted masculinity from the fight. When the speakers return to the topic of soldiers swimming, which they broached on the first page, they interpret the event succinctly:

Act IV.
What did she see when she saw men swimming.
Part III.
Examples.
Examples and examples.
All examples of children.
Now to ask guns.
Now to ask colors.

(120–21)

By the short phrase "examples of children," Stein demolishes the flattering claim by governments that military service "builds men." While recruitment slogans encourage soldiers to define men as active, strong initiators, military life instead renders each rank passively submissive to the one above it. In addition, the word *children* evocatively exposes the actual vulnerability of iron-clad men, who can easily be smashed by a shell and cry "mama" in their last moments, as Stein must have known at some point in her two years of experience as a driver of soldiers, even if she usually catered to more cheerily convalescent ones (Gregory 268, 270).

Instead of asking guns to settle the vexing question of gender identity, Stein and H.D. ask "colors" to unsettle it, in the new modernist art, whether in paint or on the page. H.D.'s incongruent juxtapositions manage to extend the picture of war, from a sketch of buddies sacrificing for the greater "good," into a panorama of military attachés assembling for the greater good of Standard Oil. These men rely on a system that imagines women as helpless Daphnes who will supposedly need laurel-crowned heroes to fight in their honor. Stein's cubist juxtapositions similarly imply that societies call sailors and soldiers "mannish" to keep them enlisting, even though war more likely reduces men to helpless children. Meanwhile, some women emerge from the dizzying whirlpool of World War I to occupy a "different" bedding to-gether or to formulate a well-thought-out literary program that slants "time-in-time," or historical context, back into the aesthetic consolations of art.

H.D.'s and Stein's supposedly "nonsensical" modernism comments, therefore, on a number of important postwar issues: to expose that the Al-lies may have fought less to preserve democracy and more to amass terri-tory and commodities; to question whether calling women helpless and men aggressive might be a construct to support war; and to demonstrate that composing juxtaposed fragments can be just as socially conscious as writing essayistic prose.

NOTES

1. Jacqueline Brogan calls Stein "the 'founding mother' of American cubist lit-erature" (250). While she does not discuss Stein's plays, Brogan characterizes cubism in literature as "multiplicity of perspectives," "repetitions," "collage-like scenes," and "self-referentiality" (250, 253).

2. In "Ear-Ring," H.D. finds the postwar condition of women little improved over that of the ancient Greeks. In *Kora and Ka* (written in 1930), H.D. further blames postwar England for heightening its misogyny, as well as for constraining men into a rigid mold as doers of violence. The character John Helforth has lost two brothers in the war, and his mother expects John to enlist next, but the war ends be-fore he can do so. Although John resents that England trained his generation into "blood-lust," he cannot shuck off the indoctrination that only "brutality" makes "masculinity" (36, 28). When he notices that he simultaneously condemns his broth-ers for docilely accepting "their casual and affable 'sacrifice'" yet wishes that he had been able to prove "masculinity" by sacrificing himself too, he evades the contradic-tion by projecting guilt onto "belching mothers," stuffed with propaganda, who then "belched out in return, fire and carnage in the name of Rule Britannia" (39, 36).

WORKS CITED

Brogan, Jacqueline Vaught. "The 'Founding Mother': Gertrude Stein and the Cubist Phenomenon." *Challenging Boundaries: Gender and Periodization*. Ed. Joyce W. Warren and Margaret Dickie. Athens: University of Georgia Press, 2000. 248–66.

Eagleton, Terry. *Literary Theory: An Introduction*. Minneapolis: University of Minnesota Press, 1983.

Ellis, Havelock. *Sexual Inversion*. 1897. New York: Arno, 1975.

Gregory, Elizabeth. "Gertrude Stein and War." *Women's Fiction and the Great War*. Ed. Suzanne Raitt and Trudi Tate. Oxford: Clarendon Press, 1997. 263–81.

H.D. "Ear-Ring." *Women, Men and the Great War: An Anthology of Stories*. Ed. Trudi Tate. Manchester: Manchester University Press, 1995. 92–106.

———. *Kora and Ka, with Mira-Mare*. New York: New Directions, 1996.

Hynes, Samuel. *A War Imagined: The First World War and English Culture*. New York: Atheneum, 1991.

Lerner, Gerda. *The Creation of Patriarchy*. New York: Oxford University Press, 1986.

Moretti, Franco. "The Spell of Indecision." *Marxism and the Interpretation of Culture*. Ed. Cary Nelson and Lawrence Grossberg. Urbana: University of Illinois Press, 1988. 339–46.

Ovid. *The Metamorphoses*. Trans. Horace Gregory. New York: New American, 1958.

Phillips, Kathy J. *Virginia Woolf against Empire*. Knoxville: University of Tennessee Press, 1994.

Richter, Alan. *Dictionary of Sexual Slang*. New York: Wiley, 1993.

Said, Edward W. *Orientalism*. New York: Vintage-Random, 1978.

Stein, Gertrude. *An Exercise in Analysis. Last Operas and Plays*. Ed. Carl Van Vechten. New York: Vintage-Random, 1975.

Stimpson, Catharine R. "Gertrude Stein and the Transposition of Gender." *The Poetics of Gender*. Ed. Nancy K. Miller. New York: Columbia University Press, 1986. 1–18.

Tate, Trudi. "Gender and Trauma: H.D. and the First World War." *Image and Power: Women in Fiction in the Twentieth Century*. Ed. Sarah Sceats and Gail Cunningham. New York: Longman, 1996. 163–72.

Winter, Jay, and Blaine Baggett. *The Great War and the Shaping of the 20th Century*. New York: Penguin Studio, 1996.

Yergin, Daniel. *The Prize: The Epic Quest for Oil, Money, and Power*. New York: Simon and Schuster, 1991.

CHAPTER TWELVE

The Forgotten Brigade

Foreign Women Writers and the End of the Spanish Civil War

ARÁNZAZU USANDIZAGA

Victory and defeat are both passing moments.

Martha Gellhorn, *The Face of War*

The Spanish Civil War was central to twentieth-century international politics and to its literary representation. As has been proved by historical documentation, events in Spain between 1936 and 1939 were of enormous relevance to the rest of Europe and even the world. In spite of a nonintervention pact agreed upon by the allies and the German and Italian fascist governments in August 1936, many foreign troops volunteered or were sent to Spain during the war. Some soldiers, mostly German and Italian, fought with Franco's troops, while others, British, American, Canadian and central European, volunteered to fight for the Republican army as part of the famous International Brigades. But not all the foreigners involved in the Spanish Civil War were soldiers. The significance of the political and military events taking place in Spain at the time attracted many journalists as well as many intellectuals and writers. Besides, once the Allies, afraid of angering Hitler, agreed against military intervention in favor of Republican Spain, a huge and increasingly important Aid Spain Committee was established in Britain and soon after in the United States. These organizations, in charge of providing mostly medical but also other kinds of humanitarian support to Republican Spain, allowed many foreign men and particularly women to directly participate in the events taking place in Spain.[1]

Foreign women went to Spain from the very beginning of the war, and several among them remained until its very end and even beyond. The power that the efficient propaganda of international communism had over the Euro-American left in a period of great economic depression convinced intellectuals of the moral imperative of transforming their ideological position into political action. Writers and intellectuals of the West felt it was their duty to save the world from fascism by fighting and dying for the Spanish Republic. The International Brigades were not allowed by the organizing communist parties to join the Republican fronts until September 1936, but some women, such as the British writer and political activist Susan Townsend Warner and her friend the poet Valentine Ackland, were so impatient to join the war that they drove all the way from England on their own in August 1936 and became the first foreign ambulance drivers in Republican Spain. The local government in Barcelona had to improvise a special pass to enable them to travel to and from the fronts and hospitals. Later, in September, several women volunteered with the foreign troops, not only as nurses, social workers, and administrative support, but as actual combatants, for the Spanish Republican government allowed women soldiers to fight along with men at the fronts during the first four months of the war. In fact, the first foreigner to die at a Spanish front was the British sculptor Felicia Brown. She fell in combat when stopping to help a soldier wounded beside her. Brown's death was not an exception. In her account of her experiences in Spain, *Red Spanish Notebook: The First Six Months of the Revolution and the Civil War in Spain* (1937), the Australian anarchist and surrealist poet Mary Low movingly narrates the death in combat of another woman, a beautiful German-Jewish nineteen-year-old volunteer called Putz.

Given the huge prestige attached to joining Republican Spain, many other women intellectuals, reporters, and writers went to Spain during the war and wrote about it. Some were already well-known novelists, journalists, and poets. Others began to write, stimulated by what they saw. They used different genres to talk about Spain: autobiographical memoirs, articles in newspapers and periodicals, short stories, poems. In some of their texts the war is used for political and moral analysis; in others it is used for interesting experimentation in the writing of modern war as well as in the tentative construction of women's self.

Foreign women's presence on the battlefields and home fronts of Spain must be connected to women's approach to the theaters of war during World War I, and their writing about Spain must be partly explained in relation to women's written responses to the previous war, though of course a number of things had changed in the eighteen years between one war and the next. As a result of World War I English and American women had been partially granted the right to vote and had acquired a certain degree of emancipation. Yet the return of the combatants to the jobs they had left to go to the fronts and the intensity of the economic depression in the 1930s seriously damaged women's hopes of economic liberation. By 1936 fascist ideology seemed to be penetrating and imposing itself in Europe, and Spain became to many European men and women the place where a central battle was taking place between forces of progress and retrograde forces of militarism. Helping Loyalist Spain was soon understood by many as fighting for the victory of intelligence over brute force. The dichotomy was rarely questioned by pro-Republican foreigners; neither was it discussed by most writers and intellectuals, by men and women who fought, often wrote, and sometimes died in Spain.

In spite of the thoroughness of many of the studies on volunteers in Spain during the war, a central fact is rarely mentioned: very few foreigners knew Spain in 1936, so their decision to go there had more to do with their own political ideas than with the actual struggle taking place. There are some significant references to this lack of knowledge in the writing of several women. Virginia Woolf writes to her friend Violet Dickinson on April 30, 1905, after her first visit to Spain: "I have three fat books about Spain to read for *The Times*. . . . You will be surprised to hear that I am an authority upon Spain—but so it is" (189). The writer Charlotte Haldane admits in her autobiography, *Truth Will Out*, that she was given considerable responsibilities by the British Communist Party in relation to Spain when the war broke out because she had spent several weeks in Spain before the war with her husband, a communist Cambridge scientist who had been invited there by the Spanish Republican government. When the war broke out, Charlotte Haldane was asked by the British Communist Party to work in the organization of British volunteers in France on their way to Spain. Similarly, Leah Manning, a member of Parliament for the Labour Party, was put in charge of conducting meetings all over Britain to convince and recruit young English men for the clandestine International Brigades. But she also visited Spain several times during the war for specific political purposes: she was responsible, for instance, for evacuating four thousand Basque children before the city fell to Franco's troops in July 1937. As a member of the left, Manning had visited the Asturias mine unions in 1934 and had written a book about her visit: *What I Saw in Spain* (1935). She became involved in the war as soon as it started.

It was very difficult for volunteers to get to know the country before and during the Civil War, not only because Spain was at the time backward and remote, but mainly because foreigners arrived with a series of preconceptions that had little to do with what was actually going on there.[2] Given the situation in 1936, most writers, men and women, carried very specific political agendas and tended to project their own ideological concerns onto a country about which they had many ideas but no true knowledge. Modern English and American notions about Spain originate in the early nineteenth century, in the Romantic period, when travel narratives idealized and romanticized Spain beyond recognition, transforming it into the fantasy of both English people and Americans in a process similar to the one described by Edward Said in relation to Western readings of the Orient. Later, many English and American writers during the Spanish Civil War observed it with an imperial eye, envisioning the less developed and poorer country from a perspective of superiority that lent itself to various kinds of exploitation. Rather than becoming involved in dealing with the country's true problems, most foreigners used the war as the arena in which to experiment with ideologies and weapons. Such approaches to the question of Spain, Romantic and colonial, lie at the heart of the misunderstanding to be found in much of the writing by foreigners about the war.[3]

The foreign women who wrote about the Spanish Civil War are very numerous and varied, yet it is surprising to see that in spite of their strongly preconceived beliefs about Spain, in spite of their tendency toward idealization, some of their texts could break free from a long tradition of colonialist and imperialist perspectives and describe the situation and the war in far truer terms than most. Several foreign women returned to peace having managed to come to terms with the clash between their expectations and what they encountered in Spain. Some broke through the obscuring veils of their own fantasy to envisage difference as something deserving respectful consideration and, given the circumstances, compassion and help. Such authors were capable of giving up prejudice and moving easily between what the critic Phyllis Lassner defines as the difficult balance in war writing between the historical, the aesthetic, and the ethical (23).

Though a great many foreigners wrote about the Spanish Civil War, few writers in English remained to see its end. Though agreed upon by the Spanish Republican government, the departure of the International Brigades in October 1938 can be understood as the starting point of the loss of international interest in the Spanish war. It was by then quite clear that the insurgents led by Franco were winning the war. Even the British government had started to secretly contact Franco's newly established government in Burgos. In September 1938 Hitler invaded Czechoslovakia, and international attention shifted immediately and almost completely from Spain to that part of Europe. Most foreign writers and journalists who had reported for some time from and about Spain were urgently called to central Europe, where Hitler was seriously challenging international stability.

Spain was gradually forgotten in the European scenario of late 1938 and early 1939. There was no time left for the Allies to try to save the Loyalist cause, led by a group whose policies had been profoundly misunderstood from the very beginning of the war and that had been made to stand for foreign anxieties about the international political situation. In late 1938 the fantasy was finally over, and the political powers that had failed to recognize the true complexities of war-torn Spain had to deal now with the imminent approach of a new version of war at home. For obvious reasons Spain disappeared from the international scene not only until the end of World War II but for a long time after. Few English-speaking writers visited the country after 1945, and it took many years for foreigners to return to Spain on a large scale. On the whole, the old Romantic and colonial attitudes continued until the end of the war and beyond. But there were some notable exceptions.

As was the case with journalists, only a few foreign writers and intellectuals remained and continued to be interested in the war until its end, but some did and kept on working and writing about it. Several English and American women could not tear themselves away from the terrible suffering of the final stages of the war. Martha Gellhorn, Francesca Wilson, Nancy Cunard, and Kanty Cooper, for example, wrote a great deal about the tragic return to peace for many of the Spanish and even foreign losers and refugees. Kanty Cooper, an English sculptor and pupil of Henry Moore, had been helping Spanish refugee children in England since the beginning of the war. In late 1937 she was told to rest from her work for reasons of health, and she decided to travel to Spain and work for the refugees escaping from Franco's troops into other parts of the country. She arrived in Spain in January 1938 and joined the Friends Service Council, a Quaker-run organization in charge of helping Spanish children. Cooper worked in the Barcelona food canteens until five weeks after the fall of Barcelona on January 26, 1939, and in March 1939 she resumed her work in France helping the great crowds of refugees arriving from Spain.

Cooper's talent as an observer and writer is proved in her autobiography, *The Uprooted: Agony and Triumph among the Debris of War* (1979), in which she covers all of her experience of the Spanish Civil War. The first chapter of her text deals with her volunteer work in England on behalf of the evacuated Basque children in July 1937. Next she writes about her work in Barcelona before and during the fall of the city, and finally she describes the tragic destiny of Spanish refugees in France in 1939. Cooper's accuracy and insight into the record of events are remarkable. She doesn't speculate about the causes, responsibilities, or possible consequences of the war. Her concern is people's suffering—the terrifying and continuous shelling they endure and the extent of the hunger and the cruelty they are subjected to: "Cats, rats and mice were eaten" (21), she informs us. What truly interests her is understanding the human responses to these terrible events, how in such conditions some people, sometimes even children, behave heroically, and how war can also stimulate the worst instincts. The dangers and difficulties of distributing food among the many hungry teach her that "[a]dversity brings out unexpected virtues and strengths. I felt as if I were looking at the people through a magnifying glass, seeing them as I had never seen them before" (26). The last three chapters of her text prove her considerable talent as a critical observer and writer. The chapter "Families Divided in Life and Death" includes narratives of two events that acquire the vividness of short stories. The first one is about Señor Morano, a man whose wife left him to join Franco's Spain at the beginning of the war and whose four sons, about whom he has heard nothing since the war broke out, are fighting on the two opposing Spanish fronts. Señor Morano's despair is convincing and painful to read. Just as tragic but more complex is the story of Benita, a young mother of a four-year-old child, whose husband was killed by the Republican police earlier in the war for having given shelter to a wounded man he found in the street, apparently a supporter of the insurgents. Benita, who works for the Quaker organization, is caught in the midst of this madness and ends up being murdered by the Franco police force when they take the city. Cooper finds out that Benita's sister-in-law denounced her involvement in her own husband's murder at the hands of the Republicans. In the terrible events surrounding Benita's life and death Cooper powerfully unveils the treachery and evil of war, particularly civil war.

But what makes Cooper's narrative historically exceptional is her accurate description of the fall of Barcelona on January 26, 1939. Though thousands of people were leaving the city in hopes of escaping to France in the confusion and chaos just before the invasion, Cooper and her collaborators decided to stay and help the many who remained in need. She is thus one of the few foreigners left to narrate the details of the arrival of Franco's troops into Barcelona; the lack of military resistance they encountered; the terrifying silence that reigned when they entered the city:

> At 8 p.m. [January 25] there was a sudden startling and complete silence. The city seemed to be holding its breath. Nothing moved, there was not a footfall. Not a voice was heard, no motor engine throbbed. . . . At 3 p.m. [January 26] two of Franco's tanks rumbled past the end of our road. A few minutes later they fired what must have been an all-clear signal for the troops to advance. . . . While the troops were passing the town was shaken by a terrific and prolonged explosion. . . . But except for this one explosion, everything remained quiet. As far as I could ascertain Barcelona had fallen without a shot being fired. (40–41)

Cooper goes on to record the many sudden transformations that took place immediately after: the bells noisily chiming in "a moment of intense emotion" (43), the sudden changes in the people's appearance and dress, the emergence of hats, the new language in the newspapers, the change of currency, the initial lack of water and food, the strange and to many citizens disturbing and difficult return to peace.

The last chapter of her text is the most painful to read, for it deals with the horrors of survival for those who managed to escape to France. Once again Cooper narrates the stories of people she knows who have become characters in her story, people with names and individual features. She is one of the first to denounce the conditions in which men are interned in the improvised concentration camps of southern France, abandoned on the sands without shelter or water and with very little food. Like Martha Gellhorn, Francesca Wilson, Nancy Cunard, and others, Cooper is very critical of the negligence she finds in hospitals, of the unnecessary separation imposed on family members: mothers from their children, husbands from their wives. She provides plenty of information, figures, and statistics, and eventually she introduces the reader to the children's colonies established in the northeast of France, where she is next sent by the charity for which she works. There she continues to observe much suffering among the refugee children. She tells the moving story of the beautiful Spanish girl Jacinta, turned into a maid/prostitute by her French mistress, who has hired her with the hope of attracting her city-loving son back to his mother's house and to his town.

Unlike Kanty Cooper, Francesca Wilson, another British back-to-peace writer, was an expert in refugee work when she traveled to Spain for the first time during a half-term leave from the Birmingham girls' school where she taught. Wilson had helped Serb and Montenegrin refugees after World War I, had worked with refugees in England and France, Austria, and Russia, and would later help Poles in Hungary during World War II. All these experiences are recorded in her extraordinary lively and well-written auto-biographical narrative, *In the Margins of Chaos: Recollections of Relief Work in and between Three Wars* (1945).

Wilson reached Barcelona in March 1937, though she immediately traveled to Murcia to do relief work for the floods of people arriving in the city between March and June. Murcia had been the meeting point for refugees from Madrid, Córdoba, and Extremadura since the beginning of the war, but at that stage new waves were arriving from Málaga. Wilson immediately joined the American humanitarian organization American Friends, already working there, and her extraordinary energy and experience proved to be very valuable. She immediately played a central role in founding a children's hospital in the city; then she organized sewing workshops for the Málaga women and found instructors to teach them how to read and write. Many of the male refugees she occupied in the manufacturing of the local rope-soled shoes, *alpargatas*—an endless job, since everyone needed shoes and *alpargatas* did not last forever. The biggest problem remained the boys, and with the help of Rubio, a local teacher of German-Jewish origin, she established a farm colony for them in Crevillente, a town located in the mountains near the city. Not only an experienced refugee worker but also a well-known educator, Wilson applied her abilities to the improvement of unprivileged war children. With Rubio's support she managed to overcome the innumerable difficulties they faced in running a colony in an old derelict building initially without electricity or water, and she proved to have a remarkable ability in turning the young into useful and respectful human beings.

Wilson returned to Spain again during her next summer holiday in July 1938. With the help of the American Friends organization and the local authorities, this time she managed to organize a children's summer camp in the city of Benidorm. Her work and the camp's success were also extraordinary. Yet unlike other social workers, in spite of her feverish activity, Wilson found time to think and write about the war, and her text carries plenty of important information and provides valuable interpretations of military and political events both in Spain and in England. She is one of the few English writers to openly denounce the considerable opinion against Republican Spain among the British establishment, particularly toward the end of the war. She also immediately understands the terrible consequences for Republican Spain of the evacuation of the International Brigades, whose departure she watches in Barcelona in October 1938. She significantly and realistically compares the precise number of foreigners leaving, 12,673, to the unknown but obviously ever-increasing figures of Germans and Italians fighting for Franco in Spain.

Wilson fully realizes the military situation and foresees the end very clearly. The title she gives to the narrative of her last visit to Spain during Christmas 1938 and January 1939 is "The End of Spain." She is now certain that her good Spanish friends "will be sacrificed like bulls in the arena" (217). Her ideas about Spain are at this stage far from romantic, and she sees the shared responsibilities in the tragedy, but she acknowledges a considerable "integrity" (211) in some of the Spaniards she encounters, particularly in rural Spain. In spite of her analytical tendency, Wilson, like Cooper, realizes that ideas are of little consequence for a people who are permanently hungry.

Although she did not return to Spain after January 1939, as Cooper did, Wilson's involvement with the war and with the Spanish people continued. She was in the south of France in Easter 1939, once again trying to help the constant waves of refugees arriving from Spain. Now she worked with the eminent British doctor Audrey Russell, who headed the International Commission and the American Friends. Wilson's narrative of life in the camps and her reflections on the behavior of the French authorities are among the most insightful to have been written on the subject. In all the horror and disorder she observes in the concentration camps, Wilson manages to look beyond the figures and generalizations and discover actual complex, interesting people. She is one of the first to publicize the destiny of the central European prisoners who fought in Spain and have no country to return to, and she realizes exactly what will happen to all the Spanish Republican soldiers as soon as World War II breaks out, a war she knows is inevitable. Again she works for all these people uninterruptedly.

The last visit she records in her autobiography takes place in August 1939, and according to her reports the situation of the refugees continues to be very tragic even though some are beginning to receive humanitarian help from several charitable organizations. The chapters of her autobiography corresponding to the description of her work during the Spanish Civil War cease at this stage. Starting in September 1, 1939, Spanish refugees were removed from the better camps. The authorities had to make room for French refugees. Paris had already begun to be evacuated. "We deserted the Spaniards," Wilson hears a French woman say. "They were the first to fight Fascism, but we let them go down alone. Now it's our turn" (232–33).

The dramatic reports of social workers, who did so much and provided such valuable and unknown details about the last stages of the civil war and the terrible conditions of peace for the losers, are confirmed and completed by the texts of several other writers and journalists. Janet Flanner, one of the best-known American journalists in Europe, who had been reporting from Paris for the *New Yorker* since the 1920s, had written very little about the Spanish Civil War in the three years it had lasted. Yet she did narrate its end. In "Exodus," published on March 1, 1939, Flanner denounces the inhuman living conditions forced upon the refugees in the concentration camps she visits in southern France. Profoundly moved by what she sees, she starts her article with "There has never been anything in modern history like the recent flight of the Catalonian army and civilian population into France" (201).

One of the most moving and interesting female voices reporting the end of the tragedy in Spain is that of the English poet and writer Nancy Cunard. She wrote important war poems about the Spanish war—"To Eat To-Day" is one of the best—in an effort to integrate the aesthetic and the political. Passionately in favor of Republican Spain, and uninterruptedly involved in the war since its beginnings, Cunard had spent long periods of the war in Spain, became acquainted with the most outstanding Spanish poets of the moment, and learned Spanish well enough to translate many of the leading Spanish poets of the time into English. In 1937 she collaborated with the Chilean poet Pablo Neruda in the organization of the International Writer's Congress in Madrid and Valencia sponsored by the Soviet Communist Party. Her intense literary activity was organized around the small printing press she ran at her own house in Rouenville in France, where she produced several collections of contemporary experimental poetry before and during the Spanish Civil War. With the help of Neruda she also wrote and printed the famous letter "Authors Take Sides on the Spanish Civil War," which they sent to the best-known writers and intellectuals of the time all over the world asking them to take sides in the Spanish Civil War. It was an unprecedented initiative, and the many answers they received were published in the *Left Review* in July 1937. It proved that most intellectuals of all Western countries were in favor of Republican Spain. But Cunard's most remarkable works in favor of Republican Spain were the articles she wrote at the end of the war for the *Manchester Guardian*. Again unlike most international intellectuals, Cunard bravely narrated the tragic ending of the war, and at this point she seemed to reach an expressiveness not found in her previous work and that she unfortunately was never again able to match. Her articles are both emotionally contained and tragic. In "The Exodus from Spain" Cunard describes all the sordid details of thousands of women and children slowly moving into the South of France in search of survival. On the next day, in a new article, "An Army Crossing the Frontier," she presents the devastated losing army forced to give up its weapons, flooding into France. In a further article, "At a Refugee Camp," published on February 10, 1939, sadness dominates over accuracy of observation: "At the great central camp of Le Boulou are thousands of men, women, and children. . . . It is a horrible sight, and all of them, men, women, and children, are in the utmost depression. This 'camp' is a large, flat, bare area, the grass trodden down into a sort of grey compost. They sleep here in the open. A few have rigged up some vague kind of shelter" (195). After uninterruptedly working for Republican Spain, Cunard was devastated by the outcome of the Spanish war, and continued to remind her readers of the Spanish refugees in articles such as "The Refugees at Perpignan, Miss Cunard's Appeal." But her effort didn't stop at describing the tragedy, for she managed to liberate several Spanish friends imprisoned in the refugee camps and take them to her own house in France in spite of the enormous difficulties she met from the French authorities.

The American writer Martha Gellhorn also remained to report the end of the war. Gellhorn was perhaps the foreign writer to have been most radically changed by her experience of events in Spain. Not only did she become committed to mitigating the suffering she witnessed during and after the war, but she was radically transformed by it because it allowed her to discover her exceptional talents as a writer of war. In "The War in Spain," the introduction to the first part of *The Face of War*, her 1988 collection of reporting from the many wars she covered as a journalist during her life, the author describes her response to her first "feeling of war" in Madrid on March 27, 1937: "I had not felt as if I were at war until now, but now I knew I was. It was a feeling I cannot describe; a whole city was a battlefield, waiting in the dark. There was certainly fear in that feeling, and courage. It made you walk carefully and listen hard and it lifted the heart" (15). Though intensely moved by events, according to her biographer Carl Rollyson, Gellhorn had not given much thought to the Spanish Civil War until she was actually in Spain (67). Her decision to join the war had been initially personal rather than professional or political; she had decided to follow her lover Ernest Hemingway, who arrived in Spain in 1937. Gellhorn doesn't mention Hemingway in her introduction, but she does recognize her ignorance of the country by admitting that she needs to study a map carefully before traveling from France into Spain and by confirming that she doesn't know a word of Spanish (5).

Yet the most outstanding moment in her short introduction to her Spanish Civil War writing is her candid description of how she became a war correspondent almost by chance. Gellhorn explains how she was able to enter Spain because her friend Kyle Crichton, an editor of the American newspaper *Collier's*, provided her with a reporter's credentials. In the early months of the war, "[t]agging along behind war correspondents, experienced men who had serious work to do," and being an incipient writer, she followed a "journalist friend's" advice and began to write about the war. *Collier's* accepted and published the first article she sent them and placed her name on the masthead of her next article. "Once on the masthead, I was evidently a war correspondent" (16).

What she experienced in Spain prevented her from ever again returning to peace, and she became one of the first women reporters to specialize in the writing of war, of all wars. Though she did eventually marry Hemingway after their time together in Spain, their marriage lasted only a few years, whereas the profession she learned during the Spanish Civil War was to have a far more lasting effect on her life. In spite of her much-criticized beauty and elegance (in her 1969 autobiography *An Unfinished Woman: A Memoir*, Lillian Hellman mentions the stylish Saks Fifth Avenue slacks Gellhorn wore in Madrid), and in spite of her love affair with Hemingway (Stephen Spender commented in his 1951 autobiography *World within World* that while in Valencia during the war Gellhorn seemed to be doing nothing but look for Hemingway), the Spanish Civil War was to be one of the most determining professional as well as personal experiences in her life.

In these very early pages of her war reporting from Spain, Gellhorn confesses her confusion about the writing she is undertaking. Finding out how to write about the war takes considerable reflection on her part. In the end she follows the advice of a reporter friend—probably Hemingway—that she write about everyday life in Madrid in the war. Indeed, political discussion will not be her main focus. Her rare political remarks are always conventional: her defense of the Spanish Republic as well as her definition of the "brave and disinterested" (17) men, both Spanish and foreign, who fight and die in Spain are clearly uncritical. Also her conviction of the international nature of the conflict and of foreign politicians' lack of vision with regard to Spain are no more than general beliefs shared by most members of the left at the time. She even gets carried away, though on very few occasions, by the idealizing that characterizes so much writing about the Spanish Civil War: "[W]e will continue to love the land of Spain and the beautiful people who are among the noblest and unluckiest on earth" (17).

But there is a deep gap between the unanalyzed ideas she may feel forced to utter as a means of defining her political position once and for all and the elaborate originality of her actual war texts, which become seriously experimental. Gellhorn's novelty lies in her decision to detach the war that she observes around her from political ideas and to interpret war as the daily event that affects human lives in ways always unexpected and usually very painful. Most of the Spanish people she writes about seem to be both uninterested in politics and uninformed. Though some hope for an improvement as a result of the struggle, what prevails is their daily experience of war, mostly their suffering. Gellhorn's writing inaugurates a radical new way of approaching war. She never mentions a battle or the name of a politician or seriously discusses ideas and ideologies, weapons, or acts of war of any kind. Her focus is always on the small detail she sees in the least prominent people. She uninterruptedly observes, visits, and talks to people, modest and ordinary people who have little to say but who inevitably show what the war is doing to them, to their larger expectations and intimate hopes. Gellhorn finds a voice in which to report the war that has never been heard before; her writing concentrates on understanding the many ways human experience is changed by the course of war.

Once she finds her voice, she moves from war to war and never stops reporting. But the learning process is far from easy, and her reports from

Spain show her anxiety about finding the right discourse for the description of this strange, new, modern war. "But how could I write about war, what did I know, and for whom would I write? What made a story, to begin with?" (16). Her uncertainty continues to be heard as late as November 1937: "How is it possible to explain what this is really like?" (36). The note of hesitancy continues to emerge in her later reports. In December 1944, though already an experienced journalist, she still confessed to a friend that her reporting of World War II was "inadequate to the enormity of the horror she had witnessed" (Rollyson 160). Yet for Gellhorn there was no return to peace from war, even though she would never again be capable of finding quite the same convincing tone she had achieved in her Spanish texts.

The Spanish Civil War is, tragically, the first modern war in history, and Gellhorn observes this very shrewdly. "What was new and prophetic about the war in Spain was the life of the civilians, who stayed at home and had war brought to them" (16). *The Face of War* collects three of the articles the author sent from Spain at different times: "High Explosive for Everyone," "The Besieged City," and "The Third Winter." The first of these was written in July 1937. What she reports in this article is unexpected: no historical explanations, no military and ideological information, no news in any conventional sense of the word. Gellhorn explains what exactly it is like to be in the midst of a radically new kind of war: the perception of the suspension of time that makes the whole experience unreal; the sounds of war; its strange sights: "the houses like scenery in a war movie" (23). She mostly follows two opposing procedures: the familiarization of destruction, suffering, and death and the defamiliarization of ordinary civilized objects and events. Following the first procedure, Gellhorn applies the same rhetoric as well as similar narrative distance in the description of the trivial and of the tragic. Thus, when describing customers sitting in a café in a Madrid square, she incidentally informs the reader that several clients died that very morning right there as a result of the bombing. But life goes stoically on. Minutes later, while she is still looking on, the shelling is resumed. Now a shoeblack who happens to be there seeks refuge in a house entrance, but a child who is being taken home by his grandmother is hit and dies instantly. The child's death is told economically, not given special relevance. Death has become an everyday event in Madrid. Later, in a shoe shop, the shelling begins again, and the customers are politely and calmly asked to continue their purchasing at the back of the shop. People have had to learn to continue to live in a state of war.

Like most foreign reporters Gellhorn was sent to central Europe at the end of 1938, but "the Spanish Civil War broke Gellhorn's heart" (Rollyson xv), and she continued to think and write about Spain, for the Spanish Civil War had become part of her self. Several of the stories included in the collection of short stories she published in 1941, *The Heart of Another*, deal with Spain and with foreign ex-combatants from the Spanish Civil War. Also the characters in her World War II novel *A Stricken Field* (1940) are connected to the lost war. Spain is again present in some of the stories in her 1958 collection *Two by Two*, as well as in several of the articles she wrote in the different theaters of war that she observed. As late as February 2, 1976, she published in the *New Yorker* an article with the title "The Indomitable Losers: Spain Revisited." But Gellhorn's most moving article on the return to peace after the Spanish Civil War is "The Undefeated," which appeared in *Collier's* on March 3, 1945. It is one of the articles she wrote after visiting Spanish refugees who were still imprisoned in southern France. Several other foreign women had written with compassion and penetration about the refugees, but Gellhorn's article is a masterpiece. Though in the second half of the article she provides the statistics on these unfortunate people forgotten by all six years after their arrival, Gellhorn starts by dramatically introducing the reader to a fifteen-year-old wounded boy: "His name is Fulgencio López and there are thousands like him; and no country, no government, no charity takes care of him" (Bessie 436). Gellhorn reproduces Fulgencio's exact answers to her questions: his hunger, his misery, his unattended wound that has turned him into a cripple, his father's deportation by the Germans, his mother's suffering: "It is hard to know whether it is worse to be Fulgencio López or his mother, who has to watch those lines forming in his forehead and the pain growing in his eyes, and has been helpless and is still helpless" (436–37). When the writer and some veterans in the ward try to console him, "The child did not believe us, but he put his grief away where he kept it always, behind the anguished eyes and the lined forehead" (436).

Very few foreign writers remembered the losers after so many years. Gellhorn was one of the very few to continue to visit and to think about them. She was exceptional in paying attention to a group of people in whom no one was interested any longer and in investing her time and energy in recalling an ideological and political cause that, though once shared by many both in Spain and abroad as a great hope, had by then been completely forgotten. She insists, "[T]he Spanish make lovely children. And also they make brave children, for if you are a Spanish Republican you have to be brave or die" (Bessie 437). Gellhorn's passion is shown in the last paragraph of "The Undefeated": "[T]hese people remain intact in spirit. . . . [T]hey have never won, and yet they have never accepted defeat. . . . You can sit in a basement restaurant in Toulouse and listen to men who have uncomplainingly lost every safety and comfort in life, talking of their republic; and you can believe quite simply that, since they are what they are, there will be a republic across the mountains and that they will live to return to it" (441).

Several well-known foreign women poets mourned the loss of the Spanish republic in verse. We can hear the British writer Margot Heineman, whose poet lover John Cornford had fallen in Spain some months before, expressing her anguish in one of her later poems about the civil war, "The New Offensive, Ebro, 1938." Heineman can only anxiously insist on the decisiveness for Republican Spain of this last battle that she is afraid can no longer be won: "This new offensive is your life and mine / One nation cannot save the world forever" (Bessie 305–6).

Several American poetic voices joined in the elegy. Genvieve Taggard wrote a powerful homage to foreign fighters in her poem "To the Veterans of the Abraham Lincoln Brigade":

> . . . they
> Knew and acted
> understood and died.
> Or if they did not die came home to peace
> That is not peace . . .
>
> (Bessie 484)

Taggard also wrote of postwar Spain in her poem "Andalucía," published in 1946: ". . . it [Andalucía] is / now a country of silences / since the war . . ." (Bessie 423).

Edna St. Vincent Millay devoted several poems in her collection *Huntsman, What Quarry?* (1939) to the tragic denouement for many Spaniards of the war: "Say That We Saw Spain Die" describes how she read events. Also mourning the losses of the war is another poem in her collection, "From a Town in a State of Siege":

> Lie here, and we shall die, but try to take me
> Before they come; their droning wings have roared
> So close so many times, that I am bored
> With death . . .

Several Canadian women poets wrote moving verse about the tragic restoration of peace in Spain. Many Canadian volunteers had joined the International Brigades, and some had died. Dorothy Livesay remembers and laments in "The Lizard: October, 1939":

No one has come from the fronts we knew
. . . .
Silent now the Madrid broadcasts . . .
To hear real voices again, to uphold the song
of one coming from Madrid . . .
Bearers of good news
From the fronts we knew.

(Vulpe 1995)

Few of the men and women who had been to Spain during the war returned during or after World War II. Time in Spain seemed to have stopped for many foreigners after the tragic ending of the war. And though much continued to be written abroad about the Spanish Civil War, Spain remained a sad dream for most writers and intellectuals. In her 1998 essay "English Poetry and the War in Spain: Some Records of a Generation," Margot Heineman revives the feelings about Spain shared many years later by foreign men and women of the left: "The mention of Spain in any gathering has always brought deep feelings of anger, unity and pride" (64).

As soon as the Spanish war was over, many foreign intellectuals initiated a long reflection on it, something that had been practically impossible to do in Spain at the time. But few returned to Spain after the war, partly because of World War II and partly also because Spain became politically very isolated during the 1940s and 1950s and attracted few foreign writers and reporters—indeed, it practically disappeared from the international scene. Yet there were some exceptions, and some of them were women writers. For example, one of the early openly postwar texts in English about Franco-dominated Spain and its relations to Europe and the world was written and published as early as 1944 by the hardly remembered American reporter Alice-Leone Moats. Ideologically disconnected from the Spanish Civil War, looking toward an uncertain future, her writing is no longer nostalgic of the past but dominated by a new curiosity about a remote and still badly known country. In spite of its title, *No Passport for Paris*, 172 pages out of its 274 are devoted to postwar Spain. It offers a first tentative outlook at a dramatically changed country in a dramatically changing world. As a narrative about

Spain's return to peace Moats's book is open to historical perspectives independent from the Spanish war and the nostalgia and bitterness of loss. She tries to understand the economic and social problems of postwar Spain without employing the traditional romanticizing approaches so prevalent in previous writing. Her book remains rather exceptional in that foreign writers, and especially historians, were to devote an enormous effort in the next decades to the analysis of the Civil War rather than to an engagement with the period of the return to peace. The conflict itself and its origins have continued to dominate the attention of the vast majority of foreign scholars and authors.

Notes

1. For the first extraparliamentary session in which the British Aid Spain Committee was founded, see Manning, *Life for Education*. For the origins and development of the Spanish Aid Committee, see Fyrth.

2. For most foreign observers in 1936 the essential Spain was still that of Washington Irving's *Tales of the Alhambra* or Bizet's *Carmen*, though of course there are some important exceptions. Gerald Brenan and his wife, Gamel Woolsey, for example, had been living in Spain several years when the war broke out, and they both knew the country very well in 1936. In 1943, Brenan published *The Spanish Labyrinth: An Account of the Social and Political Background of the Spanish Civil War*, an insightful and knowledgeable study of the origins of the Spanish Civil War. His wife published *Death's Other Kingdom* (1939), her memoir of the first six months of the conflict. After the war there would be excellent British and American historians of the war.

3. Pere Gifre-Adroher suggests such an approach.

Works Cited

Bessie, A., ed. *The Heart of Spain*. New York: Harper and Brothers, 1952.

Brenan, Gerald. *The Spanish Labyrinth: An Account of the Social and Political Background of the Civil War*. Cambridge: Cambridge University Press, 1960.

Cooper, Kanty. *The Uprooted: Agony and Triumph among the Debris of War*. New York: Quartet Books, 1979.

Cunard, Nancy. "An Army Crossing the Frontier." *Nancy Cunard: Brave Poet, Indomitable Rebel, 1896–1965*. Hugh Ford, ed. Philadelphia: Chilton, 1968. 193–94.

———. "At A Refugee Camp." *Nancy Cunard: Brave Poet, Indomitable Rebel, 1896–1965.* Ed. Hugh Ford. Philadelphia: Chilton, 1968. 195.

———. "Authors Take Sides on the Spanish War." *Spanish Front: Writers on the Civil War.* Ed. Valentine Cunningham. Oxford: Oxford University Press, 1986. 51–57.

———. "The Exodus from Spain." *Nancy Cunard: Brave Poet, Indomitable Rebel, 1896–1965.* Ed. Hugh Ford. Philadelphia: Chilton, 1968. 191–93.

———. "The Refugees at Perpignan, Miss Cunard's Appeal." *Nancy Cunard: Brave Poet, Indomitable Rebel 1896–1965.* Ed. Hugh Ford. Philadelphia: Chilton, 1968. 196–97.

———. "To Eat To-Day." *The Penguin Book of Spanish Civil War Verse.* Ed. Valentine Cunningham. Harmondsworth: Penguin, 1983.

Flanner, Janet. "Letter from Paris, Sept. 9." *Paris Was Yesterday: 1925–1939.* Ed. Irving Drutman. New York: Harcourt Brace Jovanovich, 1972.

———. "1939: Exodus (Spanish Civil War)." *Paris Was Yesterday: 1925–1939.* Ed. Irving Drutman. New York: Harcourt Brace Jovanovich, 1972.

Fyrth, Jim. *The Signal Was Spain: The Spanish Aid Movement in Britain, 1936–39.* London: Lawrence and Wishart, 1986.

Gellhorn, Martha. *The Face of War.* New York: Atlantic Monthly Press, 1988.

———. *The Heart of Another.* New York: Charles Scribner's Sons, 1941.

———. "The Indomitable Losers: Spain Revisited." *New Yorker* 2 Feb. 1976.

———. *A Stricken Field.* 1940. London: Virago Press, 1986.

———. *Two by Two.* New York: Simon and Schuster, 1958.

Gifre-Adroher, Pere. *Between History and Romance: Travel Writing on Spain in the Early Nineteenth-Century United States.* Madison: Fairleigh Dickinson University Press, 2000.

Haldane, Charlotte. *Truth Will Out.* New York: Vanguard Press, 1954.

Heineman, Margot. "English Poetry and the War in Spain. Some Records of a Generation." *"¡No Pasarán!" Art, Literature and the Spanish Civil War.* Ed. Stephen Hart. London: Tamesis Books, 1988. 46–113.

Hellman, Lillian. *An Unfinished Woman: A Memoir.* Boston: Little, Brown, 1969.

Lassner, Phyllis. *British Women Writers of World War II: Battlegrounds of Their Own.* Houndmills: Macmillan, 1997.

Low, Mary, and Juan Breá. *Red Spanish Notebook: The First Six Months of the Revolution and the Civil War in Spain.* London: Martin Secker and Warburg, 1937.

Manning, Leah. *A Life for Education: An Autobiography.* London: Victor Gollancz, 1970.

———. *What I Saw in Spain.* London: Victor Gollancz, 1935

Millay, Edna Saint Vincent. *Huntsman, What Quarry?* New York: Harper and Brothers, 1939.

Moats, Alice-Leone. *No Passport for Paris.* New York: G. P. Putnam's Sons, 1944.

Rollyson, Carl. *Beautiful Exile: The Life of Martha Gellhorn.* London: Aurum Press, 2001.

Spender, Stephen. *World within World: The Autobiography of Stephen Spender.* 1951. Boston: Faber and Faber, 1977.

Vulpe, Nicola, ed.. *Sealed in Struggle: Canadian Poetry and the Spanish Civil War. An Anthology.* La Laguna: Center for Canadian Studies, 1995.

Wilson, Francesca M. *In the Margins of Chaos: Recollections of Relief Work in and between Three Wars.* London: John Murray, 1945.

Woolf, Virginia. *The Letters of Virginia Woolf.* Vol. 1. *1888–1912* (Virginia Stephen). Ed. Nigel Nicolson and Joanne Trautmann. New York: Harcourt Brace Jovanovich, 1975.

CHAPTER THIRTEEN

Wish Me Luck As You Wave Me Goodbye

Representations of War Brides in Canadian Fiction and Drama by Margaret Atwood, Mavis Gallant, Norah Harding, Margaret Hollingsworth, Joyce Marshall, Suzette Mayr, Aritha van Herk, and Rachel Wyatt

DONNA COATES

During an interview with Margaret Atwood about *The Robber Bride*, Hilde Staels asks to what extent the writer attributed her characters' "sense of homelessness" to the Second World War (211). Atwood replies that war is the "central disruptive event in the twentieth century" (212) and that both the First and Second World Wars "caused a huge amount of social disruption," dislocating families and literally tearing them apart: "Each of the protagonists in *The Robber Bride* has a missing or altered father and that's what war does" (212). But when Staels inquires specifically about Atwood's war bride Anthea Fremont, suggesting she is the type of woman who "would not otherwise have gone to Canada" (212),[1] Atwood replies somewhat nonchalantly: "[T]he war may have brought people to Canada, but they were doing that anyway" (212). Given that nearly forty-eight thousand women made the drastic decision to wave goodbye to their families and friends and follow a stranger to the new world, Atwood's response is puzzling, for as Mavis Gallant comments, "[E]ven for a nation built on the principle of immigration it was an unusual wave: all one generation, all women, nearly all from the same racial stock" (Introduction xiv). Gallant also notes that most detested the term *war bride* (Introduction xiv), for obvious reasons: at the time of immigration, they had been married for several years or were pregnant or bringing children with them—all together, the women brought some twenty-two thousand children. Nonetheless, the term is convenient, and I shall use it throughout my essay.[2]

In spite of these huge numbers, we know little about how these courageous young women coped on the home front because war has traditionally been considered a male experience and the tale of the battlefield the privileged war story. Only soldiers, especially those who lost limbs on the battlefield, have been commemorated as war heroes, whereas the walking wounded, those women who amputated their roots to immigrate to a new land, have been, until recently, for the most part ignored. That many of these war brides existed in a state of permanent exile far away from their friends and families, most of whom they would never see again, may have prompted the war bride Joyce Hibbert to compare the pain of deracination to a serious war wound: "Leaving one's country might be compared to losing an arm or leg: until severing actually happens, one cannot imagine the strength of the bond or the terrifying wrench of separation" (48). Other war brides have made the link between soldiers' suffering and their own. In Chris Brookes's *Songs My Mother Taught Me: A Documentary Novel* (1998), a compact disc based on the experiences of British war brides who married Commonwealth servicemen during World War II and emigrated to Newfoundland, one comments that the anguish she and other brides endured was like post-traumatic stress disorder, an affliction approximately 10 percent of soldiers experienced during or after World War II; the difference was that many ex-combatants received treatment, but war brides did not. The extent of these war brides' dis-ease in the new land has been largely overlooked. So, too, has the nature of their suffering, which took many forms. Atwood's novel *The Robber Bride* illustrates this when Anthea insists that the war was harder on her than her soldier-husband Griff, for he did not go *through* the war in the way she did: her parents were killed when a bomb destroyed their house during the Blitz, whereas Griff only got into the fighting on D-Day: he was there for the "landing, the advance, the easy bit. . . . The winning" (162). All he "liberated," she taunts, was a gun (163). Or perhaps, as Anthea's daughter Tony, a military historian who conducts research on and teaches the story of war from the point of view of the victims, advances (in another context), "They were all victims. They took turns! Actually, they took turns trying to avoid being the victims. That's the whole point about war!" (23).

With the publication of Hibbert's *The War Brides* (1978), war bride Peggy O'Hara's *From Romance to Reality: Stories of Canadian War Brides*

(1983), Ben Wicks's *Promise You'll Take Care of My Daughter: The Remarkable War Brides of World War II* (1992), Barbara Ladouceur and Phyllis Spence's *Blackouts to Bright Lights: Canadian War Bride Stories* (1995), and Linda Granfield's *Brass Buttons and Silver Horseshoes: Stories from Canada's British War Brides* (2002), war brides' stories are gradually being brought to light.[3] At the same time, however, the tales of Second World War "brides" are still largely "missing" from Canadian literature.[4] Works such as Mavis Gallant's short story "Up North" (1959), Joyce Marshall's short story "The Old Woman" (1975), Margaret Hollingsworth's play *Ever Loving* (1985), Aritha van Herk's novel *No Fixed Address* (1986), Margaret Atwood's novel *The Robber Bride* (1993), Rachel Wyatt's short stories "Her Voice," "Stanley," and "Time Travel," from *The Day Marlene Dietrich Died* (1996), Suzette Mayr's novel *The Widows* (1998), and war bride Norah Harding's two autobiographical plays, *This Year, Next Year* (1995) and *Sometime, Never* (2001), have begun to fill in the gaps. To date, however, no major critical works on the representation of war brides in these texts have appeared.

This kind of critical and historical neglect perhaps takes its cue from male historians' notions that war takes place during specific time periods and on specifically militarized fronts. But as Margaret and Patrice L.-R. Higonnet point out, looking at women's experiences of war requires redefining its temporal limits: "Women experience war over a different period from that which traditional history usually recognizes, a period which precedes and long outlasts formal hostilities. Masculinist history has stressed the sharply defined event of war; women's time more closely reflects Bergson's concept of durée" (46). The Higonnets' observations are especially germane to war brides, many of whom must have uttered soon after they arrived in Canada that there was no horror like peacetime;[5] even though they landed on a calm home front, more than a few quickly became embroiled in domestic skirmishes and acts of violence that required them to show a great deal of courage and make many sacrifices. That only a small number—Wicks suggests fewer than 10 percent (*Promise* 6)—suffered defeat and returned to their homelands should not be regarded as proof that the rest "lived happily ever after," however, for the Canadian government provided only one-way tickets, and poverty prevented many from returning.[6] So did pride: although many parents wished their offspring luck as they waved them goodbye, a number of others shouted, "You'll be sorry," thereby making it difficult for these brides to return home with dignity. Moreover, many "deeply unhappy" women stayed in Canada, asserts Gallant, because they did not wish to hear their parents say, "I told you so" (Introduction xviii).[7] Even those who returned for holidays found that "the England they returned to was already not the England they'd left" (Gallant, Introduction xviii) or that they had become hybrids who did not feel at home in either place. Hollingsworth's upper-class war bride Diana Manning, for example, learns that her English family regards her as a "hillbilly" when she returns home on visits, whereas those in Southern Alberta, her adopted homeland, ridicule her clothes, customs, and manner of speaking (99).

It does not require much imagination to comprehend why so many women were attracted to the Canadian colonials, for they were, by most accounts, handsome, charming, polite, good conversationalists, and gentlemen. (The Canadian soldier Ben Harding in *This Year, Next Year* is atypically homely.) Better paid than English Tommies, Canadian soldiers could afford to lavish luxuries on impressionable young women used to wartime rationing, food shortages, and air-raid attacks. Canadian soldiers also had a lot of time to get to know women overseas because they were the first to enlist but the last to fight: as Pierre Berton informs us, "except for a brief diversion at Dieppe, no Canadian soldiers got into action until the summer of 1943" (Foreword ix). Canadian military men also spent more time in England than anyone else, including English soldiers: some were overseas for as long as six years. Service clubs and dance halls were readily available to pass the time and to ease the loneliness; not surprisingly, romance, intensified by the uncertainties of the wartime climate, began to bloom (Wicks, *Promise* 3). These amorous relationships often led to much nonviolent "action," for as Dave O'Sullivan, one of Hollingsworth's enlisted men, remarks, "[W]e're the only outfit in military history with a birth rate higher than the death toll" (56). According to Gallant, the soldiers' lengthy period away from home made them nostalgic: "men overseas . . . painted for their brides a highly idealized picture of the Canada they left behind—a picture enhanced by homesickness, youthful memories, and the passage of time" (Introduction xiv).

True to form, most of the Canadian soldiers in the literary texts promise, if not quite a rose garden (the title of the first of twenty-nine songs in *Ever Loving*), considerably more than they or the new land can deliver.[8] Hollingsworth's Dave O'Sullivan, a working-class urban dweller from Hamilton, Ontario, for example, blithely informs the Scottish Land Army worker Ruthie Watson that all Canadian families possess cars, boats, and cottages situated on the shores of huge lakes, that all Canadians have ready access to abundant supplies of inexpensive food, and that he-men like himself regularly bring home not just the bacon but the moose! (58). When Ruthie asks about the cold winters, Dave sidesteps her question by stating that the scorching summers are endless (58). Ruthie, who comes from an impoverished working-class background, is dazzled by Dave's depiction of the good life in Canada and falls straight into his arms. Similarly, Hollingsworth's Paul Tomachuk, a first-generation Ukrainian prairie farmer, misleads the wealthy Diana on a number of fronts: though he says it's "hot" on the prairies, he insists that "Canada's the greatest place on earth," that the country is ripe for social change, and that he's the man to implement it. Emphatically declaring that he will be a revolutionary writer or radical politician, not the dirt farmer he was before he enlisted, he also overstates his involvement with the Communist Party and utters iconoclastic statements about ending both "bourgeois tyranny" and colonial domination. Diana, who regards upper-class British society as stultifyingly dull and finds Paul's determination to overthrow hegemonic ideologies invigorating and his depiction of a progressive, almost utopian society exhilarating, says "Yes" to his proposal immediately. Another of Hollingsworth's soldiers who leads his future wife astray is Chuck Malecarne, an Italian-Canadian entertainer from Halifax. On their first date, when the Italian-born Luce forthrightly tells Chuck that she wants to be a singer, he urges her to marry him straightaway, for "Canada's where it's happening," and "America's on the outskirts of Halifax" (66). Luce has no way of knowing that Chuck is merely paying lip service to her ambitions or that he is misrepresenting Halifax's reputation as the entertainment capital of North America: his proposal sounds like music to her ears.

In fairness, women writers also emphasize that war brides should shoulder some of the responsibility for their subsequent unhappiness, since their reasons for marrying Canadian men are often questionable. Most of these brides were not, as Wicks asserts, unusual immigrants "motivated by fear or persecution or the need for a better way of life. They came because of the love of a stranger who one day walked into their lives and led them from the old into the new" (Preface xi–xii). In fact, Norah Harding is the only "bride" who attests that she is leaving home entirely for love. But Norah also has an overly romantic view of weddings. Once Ben proposes, she and her sister Sheila reminisce about how they "used to lie in bed planning our wedding days," how they "dreamed about floating down the aisle . . . all satin and lace . . . and roses and orange blossoms . . . with everyone throwing confetti[,] [t]he organ pealing out 'The Wedding March' and the bells ringing" (*This Year, Next Year* 12). Norah, like Hollingsworth's Ruthie, has been seduced by Hollywood, for her mother accuses her of "mixing up Canada with those movies that Nelson Eddy and Jeanette MacDonald made" (*This Year, Next Year* 66).

The majority of the other literary "brides" emigrated for the same reasons as the men who marched away to war. The latter signed on "to escape a mundane civilian life and to see the glamorous cities of London and Paris, far from the restrictive glare of parents. True, they had a country, freedom, and a way of life to defend, but few placed that ahead of their chance to run from the constant search for work and, 'if lucky,' the stifling boredom of the eight-to-five shift": most were seeking "high adventure" overseas (Wicks, *Promise* 1).[9] In these texts, women, too, have a yen for adventure, a longing to travel and to escape low-paying, boring jobs and repressive milieus. Many, adds Gallant, were "giddy, or silly, or . . . wanted to get away from home, [or] were emigrating for a lark" (Introduction xv). Accordingly, in *Ever Loving*, Luce, who comes from a traditional Milanese family that expects her to settle down and raise children, yearns to be a professional entertainer: only by getting as far away as possible from Italy can she hope to succeed. So desperate is Luce to escape her cloistered environment that she "sleeps with" almost any man in uniform who asks her (as long as he is not Italian), thereby making her husband Chuck's mispronunciation of her name as "Loose" ironically appropriate. Similarly, the affluent English-born Diana is dissatisfied with the men of her social class and hence dates foreigners exclusively. She declares that she wants to be a pilot in the WAF like her twin brother so that she can "fly or explore the Amazon in a boat" (50), and when that fantasy fails to materialize she leaps at the chance to marry an "exotic" Canadian soldier, in what is both an act of rebellion against her status-conscious parents and a means of escaping a limited social milieu. The Scottish Ruthie Watson, too, is typical of her class and time: poor and uneducated, she waits for Prince Charming, preferably a Hollywood film star, preferably Humphrey Bogart, to rescue her from drudgery in a fish shop. When she meets Dave, a Cary Grant look-alike, she pictures herself playing Jeanette MacDonald to Nelson Eddy in the Canadian Rockies.

In other stories, women wish to emigrate because their futures lack promise in England. Marshall's Molly is thirty-eight and working at a dead-end job; she falls for Toddy because he seems affable and looks nice in his

officer's uniform. Molly is also intrigued by the notion of moving to northern Quebec, a place she pictures as "strange" and "romantic" (77). Similarly,
van Herk's Lanie is a seventeen-year-old shop girl in a "sooty English town";
when both of her parents are killed in the London blitz, she is orphaned but
too old to be adopted. All it takes to woo her to Vancouver is a smile from
the good-looking Canadian soldier Toto Manteia. And a number of other
brides—Hollingsworth's Ruthie, Gallant's Mrs. Cameron, Mayr's Friedl, and
Atwood's Anthea Fremont—experience one of war's frequent consequences:
unwanted pregnancy. Friedl has had an affair with an African American,
but the text implies that he refuses to marry her, so she jumps at a proposal
from the attractive Canadian Karl. Not surprisingly, she has "some explaining to do" when she gives birth to a dark-skinned daughter. But whether
with child or not, all of these war brides marry in haste: Luce knows Chuck
for five days, Diana knows Paul less than two before tying the knot; Harding's Norah accepts Ben's proposal after six weeks of dating. (In *This Year,
Next Year*, the lengthy bureaucratic procedure the Canadian government
required before granting couples permission to marry nearly derails Ben
and Norah's wedding. Ben must request permission to wed from his com-
manding officer, and Norah, who is under twenty-one, needs her mother's
signature before she can marry. Norah is also obliged to have a "little chat"
with the padre to ensure that she is fit to be a Canadian's wife and then must
submit to a blood test to ensure that she does not have VD [14–15]). Regardless of the circumstances, however, all of the war "brides" repent at leisure.
Willfully deaf, many hear only what they want to hear: Diana ignores Paul's
anti-British outbursts, and Ruthie disregards Dave's sexism and bullying
behavior.

Like soldiers frustrated by having to wait long periods before getting
"into action," the war brides waited long periods before they could join
their husbands. After enduring interminable and often dangerous sea voy-
ages, many had to take lengthy trips, sometimes for thousands of miles, on
trains ill equipped for their needs, especially as mothers with small children. Gallant, who traveled as a reporter on a special war brides' train, confesses that she did "not know until [she] had read [Hibbert's book] how
dirty and uncomfortable Canadian trains seemed to the war brides, or how
monotonous the land appeared on the other side of the sooty windows,
with its miles of unchanging vegetation and unbroken colour patterns" (Introduction xv). But Gallant is either suffering a memory lapse or being dis-
ingenuous, for in "Up North," a story she wrote decades before, she stresses
from the outset that the English war bride Mrs. Cameron and her young

son Dennis are traveling through northern Quebec on a filthy train: "When they woke up . . . their bed was black with soot and there was soot in his Mum's blondie hair" (49). Mrs. Cameron begins to sob uncontrollably, claiming that waking "in the cold, this dark, dirty dawn, everything dirty she touched, her clothes—oh, her clothes!" is a far worse experience than being in an air raid (49). In spite of his tender age, Dennis finds the scenery— "an unchanging landscape of swamp and bracken and stunted trees"— frightening (52). Similarly, Hollingsworth's war brides Ruthie and Diana, making their way to Hamilton and Regina respectively, find these journeys across a barren landscape not so sentimental. As Yvonne Hodkinson writes, Ruth feels terror when she looks out at the vast, empty land; the menacing wilderness, one of the first images in her imagination, reflects her state of inner disarray, her emotional uncertainty and fear (22–23).[10] Like both Paul Fussell and Ernest Hemingway, who recorded the difficulty soldiers had in "naming" or "speaking about" their experiences,[11] Ruthie finds that the Canadian landscape evokes feelings so foreign that she has difficulty articulating what she sees: "It's awful . . . foreign, isn't it. I mean . . ." (80). The stage directions indicate that Ruth has *"no words to express her feelings"* (39). Diana also finds the immeasurable physical solitude of the landscape unsettling and difficult to fathom, but her response is more ambivalent: accustomed to a war-torn, ravaged landscape, she is startled by the pristine quality of the Canadian countryside. Diana finds the new land "splendidly untouched," the terrain almost "rejuvenating" after the bombed-out sites she's habituated to—that is, until she reaches her final destination, nowhere, Alberta, a place so bleak that it provokes panic. And prior to her arrival in northern Quebec, Marshall's war bride Molly thinks her destination, a town called Missawani, has an exotic ring, but she quickly becomes alarmed by the harshness of the terrain. Disembarking after a long train ride at the Missawani whistle-stop, her husband, Toddy, announces that she must then travel another thirty miles by dogsled into a barren frozen landscape, a fact he has neglected to mention earlier. As they make their "long strange journey" over the frozen landscape, the snow first "dazzle[s]," then "inflame[s]" her eyes, and the coarse snow flung up from the feet of the dogs stings her eyes (78). Molly notes with alarm the "black brittle fir-trees [and] birches gleaming like white silk" (78) and then is shocked to learn that there are no roads in winter, so that she will be trapped indoors for months.

Moreover, as Atwood's Tony Fremont points out, since most of these women had gleaned their vague and quixotic notions about life in Canada from Christmas cards (153), they were "raw" brides, unaware how truly strange and different Canada would prove to be. Only Hollingsworth's Diana has done any "homework": she knows, for example, that Mackenzie King is prime minister, that Canadians call autumn "fall," and that the maple leaf is the "national tree" (38–39), but she has apparently failed to take even a cursory glance at a map, for she frequently reminds the train conductor to wake her early so that she will not "miss" Lake Superior, a body of water so large that it takes a day to circumnavigate. Nor has she investigated the populations of Canadian cities: finding little to her liking on the brief stop-over in Winnipeg, she reassures herself that Lethbridge (one-tenth the size of Winnipeg) will be better. As these brides approach their final destinations, they suddenly realize that they have placed their lives in the hands of near-strangers, that they are entering their husbands' social environments, and that they may thus have little control over their futures: in crossing the Atlantic, they may also have crossed the Rubicon.

To escape the feelings of helplessness and insecurity evoked by the oppressive landscape, Hollingsworth's and Marshall's brides cling to the belief that once they see their houses they'll be fine. As Hodkinson observes, Ruthie's and Diana's houses represent both refuge from an overwhelming external world and the space they have been conditioned within patriarchy to consider women's only source of power (24). Hollingsworth in particular stresses the notion of "home" as a central motif. During an interview with Judith Rudakoff, she states that what her female characters most desire is "a space of their own: Finding that space and putting their seal on it," and adds that "[h]ome is a place where you are not an immigrant" (Rudakoff and Much 155). And when speaking with Cynthia Zimmerman, Hollingsworth reiterates that "[h]ome comes in again and again in my work. It's about relating to the place that you're in and finding a place for yourself in a foreign environment" (Wallace and Zimmerman 93). None of her female characters finds it easy to relate to Canada, for their houses prove as dismal as the landscape. Chuck brings Luce to a tiny room over his father's pizza parlor; only after six years do they manage to rent their own apartment. Dave deposits Ruth at his mother's house, swearing that the stay will be temporary, but the couple and their six children are still there twenty-five years later. Harding's Ben does the same with Norah, although they manage to rent their own flat in London, Ontario, within a few years' time. Hollingworth's Diana's home is not even a "little house on the prairie": it's a one-room shack with outhouse, a home where the buffalo roam, fifty miles from Lethbridge, "on the edge of "the world," as she puts it (99). Other brides find themselves in equally unhomelike spaces: Marshall's Toddy deposits his new wife in a shabby and neglected house above a sinister-looking power station that he calls his "old woman" and tends obsessively eighteen hours every day. Cut off from the town by snow and tangled bush and roadlessness, Molly, like Diana, has not even a radio to keep her company or to drown out the "loud and engulfing" noise of the waterfall. Van Herk's Lanie is disappointed in the two-room Vancouver apartment Toto brings her to, for she has expected that a Canadian soldier would be better off; her traumatic past fueling her desire for security, Lanie rushes off to work in order to buy "one of them cute little houses on the edge of town" (42). Atwood's Anthea Fremont finds nothing attractive about the house in Toronto her husband, Griff, provides; mincing few words, she describes it as a "too-cramped, two-storey, fake Tudor, half-timbered, half-baked house, in [a] tedious neighborhood" (164).

Few of these brides manage to find release from domestic confinement either. Struggling to journey vicariously away from her claustrophobic environment, Hollingsworth's Luce haunts the Halifax train station like a ghost; Ruth is imprisoned in her mother-in-law's cramped quarters; and Diana feels as if she's landed on another planet. She is terrified by the flatness of the prairie and the endless months of freezing temperatures, and she is frightened by the awesome silence, broken only by the eerie howls of coyotes and wolves. Diana identifies with the Spanish explorers who wrote the words *Aqui nada* over the top of North America, meaning "Nothing here" (99). Marshall's Molly finds there is nothing romantic about life in the bush, as the snow, "blue and treacherous as steel," produces only a "blinding glare" (79). Like Diana, she feels the isolation keenly: Toddy has no skis or snowshoes; he cannot (or will not) take the time to teach her how to drive the "snarling" and "wolfish" dogs; there is no telephone, and there are no neighbors within miles. Once a fortnight a "sweeper" brings supplies, but knowing that Toddy despises the French Canadians, he is "taciturn and barely polite," obviously uncomfortable in "this house of which she was a part" (81). And although Harding's in-laws are financially secure, they are religious fanatics who expect Norah to attend church with them several times per week, lecture her on the "Twelve Tribes of Israel," forbid drinking, and regard cards as the "tools of the Devil" that they won't allow in their house (*Sometime, Never*, 35–36).

The male figures in these texts also prove to be disappointing. Dashing and gallant in uniform, full of promise and get-up-and-go in Europe, once they land on the home front in the True North, Canadian men lack initiative and resourcefulness, failings Atwood, Marshall, and Hollingsworth are not the first to identify. A plethora of writers—Frances Brooke, Thomas Chandler Haliburton, and Martha Ostenso, to name only a few—began making similar observations centuries and decades earlier. Each of Hollingsworth's soldiers who makes up the Canadian mosaic as first-generation Canadians of either Irish, Ukrainian, or Italian descent has learned, thanks to his war experiences, that Canada is not a second-rate colony, but each is too lazy to work at making it into the promised land. Chuck declares that he wants to be a world-class entertainer, but he refuses to practice and his style is imitative. Dave has, in the current vernacular, an "attitude"; he either quits or loses his menial jobs, so that his wife and children must continue to live with his mother. Although it appears that Diana and Paul have made a success of their prairie homestead, it is Diana who does the manual labor and thinks up innovative ideas that make it a prosperous and thriving enterprise. Meanwhile, Paul goes bowling.

The opening line of Marshall's story—"He has changed"—is also a common refrain, for the men these brides greet on the station platforms are not the same ones they married overseas; having promised that the new world offered freedom and limitless possibilities, many of these men now appear to be stuck in the old ways of thinking. Hollingsworth's Chuck and Paul and Marshall's Toddy demand that their wives be submissive nurturers and caregivers who place their husbands' needs ahead of their own. Chuck envisions himself as the Great Caruso, singing to wild applause in the famous capitals of Europe, and Luce as standing "shyly" in the background, having cheerfully placed her career on hold, happy merely to give him lots of "bambinos." Paul, whose radical ideas for social change seemingly do not include equality for women, pictures Diana in the kitchen, kneading bread in his grandmother's apron and baking enough pies to feed an army (or threshing crew). Paul is threatened by Diana's industriousness and ingenuity, qualities he claimed to admire during the war but never intended to embrace. Periodically, he sabotages Diana's endeavors, canceling without her knowledge her clever plan to start a fish farm. And although he regards the prairie as his "patient lover," he refuses to allow his wife, who views the land as nothing but "dead grass," to cultivate an English garden. Dave wants a slim yet voluptuous Rita Hayworth look-alike for a mate, but his incessant sexual demands keep Ruth pregnant much of the time. He leaves the child rearing to Ruth, carries on an affair with the "girl" he left behind, and occasionally beats his wife. Marshall's Toddy does not want his wife to have any outside interests. Molly is alarmed to discover that he thinks of her as one of his machines, a generator that is "quiet and docile, waiting for him here, moving only when he tells [her] to move" (83). In *Sometime, Never,* Harding's Norah, too, finds that Ben's personality has altered after the war; he is no longer the happy-go-lucky young man who was full of high hopes about their future together. Shortly after they arrive in Canada, Ben begins to drink excessively and ignores her. In desperation, Norah returns to England. Harding's *Sometime, Never* is an exceptional text, for none of the other writers expresses the kind of sympathy for returned soldiers that she does. Norah finally learns the truth about her Irish father, Patrick McKernan, whom the family always believed had deserted them during the First World War. Her mother Maggie reveals that Patrick, having been gassed at the Somme, suffers from shell shock (51). Maggie's first husband has already been killed in the war; when Maggie meets Patrick, she feels they are simply "two lonely people" (51) who fall in love and decide to marry. But because Patrick is "sick, lonely, confused, and in a strange country" (51), he neglects to tell Maggie he has a wife and children in Ireland. Although Maggie is deeply in love with Patrick, she sends him back to his family, knowing she will then have to raise his two children (and her daughter from a previous marriage) on her own. Throughout her telling of the events, Maggie expresses no bitterness about her own emotional and financial hardship; uppermost is her love and compassion for Patrick. In another instance, Norah also learns that her sister Sheila is having a relationship with Charlie, an English soldier who, having witnessed the death of his two best friends, is depressed and having trouble with his nerves (59). He tries to pressure Sheila into marrying him; she refuses because she does not love him but feels guilty thereafter. And Norah also realizes, after Ben follows her to England, the reason he has changed so much: after the couple's wedding on June 5, Ben returns to active duty. On D-Day, he kills a fourteen-year-old German boy and, haunted by the death, drinks to wipe out the pain.

Wyatt's short stories offer an intriguing variation on the subject of changed men, for the problem that the English war bride Myra Chebs encounters is that her husband Peter does *not* change. In 1945, while still in uniform overseas, Peter has the opportunity to exchange a few words with film star Marlene Dietrich; lusting after her, he wants to ask her back to his room but, noticing her French actor-lover hovering nearby, he retreats. Back on the Ontario home front, doctors consider that Peter, who has won a medal for walking across a minefield, is suffering from the shock of the twenty-minute journey. Myra knows better, however, for she is convinced that Peter suffers more from having left Dietrich behind than if he had run away from the enemy and been shot as a coward ("Her Voice" 14); some days, she thinks, he wishes he had. Because he cannot overcome his infatuation—he has an affair with a woman whose only claim to fame is that she sounds like Dietrich, and he then takes his and Myra's vacation money to attend, by himself, Dietrich's 1965 concert in Munich—their marriage nearly founders; it is saved only by Myra's feistiness, her refusal to admit defeat.

Although there is little humor in most of these war brides' stories—perhaps because there is so little cause for it—Wyatt's stories are truly funny. While Myra feels that she cannot compete with Dietrich—she's never been thin, can't carry a tune in a bucket, and knows that even the neighbors suspect Peter calls her "Marlene" when they make love—she puts up a valiant struggle, giving as good as she gets. She never let Peter's fantasy linger for long, frequently calling him a *dreamer* ("Her Voice" 15) and insisting that Dietrich would never have followed him to Winouski, a tiny town near Lake Muskoka. Nor would Dietrich have made jellied salad for the Curling Club supper, or sung at Rotary concerts, or gotten varicose veins doing the washing up, or asked the locals to call her "Marl" for short (11). And when Peter shatters one of Myra's collector plates after a heated argument, Myra retaliates by shoving his medal in the oven, giving it a "charred" look and ruining the ribbon (16). On the day Dietrich dies, she informs Peter that the singer tortured herself to stay slim, wearing a "body stocking made of wire like a cage," and suggests she was a tramp who "slept with more men than most people've had hot dinners. Anyone in trousers. Even women" (9).[12]

Although keeping herself occupied does not appear to have been a problem for Myra, it is for other brides whose husbands who are opposed to their working outside the home. Several, particularly those who have no children (Molly is too old, Luce has none by choice), are on the verge of breakdowns. Luce vacuums without the machine plugged in, and Marshall's Molly fears that she may end up "bushed" like her husband: "Already I can feel the long sweep of the snow trying to draw my thoughts out till they become diffused and vague. I can feel the sound of the water trying to crush and madden me" (83). Diana, who also has no offspring (Paul is curiously asexual), insists that they adopt a child because otherwise she feels there is no point in continuing to struggle on the farm. And Norah, whose mother-in-law will not allow her to help around the house, gets the chance to relax only when she and her husband play cards and drink beer with the neighbors (37). Mayr's Friedl, who does have a child, cannot feed her on the paltry amount of money Karl gives her; thus Friedl resorts to stealing groceries. Given that most of these women held down responsible positions under daunting wartime circumstances—Diana was a member of the police force; both Ruthie and Marshall's Molly worked for the land army; Harding's Norah had been contributing to the family coffers since she was fourteen and during the war worked for a firm that made fittings for landing craft; Mayr's Friedl led a thrilling and dangerous life driving a car for a German general's wife who acted as a spy for the Resistance—their frustrations seem legitimate.

Mayr's, Hollingsworth's and Atwood's brides are crushed, too, by what they identify as Canada's appalling lack of culture. They come from cities where there were bookstores, libraries, museums, galleries, cinemas, or some form of culture at every corner. Friedl is appalled by Karl and his sister's repeated telling of the way they used to chew tar off the streets in northern Alberta, an activity they continue to find hilarious as adults. Similarly, Luce, who finds only "fish and fog" in Halifax, deems Canada a country that breeds only "bores," and Ruthie (married to a grown man who reads comics) misses the gaiety of Scottish society; she laments that there are no friendly neighborhood pubs where people get together for sing-alongs, and questions—correctly—why Canadians have no songs of their own. Diana declares—incorrectly, surely—that Canadians have no sense of humor, are uninterested in local politics, and do not like to get anything done but like to suffer. In a way that recalls Earle Birney's remark that "it's only by our lack of ghosts we're haunted,"[13] Diana feels uneasy at raising her adopted son in a country so young that it lacks both history and culture. Atwood's Anthea accuses her husband of carrying her off to a "narrow-minded provincial city, in [a] too-large, too-small, too-cold, too-hot country" where everyone speaks spurious grammar with a "flat" accent (164). To console herself, Anthea goes shopping, but she refuses to purchase the kind of unfashionable clothing—slacks, ski suits, earmuffs, or Hudson's Bay coats—suitable to a northern climate (153–54).

As well as struggling to survive in an antagonistic physical and cultural climate, the war brides often find the Canadian people themselves hostile. Few writers of these texts would agree with the editors' claim in *Behind the Lines: Gender and the Two World Wars* that "[w]hether [war brides] came from Axis or Allied nations, [they] were warmly welcomed, no doubt because they were fulfilling conventional feminine roles, and also because their status demonstrated that at least some of the conquering heroes had behaved admirably toward foreign women" (Higonnet et al. 12). (Despite much evidence to the contrary, the American editors cite Hibbert's and O'Hara's books as sources.) While soldiers abroad are uniformly welcomed as heroes, women on the Canadian home front are treated with animosity. Haligonians are so threatened by Luce's refusal to become a member of the community that they accuse her of being fascist and throw bricks through her windows; rural Albertans mock Diana's clothing and manner of speaking; and Mrs. O'Sullivan reinforces Ruthie's status as an outsider by constantly reiterating, "That's not how we do things here." And although Harding's Norah tells her family that her in-laws are "very nice people" and kind to her "in their own way" (*Sometime, Never,* 30), that "way" is truly inconsiderate, for they allow Ben to go to jail for drunken driving without informing Norah of their decision (49). Thus, in depicting Canadians as unfriendly, insensitive, cruel, and racist, both Hollingsworth and Harding shatter the myth that Canadians are receptive to newcomers.

All of these texts demonstrate conclusively that the aftermath of war was as destructive to women as the war years had been to men. Perhaps this is another of the reasons we have heard so few of their stories, for it is routinely winners, not losers, who tell conventional war tales; as Stein comments, "[H]istory is written backward, after the fact, by the victors" (97). Most of these fictional brides lost the home-front war, thereby swelling the ranks of wartime victims. Atwood's Anthea drinks, has an affair, and runs off to California; her mysterious death a few years later sounds suspiciously like suicide. The future also looks bleak for Gallant's Mrs. Cameron, for the story hints that she may have unwittingly married an aboriginal. Hollingsworth's miserable Ruthie, who never scrapes together enough money to take her children back to Scotland, drowns her sorrows in drink. Diana assimilates only marginally better by throwing herself into community organizing and local politics, thereby keeping at "arm's length" from her indolent husband. Their marriage survives, perhaps because Paul is the one of the only "war husbands" to admit he might be responsible for Diana's unhappiness. Harding's Norah is one of the few "literary" brides whose life in Canada has a happy ending, perhaps because Ben, like Hollingsworth's Paul, recognizes the extent to which his behavior causes her grief and hence encourages her to return to her family in England. In *Sometime, Never*, Norah decides to return to London, Ontario, with Ben after he confesses why he drinks. When she informs him she is pregnant, Ben vows to find them a flat of their own immediately. Moreover, Norah's youngest sister, Sheila, who has spent the war years lurching from one unhappy affair to another, asks to join her sister in Canada, which she deems "the country of the future" (89).

Marshall's Molly is also one of the few who emerges victorious on the home front because she finds an occupation that renders her a useful and productive member of her community. Against her husband's wishes, she becomes a much-needed midwife; drawing upon the skills she learned with the land army, she delivers babies who might not otherwise have lived. Molly, whose success brings her "fame for miles" (87), is thus one of the few who satisfies Hollingsworth's credo that a woman can be at "home" only in a place that "recognizes" her (Rudakoff and Much 155). Hollingsworth's Luce is another stalwart and courageous survivor. Having escaped from a sexist Italian society, she longs for a supportive husband who will give her freedom to exploit her talent to the full. But after seven years of unsuccessfully "waiting"—the activity commonly associated with women *during* the war—for Chuck to make a success of his career and to recognize her abilities, the thirty-year-old Luce divorces him, cognizant that she cannot hope to break into show business if she gets much older. By 1970, when the play ends, Luce is arguably a quintessential Canadian, having perfected her English and learned French. She currently lives in Toronto. (It is not, as Hodkinson suggests, the most "American" of Canadian cities; Calgary is. Toronto does, however, absorb the highest number of immigrants.) Luce has also expanded her range as an entertainer: she has hosted radio programs, cut records, written comedy skits, and learned to dance. Like Harding's Maggie, Luce is surprisingly free of vitriol, generously helping Chuck, her former husband, land a good job in Toronto. Because of her many talents, Luce's career is on the rise: after completing her 1970 New Year's Eve "gig," ironically, in Niagara Falls, the honeymoon capital of Canada, at the La Gondola restaurant where the play begins and ends, she will make her way to "the Big Apple." Luce, like Molly, has found a home that "recognizes" her, for she is asked to sign autographs in the restaurant. In the last scene of the play, Luce is singing "Somewhere over the Rainbow," a song about the elusiveness of romantic dreams. Significantly, Luce has no permanent home and thus no fixed address: she is "on the road," in process, in flux, a picara. Ever-changing, she is not, however, "ever loving." Work also plays a central role in the survival of Mayr's Friedl; after Karl contracts venereal disease and then abandons her for another woman, Friedl finds a satisfying job in a German delicatessen. Fired at the ripe old age of eighty, she suffers a nervous breakdown, but her sorrows are short-lived because she falls madly in love with another elderly German woman, who not only provides the sexual satisfaction that had been sadly missing from her marriage to Karl but also encourages her to overcome old women's perceived uselessness and invisibility by going over Niagara Falls with her and her sister in a bright orange space-age barrel! The three aged women, who suffer merely cuts, bruises, and broken dental plates from their courageous act, are offered a lucrative book deal, and Friedl agrees to pose topless (her still-magnificent breasts putting the lie to the traditional belief that old women's bodies are revolting) for a nudie magazine, thereby earning the title "nympho granny" (242).[14]

Other signs of victory—albeit less jubilant—arise, as they tend to in postcolonial texts, in the next generation. In Hollingsworth's play, Ruthie's eldest daughter, Rita, tries not to repeat her mother's life as a subaltern: at the end of the play, she has earned a degree and paid homage to her mother's Scottish heritage by becoming engaged to a Scotsman. Rita also encourages her mother to find an apartment and leave Dave. And although the war brides in both Van Herk's and Atwood's texts are minor characters, it could be argued that they have a profound and perhaps even positive effect on their daughters. While both Arachne and Tony are "hardened off" (Atwood 153) by being born to women who did not want to be mothers and as a result abandon their offspring as infants (Arachne's mother leaves her alone in her cradle while she works at a restaurant across the street, and Tony's mother spends most of her days in bed nursing a hangover), neither daughter seems to suffer permanent damage, even though their fathers aren't much better: Toto breaks Arachne's arm when she insinuates he may not be her father, and Tony's father is an alcoholic. In both texts, bitter quarrels between parents turn their homes into metaphorical battlefields or, as Atwood puts it, "raw sexes war." While this kind of upbringing could certainly break a lot of children, both Arachne and Tony ultimately thrive: they become "street smart," picking up, albeit by necessity, survival skills such as independence and resilience. As adults, both women take up unconventional careers: Arachne is, like Luce, a picara, an irreverent and promiscuous underwear saleswoman who plies her wares on the back roads of Alberta. Eschewing marriage, motherhood, and middle-class respectability, she nevertheless has a lengthy relationship with Thomas Telfer, a smart, attractive, professional man who worships her. But at the end of the novel, Arachne forsakes Thomas and, like Luce, escapes her past by living permanently as a picara: she travels, on an open road that has no end, to an *"ultimate frontier . . . where manners never existed and family backgrounds are erased"* (258).

Significantly, Atwood's Tony is, like Arachne, neither wife nor mother; she is, however, by the end of the novel, a fully integrated member of her urban community, in a loving relationship, surrounded by loyal friends, and a widely respected military historian who teaches at the University of Toronto. Undoubtedly motivated by her mother's experiences as a war bride, she wants to see "how war works" (23) for both women and men, for she focuses, not on the dates and outcomes of battles, but on the more unconventional types of war stories that offer a fascinating mix of "domestic image and bloodshed" (3). To that end, her military history lectures use the metaphors of women's crafts such as weaving, knitting, and sewing to elucidate the details of battles (Stein 100); students flock to her lectures, finding those with Steinian titles like "Tender Buttons," which identifies the problems enlisted men faced when they couldn't unbutton their pants to relieve themselves on the battlefield, entertaining and witty. But Tony also tells her students that "[h]istory is a construct. . . . Any point of entry is possible and all choices are arbitrary. Still, there are definitive moments, moments we use as references, because they break our sense of continuity, they change the direction of time. We can look at these events and we can say that after them things were never the same again. They provide beginnings for us, and endings too. Births and deaths, for instance, and marriages. And wars" (4). And, she might have added, the movement across the ocean of nearly forty-eight thousand women, all one generation, and nearly all from the same racial stock.

For most of the war "brides" whose stories appear in the nonfictional accounts, the war years appear to have been "the best of times." To be sure, there are a few "brides" who confess they found it difficult to adjust to the lack of culture, or poverty, or rural hardship, or hostile in-laws, or alcoholic and/or violent husbands, but these are rare exceptions, and the accounts of the hardships tend to be brief and sketchy, leaving readers to fill in the gaps. Perhaps, as Lisa Gabriele remarks in her review of Granfield's *Brass Buttons and Silver Horseshoes* (and her comments apply to the other nonfictional accounts), the lack of information about these women's misery may be as a result of the editors' reluctance to probe too deeply: "[T]here is an eerie, unfamiliar kind of stoicism in the lack of complaint and blame these women place on themselves or their circumstances. Perhaps by leaving these cold, troubling facts dangling, without apology or explanation, Granfield is reminding us of a time when people pulled up their bootstraps and simply got on with things" (D5). By contrast, many of the literary war brides appear to have found life in Canada "the worst of times." Perhaps the "truth" lies somewhere in between.

NOTES

1. Karen F. Stein points out that the name Anthea is an anagram for "Athena," the Greek goddess of war (100).

2. The number of war brides varies according to the source. Ben Wicks suggests that almost 48,000 women immigrated (Preface xi), whereas Joyce Hibbert says that of the 69,733 women and children who came to Canada 44,866 were from Great Britain and brought with them 21,358 children. She adds that a much smaller number came from Holland, Belgium, and France; only a few dozen hailed from Italy, Denmark, Norway, North and South Africa, Greece, Algiers, and Hungary. This much smaller group brought 632 children with them ("Appendix" 156). (Mayr's fictional German war bride is thus unusual.)

3. War brides have also recently been the focus of a number of award-winning feature films and documentaries. *The War Bride* (2001), a Canadian/UK production directed by Lyndon Chubbuck and filmed in Alberta, was nominated for a number of awards, including Best Picture. *From Romance to Reality* (2001), directed by Anne Hainsworth for Kiss the Bride Productions of Ottawa, Ontario, is a one-hour documentary on the history of World War II war brides. In 1980, CBC Film Productions aired *War Brides,* which Grahame Woods wrote, Martin Lavut directed, and Bill Gough produced.

4. Only a few war brides appear in First World War fiction. Max Braithwaite's *Why Shoot the Teacher?* (1965) offers a dismal portrayal of an English woman who is driven (temporarily) insane by the lack of culture on the Canadian prairies, loneliness, overwork, marriage to an insensitive man, and frequent childbearing. By contrast, the French war bride in Gertrude Arnold's *Sister Anne! Sister Anne!* (1919) is warmly received by her husband's *québécoise* family.

5. I am taking this phrase from Sandra Gilbert's "Soldier's Heart: Literary Men, Literary Women, and the Great War." Here, Gilbert cites a former suffragist who says, "I asked myself if any horrors could be greater than the horrors of peace— the sweating, the daily lives of women on the streets, the cry of babes born to misery as the sparks fly upward" (270).

6. In Harding's *Sometimes, Never,* Aunt Girlie insists that *thousands* of war brides returned to England from Canada as a result of "all that ice and snow," the

"primitive conditions," and the "rough" way of life (14). "What they've been through would make your hair stand on end" (13), she asserts, although there is no statistical evidence to support her claim.

7. There were also relatives who tried to frighten young women into staying put. In Harding's *This Year, Next Year*, Norah's Mum cautions her that the Canadian soldier she wants to marry could be "the next Jack the Ripper" (57), and Aunt Girlie describes Canada as an "outlandish place" with "ice and snow and blizzards all year round," where everyone lives in a "log hut" (65). Moreover, she tells Norah, there will be Red Indians "waiting to scalp [you] at the drop of a hat" (65).

8. In Harding's *This Year, Next Year*, Aunt Girlie recounts an oft-told tale about a Canadian airman who boasted that he had a huge ranch with "thousands of acres" in "some place named Detroit" (22).

9. Poverty was also a factor. Margaret Laurence's Second World War story "Horses of the Night" is a heart-wrenching account of a gentle, sensitive young man who is forced to enlist because he cannot find a permanent job.

10. In *Brass Buttons and Silver Horseshoes*, the war bride Joyce Anderson was clearly unimpressed by the vastness of the prairie landscape, stating, "You could see for miles and miles—but see what?" (12).

11. See Fussell's *The Great War and Modern Memory*, 18–35.

12. Myra's remark is heavily ironic, given that in "A Wall of Bright Stone" readers learn that her daughter Kim is a lesbian. In "Stanley," Myra and Peter also discover that their daughter is having an affair with a woman.

13. From Birney's "Can. Lit. (or *them able leave her ever*)," a poem that plays with the lyrics to "The Maple Leaf Forever."

14. Mayr's Friedl also experiences a moment of sweet revenge when Karl dies after trying the stunt himself (234).

Works Cited

Arnold, Gertrude. *Sister Anne! Sister Anne!!* Toronto: McClelland, 1919.

Atwood, Margaret. *The Robber Bride*. Toronto: McClelland, 1993.

Berton, Pierre. Foreword. *Wicks* ix.

Birney, Earle. "Can. Lit. (or *them able leave her ever*)." *An Anthology of Canadian Literature in English*. Rev. and abridged ed. Ed. Russell Brown, Donna Bennett, and Natalie Cook. Toronto: Oxford University Press, 1990. 296.

Braithwaite, Max. *Why Shoot the Teacher?* Toronto: McClelland, 1965.

Brookes, Chris. *Songs My Mother Taught Me: A Documentary Novel Recorded, Written, and Produced by Chris Brookes*. CD. St. John's, Newfoundland: Battery Radio, 1998.

Fussell, Paul. *The Great War and Modern Memory*. London: Oxford University Press, 1975.

Gabriele, Lisa. "A Boom of Brides." Rev. of *Brass Buttons and Silver Horseshoes: Stories from Canada's British War Brides. Globe and Mail* 6 Apr. 2002: D5.

Gallant, Mavis. Introduction. *The War Brides.* Ed. Joyce Hibbert. Toronto: PMA Books, 1978. xi–xix.

———. "Up North." *Home Truths: Selected Canadian Stories.* Toronto: Macmillan, 1981. 49–55.

Gilbert, Sandra. "Soldier's Heart: Literary Men, Literary Women, and the Great War." *No Man's Land: The Place of the Woman Writer in the Twentieth Century.* Vol. 2. *Sexchanges.* Ed. Sandra Gilbert and Susan Gubar. New Haven: Yale University Press, 1989. 258–323.

Granfield, Linda, ed. *Brass Buttons and Silver Horseshoes: Stories from Canada's British War Brides.* Toronto: McClelland, 2002.

Harding, Norah. Playwright's Foreword. *Sometime, Never.* Toronto: Playwrights Canada Press, 2001. n.p.

———. *Sometime, Never.* Toronto: Playwrights Canada Press, 2001.

———. *This Year, Next Year.* 1995. Toronto: Playwrights Union of Canada, 2001.

Hibbert, Joyce, ed. *The War Brides.* Toronto: PMA Books, 1978.

Higonnet, Margaret Randolph, et al., eds. Introduction. *Behind the Lines: Gender and the Two World Wars.* New Haven: Yale University Press, 1987. 1–17.

Higonnet, Margaret R., and Patrice L.-R. Higonnet. "The Double Helix." *Behind the Lines: Gender and the Two World Wars.* New Haven: Yale University Press, 1987. 31–47.

Hodkinson, Yvonne. *Female Parts: The Art and Politics of Women Playwrights.* Montreal: Black Rose Books, 1991.

Hollingsworth, Margaret. *Ever Loving. Willful Acts.* Toronto: Coach House Press, 1985. 35–111.

Ladouceur, Barbara, and Phyllis Spence, eds. *Blackouts to Bright Lights: Canadian War Bride Stories.* Vancouver: Ronsdale Press, 1995.

Laurence, Margaret. "Horses of the Night." *A Bird in the House.* Toronto: McClelland, 1973. 128–54.

Marshall, Joyce. "The Old Woman." *A Private Place.* Toronto: Oberon, 1975. 77–91.

Mayr, Suzette. *The Widows.* Edmonton: NeWest Press, 1998.

O'Hara, Peggy. *From Romance to Reality: Stories of Canadian War Brides.* Cobalt, ON: Highway Book Shop, 1983.

Rudakoff, Judith, and Rita Much. *Fair Play: Twelve Women Speak. Conversations with Canadian Playwrights.* Toronto: University of Toronto Press, 1990.

Staels, Hilde. "You Can't Do without Your Shadow: An Interview with Margaret Atwood." *Margaret Atwood's Novels: A Study of Narrative Discourse.* "Appendix." Basel: Frank, 1995. 207–14.

Stein, Karen F. *Margaret Atwood Revisited.* New York: Twayne, 1999.

Van Herk, Aritha. *No Fixed Address: An Amorous Journey.* 1986. Red Deer: Red Deer College Press, 1998.

Wallace, Robert, and Cynthia Zimmerman. "Margaret Hollingsworth." Interview. *The Work: Conversations with English-Canadian Playwrights.* Ed. Robert Wallace and Cynthia Zimmerman. Toronto: Coach House Press, 1982. 90–101.

Wicks, Ben, ed. *Promise You'll Take Care of My Daughter: The Remarkable War Brides of World War II.* Toronto: Stoddart, 1992.

———. Preface. Wicks xi–xiii.

Wyatt, Rachel. *The Day Marlene Dietrich Died.* Lantzville, BC: Oolican Books, 1996.

———. "Her Voice." *The Day Marlene Dietrich Died.* 9–17.

———. "Stanley." *The Day Marlene Dietrich Died.* 29–37.

———. "Time Travel." *The Day Marlene Dietrich Died.* 197–204.

Zimmerman, Cynthia. "Margaret Hollingsworth: Feeling Out of Context." Interview. *Playwrighting Women: Female Voices in English Canada.* Ed. Cynthia Zimmerman. Toronto: Dundurn Press, 1996. 100–132.

CHAPTER FOURTEEN

Ta(l)king War into Peace

Marguerite Duras's La douleur, *History and Her Stories*

C A M I L A   L O E W

A man is so much cleverer than we,

Conversing with himself of truth and lie,

Of death and spring and iron-work and time.

But I say "you" and always "you and I."

Gertrud Kolmar, "The Woman Poet"

An important part of war witnessing—the witnessing that becomes war narrative—actually begins once the (official) war is over. As the witnesses of war take pains to go back to peace, they simultaneously strive to put their experience down on paper, and in this process the transition between war and peace is reassessed (conversely, one could also argue that narrative strategies inherent in war telling are already at work during war; in this sense, war victims and participants both *tell to survive* and *survive to tell*). In recent years a new understanding of the notion of war testimony has developed. This change can largely be credited to the radical alterations in warfare—and also war narrative—brought about as a consequence of the conflicts of the twentieth century, in which civilians were thrust into the reality of war and came to form a part of it just as much as the soldiers did. As a result, the criteria that determine what an "authentic" war narrative is have been stretched to include other voices; the canon of what we now call war texts encompasses a myriad of stories no longer limited to the tale of physical combat on the battlefront: "Each story told by someone who experienced a war, or someone who saw someone who experienced a war, or by someone who read about someone who experienced a war becomes part of a mosaic, the many colors of which make up the totality of that war" (Cooke 4).

In the pages that follow I shall read Marguerite Duras's *La douleur*, an autobiographical recreation of her experience during World War II, as a revision and critique of traditional, patriarchal representation of war. The main purpose of this essay is to show the complexity of *La douleur*, not only in its moral implications but also as a tale of war in itself and, by extension, a meditation upon the genre of war narrative. As we shall see, Duras's postwar written struggle to go back to peace is tainted by an attempt to erase the strict spatial and temporal boundaries between times of war and times of peace. I suggest that Duras performs her reassessment of war narrative through a literary practice that results in a complex textual pattern that brings together many different theoretical strands. By reuniting ethical and metatextual issues pertaining to war and the Holocaust, as well as meditations on gender and autobiography, Duras proposes that the patterns of war are deeply inscribed in the domain of what we usually call "peace." To reach this conclusion, I shall examine the multiple aspects of *La douleur* that permit us to call it a war narrative.

Duras incorporates a metatextual revision of war narrative into her own tale of war. In this process, an important factor is the relationship Duras constructs between her text and the memoirs of her then-husband Robert Antelme about his camp experience. The author and narrator's husband is thus present at two different stages: as a character of the plot and as an authorial voice Duras responds to. In her addresses, Duras redefines the nature of witnessing and questions the ethical issues Antelme discussed from a different standpoint. In her subversion of previous ethical assessments on war and after-war, gender plays an important role. As we shall see, Duras focuses mainly on female personae in the texts of *La douleur* and represents them with a power of agency that women lack in many other war texts. The constant boundary erasing that Duras performs (between battlefront and home front, times of war and times of peace, female and male, language and experience) takes the ethical implications of Antelme's text to a different, perhaps even more obscure level. In this way, the testimonial text becomes a denunciation of certain discursive practices inscribed in Western culture and representation.

Duras's testimony is apparently presented not as a firsthand assessment of the Holocaust but in a sense as a secondhand narrative, in which the "real" witness to horror is the absent husband the narrator is anxiously awaiting. Because Duras herself was neither a prisoner of the camps nor a soldier on the battlefield (she never left her Parisian home), she is arguably not a "true" witness to the war. However, the question of the authenticity of testimony acquires a new light in relation not only to Duras's text but also to Antelme's testimony of life in the camps. Titled *L'espèce humaine* (1947), the book was published by Les Éditions de la Cité Universelle, a publishing house established by Duras and Antelme, as one of the first testimonies about the concentration camps and one of the first attempts to analyze the consequences of the Holocaust for the human race.[1] Duras's reassessments of Antelme's main conclusions lead to ethical reflections on the nature of war and peace.

Although Duras herself was not a prisoner of the camps, *La douleur* is by all means a war story and, like *L'espèce humaine*, can be read as a meditation on the human condition after Auschwitz. Duras reopens the issues Antelme raised in his writings on his experience of the war. Precisely because of Duras's reinscription of the category of "war" into "peace," the fact that she is removed from the front lines and the camps becomes ultimately superfluous: hers is also a tale of war and its aftermath in "peace."

Moreover, Duras's stance "on the line" or margin of different war roles, as simultaneously fighter, victim, and onlooker, is arguably what grants her the position to observe and express the patterns of war in peace. In this sense, Duras's testimony is unique, and its value lies in the fact that we cannot place her on any of the traditional "sides" of war. Duras deals with the Holocaust as witness to Antelme, a prisoner of the camps, but also as a victim, affected by the war and the concentration camps in her own way. *La douleur* aims at revealing that to deal with our own past and its repercussions in the present we must understand that the patterns of war are deeply inscribed in and inherent to what we call "peace."

The incorporation of war into peace in Duras's writing is closely linked to her representation—and criticism—of the traditional roles assigned to men and women in times of war (and times of peace). In this sense, Duras follows a tradition inaugurated by Erich Maria Remarque's 1929 World War I novel *Im Westen Nichts Neues*, one of the first major unmaskings of

masculine military glory in war narrative. Remarque "feminized" his soldiers to counter the stereotype of heroic representations of war (like those
of Ernst Jünger, for instance) and reveal the absurd, senseless nature of war.[2]
Like Remarque, Duras denounces certain myths and artificial constructions present in the discourse of war; however, she goes about this task by
examining the roles assigned to *women* in times of war.

While many soldiers' tales of war reassess the opposition between men
and women's "fixed" places in war, Duras writes against this war narrative
tradition by subverting the conventional gender roles and depicting some
of her women as aggressive warriors rather than the submissive, docile figures men must protect in traditional tales of war. Duras represents herself
during the war not on the front line of battle but in the heart of Paris, where
another kind of war was going on, a war not as clear as the physical battle
and much harder to call "war." Part of this reassessment of gender roles
concerns the author's own role in war. Although Duras is not a soldier, she
participates in war as an active agent rather than a passive onlooker and in
doing so foregrounds issues relevant to the nature of bearing witness and
writing war.

La douleur is a collection of texts written by Duras during the war
years, but it was not published as a book until forty years later (some fragments of the diary extract "La douleur" were published anonymously in
Sorcières magazine in 1976).[3] The book is divided into two major parts: a
long diary extract, titled "La douleur," that describes the author-narrator's
painful wait for her husband's return from Nazi concentration camps and a
collection of five short texts that narrate various daily events of wartime
and immediate post-Liberation France. Each subgroup of texts is preceded
by commentaries provided by the author in which she addresses the reader
to prescribe and frame how the reader should interpret each text's hold on
truth: some of the texts are "vraie jusque dans le détail" (90), while others
are "inventé" or "de la littérature" (194).

The diarylike text "La douleur" tells of the author-narrator's experience
while she struggles through her day-to-day life in recently liberated Paris,
anxiously awaiting news from her husband. Robert Antelme was deported
by the Gestapo in 1944 due to his clandestine work as a member of a French
Resistance group (in which Duras also took part). In the final section of the
text, the husband (barely fictionalized in the name Robert L.) returns—or
rather, what remains of him does—in a state of desperate struggle between
life and death. The narrator's life—and the text's plot—goes forward moved

solely "par la passion de sauver Robert L. de la mort" (71). In this sense, "La douleur" bears witness to a witness. This metawitnessing is a key aspect of Duras's text.

In *La douleur* Marguerite Duras represents herself as a witness on three different levels. These three levels of witnessing have been described by Shoshana Felman and Dori Laub, in an insightful analysis of twentieth-century after-war testimony, as three distinct moments in post-Holocaust texts: the level of being a witness to one's own experience, the level of witnessing testimonies of others, and the level of witnessing the process of witnessing itself (75). Duras is thus a witness to herself, to her husband the Holocaust survivor, and to the mechanisms that the process of witnessing involves. The narrator testifies, through her own suffering and pain, not only to the traces of horror written on the emaciated body of her husband but also to her own experience of the war in Paris and to the reaches and limits of these experiences when they encounter the written word.

The simultaneous presence of these three stages determines the uniqueness and novelty of Duras's text in relation to texts of previous women writers of the Holocaust. Initially, the texts by women on the Holocaust that became well known were mostly those of women who had written during the war but died before its end. Authors like Anne Frank, Etty Hillesum, and Gertrud Kolmar wrote texts in which some of the issues Duras brings up had already been introduced. However, the writings of these women authors lack the temporal distance that gives Duras a theoretical and metatextual dimension, as well as an insight into the postwar issues that arise once war fades and blends into peace. In this sense, Duras's text raises issues relevant to the process of going back to peace, which until recently had been read mostly in men's testimonies (for example, in texts by survivors like Primo Levi or Jorge Semprún), by exploring the way we deal with the memory of war from a "peacetime" standpoint.

The universe of the concentration camps looms over Duras's whole text. Martin Crowley reads its proximity as a presence *in absentia*, "as the texts mostly describe an *elsewhere* of the suffering of the camps" (174), the space occupied by the families of those deported to the camps, and Paris at the end of the war (that is, if we can call this an end; Duras's testimony shows that it isn't). Although they are represented only obliquely, the camps "represent the condition of possibility of the text's existence" (175).

The transferential nature of Duras's suffering should not lead us to believe that she is suffering the camps only indirectly. If we read this text in the frame of the rest of the texts that form the volume, *La douleur* shows that Duras's war experience goes beyond the eternal waiting for her husband and her desperate uncertainty about his welfare. The suffering of the camps is displaced onto Duras's day-to-day life in Paris as she imitates his hunger and pain, which become confused with her own: "[L]e pain est celui qu'il n'a mangé, celui dont le manque l'a fait mourir" (19). Crowley reads this mimicry of suffering as a "generous doubling, a refusal to let the suffering of her husband go unaccompanied" (176). In a similar vein, Colin Davis argues that *La douleur* (and specifically the text "La douleur") presents itself initially in a place of dependence and secondarity, both literally, in relation to the previous *L'espèce humaine,* and thematically, as the story of a waiting wife solely preoccupied with her husband's destiny (172). According to Crowley and Davis, her primary role seems to be mainly that of listener. I believe, however, that the transferential nature of Duras's suffering is meant as a statement on the nature of war and the extent of its devastation.

Duras's portrayal of pain may be read as inevitably tied to the experience of the concentration camps but independent from the experience of those deported to them. *La douleur* deals with other aspects of war, with facets that the victims of the camps were not witnesses to, just as Duras was not a "direct" witness to the camps. This is what makes the text so complex: it is a tale of the Second World War and the Holocaust, but from a perspective that has not been adopted before. From her original space as listener, and because of the fundamental role the listener occupies in testimony, she makes herself an active participant in these re-called events. As Lawrence Kritzman argues, "[T]he desire for an audience permits the listener to assume the role of witness which the survivor had previously experienced alone" (68).

As a "companion on the eerie journey of testimony" (Felman and Laub 76), the listener participates in the re-membering (putting back together) and re-calling (naming) of the experience. In this phase, one must go beyond what was lived to tame somewhat its horror, giving form to the extreme deformity of its horror through language and converting the chaotic unnamable into a comprehensible linguistic sequence. In this sense, the witness functions as mediator between darkness and light, between death and life. As Primo Levi stated, only "the saved" can take on this task, but theirs will somehow always be a secondhand narrative; they are not the "true witnesses" to horror because these are no longer here to express their experience in language (83).

The process of becoming an active witness is particularly revealed in the strong identification the narrator feels with her husband while he is still away from home. This identification becomes even stronger when Robert comes back home. Marguerite's developments are parallel to his: "Moi aussi, je recommence à manger, je recommence à dormir. Je reprends du poids. Nous allons vivre. . . . Mon identité s'est déplacée. Je suis seulement celle qui . . . veut à sa place, pour lui" (78–79). This strong identification can be read as a female submission to a man's war experience, but it can also be understood as an insight into the process of back-to-peace testimonial writing. For Duras, in her home, removed from the battlefront but ever so close to the effects of war, the experience of *la douleur* is what reveals that she is alive and, simultaneously, how she reveals this to herself and the reader. In that experience of pain, *the other* is a necessary, fundamental element. As a witness to the war, Duras shows that to feel pain there must be another subject, an objective other to feel it *for*. "Douleur" is equivalent to hope: "la douleur est implantée dans l'espoir" (79). The pain is what allows her to keep waiting and hoping for change—be it the end of the war, the return of her husband, or, on a larger scale, a significant alteration of the patterns of evil in society, present in both war and peace. Without the objective other that serves as figure of mediation, the subject cannot constitute itself as such. The figure of the female narrator, caught between the war that caused her husband's absence and the oncoming peace of the "liberated" city she lives in, thus highlights mediation in the postwar text.[4]

The metatextual dimension of Duras's narrative is common to many testimonies and post–World War II texts whose authors find themselves forced to share the newfound uncertainties regarding the relationship between language and experience with their readers. The Holocaust has significantly altered our understanding of humanity and our relationship to extreme evil, but in the telling and retelling of its history it has also changed the ways both collective and individual history or testimony are read. In the preliminary words to "La douleur," Duras broaches a meditation upon the fragile, shaky relationship between literature and memory, between the objective textual representation of the extreme and the uncertain space these memories occupy in the author's lifetime. Duras confesses to having found the long-forgotten pages of her journal in a closet over forty years after the war's end.[5] Although her memory of writing about this period of her life now fails her, she doesn't think it's possible that she wrote these lines during the actual waiting for her husband, a statement that implies that the diary format given to the text is an artifice.[6] She acknowledges that "*La douleur est une des choses les plus importantes de ma vie*," signaling, through the use of italics, the title of the book but also suggesting that the pain she truly went through is inherent to her own experience. Duras sets the neat, regular writing found in the notes of her journal against the chaotic disorder of thoughts and feelings "*au regard de quoi la littérature m'a fait honte*" (12). However, she did decide to have it published.

The pronouns of the phrase "*Je sais . . . que c'est moi qui l'ai écrit*" (12) condense the unfolding of subjects that all testimonial writing implies. *Je* is the well-known novelist who put together these rediscovered pages in 1985 to give form to a new book. *Moi* refers to the subject represented in the text, a woman supposedly writing in Paris in 1945, a literary persona that, through the use of the first person, coincides with the author and narrator.[7] The expression *c'est* allows this persona to be represented or signaled at a distance, as an external other, different from (yet the same as) the Marguerite Duras who acts as editor of her own texts. Finally, the first-person singular *passé composé* of *ai écrit* comprises both *je* and *moi* in one verb, placing author, narrator, and protagonist together (Phillip Lejeune's sine qua non for autobiographical literature) as disrupted pieces of the same puzzle.

This unfolding of subjects is the central aspect highlighted in the theory of modern testimony. Through the use and abuse of different pronouns and personae, Duras explores the complex relationship between witnessing, experiencing, and writing. She plays on the unfolding of the act of bearing witness in many other moments of *La douleur*—for example, through the use of pronouns, by switching from first to third person, from *je* to *elle:* "Qui est ce Robert L.? . . . Qui est elle? Qui elle est, D. le sait. Où est D.? Elle le sait, elle peut le voir et lui demander des explications. Il faut que je le voie" (50). In this way, Duras's text inaugurates a whole new dimension of testimonial and textual issues: the metatextual mediation, a meditation on how history is received and passed on, how the story (or manifold stories) of war becomes history once we go back to peace.

The third level of witnessing—that of witnessing the process of witnessing itself—is the central aspect that distinguishes Duras's style of representation from Antelme's; it reveals that we are dealing with a narrative inserted in a much more contemporary context than Antelme's immediate, urgent postwar writing. Duras is by now well aware of the nature of language and its inability to represent the extreme, a common topos of Holocaust literature. In Antelme's text, the urgency to communicate what he experienced in the realm of Nazi terror is stronger than the difficulties he encounters in searching for an appropriate means of representation in language (even though those difficulties are explicitly acknowledged). Duras questions the possibility of objective, neutral historical representation in testimony—and this is what makes her a witness of the process of witnessing. Once we go back to peace, the past war experience can only be alluded to, but its pastness eludes us as writers/readers/witnesses. *La douleur*, as Leslie Hill states, is "a work that bears witness to the sheer impossibility of bearing witness" (129). *La douleur* intends to show that in contemporary representation the Holocaust is no longer merely a historical period but that it is also more than a metaphor for the estrangement from humanity and moral truth, as Antelme interprets it. In Holocaust texts contemporary with *La douleur*, the metatextual debate about how to represent (horror) has necessarily become a part of the work itself.

Antelme, writing in 1947, is already aware of the breakdown of the relationship between language and experience, between the urgent need to tell what has happened and the impossibility of telling it adequately. He speaks in the name of all witnesses to horror when he tries to describe this gap. He alludes to the vast distance he has discovered between the language we dispose of and the experience that is still going on in the survivors' bodies. The tie to language is frustrating, for language is required and desired as the only link with the outside world but is also detested because it fails to embrace their experience in its totality. The inadequacy of language to express horror is perhaps the problem most difficult to solve textually; it is the problem that appears most often in Holocaust testimonies. Nevertheless, Antelme's faith in the strength of language proves unshakable; he needs it to be unshakeable so that he may survive and return to the realm of the living. Although the world as he once knew it has fallen apart, Antelme still believes in the redeeming, resilient capacity of language, which is one of the strongest confirmations of the prisoners' ultimate independence and identity. Through language Antelme can claim that all men—both Nazis and *Häftling*—belong to the human species. This is why the conclusion to *L'espèce humaine* is a proclamation of the need for all the individual stories to be told. Only the ability to tell can help communicate the events and undermine the incredulity that such extreme truths can provoke. Antelme proposes to bring all the individual testimonies together, one after another, in an invisible, eternal string of narrative. Although the traces of their fracture are apparent in Antelme's work, memory, history, and writing still form an indivisible bond, because if we ceased to believe in the possibility of representing the truth the concentration camps wouldn't exist.

Antelme's plea for the thousands of narratives to come forth is still being answered today by those who choose to bear witness through testimony. Almost sixty years after the liberation of the concentration camps, the abundance of testimonial production has revealed an unending attempt to keep these events present and represented. However, faith in the possibility to communicate what went on behind the barbed-wired walls of Auschwitz has grown ever weaker, resulting in a collapse of the transparency of "objective" testimony. In fact, today we read this genre for the stylistic devices involved as much as for its documentary value.

La douleur is a much more fragmentary, unstable text than *L'espèce humaine*. Duras, revising her notes in the 1980s, is by now well aware of the lack of transparency inherent in autobiographical language and particularly in the telling of atrocity. Her narrative has a much less mimetic intention than *L'espèce humaine*.[8] This can be illustrated not only when Duras claims that Antelme's text is the representation of what he believes he lived but also when she describes her encounter with two of Antelme's fellow prisoners of the camps. Although they have just been freed, they cannot remember the recent, horrendous past enough to give her any clear indication of her husband's whereabouts: "Perotti ne sais plus raconter rien, il a la mémoire en miettes" (54). The survivors can narrate only disrupted fragments because "du reste, non, ils ne se souviennent plus" (55). Duras is implying that after this war we have passed on to a new stage of humankind: the story of what has just become history is, in its extremity, no longer clear or certain enough to be told as a coherent narrative. The "crumbs" that make up Perotti's memory are the fragments one must strive to put together in the return to peace in which the telling takes place. However, this return from wartime back to everyday life is not a simple one-way journey. Duras's text works to show the reader that the supposed after-war peace is not a separate realm from war. As in Perotti's stuttered memories, the path of "crumbs" traced by war marks the instinctive path of humanity toward evil and the infliction of pain on other human beings. With the image of a witness's memory crumbling into pieces, Duras reveals the operations of war: she both metatextually denounces the mediation inherent in all war telling (and particularly in this tale, due to its extremity) and makes a statement on the ethical status of war and humankind in the twentieth century. The extremity of this particular conflict leads both Duras and her husband, to whom she appeals, to question the nature of good and evil and our relationship to them in the system of war and peace. The representation of the human species in the characters of *La douleur* reveals Duras's belief that, against Antelme's ultimate optimism, humans are much closer to evil than they are to good. In this sense, war is a presence that extends beyond the bounds in which history books tend to enclose it.

Duras's insistence on the presence of war in peace is best revealed in the constant foregrounding of her indifference toward the traditional oppositions on which much of war discourse is based. The breakdown of oppositions like good/evil, torturer/victim, and right/wrong can be read thematically and discursively on various levels of the text. In this sense, it would be possible to read a first apparent contradiction in the relationship with her husband in "La douleur." The long, painful wait for Robert L. ends, not with a happy reunion of the couple, but with their separation. After mourning his absence and nursing him back to life, Duras decides to divorce him.[9]

Three autobiographical texts in the book complement "La douleur" in their portrayal of different types of war victims and perpetrators, and of victims as perpetrators. Whereas "La douleur" is apparently the text of a victim subjected to anguish and pain, in the other texts it is no longer clear who imposes the pain on whom. The narrator of "La douleur" suffers during her "passive," patriarchally "feminine" wait for her husband's return. In the other texts, the main character is a victim who uses and abuses her position of power as a member of the Resistance. Although Duras hardly mentions these activities in "La douleur," they supposedly coincide chronologically with the first tale.

The plot of "Monsieur X dit ici Pierre Rabier" is directly interwoven with that of "La douleur": the narrator maintains her relationship with a Gestapo agent because he has the power to give her information on her deported husband's whereabouts. This strange, ambivalent relationship is not even mentioned in "La douleur." "Monsieur X . . . ," however, is not written as a journal; instead, it takes a linear narrative form. The author uses the present tense to give the events an illusion of immediacy and eyewitnessing. The encounters between the narrator and Rabier become more and more frequent; both parties see the other as holding a certain power for different reasons. Rabier envies and admires Duras because she is a writer and "Rabier était fasciné par les intellectuels français, les artistes, les auteurs des livres" (98). From his point of view, she is successful as an artist where he has failed.

Although fear is the theme that the author foregrounds in this text, just as pain seeps through each word of "La douleur," one cannot help noticing the dangerous game of seduction going on between them. The narrator is lost in this unsettling game; not only does she lose contact with the members of her Resistance group, who are aware of their frequent outings, but she also starts to lose her grip on her original motivation for engaging in these encounters. Logic no longer has a place here. Rabier should naturally want to erase a dangerous witness like Duras from existence: she is a writer and the wife of a Resistance fighter. However, he continues to narrate his detentions and persecutions in full detail, as if he were implicitly pleading to her to make literature out of them. As for Duras, she continues to forget her identity, both as a member of the Resistance and as the wife of a prisoner of the Nazis, and totters on the brink of thinking of herself as a prospective prisoner and simultaneously a perpetrator acting on the Nazi's violent impulses.

These recurrent encounters reveal an erasing of both spatial and temporal delimitations of war; just as there are no clear borders between battlefront and home front, we cannot speak of clear boundaries between war and peace. Duras intends to show that moral sins are not exclusive to the enemy; they are also committed on what is believed to be the "good side." "L' habitude est telle, de punir, de se défendre, de se débarasser, et surtout de 'n'avoir pas le temps,' que la décision est prise d'abattre ce camarade à la Libération" (104). The chain of treason and accusation functions in the same way on both sides and in a sense continues the war even after the war is officially over: Rabier proposes to give her back her husband if she turns in François Mittérand (called Morland), the leader of her Resistance group. Now she is the one who has the power and the strength to determine Rabier's fate. Although she does not give in, and Rabier is, through her agency, caught and tried in court, her oral testimony during the trial reveals the uncertainty and lack of conviction that are the prevailing themes of La douleur. Since the discoveries that resulted from the liberation of the camps, we have entered a new time, no longer "vierge et virginale" (123); we cannot speak of moral truth and transparent telling. This is the lesson the narrator has learned from her encounters with Rabier.

In court, Duras claims that she wants only to "dire la vérité, afin qu'elle ait été dite" (134), but to reveal this facet of the truth is something too complex for the court to bear. "La vérité," for whatever it is worth, is left unsaid. The war ends, and its trials aim to achieve a kind of closure in order to go back to peace. However, as Rabier himself suggests, it is no longer possible to think of war in terms of winning and losing: "[L]a guerre ne s'arrêtera pas pour des gens comme moi" (130). The Allied forces' victory over Nazi Germany does not come untarnished. The court scene grants a legal frame for the continuation of the patterns of war into peace. The war lives on in its victory over ethical certainty and the impossibility of speaking of moral truth: "[C]'est dans ce silence-là que la guerre est encore présent, qu'elle sourd à travers le sable, le vent" (83).

The indivisibility of war and peace is inseparable from Duras's notions of good and evil in human behavior. The consequences of war trauma for individuals and for postwar society are thus very different in *La douleur* from those that *L'espèce humaine* proposed in 1947. Whereas Antelme affirms the indivisible unity of humankind in spite of the atrocious Nazi crimes, Duras affirms this unity precisely in a shared human capacity to destroy one another (Davis 176). These differing views have both ethical and aesthetic implications. The ethical implications may be related to the fact that, as a survivor, Antelme clings to an ultimate faith in humankind; he can thus also believe in testimonial truth. Duras's disbelief of positive unity is revealed in the fragmentation of her own narrative subject, and also in this subject's calling forth the many uncertain aspects and unresolved truths of the texts. By foregrounding a lack of ethical significance in her representation of the war years, Duras also questions the capacity of language to represent the past. Historical witnessing and testimony become more literary than literal; there is no longer any possible objective, absolute truth in narrative.

Just as Duras refuses to see a temporal boundary between war and peace, she erases the dividing line between the supposedly opposing sides of the war. The idea that the two sides are the same is notably present in "Albert des Capitales," the story of the imprisonment and torture of a Nazi collaborator by members of the French Resistance. In the preliminary words to this text and the one that follows it ("Ter le milicien," in which the narrator is sexually attracted to a collaborator),[10] the author states that she is the person behind the main characters of the texts, and she affirms that these are "des textes sacrés" that we must learn to read among the rest of the texts of *La douleur* (138). Literature serves as a privileged space that can show the blurring of the dividing line between war and peace and between victims and perpetrators of war. If *La douleur* has antiwar intentions, these must be read in the lack of a "moral," understood both as an ethics and as a guiding principle that can be extracted from the story.

The plot of "Albert des Capitales" takes place one week after the liberation of Paris; the Resistance group Duras belonged to was then in charge of hunting down the informers who had handed Jews over to the Nazis. But instead of speaking of this task as a way of righting a wrong, or even as a vengeance on the performers of evil, the narrator starts out by explaining her participation as an act of curiosity: "[O]n était déjà plus curieux de ce qu'on avait vécu aveuglément sous l'Occupation que de ce qu'on vivait d'extraordinaire depuis un semaine, depuis la Libération" (141). Once the collaborator is (literally) in their hands, and before the torture session begins, the narrator, through the use of free indirect style, makes the main character, Thérèse—the only woman among the group—pause to look upon both "Resisters" and collaborator with a distant, standoffish glance. The differences between men are merely accidental; the collaborator, about to be questioned and tortured, undresses just as any other man would (153).

When Thérèse pronounces her first sentence in the scene, the narrative shifts suddenly from reflective description to action; Thérèse abandons her remote point of view and becomes one with them, or rather becomes the leader of the session of violence. Duras thus reveals that war is not temporally circumscribed: while Paris celebrates its "liberation" in the streets, this dark chamber in the heart of the city is the heart of darkness itself; "ni la tristesse douce ni la fin ne sont possibles" (154). In the streets homecoming soldiers are reunited with their sweethearts, but in this dark cell evil and the infliction of pain go on indefinitely. The role of torturer has been switched to the "good" Resistance fighter; that of victim now belongs to a former Nazi. The patterns of violence are perpetrated and perpetuated, indifferent to the victory the Allied forces have claimed for themselves.

Though Duras and Antelme would agree on the unity of humankind, they arrive at this conclusion through opposing arguments; he sees human strength where she emphasizes weakness. Whereas Antelme reaches this conclusion on a positive note, revealing the strength of humankind in its indivisibility and assuring the defeat of Nazi ideology, Duras highlights the weaknesses of humankind as a foundational element of its unity:[11] "La seule réponse à faire à ce crime est d'en faire un crime de tous. De le partager. De même que l'idée d'égalité, de fraternité. Pour le supporter, pour en tolerer l'idée, partager le crime" (64–65).

Duras presents her conclusions with a lack of closure that suggests that the discourse of war must be revised and renewed. By examining the unstable nature of war testimony she inscribes her text in a new form of discourse that aims to recontextualize the memory of the war and under-mine narratives based on traditional, patriarchal oppositions that conceive of war and peace (or victim and torturer) as excluding one another.

The exercise of uncertainty is notably acted out by the female personae that appear in the different texts of *La douleur*, through a gender subversion that accords with and implies the erasing of other boundaries. Duras fore-grounds the female figure to reject that the war is a story about "elsewhere," told from the point of view of peace once war is over. On the contrary, the tale of war Duras gives us inscribes the "other" in the here and now, in the heart of darkness of each human being, in any city, at any time.

Martin Crowley argues that the torture performed by the Resistance members on the Nazi collaborator is Duras's way of exploring the ultimate implications of Antelme's central thesis, that of the unity of the human race. In his view, Duras presents the victim as indistinguishable from the tor-turer, proposing that both are equally human and that "to torture is as much a part of this shared condition as to suffer" (182). I would suggest that, as opposed to the activities and discourse of the Resistance represented in *La douleur*, Duras proposes other sorts of resistance. The upper- and lowercase letters here call our attention to the different meanings of the word *resis-tance*. The resistance that actively opposes an attacking force using the same means of arms and violence as the attacking force is revealed in the torture scene of "Albert des Capitales" to be just as dangerous as the aggression that awakens it. Duras is highlighting a very human tendency toward inhuman-ity—that is, a violent denial of the other's humanity. In this sense, Duras's text reveals the pattern of action and reaction as a human tendency and foregrounds its dark ethical implications so that its most dangerous conse-quences can be resisted: "Duras's insistence is that this material must be confronted *in order that it not reproduce itself*" (Crowley 189, emphasis in original). If this reactive pattern is not revealed and undone, the chain of massacres will never be broken and war will continue to imitate war narra-tive, which itself imitates war (Huston 273).

Another meaning of *resistance* is a refusal to comply with what is im-posed. This sense is usually called passive resistance. Nevertheless, Duras converts any passivity implied in this sense of *resistance* into a significant action: the action of countering the perpetuating narrative scheme that reads war as based on antagonistic, exclusive oppositions. In this process, women are written into the war story as participants in war. They play a se-ries of roles that range from the waiting, wailing women who mourn their husbands' absence in "La douleur," to the vengeful torturer of "Albert des

Capitales," to the innocent, defenseless young girl of "Aurélia Steiner." In each text, through the female characters, Duras proposes a reinscription of the ways we read war (narrative) once we are back "in peace." The voices of victims are transformed into active statements of subjects who have something to say, survivors who want to resist the master narrative of war.

The women of the journal "La douleur"—not only the narrator but also the other women that appear in the text—are mainly portrayed in the role of waiting: "Il faut que je sois raisonnable: j'attends Robert L. qui doit revenir" (14); "Nous sommes à la pointe d'un combat sans nom, sans armes, sans sang versé, sans gloire, à la pointe de l'attente" (48); "Il n'y a nous qui attendions encore, d'une attente de tous les temps, de celle des femmes de tous les temps, de tous les lieux du monde: celle des hommes au retour de la guerre" (60). These women are not perpetuating the binary scheme of war in which men are active and women passive. On the contrary, the women have turned their wait into a cause in itself, a political battle against the system that confines them to the outskirts of war. The women refuse to accept the loss of their men, and although they are confined to the margins of the official repatriation activities their role must be understood actively, as a resistance against the obsolete discourse of the official figures, based on abstract concepts that only perpetuate the War Story.

This official discourse is embodied in the character of the priest, who speaks to the women of faith, absolution, and forgiveness, even though he himself has experienced neither deportation nor the pain of the wait. The women disregard the priest and reject his unfeeling words: "Restait d'un côté le front des femmes, compact, irréductible. Et de l'autre côté cet homme seul qui avait raison dans un langage que les femmes ne comprenaient plus" (35). The women resist the stale language of the priest in their refusal to comply with a discourse that ultimately justifies war. Their resistance takes place precisely through their embodiment of "la douleur"; they suffer compassionately with their absent husbands, repeating or re-presenting the men's suffering, refusing to leave them unaccompanied in their pain.[12]

Along with the abstract language of religion, another type of discourse that the text denounces as based on a rigid and sterile structure is that of politics. De Gaulle is portrayed as excluding all allusions to the camps from his speeches. He refuses to include the people's suffering in his construction of victory and military glory. The women reject De Gaulle because he will not allow them to confront the reality of that pain and deal with it as a (human) part of the war. In his speech, "le deuil du peuple ne se porte pas" (45–46). Although De Gaulle's discourse is one of war and not of peace, it approaches the priest's values in its insistence on binary oppositions that exclude the mingling of pain, grieving, and violence in peacetime, a combination the group of women is experiencing. The women are paradigmatic representatives of Duras's notion of war and peace as a continuum because they embody the grieving, violent conflicts that live on once those who were at the battlefront come home. The battle does not cease to exist; many of its schemes and patterns are reproduced in ways that are more complex because they are not as clearly determined as the stark borderline between war and peace could lead one to believe.

As we have seen, in "La douleur" Duras explores the role of women as agents who re-produce the suffering of war. In "Albert des Capitales" she focuses on another facet: that of women as agents capable of inflicting pain. In this text Duras broaches the issue of violence, which shows the human race to be executioners as much as victims. Female characters are again highlighted. Thérèse wants to kill the German prisoner and shows no mercy whatsoever for the Nazi collaborator she tortures. On the other hand, the group of women onlookers cannot bear the torture session. Crying out from the shadows, these women protest by placing themselves on the side of the victim—a victim who was the first executioner. The women are overruled and finally leave the room, though it is not clear if they do so by force or by choice.

By contrast with the victorious patriotic constructions of the French Liberation, in Duras's depiction of (war in) peace everyone loses: the informant, the women—unable to make the others refrain from the violence—and Thérèse, whom the other women silently leave, and who can only break into tears as she confirms her own ambivalence: after having tortured the informant mercilessly, she orders him to be freed. The text closes leaving all its characters—and the reader—with a sense of the total absurdity and lack of moral of the situation. No meaning can redeem the experience of violence; good and evil are no longer certain categories.

The ambiguity and apparent lack of meaning to be derived from *La douleur* link Duras's representation of war to what the historian Saul Friedlander calls a postmodern aesthetics of history that accentuates the dilemmas of history telling: "Works in this vein acknowledge both the moral obligation to remember and the ethical hazards of doing so in art and literature." Friedlander conceives of "an aesthetics that devotes itself primarily to the dilemmas of representation," in which "an antiredemptory history of the Holocaust . . . resists closure, sustains uncertainty, and allows us to live without full understanding" (qtd. in Young 6).

Following this aesthetics, Duras's women show the ultimate failure of the reactive and redemptive pattern of war. The women who abandon the torture chamber are actively rejecting the role of agents and witnesses to war by refusing to take part in the perpetuation of the pattern of war. However, an important nuance does not allow the reader to interpret their action in a binary scheme in which women are "good" and men "evil." Due to the lack of closure and the ultimate inadequacy of Manichean interpretations that Duras's writing foregrounds, the reader is left wondering whether these women are not also perpetuating the acts of violence by simply closing their eyes to them.

Violence and the capacity to inflict pain are as much a part of human nature as the capacity to suffer. To deal with the issues the return to peace comprehends—such as expressing the experience in language through a mediated representation, telling the story of battle, and converting the story into history—the human species must face up to the patterns and traces of war in peacetime. Duras's ethics of writing must be read as a revelation not only of the nonessential quality of moral truth but also of a failure in the ways history has understood war and the return to peace. In *La douleur* the infliction of evil, the acting out of violence, is dangerously omnipresent throughout history, in which times of war and times of peace lie on a continuum with no perceptible distinction between them. Duras shows that good and evil (perhaps especially evil) are inherent aspects of the human race: "Autour de nous les mêmes océans, les mêmes invasions, les mêmes guerres. Nous sommes de la race de ceux qui sont brûlés dans les crématoires et des gazés de Maïdanek, nous sommes aussi de la race des nazis" (60–61).

The transitional period of time represented in *La douleur*—the liberation of Paris and the beginning of the end of the war—is portrayed by Duras as a continuation of the values and behavioral patterns of wartime; there is no so-called "beginning" and no end. By ignoring this continuity the "human species" makes each return to peace an eventual, inevitable return to war.

Notes

1. Duras briefly alludes to Antelme's book twice in *La douleur*. The first time, she describes it as "*un livre sur ce qu'il croit avoir vécu en Allemagne*" (82, emphasis added), thus stressing the difficulty (or impossibility) of the representation of that

experience. It is implied that the book had a cathartic function; Duras says that after completing it he never again mentioned a word about the camps or about the book. The second allusion appears in the text "Monsieur X" when Duras refers to her obscure encounters with a Gestapo agent in their 1944 context as a still innocent time because the horrors of the Holocaust had not yet been made public: "Nous sommes aux premières temps de l'humanité, elle est là vièrge, virginale, pour encore quelques mois. Rien n'est encore révélé sur L'Espèce Humaine" (123).

2. For a further discussion of the feminization performed by Remarque's text, see Marcus.

3. Of course, by the time *La douleur* was published, many years after the events it describes, the gruesome details of the Holocaust had long since become common knowledge. This circumstance alters the text's reception. Leslie Hill argues that the recontextualization of Duras's text in 1985 acquires new meanings because at this time in France the "revisionist" accounts of the war that denied the Holocaust were being published (126).

4. Duras's tale is twice removed: if the horror of war can be told only through indirection, *La douleur* is doubly indirect in that the narrator is witness to a witness of the horror of the camps. The importance and novelty of this text lie in its unveiling of the mediation of *all* (post)war telling. The narrator's indirection serves as epitome of the mediation inherent in all telling of horror. The consciousness of mediation in testimony we find in Duras's writing is characteristic of what later became the central preoccupations of "second-generation" Holocaust literature. According to James E. Young, the writers and artists of the "second generation" were faced with the inevitable problem of mediation: they could not "remember" the Holocaust apart from the ways in which it had been passed down to them, not only by the survivors themselves, but also through photographs, film, histories, novels, poems, plays, and testimonies. "It is necessarily mediated experience, the afterlife of memory, represented in history's after-images: the impressions retained in the mind's eye of a vivid sensation long after the original, external cause has been removed" (3–4). In this sense, *La douleur* could be a precursor to the dilemmas of representation foregrounded in second-generation Holocaust texts, in which the experience of the memory act is as central to the telling as the memory of the experience itself.

5. Although this claim is a traditional literary device that gives veracity to autobiographical texts, the journals of *La douleur* were actually found and are conserved to this day at the Institut Mémoires de l'Édition Contemporaine in Paris.

6. The artificiality of the chronological time span is also revealed in a "slip" in the diary entry under "April 1945," when the author alludes to an event that occurs in November of that same year—that is, at a later time (58).

7. When the third person is used, the author states that the main character "c'est moi" (138). See also 14 and 150, and the preliminary words to "Albert des Capitales" and "Ter le milicien," where the author-narrator explains that she is truly the person behind the main characters of these two texts.

8. However, I would not go as far as Lawrence Kritzman, who affirms that in Duras's text we can see that testimony belongs completely to the domain of literature (64).

9. In fact, she later had a child with Dionys Mascolo, a close friend of the couple, the "D." of "La douleur" who accompanies Marguerite through all her agony.

10. Sex is also paralleled to violence and torture in "Albert des Capitales" when the narrator notes that "c'est le primier fois de sa vie qu'elle se trouve avec un homme nu sans que ce soit pour l'amour" (154).

11. For a detailed analysis of the theme of the unity of the human race in the two texts, see Crowley.

12. Crowley reads this complicity as yet another representation of Duras's "generous doubling" of suffering, as a means of approaching the difficulties in representing a traumatic event. Because atrocity is impossible to represent, it must be doubled or re-represented: "the uniqueness of trauma cannot be represented as such. So, it is never allowed to live alone in its singularity" (176–77).

WORKS CITED

Antelme, Robert. *L'espèce humaine*. Paris: Gallimard, 2000.

Cooke, Miriam. *Women and the War Story*. Berkeley: University of California Press, 1996.

Crowley, Martin. "'Il n'y a qu'une espèce humaine': Between Duras and Antelme." *The Holocaust and the Text: Speaking the Unspeakable*. Ed. Andrew Leak and George Paizis. New York: Macmillan, 1999. 174–92.

Davis, Colin. "Duras, Antelme and the Ethics of Writing." *Comparative Literature Studies* 34.2 (1997): 170–83.

Duras, Marguerite. *La douleur*. Paris: P.O.L., 1985.

Felman, Shoshana, and Dori Laub. *Testimony: Crises of Witnessing in Literature, Psychoanalysis and History*. London: Routledge, 1992.

Hill, Leslie. *Marguerite Duras: Apocalyptic Desires*. New York: Routledge, 1993.

Huston, Nancy. "Tales of War and Tears of Women." *Women's Studies International Forum* 5.3/4 (1982): 271–82.

Kritzman, Lawrence. "Duras' War." *L'Esprit Créateur* 33 (Spring 1993): 63–73.

Levi, Primo. *The Drowned and the Saved*. New York: Summit Books, 1988.

Marcus, Jane. "Afterword. Corpus/Corps/Corpse: Writing the Body in/at War." *Not So Quiet . . . : Stepdaughters of War*. New York: Feminist Press, 1989. 241–300.

Young, James E. *At Memory's Edge: After-Images of the Holocaust in Contemporary Art and Architecture*. New Haven: Yale University Press, 2000.

Contributors

WILLIAM BLAZEK is a Senior Lecturer in English and American Literature at Liverpool Hope University. He is a co-editor of the *F. Scott Fitzgerald Review* and co-editor of *American Mythologies: Essays on Contemporary Literature* (Liverpool University Press, 2005) and *Twenty-first Century Readings of* Tender Is the Night (2007). His other recent work includes essays on E. E. Cummings and Louise Erdrich.

RENNY CHRISTOPHER is Associate Professor of English at California State University, Channel Islands. She earned her PhD in American literature from the University of California, Santa Cruz. Her book *The Viet Nam War/ The American War: Images and Representations in Euro-American and Vietnamese Exile Narratives* (University of Massachusetts Press, 1995) was named Outstanding Book on Human Rights by the Gustavas Myers Center for the Study of Human Rights in North America. She has an MA in linguistics from San Jose State University and a BA in English/creative writing from Mills College. Her teaching and research interests focus on issues of race, class, and gender in U.S. literature and culture.

DONNA COATES teaches in the English Department at the University of Calgary. She completed her doctoral dissertation on Australian and Canadian women's fictional responses to the Great War. She has published "Myrmidons to Insubordinates: Australian, New Zealand, and Canadian Women's Great War Fictions," in *The Literature of the Great War Reconsidered: Beyond Modern Memory*, ed. Patrick J. Quinn and Steven Trout (Palgrave, 2001); and "Pot Shots to Parting Shots: Wendy Lill's The Fighting Days," in *Women, the First World War and the Dramatic Imagination*, ed. Claire Tylee and R. Athfield (Edwin Mellen Press, 2000). She also wrote the entry for "War" in *Reader's Encyclopedia of Canadian Writing*, ed. W. H. New (University of Toronto Press, 2002). Additional articles on women's wartime fiction of the First and Second World Wars appear in recent issues of the *Journal of Commonwealth Literature, Antipodes, Canadian Literature, Australian Literary Studies,* and *Australian and New Zealand Studies in Canada.*

JANET DAWSON graduated from Nottingham University with a BA (Hons.) in French studies. She also has an MBA from Manchester Business School. Since coming to live in Spain she has obtained a degree in English language and literature from the University of Seville, for which she was awarded the prize as the best graduate from the Faculty of Philology in 1998. Her postgraduate interests include postmodern political and philosophical theories, early modern drama, and rewrites and revisions of Shakespeare and Ovid. She has published on aspects of chaos theory in Edith Wharton's *The Age of Innocence* in *Philologia Hispalensis,* 1999, and on order and disorder in *Troilus and Cressida* in *SEDERI* in 2002. She currently teaches English in Seville.

BRIAN DILLON earned his PhD from Washington State University and is currently Professor in the Department of English and Philosophy at Montana State University–Billings, where he teaches a wide range of courses, including Literature of World War I. His essays on Irish literature have appeared in *Genre* (on W. B. Yeats and Maud Gonne), *Nua* (on Ciaran Carson), *Canadian Journal of Irish Studies* (on Eavan Boland), and *Working Papers in Irish Studies* (on Samuel Beckett).

DON DINGLEDINE, Associate Professor of English at the University of Wisconsin–Oshkosh, is the editor of *Waiting for the Verdict* by Rebecca Harding Davis and is currently working on a book-length study of American literature from the Reconstruction era. His essays and reviews on nineteenth- and twentieth-century American literature have appeared in *PMLA, Women's Studies, Journal of Southern History, Legacy,* and *Studies in American Fiction.*

LAURIE KAPLAN is a Professor of English and Chair of British Studies at Goucher College, Baltimore, where she teaches courses in eighteenth-, nineteenth-, and twentieth-century literature, including seminars on the

Great War and postcolonial fiction and drama. Recent publications include "'How funny I must look with my breeches pulled down to my knees': Nurses' Memoirs and Autobiographies from the Great War," in *Dressing Up for War* (Rodopi, 2001); "Over the Top in the Aftermath of the Great War: Two Novels, Too Graphic," in *The Graphic Novel* (Leuven University Press, 2001); and "Bring in the Clowns: The Comedic Monologues and Dialogues of Austen's Fiction," in *Sensibilities* (Jane Austen Society of Australia, 2003). Currently, she is completing a project on Mary Borden's *The Forbidden Zone* for the Imperial War Museum in London. She is the editor-in-chief of *Persuasions: The Jane Austen Journal* and *Persuasions: The Jane Austen Journal On-Line* (www.jasna.org).

CAMILA LOEW has lived and worked in Argentina, the United States, and Spain. After receiving a degree in literary theory from the University of Buenos Aires, she joined the Humanities Department of the Universitat Pompeu Fabra (UPF) in Barcelona, where she is currently finishing her dissertation on women's testimonies of the Holocaust. At the UPF she belongs to a research group on the discourse of war in twentieth-century literature and visual arts. She currently teaches literature and film at the Hispanic studies program of the UPF and the Institute for International Education of Students. Her most recent publications include articles on contemporary Spanish film and on twentieth-century women's war writing.

ANDREW MONNICKENDAM studied literature at the University of Essex, then took a PhD at the Universitat Autònoma de Barcelona, where he currently teaches as Professor of English Literature. He specializes in Scottish literature; his most recent publication has been a critical edition of Christian Isobel Johnstone's *Clan-Albin* (1815), one of the few, if not only pacifist historical tales. Together with Aránzazu Usandizaga, he edited *Dressing Up for War: Transformation of Gender and Genre in the Discourse and Literature of War* (Rodopi, 2001).

KATHY J. PHILLIPS has a PhD in comparative literature from Brown University. Now a Full Professor at the University of Hawaii, Phillips has published two books, including *Virginia Woolf against Empire* (University of Tennessee Press, 1994), and twenty articles. With photographer Joe Singer, she published *This Isn't a Picture I'm Holding: Kuan Yin* (University of Hawaii Press, 2004), a book of poems celebrating this Buddhist figure. Her most recent publication is *Manipulating Masculinity: War and Gender in Modern British and American Literature* (Palgrave Macmillan, 2006).

MARY ANNE SCHOFIELD, PhD, is a member of the Core Humanities Program at Villanova University. A scholar of the novel, she has published widely (with Macmillan, G. K. Hall, Popular Press, and the University of Delaware Press) on eighteenth-century feminism and how it functions in the novels of the period. Recently, she has shifted her attention to issues of women and war and, again, has published extensively in this area, especially on women and the Second World War; her articles have appeared in the *American Journal of Semiotics, Phoebe: An Interdisciplinary Journal of Feminist Scholarship*, the *Journal of American History*, and others.

JENNIFER TERRY is Lecturer in English Studies at the University of Durham, UK. Her research interests lie in American literature, postcolonial studies, and writings of the black diaspora. Her doctoral thesis, completed at the University of Warwick, examined the novels of Toni Morrison. Current projects include a comparative exploration of African American and Caribbean fiction.

BEATRICE TREFALT is Senior Lecturer in Japanese Studies at Monash University. Her research field is postwar Japanese history and in particular popular and public memories of the Second World War as well as discourses of national identity. Her most recent publication is *Japanese Army Stragglers and Memories of the War in Post-war Japan, 1950–1975* (Routledge Curzon, 2003). She has also written on the commemoration of war for the volume *Nation and Nationalism in Japan*, edited by Sandra Wilson (Routledge Curzon, 2002). Her current research project focuses on processes of repatriation in the late 1940s and early 1950s.

CLAIRE TYLEE taught at the University of Málaga and is currently Senior Lecturer in English at Brunel University. She has a particular interest in feminism and women's writing, especially in the area of drama. She has written a number of articles and is particularly known for her book *The Great War and Women's Consciousness* (Macmillan, 1990). She has spoken at international conferences in Paris, Washington, and London.

ARÁNZAZU USANDIZAGA is Professor of English and American Literature at the Universitat Autónoma in Barcelona. She has published mainly on gender, and more recently on gender and war. In 2000 she edited in Spanish a selection of women's writing in English on the Spanish Civil War: *Ve y cuenta lo que pasó en España: Escritoras extranjeras y la Guerra Civil* (Editorial Planeta). In 2001 she edited with Andrew Monnickendam a collection of essays: *Dressing Up for War: Transformations of Gender and Genre in the Discourse and Literature of War* (Rodopi, 2001).

Index

82 Mass Observation re 1945 return home (also 85)
86 need for 'magical fictions' after 1945 & VIP 89
(see agst Valentine's rejection).

230 Es? re foreign women writers & Span Civil War
231 re Townsend Warner etc
232 re recruiting & ignorance re Spain
233 re preconceived ideas etc
234 Curand etc
235 Kartic Cooper's experiences (ge date 1st pub)
236 of Koestler
237 Francesca Wilson
238 Wilson continued
239 Curand
240 Authors Take Sides – & Gellhorn 241–2
243 Gellhorn 244–5–6